NIGHT OF THE LIVING DAD

Also by Sam Delaney

Get Smashed! The Story of the Men Who Made the Adverts
that Changed Our Lives

NiGHT OF THE LiViNG DAD

CONFESSiONS OF A SHABBY FATHER

SAM DELANEY

JOHN MURRAY

First published in Great Britain in 2009 by John Murray (Publishers)
An Hachette UK Company

I

This is a true story although some names and identifying characteristics have
been changed to protect people's privacy

A CIP catalogue record for this title is available from the British Library

ISBN 978-1-84854-093-4

Typeset in 12.5/16 Bembo by Servis Filmsetting Ltd, Stockport, Cheshire

Printed and bound by Clays Ltd, St Ives plc

John Murray policy is to use papers that are natural, renewable and recyclable
products and made from wood grown in sustainable forests. The logging and
manufacturing processes are expected to conform to the environmental
regulations of the country of origin.

John Murray (Publishers)
338 Euston Road
London NW1 3BH

www.johnmurray.co.uk

FOR COCO

CONTENTS

CONTENTS

viii

1
TRAVELCARD

We are in the bathroom. It's late. I've just cleaned my teeth and gobbed the minty residue down the plughole. I feel sexy. My wife is standing beside me, rubbing some sort of gunk into her face, when I turn to her and say, 'I think we should start trying for a baby right now.'

She stops rubbing and adopts this 'I don't know what to say, this is all happening so fast' look. At least, I think that's what it is. She may even be going a bit teary. Or maybe that's just some exfoliating grit in her eyes.

Then she says, 'OK, great. I'll come off the pill. We should be ready to get going in a couple of weeks.'

'A couple of weeks!' I think. 'When I said right now, I meant right now!' But apparently it takes a fortnight for the pill to wear off. Stupid pill.

I begin to realise that there's been a bit of a misunderstanding. When I said, 'I think we should start trying for a baby right now,' she must have thought I meant 'I think we should ACTUALLY start trying for an ACTUAL baby right now'. Whereas what I really meant was 'Shall we have sex right now? Please?'

But there you go. Now we're going to start trying for a baby. All because I couldn't think of a more elegant sexual advance on a run-of-the-mill Wednesday evening. Oh well. It was bound to happen sooner or later, I suppose. We both want kids. We just hadn't discussed exactly when. We've been in love for, like, ever. And one of the lesser-mentioned characteristics of a loving relationship is the lack of discussions you have about stuff. Not because, as cynics would have you believe, you're bored and have absolutely nothing left to say to each other. It's just that you know each other far too well to bother with much in the way of conversation. You share thoughts instinctively. She's hungry when I'm hungry. I'm happy when she's happy. Sometimes, although only occasionally, we simultaneously find ourselves inexplicably wanting to listen to Cyndi Lauper records. That's love. It gives us a mental affinity that makes talking largely unnecessary. Like that magical telepathy shared by Tony Cottee and Frank McAvennie in West Ham's legendary 1985/6 season. Each of us just knows what the other is thinking.

I've known my wife since school. I had a crush on her when I was about fifteen and finally managed to get together with her when I was twenty. We've been through all of life's key moments in each other's company. We collected our exam results together. We went to each other's grandma's funerals. We watched 9/11 unfold on the box, clutching each other's hands. We did the same when Take That broke up. Once we went on a daytrip to Alcatraz and took the audiotape guided tour together. Those kind of shared experiences fuse your very spirits together. She is pretty much better company than any of my friends. She's funny and gorgeous and smart. She devours a couple of books a week. Not only that, but she's thoughtful enough to buy me stuff to read while she's ploughing through her latest work of literary genius. The other day she got me a book of prison slang. Best thing I've ever read. See what I mean? She's my soulmate.

We've had a few ups and downs, I suppose. Once, about twelve years ago, I thought it'd be funny to hide from her when we were alone in my mum's house. It was just supposed to be a joke. I crouched behind a cabinet in the front bedroom. She started calling out for me, but I just stayed there giggling to myself. She hated it; it freaked her out, and she said she'd dump me if it ever happened again. What else? Oh yeah, once she had a dream about me and an imaginary foxy redhead ganging up on her at a party and ending up snogging in the corner. She was furious when she woke up. 'Don't worry baby, I won't leave you for the imaginary foxy redhead,' I said. And I wouldn't. But I must admit I still fantasise about that fictitious crimson beauty from time to time. Hey, it's not my fault. She was the one who invented her.

I can't really remember her ever upsetting me much. There was the time in New York on new year's eve in 1998. She got so drunk that I found her asleep with her head on the shoulder of a Chinese businessman in the queue for the bogs. He looked petrified. Later that night she puked on the bed in my cousin's apartment. I was briefly pissed off at her for about six hours the next day, but since then I can't recall many complaints.

I can't imagine what she sees in me. I'm not rich. My looks are adequate at best. I am intellectually inferior to her on a grand scale, and my line of chatter can, by common consent, be really, really irritating. Mind you, I have always been quite lucky when it comes to finding parking spaces. So I suppose I've got that going for me.

Anyway, the point is, I think we're probably ready to have a kid together. We both love kids. There's always been a tacit understanding that we would have them one day. We've never discussed exactly when – it just always seemed to be something we would do in 'the future'. Well, I suppose the future is now. Yes, I know that's a slogan from a mobile phone advertising campaign. But what better way is there to navigate yourself through life's biggest and most confusing decisions than via reference to advertising slogans? This is the game of life we're playing, and advertisers are pretty much the only ones who are bothering to show us the way it should be played.

I reckon we're ready to do this. We're not destitute. We've got our own place. Neither of us is mad or drunk or racist. We probably pass for reasonable parenting material. People have been asking us for some time when we might start a family. Nosey bastards.

'I don't know when we'll get round to all that,' I tell them sheepishly.

'Why not?' they persist.

'FUCK OFF! That's why not!' I reply.

I mean, what's it got to do with them? And what makes them assume that we're going to let social convention dictate our every life choice? Do we really seem so traditional and dull? My wife's a vegetarian, for fuck's sake. I moisturise. We're hardly Terry and June.

While I'm thinking over all of this crap, my wife seems to have warmed to the theme of me impregnating her. She is talking about maternity leave cover. There's no turning back now.

'We'll need a bigger car, I'd imagine,' I hear her say.

'Yep, you're not wrong,' I interrupt, clambering into the bedroom wearing a towel. 'Right then, better get started. These babies don't make themselves you know.'

And, do you know, I am having it off not five minutes later? If only I'd used a line as pithy and romantic as that in the first place.

After the sex she isn't pregnant. A couple of days later we do it again, and she still isn't pregnant. A whole month goes by, and still no sign of a baby. Frankly I am disgusted. What sort of a bloke am I? The sort of bloke who needs his testicles examined in case of deficiencies, that's what sort.

The last time I went to the doctors to have my nuts examined, I fainted, had a seizure and pissed myself. I'd thought I could feel a lump. So I went down the health centre and told them they'd better have a look. The doctors were busy, so the nurse had to do it in a side-room. I know, I know: it all sounds like an ill-thought-out plotline to a porno doesn't it? But it really happened. She told me it'd be easier if I stayed standing and dropped my pants. I did so, and she started tickling my scrotum. Sounds nice, right? Only it wasn't – it made me feel nauseous and dizzy. And the next thing I knew I was coming round on the floor in a puddle of my own piss with a couple of doctors fussing about me.

'Are you epileptic?' one of them was asking over and over again.

'What does it look like to you?' I said. From past experience it was immediately clear that I'd spent the last couple of minutes spazzing about on the floor, spraying wee all over the place and gurning like the big eppy bastard I am.

'Yes, it looks like you're epileptic,' said the doctor. Then he just walked out of the room.

'Are you on medication?' asked the nurse.

'No,' I mumbled, pulling my saturated trousers back on. 'It's not bad enough for medication. I only tend to have fits when I'm, erm, you know, in a state of high anxiety.'

An awkward silence befell the room. I decided to go. She showed no signs of stopping me.

'What about my balls?' I said as an afterthought, just as I was leaving.

'Oh yes, them,' she said. 'I definitely felt something strange. You should probably get them looked at by a doctor.'

I didn't say anything. But I did give her a look that I hoped said something along the lines of 'No shit, Florence Fucking Nightingale!'

Anyway, I didn't have ball cancer, if that's what you're waiting for. It was just a harmless testicular cyst, which is actually still there today and . . . hey, hang on a minute! What the hell has this got to do with anything? You don't need to know about my harmless testicular cyst.

Suffice to say, going back for another examination on my nuts isn't something I'm likely to enter into lightly. In fact, it isn't something I enter into at all. I decide instead to continue worrying about my virility in tortured silence. More months go by. Every time my wife has her period, she cries a bit. Increasingly, I find myself standing naked in front of the bathroom mirror angrily chastising my own genitals.

'You useless, lazy bastards!' I shout at them as they hang there all apologetically like a dog that's been caught pissing on the duvet. 'All you've ever done is cause me trouble! You've been like an albatross around my neck from Day 1! And now this! This really is the last straw. I've half a mind to cut the pair of you off!' But they refuse to respond to bullying tactics.

I fell into this situation almost by accident, and now it's dominating my every thought. Communication with my wife has all but disintegrated beyond blunt, emotionless texts and e-mails that say things like 'prgnt yet?' She responds with things like 'period strtd. ☹' Trying for a baby truly sucks the poetry from a relationship.

I'm probably approaching the whole thing in the wrong way. You're supposed to relax, chill out, think positive thoughts and have it off with your wife just like it was any other romantic night. Forget about the whole insemination process. Light some candles, put on some Luther Vandross, do it all slow and gentle. But come on: how likely is that? Once you know the sex is for something other than mere, frivolous pleasure, you're stuffed. You approach the whole thing like a robot. I can't get going without images from one of those spooky sex education films they showed you at school flashing through my brain. The sperm swimming its way towards the egg and all that. For some reason I start to hear David Attenborough commentating on my sexual performance while I'm trying to go at it. It's not nice. I try to refocus my brain, but all that pops in is Bruce Forsyth prancing about in flares singing 'Life is the name of the game'.

Another week goes by. Still no baby. Why am I so

.ed by rampant consumerism probably. I've
having my every material wish fulfilled at
a mouse. iPods, Japanese carving knives,
memorial plates: all I have to do is type in my
AmEx mber and they're on my doorstep within a
couple of days.

But you can't get a baby from Amazon.co.uk. Madonna's
probably tried it, mind you. But me, I'd rather grow one
organically in my wife's tummy if I can.

It is Friday night, and I am getting drunk in a pub. My wife
texts: 'When r u cming home?' It's rather more verbose
and polite than our recent communiqués. 'Something
fishy's going on here,' I think to myself. 'Gtng drnk,' I text
back. 'Dn't get 2 drunk ;),' she responds. Hang on a
minute! Semi-colon followed by closed bracket equals
saucy emoticon! Of course: it's sex night! Like I say, the
poetry has temporarily been removed from our relationship. We're no more than colleagues working on an
important joint project.

A couple of weeks ago we paid a doctor with a double-
barrelled name 250 quid to help get us pregnant. After a bit
of jiggery-pokery he managed to pinpoint the exact days
my wife would be fertile. He even wrote them down for
us on a bit of embossed notepaper (which I thought represented fantastic value for money). Turns out, there's only
two days a month she's actually ovulating. Having it off at
any other time is basically a waste of time. But tonight is
one of the special nights.

'How could you forget?' she asks when I get home.

'I lost the list of dates!' I tell her.

'I've got the list of dates!' she exclaims, waving the embossed notepaper at me.

'But I copied them out on to a Travelcard and put it in my jeans pocket but then I put the jeans through the wash, and now the Travelcard's gone all crumbly and illegible!' I niftily explain.

That's the kind of chat that passes for foreplay these days.

Next, we settle down for some of the most mechanical, half-cut but technically efficient sex we've ever had. As I'm doing it, I mentally recount all the beer and wine and crisps I've consumed that evening. 'Probably best we don't conceive tonight,' I think to myself.

We conceive that night.

2

COKE

'Can you ever forgive me for all those terrible things I said?'

I am standing in front of the mirror, stark naked, cupping my genitals in my right hand.

'I was confused. I was angry. I didn't mean it. How could I have not trusted you?'

My testicles just sit there as silent and inscrutable as ever. But somewhere amidst those gruesome folds of skin I think I can detect the smallest twinkle of pride. Perhaps even a little smugness. I don't mind. Let them have their moment – they've earned it. They've come through for me big-style this time.

'You and I have done this, old friends!' I beam at them. 'You and I have created a human life! We've had some adventures together in the past – but this? This must be our crowning glory!'

How do you feel when you find out you've impregnated your wife? Proud? Astonished? Warm and fuzzy? Terrified? No, you feel victorious. You clench your fist, punch the air, adopt an aggressive snarl and shout out loud, 'Get in there you bastard!' like you've just scored the winner at Wembley. At least, that's what I did. The tiny

Indian nurse who'd just given us the good news didn't know where to look.

The whole thing had developed into a sort of game in my head. For months I had become obsessed with hitting my wife's ovaries in the right place at the right time. During sex I would sometimes shut my eyes and picture that scene from the end of *Star Wars* where Luke fires his successful shot at the Death Star's vulnerable exhaust port, blowing it to smithereens. I can honestly say that when that softly spoken nurse gave us the results, I couldn't have been happier even if I really had just destroyed an evil intergalactic space station. But after a few days of rampant triumphalism, it was time to take stock.

After this one last rousing address to my testicles in the bathroom mirror I breathe deeply and ask myself, 'Are you ready to be a dad?' I dwell on my reflection for a while longer and conclude that I don't really look like one. Dads should be bigger. And hairier. And altogether more man-like. I'm still kinda skinny and awkward – like an adolescent who'd probably get picked last for a five-a-side. Plus, I have this perennially stupid look on my face that suggests I've just stuck a flaming dog turd on someone's front step, knocked on their door and run away. Dads shouldn't look mildly amused. They should look authori-tative and grumpy.

'Nope, you definitely don't look the part,' I say to myself in the mirror. 'At best, you look like a warm but slightly retarded uncle – which is basically what you are. Still, you've got nine months to work on your look. The question is: can you *act* the part?'

★

It's about a month later. I'm in a beer garden in Norfolk. We're on holiday. My eldest brother is sitting beside me playing about with his phone. His daughter Daisy is there too. She's eight and has read all the Harry Potter books, like, four times. She reckons this qualifies her to verbally outwit me. She reckons right.

I've just ordered a Diet Coke. It's part of my training for fatherhood.

'A *Coke*?! Didn't you say Coke was bad for us?' Daisy says.

'Yeah, I did. But this is Diet Coke. It's different.'

She looks incredulous.

'Diet Coke, Coke, surely they're all the same?'

'No. It's the sugar in Coke that's bad. This is sugar-free – see?' I point at the words on the side of the can.

She examines them sceptically then looks at her dad and asks him, 'Does that mean I can have Diet Coke?'

'Erm, no,' he says, looking up from his mobile phone for a moment.

'Why not?' she asks.

'Um . . . well.' He glances at me worriedly. '*Don't get involved, go back to your precious phone,*' I snarl at him with my eyes. 'The thing is, Diet Coke has other things in it that are bad for you. Sweeteners and caffeine . . . and . . . that.'

Why did he have to go and tell her that? She's a Rottweiler, this girl. Give her a glimmer of an argument, and she'll clamp hold of it and not let go until she's tasted blood.

'Cock!' I shout at my brother almost involuntarily.

'Pardon? What did you say?' says Daisy.

'Coke!' I say. 'I said "Coke".'

'I thought you said "cock",' she persists.

'No, merely "Coke",' I mumble absent-mindedly, pretending to have seen an interesting bird hovering somewhere overhead. But she won't be distracted. It's like having Jeremy Paxman for a niece.

'What about it?' she demands.

'What about what?' I say. I have no idea where I'm going with this.

'Coke! What about Coke?!'

I feel like I'm being interrogated. Any minute now she's going to grab me by the hair and start slamming my face into the table.

'Coke . . . is . . . it!' I say, meaninglessly. 'It's The Real Thing! Always Coca-Cola!' For some reason I deliver the last line in a tuneless little sing-song.

'Hmmmm,' she says, dismissively. 'It's strange that you took so much time the other day telling me how drinking Coke was like drinking . . . what was it again?'

'Petrol,' I mutter, hanging my head in lament.

'Yes, like drinking petrol. So why are you drinking Diet Coke? Are you on a diet?'

'NO!' I bark, noticing my voice cracking slightly.

'My dad says Diet Coke is even worse than the normal stuff. You're drinking something that's WORSE than petrol.'

Clever little shit. You'll have something worse than petrol all over your head in a minute, I think to myself.

'Now, now – I didn't say it was worse,' my brother interrupts, rightly trying to sort out the mess he created. 'I just said it was probably as bad.'

She scowls at him. He shuts his mouth and goes back to his phone. Over the past eight years I've seen her systematically break his will and erode his spirit. Now he's not so much a dad as an obedient automaton, trained to do her bidding.

'Well?' she says, turning her death-glare back on me.

'Well what? What do you want?' I ask.

'Are you going to say sorry?'

'Sorry?'

'Yes, sorry. Sorry for telling lies. And for saying one thing and doing another.'

She is deadly serious about this. My mouth goes dry. I look around for help, hoping someone may intervene. My brother glances up and gives me this pleading look as if to say, 'Just give her what she wants. It's easier that way.'

No. Screw that. I won't be bullied by an eight-year-old. So what if she's read a load of books about some gaylord little wizard? I've got a degree and a driving licence. I'm a grown-up. I'm VAT-registered, for fuck's sake.

I straighten my back and broaden my chest.

'Look, I'm only trying to give you some guidance OK?' I bark. She grins. My brother gawps and looks like he's about to cross his chest and jump under a table.

'I'm your uncle and I'm trying to give you the benefit of my experience. That's what uncles do!' I'm getting louder. 'Yes, I drink Diet Coke! There, I've said it. Know what? I sometimes drink normal Coke too. I'm a *bad* man, aren't I? But it's too late for me now. See?'

I pull my lips open to reveal the semi-derelict condition of my teeth and gums.

'That's what drinking Coke does to you. Do you want

to grow up with teeth like mine? I doubt it. That's why I've tried to warn you. But frankly, if you just see my advice as a chance to point-score . . . if you just want to throw it back in my face . . . then I don't care if you drink Coke. I'll buy you a can right now if you want!' I'm actually reaching into my pocket for the money. 'And why don't you buy yourself a packet of fags while you're at it? They give you cancer by the way – but you probably know best, right?!'

I pause for breath. She looks thoughtful.

'How much are fags?' she asks.

'I dunno. About a fiver?' I say.

'Can I just have the cash?' she beams.

I've gone red in the face now. 'No, you cannot!' I say.

'Why not?' she asks, remaining irritatingly calm in the face of my increasing hysteria.

'Because,' I say, moving in closer and lowering my voice to a menacing whisper, 'you are a rude and selfish little girl.'

Her eyes well up a bit. I drain my Diet Coke, slam the glass on the table and stride off to the bogs. I feel like Clint Eastwood. To everyone else in the pub I'm just the six-foot-two bloke who shouts at cute little girls with pigtails until they cry.

'In retrospect, I probably could have handled that better,' I say to my brother later that evening. We are slumped in front of an open fire with large glasses of brandy balanced on our chests. He stares blearily into the flames and contemplates the matter for a moment. 'Possibly,' he muses. 'When it comes to dealing with kids, it's like what the police tell you when you have to go to prison.'

'What's that then?'

'Don't make eye contact, and don't enter into any sort of conversation.'

I'm not exactly sure what he means by this, but I think I catch his general drift. Don't fuck with Daisy.

I have three older brothers. All of them have children who are more confident, more articulate and miles better-educated than them. Even the ones who are still at nursery have already attained more academic qualifications than all of the grown-ups in my family put together. They go to good schools where they're sitting French vocab tests at the same age that the rest of us were still taking lessons in how to shit into a potty. Then there's the high-falutin attitudes they pick up in those places. Socio-economic advancement may seem like a good idea at first, until your kids come home from school and start sneering at you for spreading Flora on your bread roll instead of dipping it in chilli-infused olive oil.

My brothers and I grew up in an environment where there wasn't a particularly strong emphasis on the completion of homework – by our teachers or our parents. That's not true – I think my dad probably thought it was very important we did our homework. But seeing as he was living with his new girlfriend on the other side of town, he didn't have much of an opportunity to monitor the situation. My brothers probably completed about half a dozen pieces of homework between them over the years. And at least one of those would have been a picture of a teacher with a giant penis growing out of his ear, scrawled in crayon on the back of one of our mum's final demand statements. Creative but never likely to get you fast-tracked into the sixth form's Oxbridge entrance classes. That's if our schools had had a sixth form or any Oxbridge entrance classes, which they didn't. Mind you, mine did have two Commodore computers and a well-stocked snack machine in the sports hall foyer, so I can't complain.

Once I had muddled through school and into a sixth form college, I started to buckle down a bit harder. I'd learned from my older brothers' mistakes; I didn't want my education to pass me by. But still my academic efforts were often undermined by their boisterous horseplay around the house.

'What the fuck are you doing?' they would burst into my bedroom and ask me, just as I felt I was getting to grips with the second act of *A Midsummer Night's Dream* or the meaning of photosynthesis.

'Homework,' I'd say.

'Homework?' they'd scowl, their noses running with snot (they would usually be inebriated on strong industrial solvents). 'Homework?' they would say again, this time doing a special 'gay voice' and performing a little fairy-like twirl. 'I'll give you some homework.' Then they would kick over the small bookshelf beside my bed and give me ninety seconds to re-shelve every item.

I know that makes them sound like wankers, but they're all right really. I can't blame all of my educational deficiencies on them; I was also hindered by my own laziness and naturally average intelligence. That and the fact that there never seemed to be enough pens in our house. No matter how many my mum nicked from the stationery cupboard at work, they would always disappear. We eventually realised the dog was eating them when she started to puke up dark blue ink. Eventually she died of pancreatic cancer. Coincidence? Unlikely.

Anyway, the point is, I may not be Professor Stephen Hawking but I'm not exactly Benny from *Crossroads* either. While I'm not catastrophically stupid, I'm just dumb enough to be intimidated by small children with precocious vocabularies and the courage of their convictions. I get drawn into arguments with them, allowing them to get me all cross and confused. They toy with my mind and my emotions like a cat toys with a badly injured mouse that it can't be bothered to actually kill. I am beginning to realise that this has less to do with cleverness and more to do with maturity. At thirty-two years old I am not yet mature enough to communicate effectively with small children, let alone command their respect. Sometimes my nieces and nephews find me funny. Occasionally they may find me interesting. But I'm not sure how much they actually respect me. The only way I've ever been able to get any of them to do anything (such as stop crying or give me back my car keys) is by paying them. Putting all of this together, I begin to realise that I lack any semblance of fatherly *gravitas*. Which is bad enough when you only have to cope with other people's children every couple of weeks. But what about when I've got one of my own knocking about the house full-time? This is something that's starting to worry me.

I look at my brother (who is now asleep with a large glass of brandy spilt all down his front) and think that he may not be such an obedient automaton after all. He's more like a clever, white-collar criminal who has learned to survive among the savage bullies on the inside. He knows when to keep his mouth shut. He knows how to keep his nose clean. He knows where he can buy a crudely fashioned shiv with which to protect himself should things get dicey in the showers.

'You're the sort of con a bloke can rely on,' I slur at him drunkenly, patting him on the shoulder.

'Hrrrumph! What!' he says, waking up all of a sudden.

'Oh, I just said you know how to . . . y'know . . . do your porridge with dignity.'

'Fucking right,' he slurs, then quickly falls asleep again.

I notice that I'm making more and more prison analogies in relation to fatherhood. This is another thing that's starting to worry me.

3

SNICKERS

There's a nurse rubbing a big electronic stick all over my wife's stomach. It's covered in gel. The room is dark and quiet. Altogether, it's the sexiest experience I've had in weeks.

'See that blinking little light?' she says, nodding at the monitor in the corner of the room.

'No,' I think. 'Yes!' I say.

'That's baby's heart,' she explains flatly.

I squint and hear myself saying something like 'Wow' or maybe 'Cor blimey'. It seems important that I pretend to be able to see what's going on. And be moved by it. All I can actually make out on the crappy little screen is a load of pointless, grainy shadows. It's like the sort of rubbish telly a student would hire from Radio Rentals. The sort that doesn't even have Teletext.

'And that long line on the left-hand side?'

'Uh-huh,' I say, pulling my special fascinated face.

'That's its spine.'

I stop smiling and turn away. I don't want to see its spine. I don't even want to think about what this baby looks like until it's warm and cuddly and giggling at the array of hilarious faces I am planning on pulling for it once it's out. Spines aren't warm or cuddly – they're all spiky and cold and rubbish. Now the nurse is talking about the outline of the skull and the half-formed fibula. She's making it sound like a stupid fossil or one of those tiny, translucent, featherless birds you used to find lying dead in the bushes when you were a kid. I feel like I'm going to puke. I squeeze my wife's hand just a notch too hard. It's a squeeze that tries to say 'I love you and I love looking at tiny human life forms in their early stages of development'.

My wife blinks worriedly at the screen. I think about how she must feel: she's the one with this grotesque bag of flesh and cartilage swimming around inside her stomach, or womb, or whatever you want to call it.

'And that black splodge there looks like an ocular cavity', deadpans the nurse.

I don't feel sexy any more.

Back outside in the waiting room I have to stand around while they book my wife in for another round of unedifying intrusions. The receptionist hands me a Polaroid version of the black shapes we've just been looking at on the screen.

'Something for your pinboard in the office,' she smiles.

I stare at the baffling image, trying hard to muster some sort of emotional response, but it's no good. It just looks like the sort of picture your mobile phone accidentally takes in your pocket when you've forgotten to activate the keypad lock. People put pictures of their children up at work to brighten up their day and make people think of them as balanced and warm. If I stuck this up, people might think I was a cynic or a murderer or some sort of goth.

As it happens I don't have an office or a pinboard. Still, the receptionist wasn't to know that. Or was she? The only other bloke in the waiting room has 'office' written all over him. He looks like he probably works in a big, oak-panelled office with leather-bound books on the shelves, a decanter of scotch in the cupboard and an electric pencil-sharpener on his desk. He is shaved and suited and reading a broadsheet paper. His shoes are shiny, his face is big and red and his expression is serious. I am scruffy and scoffing a Snickers bar I just bought from the snack machine. I worry that he looks more like dad material than I do. He's not the sort of idiot who'd eat a Snickers for his breakfast. I bet he had something fatherly before he came out. Kippers, I'd imagine.

I keep one jealous eye on him while flicking through the leaflet rack, hoping to find one about sexual diseases with pictures of gigantic knobbly tumours growing out of someone's helmet. Meanwhile, the other bloke is carefully analysing the business pages. At least, he's wearing an expression that suggests that's what he's doing – I can't actually see the pages. Maybe he's just got a copy of *Take a Break* concealed inside. I doubt it, though, not with shoes as smart as his.

I should mention that we are in Britain's poshest NHS hospital. It's in a salubrious district of London where people could not only afford to go private if they wanted to but probably also refurb Claridge's with medical equipment and staff it with specially shipped-in obstetricians and élite midwife teams from California if they really needed to. But they don't, because they've got this place offering a similar level of service on their local high street. We qualify for this privilege by living right on the edge of the same borough in a not-quite-so-salubrious district. We are the beneficiaries of a massive postcode injustice. I think about the stinking, falling-to-pieces infirmary down the road where my mum had to have eyes lasered a couple of years back. I feel mildly guilty. I am quickly distracted from my guilt by the smart man, who I notice is looking at his watch and sighing irritably. 'He's got the right idea,' I think to myself. 'That's what a dad would do. Look at his watch and sigh irritably. Not sit here grinning and eating chocolate.'

If I was in a crappier hospital there'd be fewer blokes like him and more blokes like me. Maybe some of the blokes would be even worse than me. There'd be drunk men, smelly men and men who smoked fags and blew the smoke into their pregnant wives' faces; men dressed in their pants, men who had wet themselves and men with racist tattoos. In short, men who would make me feel better about myself. Men who, by comparison, would make me look like the very model of a sober and serious-minded father. I'd probably feel just like that man in the suit does now: superior, expertly groomed and a bit irritable in a calm, authoritative sort of way. On the downside, my wife might catch the MRSA virus and end up having the baby delivered by a work-experience porter using a maths compass in the corridor.

On balance, we're probably marginally better off being here.

The man with the shiny shoes looks up as his wife shows

him the pointless Polaroid image of their barely formed offspring. He glances at it with unconcealed ambivalence and checks his watch again. 'Yeah, you tell her!' I think. 'There was me wasting my time pretending to look at the stupid picture when I could have been, I dunno, checking out how Procter and Gamble shares were doing on the Nasdaq or something. They probably hand the same bloody picture out to everyone anyway. I feel like such a fool. If only I had the confidence of the man with the shiny shoes.'

My wife comes back over from the reception desk.

'What are you singing?' she asks.

'Singing? I wasn't singing,' I say.

'Yes you were,' she insists. 'Under your breath. It sounded like the theme tune to *The Man with the Golden Gun.*'

Oh yeah, hang on, I think I was singing.

'"Shiny Shoes",' I say.

'What?'

'I was actually singing "The Man with the Shiny Shoes". I changed the words.'

She looks incredulous, then glances around the room. She sees The Man with the Shiny Shoes. Then she looks back at me.

'Have you invented a song about that man?' she asks.

'Keep it down,' I hiss, ushering her towards the exit.

Outside she asks me again. 'Well, have you?'

I tut, sigh, look at my watch a bit then say, 'Yes, OK, I have invented a song about that man.'

She looks disappointed.

'The Man with the Shiny Shoes was a dick,' she says.

'Oh . . . yeah . . . total dick,' I chuckle.

'Are you sure you didn't think he was a bit cool?' she says calmly. She knows about my roving eye. The way I look at other men. How I worry that I should be more like them and less like me. And how I sometimes express those worries via the medium of song.

'Yeah. The original words I was singing were . . . er . . . The Man with the Stupid Face,' I insist.

She ignores this.

'He ignored his wife the whole time he was there and didn't even bother looking at the crappy picture. I mean, come on! At least you pretended.'

I narrow my eyes. 'Who says I was pretending?'

'It's OK,' she says. 'I was pretending too. If you don't act interested, they might report you to social services in advance or something.'

We get in the lift and fall silent. I think about the possibility of social services receiving advance intelligence on us. I resolve to feign interest even harder next time we're here. Then I think about The Man with the Shiny Shoes. Maybe he wasn't so great. His wife didn't seem to like him much. I didn't once see him reassuringly squeeze her hand a notch too hard.

By the time we step out of the lift I'm feeling much better about myself. Just because I don't eat kippers for breakfast or understand the money markets doesn't mean I'll make a bad dad. This is 2007: get out of the '90s, you shiny-shoed dick! Everything you know is wrong! You're looking at the new face of modern parenting! Yes, that's right, it's covered in melted Snickers. Deal with it.

★

It's early evening, and I'm standing in a pub with my mate Dave. He is looking at me blankly while I brandish my black, pointless Polaroid in his face.

'That's baby's spine!' I beam, pointing at an arbitrary area of the photo. 'And that bit on the left is either its fibula or its ocular cavity, I'm not sure which.'

4
GREASE

I'm not really living the lifestyle of a responsible adult. This isn't how a dad goes about his business. I don't have a proper job. I'm a freelancer. When you tell people that, they think you're basically a layabout with pretensions. In fact, I work reasonably hard, but most of what I do is just namby-pamby nonsense. Writing stuff, talking jibber-jabber on the TV and radio: it's hardly the gritty and industrious vocation of an honest-to-goodness father figure. I don't come home from work with roughened hands and weather-battered features; I usually pull up in a black cab with a takeaway. And I don't have a pension or savings or anything like that either. I have not really been cultivating a safe and secure nest in which to raise this child.

Still, I've managed to wrestle my way out of that long post-student period of constant financial peril and into a strangely comfortable position where I can spend long afternoons in the gym or the pub and still manage to pay my mortgage every month and have a bit left over for new trainers and sweeties and that.

My flat is swish: the floors are made out of black rubber, and the kitchen is made out of imported Italian wood or something – I dunno, the people we bought it off had it installed. There is a widescreen plasma mounted on the wall and stupid pieces of 'art' hanging everywhere. There is an expensive sound system, an elaborate, unused coffee machine and a stylish, profoundly uncomfortable L-shaped sofa. Altogether, my flat is what can only be described as a bit poncey. It's like I'm some sort of cut-price Patrick Bateman out of *American Psycho*. There are no dead prostitutes in my fridge, but I sometimes wonder whether there might be if I weren't married to a level-headed woman who simply wouldn't stand for that sort of thing.

'Where are those Quorn sausages I bought, darling?'

'Behind the hooker's skull on the second shelf down. The one with the eyeballs removed.'

Also like Bateman, I have a tendency towards obsessive materialistic fetishism and conspicuous consumption. Nevertheless, I feel almost certain that I would never kill and refrigerate a sex worker.

This kind of lifestyle is quite nice, I suppose. It's better than I expected when I was a kid. The best-paid person in my house back then was my brother, who was working as an entry-level postman. I dreamed of living his life of 4 a.m. starts, cold days tramping the rainy streets, wearing a stinking nylon uniform. He told me such enchanting tales of stealing cash out of children's birthday cards and occasionally winning a tenner on the canteen fruity. The Royal Mail sorting office sounded like bloody Xanadu to me when I was ten. I could hardly dare to dream of one day living the same exotic lifestyle enjoyed by my brother. He had a motor bike and a girlfriend and a music system in his room. To my young eyes he was like Faceman out of *The A-Team* and Dex Dexter from *Dynasty* rolled into one.

But I didn't think I really had it in me to follow in his footsteps. He seemed to have a certain charm and mettle that I sensed were lacking from my flimsy soul. I figured I'd probably end up miserable, unemployed and alone in a shit-smeared bed-sit in Isleworth, crying my tits off in front of the snooker on a black-and-white telly.

So, all things considered, I can't complain about the way things have turned out. If I could travel back in time to 1985 and meet my younger self, he'd wet himself with excitement. Then my brother would probably come back from his night shift at the sorting office feeling grumpy, beat me up and steal my wallet. But it'd be worth it just to see the look on my podgy ten-year-old face.

Mind you, there's been a small concern nagging in the back of my mind for some time now that I am, in fact, entirely pointless. I'm making about as much valuable contribution to the progression of mankind as a member of the Pussycat Dolls. And not the fit lead singer one, either – one of the others who just stand around at the back.

God, I've wasted what little spare money I've earned. The iPod attachments, the games consoles, the taxis. All those luxury, overpriced biscuits. Maybe they are just a sorry excuse for something else. Something bigger. Something soft and cuddly that pukes on your new trainers when you're just about to head down the pub. I'm guessing that, once I have a baby and look into its cute little baby eyes, I will realise once and for all that all those shiny things were just worthless surrogates. There is also a slim chance I may get bored of the baby after a few months and realise that Pro Evolution Soccer wasn't such a waste of time after all. But by that time it'll be too late: I'll have eBayed my Xbox and used the proceeds to buy a papoose.

This flat is not child-friendly. There are breakable ornaments and dangerous spiky edges everywhere. Plus, I'm a weirdo neat freak who doesn't like it when my nephews and nieces come round in case they move a magazine.

The building is on a dirty street full of traffic and madmen. Some nights a drunk man stands out on the pavement shouting, 'You're all fucking wankers!' over and over again. He's probably angry at the world. But when I'm lying in the darkness unable to sleep, I worry that he might be angry at me personally. 'Who? Who are the fucking wankers?' I think to myself nervously. 'Am I one of them? Was I a fucking wanker to you in the past? I'm sure you've made a mistake. I've never been a fucking wanker to anyone! I swear on my life! I've been a twat. I've been an idiot. But a wanker? A *fucking* wanker? No, this must be some sort of terrible mix-up!' I think about going out on to the balcony and shouting, 'I'm not the fucking wanker you're looking for!' But instead I just lie there fretting for a few more hours until he goes away.

He's not the only problem. The other day some kids stole and vandalised my scooter. The same ones lobbed a water balloon at my mates on their way into the house. It was an ambush. I tried to have it out with them, but they pulled a knife. I told my wife I was going to go and get my Leatherman, but she stopped me by saying, 'What are you going to do? Have a knife fight like someone out of *West Side Story*?' She had a point. I can't knife-fight. Especially not rhythmically to music like they do in *West Side Story*.

In the hallways and stairs that lead to my flat there is a nasty, musty smell. The carpet is loose, and there are old fag-ends and chocolate bar wrappers lying around on the floor. I think there are about six or seven other flats inside. I can't be sure, because the faces I encounter on the stairs are always changing. When I see one of them, I stare at my feet and mutter. They do the same. All of us are trying to ignore the fact that we live cheek by jowl with strangers in a lonely building on a stinking polluted street where screaming and sirens punctuate our anxious nights. We're trying to tell ourselves that this urban nightmare is OK. That it's cool to be terrified and alienated. But I'm not sure I can suspend my disbelief any more; I fear my mask of sanity is beginning to slip.

From what I've seen of them, the neighbours are mostly bastards. They steal our mail and have parties. The bloke who lives upstairs is auditioning for an appearance on the ITV reality show *Grease is the Word*. He wants Simon Cowell to select him as the new Danny Zucco. He rehearses the song 'Sandy' continuously throughout the day. While I'm on the phone to the bank, all I can hear is him warbling on about being stranded at a drive-in.

'What was that?' says the woman in the Indian call centre.

'I said I wanted to extend my overdraft,' I reply.

'You mentioned something about a drive-in?'

'Forget the drive-in. Just give me the money.'

The same neighbour also enjoys singing 'Walking in Memphis', by Marc Cohn. 'That won't get you anywhere with Cowell,' I think smugly to myself. 'It's not even in *Grease*. Do your bloody research you shithead!' By late afternoon I start to think about going upstairs and cutting out his larynx with a tin-opener.

When I do eventually go upstairs and bang on his door, he falls silent and refuses to answer.

'I know you're in there,' I shout. I hear his breathing. I think about kicking the door down. 'I'm gonna kick your door down!' I shout.

But when push comes to shove, I don't think I've got it in me. I'm just hoping I can scare him into thinking I might. In the end I just write an indignant note and slip it under his door. That evening, while my wife and I are watching telly, the singing starts again. I jump up from the sofa and head upstairs for a confrontation. 'Don't be a dickhead about it,' my wife calls after me. But she knows I'm going to be a dickhead about it. I'm doing my special dickhead walk.

BANG! BANG! BANG! I am slamming my fist against Danny Zucco's front door. 'Open the door!' I shout. The singing stops again. 'I'm going to kick your door down,' I say. The neighbour from across the hall pokes his head out.

'Everything OK?' he asks.

'Fine,' I smile all politely. He disappears.

I hurry back to my flat and start rummaging around in the cupboard under the sink.

'What are you going to do?' asks my wife.

'I'll set fire to his flat,' I explain. She seems unconvinced.

'You can't burn his flat down. You'd never be able to isolate the flames! We'd all go down. You'd be burning your own home.'

She's probably right. And besides, all I can find is an old pan scourer and some Brasso. No one ever started a fire with that.

My wife e-mails Danny Zucco's landlord. The landlord threatens to evict him unless the singing stops. He moves out and things go back to normal. But it all leaves a nasty taste in the mouth. This doesn't feel like the sort of environment in which to raise a child.

Plus, the whole episode didn't reflect well on me personally. I didn't respond to the problem with what you might call fatherly aplomb. For starters, any father should possess a certain amount of calm, diplomacy and fire-starting know-how. I have proved deficient in all three.

It's this flat. It brings out the worst in me. It makes me look, feel and act like a twat. I want to live in a place where I will feel like a responsible adult capable of raising a child. I want there to be a shed where I potter about at weekends. I want there to be four different types of recycling bin for various forms of household waste, each with its own subsections. I want there to be tiles that need grouting. I want to know what 'grouting' means. I don't want to knife-fight with my neighbours; I want to have them over for a barbecue on a sunny bank holiday. Then, maybe if we've had enough to drink, we might choose to have a musical, *West Side Story*-style knife-fight. But just for fun, as consenting adults.

I'm lying awake in the middle of the night worrying about the twatty flat and the horrid area and the way it all makes me feel so stupid and incapable. It's dark outside. No one is shouting swear words. No one is singing 'Sandy'. All I can hear is the gentle whirr of the air-conditioning system. That's because I am on the twenty-eighth floor of a hotel casino in Las Vegas. We flew here on a whim two nights ago to celebrate a friend's birthday. Which somehow encapsulates everything that needs fixing about my stupid lifestyle before the baby arrives. I am full of jet lag, over-priced sushi and self-hatred. I look at my wife on the other side of the gigantic bed. She's all sleepy and pregnant. I think about the chaos and the grime and the knives and the singing and the water balloons back home. I grab her arm and shake it.

'We should move to the suburbs,' I tell her.

So we do.

5

SAINSBURY'S

I am standing outside our new house clutching a hammer and some pliers. They're just two elements of the whole new tool set I bought down at Homebase earlier this morning. That's the kind of guy I am these days: a tool set kind of a guy. I'm using them to remove the 'For Sale' sign from our front garden. My next-door neighbour knocked round earlier and complained that it was blocking out her sunlight.

'No problem, I'll get rid of that sign for you,' I told her perkily. 'I'll just go and grab my hammer and my pliers. From my toolbox. Which I keep in the cupboard under the stairs. Because that's the kind of guy I am!' She looked at me strangely and walked off.

I now own a house with a front garden that's got a tree in it. I am a tree owner, and there's nothing more grown up than that. I am wrestling with the 'For Sale' sign when my hand slips and I whack myself in the face with the pliers. 'FUCK OFF!' I shout loudly in pain. The neighbour comes to her front window and looks at me crossly. I shrug back at her boyishly in a manner that I hope suggests that I'm not the sort of guy who usually goes around shouting 'FUCK OFF!' all over the place.

You'll have also noticed that I'm now the sort of guy who refers to himself as a 'guy' instead of a 'man', 'bloke', 'geezer' or 'hobbledehoy'. A guy is more informal than a man, more sensible than a bloke, more approachable than a geezer and more reliable than a hobbledehoy. A guy is the sort of guy who has a toolbox in the cupboard under the stairs. The most unpredictable and crazy thing that happens in a guy's life is whacking himself in the face with some pliers during the course of a domestic chore.

I pick up the pliers and get back to work. As pedestrians walk past the house, I sense them looking at me and thinking to themselves, 'What a studious and adept young man. He'd doubtless make an excellent husband and father.'

They're a funny bunch round here. Where I used to live, there was such a mix. Rich kids with preposterous hairstyles and imported Japanese trainers shared the streets with dipso geriatrics wearing cats round their shoulders like scarves. There were American hedge fund managers, demented crack whores, yummy mummies, hoodies, kids armed with water balloons, kids armed with knives, Nobel Prize winners and a whole host of famous faces off the telly all living together in one square mile. All the rich ones pretended the poor ones weren't there. It's what they call a 'melting pot'. Round here there's more uniformity. For instance, I've noticed everyone – man, woman or child – wears sleeveless body warmers. Some are fleecy, some are waterproof, some are padded, but the one rule is that they can't have any sleeves. It's a universally observed dress code. It's like the parish council have passed a law on it or something. I shall have to start cutting off the sleeves from all my coats and jackets in case they fine me. It'll be another chance to use an item from my new tool set.

So far we haven't made any friends. We came close the other day, when we were approached by a crowd of posh-looking middle-aged people on the high street. They were handing out leaflets that publicised the opening of a new supermarket in the area and twittering loudly to anyone who'd listen. Usually I don't do stop-and-chats with strangers. If a gang of strangers had approached me in the street back where I used to live, I would have instinctively kicked the closest one to me in the nuts and then run for it screaming. But this was a new area, a new me and a new set of strangers, who, it has to be said, looked less likely to stab, rape or vomit on us. In the spirit of mature, convivial, suburban neighbourliness I smiled and approached them warmly, accepting their leaflet with a feigned expression of interest. My wife took one too and examined the headline.

'Ooh, they're opening a Sainsbury's!' she said excitably. 'Great!'

No. Not great apparently. Not great at all.

'Great?' frowned one of the leafleting throng. 'What's so great about it?'

My eyes quickly scanned the leaflet more closely, consuming enough invective to realise that this was no promotional campaign.

My wife had got the wrong end of the stick. In fact, she'd got so confused that it was debatable whether she had the stick at all. But there was no stopping her now.

'Well, most of the shops round here are crap, aren't they?' she grinned.

She was right, of course. We have moved to one of the last few districts of London that has more or less managed to resist the onward march of major retail chains. The high street is occupied by the sort of small local businesses that your modern ethical, eco-fascist is so fond of harping on about: there's gift shops and fishmongers, haberdasheries and florists, numerous independent wine merchants and an abundance of 'charming' little outlets purveying trinkets, curiosities, forget-me-nots and other useless crap. But if you want to buy a tin of baked beans, some J-cloths or a pound of spuds after 5.30 in the afternoon, then you're stuffed. The locals don't mind this because the twee inconvenience of it all makes them feel like they're living in some rose-tinted 1940s' fantasy – only with less rickets and rationing.

Still, this was neither the time nor the place to point any of this out to them. These people were zealots. A fire of hatred burned in their eyes. Hatred for convenience stores with their array of fresh, reasonably priced produce and late-night opening hours. Hatred for the modern way of life that these supermarkets embodied. And hatred for the likes of us with our fully sleeved outerwear and weak-minded susceptibility to Nectar points promotional schemes.

A hush befell them. They seemed to be forming an angry circle around us. They fixed us with glares that screamed, 'You evil, ignorant, supermarket-loving bastards.'

Then one of them let rip.

'It'll tear the heart and soul out of the neighbourhood!' she spluttered in a shrill falsetto.

'There'll be neon signs and trolleys! It will be an eyesore!' said another. Their voices formed an indecipherable cacophony. Everyone wanted to get involved. My wife and I took a step backwards, only to find our paths blocked by more angry campaigners keen to point out how stupid and selfish we were. Someone said something about the ozone layer. Another mentioned traffic density. I heard somebody use the phrase 'carbon-neutral zucchini'. None of this made any sense. I began to feel like we were in *The Wicker Man*. 'Oh God! Oh Jesus Christ!' I muttered like Edward Woodward being dragged to his death in that giant burning effigy. How will they kill us here? Tear off our arms with their bare hands then shove a load of organically grown, locally produced asparagus up our arses before dragging our corpses around the local streets tied to the back of a Toyota Prius as a warning to other non-believers? Suffice to say, we had yet to acclimatise fully to the local culture and customs.

People haven't stopped wanting to stop and chat, mind you. It's weird. On a sunny day like today they even come up to you in your own front garden for an unsolicited chinwag. For instance, right now, an elderly woman is asking me about the flowers growing in my garden.

'Is it evening primrose?' she is asking while pointing at something on my front wall that, to my eyes, looks like a colourful clump of bird shit.

Before I can respond, she's wandered up the garden path to take a closer look. If I didn't know better, I'd think this was some sort of stitch-up. I know she looks posh and old and respectable, but she could easily be a pikey casing the joint. She could have a couple of accomplices hiding round the corner ready to pounce out and cosh me over the head with a sock filled with gravel once she's distracted me with her phoney flower chat. They'll be moving in with their eighteen grubby-faced children before I know what's happening. Burning tyres in the back garden, keeping ferrets in the bath, trying to sell me back my own plasma. That's how these people operate. Well, they've picked on the wrong bloke this time. I'm not just any old suburban mug.

'Look, luv, I don't know what you're on about,' I interrupt. 'I'd like you to get off my property please.'

She looks a bit taken aback. The door opens, and my wife appears. She smiles warmly at the old woman. She's very naive sometimes, my wife. Wouldn't know a confidence trickster if one came up and kicked her in the arse.

Luckily I've already done enough to get rid of the old bag, who's scuttling back down the garden path looking well and truly rumbled. And upset. And a little bit scared too. 'Hmmm,' I think to myself, 'maybe there's a chance she wasn't a gypsy confidence trickster after all . . .'

'What did she want?' asks my wife.

'The plasmas and the laptops, I reckon,' I say casually, 'but she might just as easily have been after the copper wiring out of the walls. You can get a packet for that these days.'

My wife looks back at the woman's retreating figure. She is tiny and wrinkled and slightly harassed-looking.

'Blimey, good job you had your pliers then,' says my wife after a bit of contemplation. Then she walks back inside.

I suppose I'm just not quite ready to be a talking-to-strangers-kind-of-guy yet.

6

LOVE

I clamber through the front door wrapped in a thin membrane of sweat and pollution. I chuck my keys in the drawer, drop my bag on the floor and peruse the pile of mail sitting on the table. And then I see it, sitting ominously on top of all those unopened bank statements and final reminders. A brown A4 envelope with my name written on it. My name written on it in pink highlighter pen with bits of gold glitter glued all around the outside. A chill tingles up from my stomach and karate-chops me in the windpipe. I know what this is, and it's worse than anything from the bank or the gas company. This is a valentine's card. And not just any valentine's card either. It bears all the hallmarks of a home-made valentine's card. The sort that requires a visit to W.H. Smith to buy some coloured card and Pritt Stick. The sort of that requires real effort. The worst sort of valentine's card.

Especially when you've got in from work with nothing to offer your thoughtful wife in return. Mind you, why should I have? There has been a mutual understanding in this marriage for some time now that we just don't do valentines. Didn't we discuss this? Didn't we decide that all the tacky cards and overpriced roses and romantic set menus

cheapened and homogenised our love? Or something like
that anyway. I definitely remember us dressing up the decision with some sort of clever-sounding twaddle. We have
both stuck faithfully to the deal ever since. It depends
on both of us observing its unwritten principles. Instead of
cramming a large dose of cheap, nasty, commercialised
romance into a single day each February, we have resolved
to sprinkle it evenly across the entire year. Just little touches
here and there, like making unsolicited cups of tea or
remembering to flush the toilet after you've used it. Those
are the sorts of things that keep the magic alive. The point
is, our valentine's amnesty has been functioning perfectly
well for years. But it depended on neither of us blinking first
– a bit like the Cold War. Well, now my wife has blinked,
and we find ourselves in our own personal Bay of Pigs.

I cautiously open the envelope and slip the top few
inches of the card out. Oh God. Oh, Jesus Christ. It's
worse than I thought: a whole bloody cartoon strip. With
pictures of chimpanzees cut out of magazines depicting my
wife and me in a satirical rendition of our relationship history. I can't bring myself to read this. I feel guilty enough
already, without finding out how hilarious and touching it
might be.

Why has she done this? She must have known I'd have
come home empty-handed. How am I supposed to
respond at this late stage of the day? She may not have
heard me come through the door. I could sneak back
down the shops, I suppose. But what am I going to get
round here that comes anywhere near the level of poign-
ancy of a hand-crafted chimp-based photo story? A box of
Miniature Heroes and a dusty old birthday card which I'd

quickly have to modify with a biro on the way home? That's just insulting. I may as well face the music.

I shuffle sheepishly into the living-room wearing a flustered, unconvincing smile.

'This is hilarious!' I blurt as she gazes up at me from the sofa. Then, as if to really hammer the point home, I glance at it again and emit a theatrical and rather too loud 'Ha!' It comes out sounding a bit sarcastic.

'Happy Valentine's,' she beams. I sit beside her and give her a kiss on the lips

'Thanks! I haven't got you anything,' I say, spontaneously, deciding on a come-right-out-and-say-it-we're-all-adults-here-after-all sort of approach. She half-smiles. 'I thought we didn't do that sort of thing any more,' I continue, 'although this really is brilliant.'

She looks a bit upset. Her eyes glaze over, and she gives a weak smile, then says, 'Don't worry, I don't mind.'

None of this makes sense. My wife doesn't play these sorts of mind games. She doesn't go in for melodrama, sentimentality, emotional trickery or any of that other stuff that can muddy the waters of an otherwise sensible relationship. She tells it like it is, my wife. She gives it to you straight. And if you don't like it quite as straight as she gives it, then you'd better get out of the way because you're liable to end up losing an eye. It can be harsh, but at least you know where you stand. If anyone has a tendency to come over all emotional and unnecessary in this relationship, it's me. But right now, I have to say, my wife is acting like some sort of . . . girl.

'If I'd known the policy had changed, I'd have . . .' I begin, but it's too late. She is now crying. Properly crying, with tears dribbling unapologetically down her reddened cheeks and snot coming out of her nose and everything. I get that punch-in-the-stomach feeling I get whenever she cries.

Then she blubs, 'I'm just being silly.'

She's right, of course – she is being silly. But this is what life is like in our house these days. All the usual rules and procedures have been turned upside down. I am having to learn to expect the unexpected. It's this pregnancy business, see? My wife is unusually delicate and touchy. She is sensitive to the things I say. Over the years she has learned to be pretty resistant to the endless tirade of ridiculous, boorish and offensive balderdash that spills from my lips. She has developed an internal filter that helps drown most of it out. But lately the filter seems to have malfunctioned. Now she's listening to almost everything I say. That's all I need.

I hold her close. There's no point in trying to reason with her. Reason has taken a nine-month vacation and been replaced by hysteria. I just have to be 'understanding' and 'sympathetic'. I express these sentiments by stroking her hair and making her loads of tea. 'Wanna cup of tea?' I say in a special baby-like voice designed to denote sympathy. She accepts. I bring it to her with a garibaldi biscuit. She looks happy. I feel like I have fixed the situation.

Later on, while she is in bed with a book, I sit on the bog reading the card. It is as touching and hilarious as I had suspected. Damn. I feel guilty all over again. I am overwhelmed with an urge to do something, anything, to show her how much I love her. In the absence of anything material to give her, and it being too late to offer her another cup of tea, I resolve to try and have sex with her. I mean, what's more romantic than that?

'What are you doing?' she says. I am clambering around under the bedclothes in my own uncoordinated version of foreplay. I am clumsy and oafish. Even after all these years together she still can't really tell whether I'm trying it on, having a fit or looking around under the sheets for the remote control.

'I'm trying it on!' I grin, all proud of myself.

'Why?' she asks.

'Coz it's Valentine's?' I explain.

'But I'm in the middle of a chapter.'

I shrug and fall silent for a bit. She returns to her book. I keep staring at her. In my head my expression is seductive and predatory. I am burning through the pages of her weighty novel with sheer sexual electro-power. Soon the stupid book will fizzle and burn in her hands. And then her bra will burn also, but not so badly that it will harm her breasts in any way.

'What are you looking at me like that for?' she eventually asks.

'You know why,' I say, a bit like Roger Moore.

'Why are you talking in that stupid voice?' she enquires.

It's beginning to feel like *Twenty Questions*, so I decide to snatch the book from her, fling it across the room, switch off the lights and just make a lunge in the darkness. Sometimes a woman likes a man to be a man. To take control. To grab the night by the scruff of the neck, look it square in the eyes and tell it, 'Library time is over Daddio, it's time to get down and boogie with Dr Love.'

'What the fuck?' she exclaims.

'Oof,' I blurt as she accidentally skims my nuts with her foot. At least, I hope it was an accident.

'What's the problem?' I say. 'I'm just trying to be . . . what d'you call it? Affectionate.'

She flicks the light back on. 'I'm not up to it,' she says. 'I feel rubbish and tired. Sorry.' She turns on her side and shuts her eyes.

I decide to stay awake for a while, staring at the wall and feeling sorry for myself. I may be gormless and ungainly in the bedroom but she knew that when she married me. It's never bothered her before. Hanky-panky has been pretty much off the agenda for weeks now. She is always tired and tense. She says she feels unattractive. I've tried to tell her that, what with her breasts looking all pregnant and inflated, I actually find her more attractive than ever. It doesn't seem to help.

'Can I make you a cup of Horlicks?' I ask in the darkness.

'No,' she mumbles in a state of semi-consciousness.

'Ovaltine?' I venture.

'Shut the fuck up and go to sleep,' she says.

Times are tough, all right. The dynamics of this rela-tionship have changed lately. She's usually so calm and in control. She's the rock we build our lives on; the voice of reason and the flag-waver for common sense. She's the one who stops me from doing stupid, irrational stuff like trying to burn people's flats down. If I tried to burn someone's flat down now, I don't know what would happen. She'd probably be too tired or tense to stop me. And then where would I be? Actually committing an act of stupid arson, that's where. It's a frightening thought.

It's not just that. My wife usually trims the hedges in our garden, sets up the direct debits at our bank and knows where all the heating controls for the house are. Let's be honest: she's the man of the house. Yes, it sometimes feels a bit humiliating. But not quite so humiliating that I have been bothered to learn how to do any of this stuff for myself.

Well, I'm having to learn now – and fast. She is becoming emotionally and physically incapable of performing her usual role as our home's father figure. It's time for me to step up to the plate.

The new house still needs a bit of work done on it. She has developed a fixation about every last detail being finished and perfect by the time the baby arrives. I'm not just talking about the flat-pack cot being assembled either. She wants the walls painted, the carpet fitted and those dangerous-looking wires hanging out of the wall in the baby's bedroom dealt with too.

'Don't worry, don't worry, I'll get it all sorted in time,' I tell her.

She looks at me sceptically. I can't even change a light bulb without lengthy reference to my *Reader's Digest DIY Manual*. Besides pulling down that For Sale sign, all I've used my tool set for so far is smashing up ice cubes to put in a glass of Dr Pepper.

Besides, even if I had the know-how, I wouldn't have the time. My days are busier than ever right now. With the birth drawing nearer, I feel under increased pressure to earn money: the child will doubtless be needing it to fritter away ungratefully on sweets and nappies and *Transformers* or what have you. And when I'm not actually out earning money, there is important time-wasting to be done. I figure once I'm a dad I won't have much opportunity to waste time any more: my life will become too hectic and filled with responsibility. That's why I'm trying to waste plenty of the stuff while I still can. I set aside a few hours each day to play Tetris on my laptop or just stare into space while idly wrapping my own hand in Sellotape. The other day I managed to sit through the whole of *Three Men and a Little Lady* on Sky Classics in the middle of the afternoon. I felt as if I owed it to myself.

There's no point trying to explain my frenetic time-wasting schedule to my wife, though. I just couldn't find the words to make it sound like a credible excuse for why the kitchen is still devoid of all essential appliances and we are keeping fresh food in a chilled picnic box next to the sink.

I make an executive decision to hire some men to do it all for me. My mate Simon is an expert painter and decorator. He says he can paint the entire inside of our house in three days. I hire him for two weeks, which he foolishly interprets as an act of generosity. What he doesn't realise is that I'll be needing him to fit light bulbs, install fridges, hang pictures and fiddle repeatedly with the heating controls during this period. Admittedly, these aren't the sorts of menial services he usually provides. But the bloke owns a van and a portable radio splattered with paint: if that doesn't mark him out as 'handy', I don't know what does.

I don't want to insult him by coming right out and asking him to do these odd jobs. I think it's more polite to subtly trick him into it. While he's on his lunch break, I ask him if he minds helping me hang this giant round mirror in the front room.

'Just stand there and tell me if it looks straight,' I say, holding it in position.

'Yeah, that looks about right,' says Simon, chomping on his sandwich.

I reach into my toolbox and fish out the hammer and a nail. I call it a nail – it's more of a tack really. It'd struggle to hold the weight of a set of door keys, let alone this 12-stone mirror I'm trying to put up. But it's all part of my ruse, see?

'What the fuck is that?' asks Simon in disbelief.

'It's a nail! What d'you think it is?' I say all casual, as I start to bash it cack-handedly into the wall.

Simon walks over and nabs it from me. 'You're not gonna hang anything on that. That's a girl's nail,' he says.

'Really?' I say. 'Well, it's the only sort of nail I've got. Maybe I should put a couple in?'

'No. You'll need more than just a nail. And you'll need more than that poxy craft hammer as well. I'll go and get my drill.'

And with that simple exchange I have Jedi mind-tricked Simon into performing what will be the first of many domestic chores over the next fortnight. I feel pretty clever, if a little hurt by what he said about my hammer. I make a mental note to go back to Homebase and buy something a bit chunkier as part of tomorrow's time-wasting itinerary.

Over the next few days, in between his painting obligations, Simon helps me wall-mount a TV in the bedroom, stick handles on all the cupboards in the kitchen, fit a new toilet seat and sort out those rogue electrical wires in the baby's room. He also helps me get in through the back door after I lock myself in the garden. Twice. I should feel like I've got him in the palm of my hand – but I don't. It hasn't taken him long to flip the dynamic back in his favour. Without asking, he has brought in an assistant called Ted, whom I have to pay extra for. The pair of them have started talking me into extra work that I never knew I needed.

'We can get hold of some cheap tiles to sort out that problem in the kitchen,' Simon tells me.

'What problem in the kitchen?' I ask.

'Damp,' says Ted. 'It's not too bad at the moment, but if you don't re-tile, it could be chaos in about a year.'

'How will re-tiling help?' I say.

'These are special damp-resistant tiles. They'll stop it penetrating any further.'

I stand there pretending to think about what they're saying. The truth is, whenever they go into the details of their work, my brain zones out and I start to visualise the Kleenex puppy in a pair of Ray-Bans dancing around to 'Money for Nothing' by Dire Straits. By the time I zone in again, they're explaining that they can get me the tiles at 50 per cent discount through a mate. I find myself agreeing to the deal.

'Great, well, are you gonna be in Fulham any time this afternoon?' Simon asks.

'No,' I say. I mean, why would I be in Fulham this afternoon? There's absolutely no precedent for me being anywhere near Fulham at any time of day.

'Only that's where the tiles need picking up from,' he continues, fixing me with his 'You're not going to make a big deal out of this, are you?' look.

Needless to say, I'm soon on my way to Fulham to pick up the tiles from a grumpy old codger on the North End Road. He's offish with me to begin with, until I tell him that Simon sent me. Then he perks right up.

'You his boy, are you?' asks the codger.

I'm not sure if he means this in a romantic or professional sense. Either way, I reply with an indignant 'No!' But he doesn't hear because his mobile has just started to ring. Only it's not actually ringing; it's bellowing out this 'comedic' announcement, which says, 'Can the man with the ten-inch penis please answer the phone immediately.' He answers the phone, shooting me a matey wink. I try my best to look unamused.

'Like my ringtone, did you?' he chuckles once he's finished his protracted chinwag.

'Not really,' I say, acting a bit sulky because he's treating me as if I were a teenager.

'Course you did!' he says. 'Now load them tiles in the motor and get back to the site before your boss gets the hump.'

'Site? Boss? Hump?' I think angrily to myself as I leave. 'This daft old loon has clearly got the wrong end of the stick about what the deal is between me and Simon.'

Only he hadn't. When I get back to the house, Simon tells me off for taking so long. 'But it was that mad old bastard with his ringtone!' I start to explain.

'Don't want to hear it,' says Simon. 'Me and Ted are gonna have to work late now.'

By 'late' he means past five o'clock.

I should put my foot down and remind everyone who's paying the wages around here. But I can't. Like I say, Simon is a mate. And anyway, I am in thrall to him and Ted: their magical handyman skills, their blokeish banter, their array of mystical tools and gizmos. Sure they patronise me, fleece me and mock me for what they see as my effeminate and flighty lifestyle. But they also let me use their sledgehammer to break up old tiles in the back garden and give me Jaffa Cakes. I'll miss them when they're gone. Which, as it happens, won't be any time soon. They claim to have discovered more damp and have, in response, smashed the whole room to pieces. We've got no sink or anything. We're having to do the dishes in the bath. I've no idea where the cooker has gone. I think they said something about putting it out back or throwing it in the canal or something. We are having to survive on whatever raw foods we can find in our bomb-site of a home. The other night I ate twelve Cola Bottles covered in brick dust for dinner. It's got so bad that my wife's almost starting to wish I'd taken care of all the chores myself. Almost.

She wakes up feeling too sick and weary to go to work one morning. 'Take the day off, it's important you look after yourself,' I say. There's something exciting about her being around the house during the day. It feels like when the teachers go on strike when you're a kid and you get an unexpected day off school. You've suddenly got a licence to muck around while everyone else is out at work. It's anarchic. Of course, I really should be at work myself. Or wasting time. Or running errands for Simon and Ted. But

I tell myself that hanging out with my wife is more important: she needs my support.

We sit around watching telly and eating biscuits. We go
out for lunch together. We basically act like a retired
couple for the day. Over lunch we talk about possible
names for the baby: I like Napoleon, Zeus or Jesus (pronounced 'Heyzus', like some sort of maverick South
American centre forward) for a boy and Shee-ra or Princess
for a girl. She remains non-committal about all of them.
Ultimately, I don't suppose I'll get the final say on the
matter. I guess I'll just wait and see what her decision is on
the day of the birth.

One other development: she suddenly wants to have sex
again. Like, all the time. It's weird – this happens in the
final few months of the pregnancy apparently. Trouble is,
her bump has now grown so large that the sheer mechanics
of congress are too complicated for me to even attempt.
I'm not the most dexterous fella at the best of times. I
struggle to perform even the most rudimentary sexual
manoeuvres. To attempt anything saucy with her now
would just be dangerous – I could pull a hamstring, crack
a vertebra or worse. Plus, the baby's on the move. It's
kicking and dancing around in there like nobody's business. You can actually see its little hands trying to punch
their way out of the womb while my wife lies on the bed.
It's off-putting. I don't want to feel my unborn child
moving while I'm trying to get busy with my missus. Let's
be honest, it's noncey.

'I'm not up to it,' I tell my wife.

'What's up?' she asks.

I don't want to make mention of the size of the bump

or its tendency to move and jerk about. Those are sensitive subjects. So I just say, 'I feel, erm, you know, tired and tense and . . . unattractive.' Well, it worked for her.

She laughs a bit. Then does a bit of a cry. I hold her apologetically and contemplate the fact that this is the first time in my life I have ever been in a position to turn down sex. And it'll almost certainly be the last.

7
BOBA FETT

I've been awake for what feels like hours. I wonder why my eyes won't adjust to the darkness. It may be that I've lost track of whether they're open or shut. 'I wonder what it would be like to go blind,' I think, in a way that only someone who's been lying awake in bed for hours can possibly think. 'Shit, maybe I am going blind. I keep getting those headaches. Must go to the optometrist. Or optician. What's the difference? Nobody knows. They don't just check your vision; they examine your eyeballs for cancerous growths. Eye cancer. Imagine if I had that. Blood seeping out of your corneas like tears. Jesus, anything but that. That or throat cancer. Or brain cancer. Anything inside the head. Cancer of the goolies I could manage. OK God, here's the deal: if I have to have any form of cancer, I'll take goolies. I've already got my missus pregnant – they can lop the bastards off now for all I care. We'll adopt a second. From Africa maybe. They could do with a few more black faces in an area like this, it's like *Village of the Damned* round here. Either way, I'm calling the optometrist first thing in the morning. What time is it? 4.19 a.m. Already? Now I'll never get back to sleep. Shit! Why did I check the clock?'

My wife fidgets beside me, trying to negotiate her ripened bump into a comfortable position. Her irritable night-time sighs are the only sounds that punctuate the pitch-black suburban silence. There are no street lamps outside our house and no traffic either. It's spooky. For a brief moment I miss the man who used to call us all fucking wankers at night. At least he reminded me that I was alive. But I suppose peace and quiet was one of the reasons we came here. It's just proving more of an acquired taste than I imagined.

Engine noise is what I miss most. The rumble of freight vehicles. The violent whine of super-bikes racing in the dead of night. The hiss of brakes on a National Express coach. These are the sounds that soothed me to sleep throughout my childhood. Our house was perched on the side of the A4 in west London. My bedroom windows shuddered with the vibrations of lorries and buses as they trundled by each night. It was rhythmic and comforting – like sleeping on a train. Plus, all the pollution formed a sticky black residue on my bedroom windows, which helped dull the neon glare of the street lamps that shone outside.

We'd been living on the grim sprawling estate down the road until our dad did the off. Understandably, my mum went temporarily loony and the family doctor identified us a family at risk. At risk of what was unclear: but four young sons plus a half-mad mother living on an estate where the opportunities for trouble were plentiful was probably considered a recipe for disaster. So they moved us to the little house on the motorway. I guess they figured that the carbon monoxide in the atmosphere would be slightly less damaging to our health than the inexpensive heroin that was available back on the estate.

Mind you, the new place was hardly a sanctuary of peace and quiet. Anarchy reigned from the moment we moved in. I was about six, and my three brothers were in their mid-teens. They fought and swore and abused drugs. My mum was traumatised, abandoned and skint. She worked as a part-time secretary, finishing at half three every day so she could pick me up from school. Driven to desperation by household overheads, the financial demands of her adolescent sons and her own cavalier use of a Dorothy Perkins store card (which she used to indulge in a rather perverse, prototype form of retail therapy before the term had even been invented), she ended up going to loan sharks for assistance. Even my school uniform was financed by a local Irishman in a grubby suit with a thin, insincere smile and a competitive line in 75 per cent interest rates. Every Friday evening he'd knock round for the latest repayment, then outstay his welcome by sitting on the sofa and trying it on with Mum while I tried to concentrate on *Play Your Cards Right*.

A constant stream of unsuitable dossers passed through our house. Drunks, degenerates, thieves, scoundrels and thugs all used our home as a place to stay for a night or sometimes more. And those were just the ones Mum invited back.

She sympathised with lost souls and offered them sanctuary under our roof: the dipso Glaswegian milkman, the hunchback machinist from the signage company where she worked, the flighty junior from the typing pool who'd just split up with her husband. That particular dosser actually came downstairs one night dressed in a slinky négligé and tried it on with my brother, who must have been at least eight years her junior. That sort of thing never once happened to me when I reached seducible age, which is just another indication of the rampant injustice that prevailed in our household.

Late one night I answered the door to a middle-aged woman who looked like she'd just gone eight rounds with Lloyd Honeyghan. Beside her stood a small boy about two years younger than me, dressed in his jimmy-jams and crying. She turned out to be the lady who brought round the sandwiches at Mum's office. They were invited to stay for as long as they liked. Looking back, it was an admirable act of instinctive compassion by my mum. After all, this woman wasn't even a close mate – she'd just tipped up knowing that my mum was the sort of person you could turn to in those sorts of situations. But as Mum uttered her invitation, all I could do was look at that poor, traumatised lad – a boy who had obviously witnessed despicable scenes of domestic violence that no child should ever have to see – and think to myself, 'That little shithead needn't think he's kipping in my room.'

Yeah, his dad may have knocked his mum around a bit. Yeah, he'd had to flee his family home in the dead of night and move in with a bunch of strangers. All that might have gone some way to explaining WHY he was a little shithead but it didn't make him any less of one to my mind. Needless to say, he DID get to kip in my room, play with my toys, wear my clothes, nick stuff from my lunchbox and generally fuck with my shit for the three

months they stayed with us. He'd pester me and attack
me, verbally abuse me and continually switch the telly
over when I was trying to watch *Saint and Greavsie*. I'd
always been the little brother of the house. Suddenly I had
one of my own and I didn't like it. If I complained, or
moaned or punched him in the stomach, I'd be the one
who was condemned.

'Poor little Jimmy, all he's been through! Why don't
you give him a break?' my mum would ask.

'Jimmy's a wanker,' I told her.

She'd just tut, shake her head and give him the last
packet of Golden Wonders from the bread bin to make
him feel better. Even my brothers were on his side. They
never made him do the bookshelf challenge once. They
quickly worked out that taking his side in any conflict was
a brilliant way of winding me up into an incandescent state
of frustration.

'Jimmy, you took that pound coin from my piggy bank,
didn't you?' I once shouted at him in the living room.

'Tell him to fuck off, Jimmy!' my brothers chuckled.

'Fuck off!' Jimmy grinned. Instinctively I lunged for
him, only to be intercepted by my brothers, who encouraged Jimmy to execute a 'free slap' around my face while
they held my arms.

When Jimmy and his mum finally left, I caught him
smuggling about fifteen of my *Star Wars* figures out of the
house in his bag.

'Give me them back, you thief!' I said. Jimmy started to
cry.

'Don't be so mean!' my mum chastised. 'Let him have
the figures, you've got loads of others!' Like they were

spares! The whole point was that you had to try and collect every individual character from all the *Star Wars* movies. I couldn't afford to just give fifteen away! That act of enforced charity set my collection back by about three years. Boba Fett, Luke in his Bespin Fatigues, C3PO with removable limbs, the Imperial Storm Trooper in Hoth battle gear – that little shit waltzed out with some of my most prized assets.

A few months later some bloke we knew got slung out of his flat for not paying the rent. Suffice to say, he wound up kipping on our sofa for about a year. He'd turned up with three carrier bags of clothes and a fat tortoiseshell cat. Only it turned out to be not fat but pregnant. Our house was already overrun with pets – we had two cats and a dog of our own that seemed to be forever spewing out litters of offspring. So when the lodger's cat gave birth to six kittens, no one was best pleased. Anyway, we must have made him feel pretty guilty about it because one night he drowned them all in a bucket of water in our front room. My brother caught him at it while he was going downstairs for a glass of water. Using our broom to hold the little blighters down, he was. He'd turned the volume right up on the telly to try and drown out their terrified meows. It being the middle of the night, *The Hitman and Her* happened to be the only thing on. The last sound those cats would have heard was something like 'Boys, Boys, Boys', by Sabrina. I don't care if you're man or beast; no one deserves that kind of undignified send-off.

To my brothers and their friends our home was a truancy safe house in which they could doss on weekday afternoons with impunity, whiling away the hours with solvent abuse and marathon sessions on our Atari games system. Three or four times a month I'd pretend to be ill in order to get out of school. Mum couldn't afford to take the day off to look after me, so usually all three of my brothers would volunteer to stay home and make sure I didn't drink any bleach or anything. Rather than have to choose which one got the nod, my mum would invariably let all three of them stay home just to keep the peace.

My pointless days around the house would be measured out by episodes of *The Sullivans*, *Sons and Daughters*, *Crown Court* and *Falcon Crest*. I'd watch anything and everything, me, even the test card. My brothers and their mates would only bother me sporadically. Sometimes their respective groups of friends would all come round at once, and a fight would break out between them. I remember having a particularly enjoyable episode of *The Waltons* interrupted by a disagreement between my youngest brother and the friend of one of my older siblings. Things got physical and my brother produced a knife from his back pocket. It was just a craft knife really – the sort where you had to push the tiny blade out of the plastic handle with a little button. Even as an eight-year-old, unseasoned in the mechanics of street fighting, I could see it was a pretty pathetic weapon. He wafted it half-heartedly at his assailant, making unconvincing threats to 'carve him up' before the whole daft fracas was broken up and I got back to watching Jim-Bob trying to cop off with Aimee Godsey.

Soon they graduated to more elaborate weaponry. One afternoon they got hold of a Gat gun, which fired lead pellets out of a spring-loaded barrel. They accidentally shot a light switch, causing it to explode and leave large scorch marks on one of the bedroom walls.

'When Mum gets home, tell her you did it,' they told me.

'What with, the gun?' I asked. 'No you dickhead. Not the gun. She mustn't know about the gun.'

'Well, with what then?' I asked.

They looked at the damaged light fitting for a moment and stroked their chins.

'A hammer,' said one. 'Tell her you were playing with a hammer and accidentally smashed the light switch to pieces.'

'Until it exploded?' I asked sceptically.

'Yes!' they said angrily. 'Until it exploded!'

'I dunno,' I said, shaking my head and regarding the damage. 'It doesn't look like it's been smashed with a hammer. It looks like it's been shot with a gun.'

One of them grabbed me by the face. 'Look, you little bastard. I don't care what you think it looks like. Just tell Mum your story and stick to it.'

Suddenly the other brother came over all good-cop and intervened. 'Look, if you do this, we'll get you a toy,' he said. 'Any toy you like.'

I knew the story was unconvincing. I knew I'd get into trouble. But the deal was appealing. I'd had my eye on an Action Man with Deep Sea Diving Kit in the Argos catalogue for months. I told them my price.

'Fine,' said good cop, perusing the catalogue I'd just handed him. 'Deep Sea Diving Action Man. Good choice. It's yours come the weekend.'

When my mum came home and saw the damage to the wall, I took the blame. It was the first and last time I'd ever take the rap for a blag I hadn't done. She went berserk. Not so much about the damage to the wall but at the insulting nature of our flimsy explanation.

'You expect me to believe that?!' she shouted. 'We haven't even got a fucking hammer!' I looked around for help, but by that time my brothers had scurried out the front door.

The point I'm trying to make is, I grew up in a house where there was simply too much going on and too many people coming in and out all the time. Chaos and uncertainty reigned. Anxiety and menace hung in the air. People nicked your *Star Wars* figures and got away with it. I felt loved and reasonably safe but never that relaxed. Boo-hoo. Poor me. A nasty man drowned some cats in my front room. Hardly the stuff of a half-decent misery memoir, is it? Well, my traumas may be lame, but at least I'm not making them up.

'They still owe me that Deep Sea Diving Action Man, the tight bastards,' I think to myself angrily as I lie in bed twenty-five years later, still wide awake and staring at the ceiling. 'I bet Argos don't even do them any more. Well, they'll just have to find a vintage one off eBay instead. Some nerd will probably charge them a hundred quid for it these days. They could have got it for about a tenner back then. So who's the mug? Me or them?'

The bedroom still smells of paint and fresh carpet. There are empty boxes of flat-pack furniture stacked neatly in the corner. Each of the electrical sockets is covered with little glowing plugs with pictures of bunny rabbits on them. These are the last-minute refinements I've been making in time for the baby's arrival. This household will be a neat, tidy, quiet and hopefully slightly boring place to grow up in. I'm not quite responsible enough to make too many guarantees to my unborn offspring just yet, but I can promise that it will never be woken in the night by an act of cat murder. And, what with the precautions I've made, I also feel pretty confident that it will never be allowed to electrocute itself in one of the plug sockets. It's not much of a fatherhood manifesto but it's the best I can do right now: no cat killing, no electrocutions. And absolutely no one kipping on our sofa for more than one night at a time.

Solitude: that's what I want from my new life in this house. Don't get me wrong: I'm all for neighbourliness. If you live within three doors of me, then by all means come on over, put your feet up, have a cup of tea, help yourself to a Mr Kipling and spend some time admiring my impressive array of fashionable compact discs. Just make sure you've got an invite and it's all arranged in advance. Don't surprise me with an impromptu visit or I'm liable to blind you with the can of Mace I keep by the door for security purposes. It won't be my fault either: when unidentified visitors turn up on my doorstep, I'm afraid I follow a strict policy of spray first, ask questions later.

It's later in the day, and my wife is out front sorting out the recycling bins: paper, plastic, glass, flakes of skin, dust, unwanted Savage Garden CDs. There's a separate bin for everything these days. Whatever happened to loading all your rubbish into a stolen supermarket trolley and pushing it into the canal? Progress, I suppose.

Suddenly she waltzes into the house with a friend in tow. An unexpected, off-the-cuff, 'I-was-just-passing-and-thought-I'd-pop-by-and-say-hello' sort of a friend. The worst sort.

'You remember Flo, don't you?' she beams. Flo waves at me soppily over my wife's shoulder. I don't remember her, but she is just pretty enough for me to wish I wasn't sitting in front of the racing from Aintree while idly scratching my testicles. I emit a phlegmy cough by means of a greeting and splutter Rich Tea biscuit crumbs down my front.

See what I mean? No good can come from a house that's got too much of a welcoming air about it. Apart from anything else, I would have prepared myself better had I known Flo was going to make an appearance. I would probably have been back out in the garden with my tools. And not just the hammer and pliers either – the spirit level and Stanley knife would have made an appearance too. I might even have donned the tool belt. At the very least, I would have made sure I was munching on biscuits rather more sophisticated than boring old Rich Teas. Something like shortbread fingers I'd imagine. In any case, welcoming the likes of Flo in with such breezy spontaneity is a slippery slope. Before we know it she'll have made herself up a little bed on the sofa and be insisting that we watch *The X Factor* on Saturday night instead of *Strictly Come Dancing*.

'You're just the thin end of the wedge,' I mutter

under my breath, as she and my wife totter into the kitchen.

'What was that?' smiles Flo.

'Oh,' I splutter, 'I said d'you wanna Rich Tea?'

8

PLAYBOY

Luckily, I have some proper friends who live round here who I can meet up with under more controlled circumstances. Like Dave, who, I suppose, is kind of like my best mate. I've known him since school, was best man at his wedding and am godfather to his five-month-old daughter.

Dave and I are in his local pub. I suppose it's now my local pub too. Having a local pub already sounds like a step in the right direction towards sensible fatherly behaviour. While my current tendency towards long periods of abstinence punctuated by catastrophic bouts of binge drinking is deemed by society to be immature and stupid, the sort of inoffensive alcoholism that suburban dads cultivate nightly in pubs like this is still considered a wholly grown-up and somehow cosy form of addiction. It's one I intend to experiment with over the coming months.

'What are you drinking?' I ask Dave.

'I dunno. What are you drinking?' he replies.

This is what conversations with him are like. He can't make a decision without first knowing what you're going to do.

He's the anxious type. Always biting his nails and

thinking the sky might fall in on us at any moment. Dave sees the glass neither as half-empty nor half-full; he sees it as a potential health hazard that is likely to get tipped over on to some exposed wiring at any moment, causing a massive electrical fire in which we shall all be engulfed in flames and quickly reduced to charred, screaming corpses like those ones at the end of *Raiders of the Lost Ark*.

'Do you want any crisps?' I ask Dave.

'I dunno. Do *you* want any crisps?' he replies.

There's something else you should know about Dave: his name isn't really Dave. He wouldn't like it if I committed his actual name to print. This despite the fact that his real name is as generic and innocuous as the phoney one I've selected for him. And despite the fact that you wouldn't know or care who the hell he was even if I published his entire name, address, social security number and a small illustration of his face. I don't even have anything particularly unkind or incriminating to write about him either. But, like I say, he's the anxious type – and just a little paranoid too. He already thinks the government are trying to steal his thoughts. Imagine if his real name got used in a book. Then he'd know they were on to him. He'd probably buy a shotgun, run off into the hills and wind up blowing his own brains out. I don't want that kind of blood on my hands.

So I've decided to call him Dave. Just so you know, I am changing most other people's names in this book too. All I can guarantee is that my name really is Sam Delaney. But, for the record, if I were to use a pseudonym, it would probably be Thunderhawk Jones. Or Ricardo St Tropez.

Anyway, here we are in the pub. The very pub in which Dave first convinced me to move to the area. I told him all the worries I had about my fatherly credentials. About how I thought it was time for a calmer, more austere, more predictable way of life. I looked around at the roaring fire, approachable bar staff, dozing canines and bunch of retro old crap hanging from the walls of his local and said, 'I need to move to the suburbs.'

For once, he was unequivocal in his response.

'You wanna live where I live, mate,' he said before the words were barely out of my gob.

This is what all blokes say when you tell them you're thinking of moving. That's because most blokes think that giving sage advice just means telling people to make the exact same decisions as they have made. Even if they spend most of their time moaning about the decisions they have made.

Conversations between blokes usually go something like this:

BLOKE: I wish I'd never bought that motor. It's uncomfortable, the boot space is rubbish, it's always breaking down and it drinks petrol like nobody's business. Plus, it looks like something a bleeding hairdresser would drive.

BLOKE'S MATE: Yeah, I know what you mean. I'm thinking of getting a new car myself.

BLOKE: Are you? You wanna get what I drive, mate.

BLOKE'S MATE: But weren't you just saying how much you hated your car?

BLOKE: Well, yeah, but what else are you gonna get?

BLOKE'S MATE: I dunno, I was thinking of a Saab.

BLOKE: A Saab? A Saaaaab? What are you? A dentist from Sweden?

BLOKE'S MATE: Erm, no.

BLOKE: Some sort of architect called Steven who listens to Coldplay?

BLOKE'S MATE: No, I'm not that either.

BLOKE: Well what are you getting a Saab for then?

BLOKE'S MATE: I didn't say I was getting a Saab . . . I just said I was thinking about it.

BLOKE: Well, are you still thinking about it now I've told you what sort of people drive Saabs?

BLOKE'S MATE: [staring hollow-eyed at his pint glass and muttering sheepishly] No.

BLOKE: So what are you thinking of getting instead?

BLOKE'S MATE: [hanging his head, utterly defeated] The same car as you drive.

BLOKE: Good. That's that sorted then. Now, what are you drinking? Same as me?

We talk like this because we are confused and baffled by the incessant challenges life spews up. Each and every day a man is faced by difficult questions like 'What mortgage?' 'What car?' 'What sandwich filling?' 'What mid-price pair of smart casual trousers?' and other dilemmas that sound like titles of helpful magazines. In fact, I think the first two already are titles of helpful magazines. The second two aren't but should be and, should any shrewd magazine publishers reading this agree, then may I be the first to throw my hat in the ring for the role of editor-in-chief on either publication. Particularly the one about sandwiches.

Anyway, none of us knows how to answer these important questions with any degree of certainty or confidence. We can never be sure that we have made the right choice about anything. Our only means of judging our decisions is to compare them with those of our peers. By subtly bullying our peers into making the same decisions as us we can feel slightly more comfortable about our ridiculous, transient and ultimately futile existences. All of our fates are pretty much in the hands of outrageous fortune or the Gods or The Power of Greyskull or whatever you want to call it. We have control over so little – but we can sometimes maliciously influence the decisions of our best mates for no other reason than our own petty-minded sense of self-satisfaction.

So, in a way, we're all like Dave.

'Becoming a dad is . . . a journey,' he'd told me that night in the pub, gingerly placing his pint on the table and affecting a faraway look in his eyes. 'It's like discovering what life is really about. I'm suddenly, like, "What have I been *doing* all these years? Life's not about drinking and drugs and, y'know . . . French electronic dance music."' Yeah, I know, I found that last example strange too, but I let it pass. 'It's about *human beings*! I mean, I look at my little girl's face in the morning and everything is in perspective.'

I nodded politely. But inside my head I thought: 'That's funny. It's not like Dave to speak in a series of meaningless clichés. Maybe those meaningless clichés are in fact true, that's why people say them all the time.'

Next he started going on about the area like some sort of crappy, half-pissed estate agent.

'The schools are great, the pubs are great and the transport links to town are plentiful!' he slurred.

Ordinarily, I don't like 'transport links' as a term or a concept. And on this occasion I found his strange use of the word 'plentiful' a bit disconcerting too. But I nevertheless noticed myself treating his words with slightly less disdain than they perhaps deserved. I never thought there'd be a day when the quality of local schools or even pubs would be factors in my assessment of an area. If anything, I would have actively sought out areas with rubbish schools and disgusting pubs just to make a point.

'Just how disgusting are the pubs round here?' I would ask the estate agent.

'Oh, they're truly disgusting, sir. Full of murderers and racists with rude words smeared out in human faeces all over the walls!' would come the reply. Or at least it would have done, had the estate agent had his head screwed on.

'What about the schools?' I would venture.

'Piss-poor. Not one pupil has ever passed so much as a spelling test, and the teachers are all paedos.'

'Great! Where do I sign?'

But my mindset was clearly altering. Sitting in the pub listening to Dave drone on about the mundane appeal of his locality, his words began to sound strangely appealing. It was like I was one of those world leaders you see sitting in the middle of an international summit. Someone had stuck a special pair of headphones on my ears that helpfully translated all the seemingly meaningless foreign babble into a semi-coherent form. I had seen the light. No, that doesn't sound right. I had seen the darkness? No, what I had seen was the dimly lit greyness of suburban family life. And I quite liked it.

So I convinced my wife that we should move here. And now I'm back in the same pub drinking the same beer and eating the same flavour crisps as Dave. The baby is due in a couple of weeks. Dave is giving me some last-minute advice on the matter.

'Mate, these are the most important two weeks of your life', he says.

'I know. Buying nappies, getting the birth bag ready, planning the route to the hospital,' I reply.

'No, mate. Fuck all that,' he says fixing me with a grim stare. His eyes are baggy and his face unshaven. He has been outside for a fag about eighteen times already. We've only been here three-quarters of an hour. 'You've got to understand that having a baby ruins your life. So you have to squeeze as much living in now before it's too late.'

I look at Dave's mad face. His right eye twitches manically. He needs more sleep. I think about what he's said. Have I really done enough living over the past thirty-two years? Depends on what he means by 'living'. If he means travelling to the farthest reaches of the globe, meeting strange and fascinating people, enriching my soul, invigorating my mind, witnessing the extremes of nature in all its many guises, unlocking the secrets of the human condition and discovering the whispered truths of the universe, then the answer is undoubtedly no. Mind you, me and the missus had a great weekend in Rome last year. Went right to the top of the bloody great tower at the Vatican we did. The staircase was steep and windy and my wife started to go all dizzy, so we didn't stop for long. But for the brief few moments we were up there I remember looking out across the majesty of all those stunning buildings and thinking, 'Blimey, what an achievement. I could never make something as good as this. No patience. Never even finished so much as an Airfix Spitfire model without getting distracted. But of course, I don't believe in God. Maybe if I did I'd have had more of an incentive to finish that rotten Spitfire. Would a plastic rendition of a Second World War fighter plane be an appropriate tribute to a deity? Probably not. If anything, He might find it a crude and offensive reminder of man's tendency towards self-destruction. I would probably incur his mighty wrath and be struck down with righteous fury. Or something. So, all things considered, probably best I stick to being a Godless heathen after all.' It was probably the most profound thought world travel had ever inspired in me. By the time I'd finished having it, we were back at the bottom of the steps buying overpriced Cornettos from a street vendor.

Personally, I don't see why the notion of enlightened, fulfilling, wholehearted living is always associated with travel. In particular, it seems to be associated with doing outlandish outdoor activities in places like New Zealand or Wales. There's a couple of idiots who live down my street – outdoorsy types they are – who have got a bumper sticker on their Land Rover that says 'One Life, Live It'. Well, what else are we gonna do with it? Lick it? Frame it? Buy it a kebab? I know what they're really trying to say with their stupid sticker. They're trying to say that you should get outdoors and climb up a rock. Or piss about inside a cave wearing a helmet with a light on it. Or buy a mountain bike. The implication is that, unless you're spending at least fifty quid a month in Millets on Gore-Tex-based outdoor wear, then you're pissing your life up the wall. Which strikes me as a bit narrow-minded. I mean, I've done my fair share of adventure sports, and I can't say it taught me much about the meaning of life. In the summer of 1984 I attended Camp Dolphin Adventure Camp in Wales with my mate Alex. We did rock climbing, abseiling, potholing, kayaking, the lot. I spent the week making a bit of a prick out of myself if I'm honest. I'm just not cut out for that sort of thing. The instructor fined us a Lion bar every time we used our knees for support during rock climbing. I was the poor bastard who owed him twenty-five Lion bars by the end of the week. I blew my entire tuck budget on that idiot. Sums up the sort of fascistic mentality of the people who go in for that sort of outward-bound crap if you ask me. I mean, OK, I admit it: I'm not that good at extreme sports. I'm not a particularly co-ordinated sort of a bloke. Does that mean that I am unable to make the most out of life? Just because I can't climb a rock without using my knees? Is that what those Land-Rover-driving bastards up the street reckon? Well, screw them and screw their sleeveless, Gore-Tex jackets too.

In any case, none of that matters because that sort of stuff isn't what Dave means by 'living'.

When Dave says that I should cram as much 'living' as possible into the next two weeks, he means I should cram as much 'drinking' as possible into the next two weeks. Maybe throw in a bit of drunken leering at girls for good measure. Spend a couple of soul-corroding evenings in a lap-dancing bar. Perhaps nip into the bogs once in a while to shovel drugs up my nose off the edge of my Oyster card. That's the kind of living he's got in mind. Because that's the kind of living he misses from his carefree childless days. Of course, the irony is, he didn't really spend much time doing any of those things during his carefree childless days. But at least he always had the option of doing them. That option has now been removed. Not by his wife but by himself. He's responsible enough to know, deep down, that's no way for a decent adult to behave. But it suits his inner narrative, his carefully constructed self-mythology, to pretend that he's some sort of rampant hedonist who's having his rock 'n' roll instincts cruelly restrained by the chains of domesticity. Like many blokes, Dave likes to think of himself as some kind of maverick Lizard King living on the edge of reason and decency. He usually thinks these thoughts while trimming his front hedges on a Sunday morning, listening to Elaine Page's Radio 2 show on his transistor radio. The mundane truth, which he can't bring himself to confront, is that he's actually a good, honest husband and father.

This is a form of self-delusion I must take care to avoid. Hard times lie ahead. Parenthood won't be a walk in the park. But I've gone into this with my eyes wide open. I can't allow myself to start thinking that a life of buttoned-down responsibility has been somehow imposed on me. That way madness lies: I just have to look at Dave's right eye to realise that.

Anyway, I figure I've done my fair share of mindless, low-rent hedonism. Over the years I've spent three separate Friday nights in three separate A&E wards across

London. I've wet myself in a coffee shop in Amsterdam. I've bought drugs off a Hispanic gangster in New York who threw me out of his moving Cadillac. Only the other month I got slung off a train in Stevenage for nicking a miniature bottle of gin from the buffet car. Oh yeah, I've lived life on the edge all right. I even attended a party at the *Playboy* mansion once. I was in LA on an assignment for a magazine and somehow wangled an invite to some daft party Hugh Hefner was throwing. It wasn't all that, to be honest. The snacks were dry and boring, the beer was watery and the bunnies' conversational skills were nothing short of pathetic. Their smiles were sparkly, their bosoms heaving, but their eyes were cold and dead. I know it may sound strange, but they seemed somehow indifferent, as if they wished they weren't talking to me and the other idiots who were slouched around the place but were far away with someone else. Or maybe they were simply wishing they were dead. Who knows? Suffice to say, I've been to the edge of reason and decency, and it wasn't all it's cracked up to be.

On the other hand, if Dave is simply pointing out that I'll have no spare time left once I'm a dad, then good. I hate spare time. Makes me itchy and irritable. Once I've finished work, had my tea, done the washing up and watched a DVD, I'm usually stumped about what to do next. I find myself staring out the window at the neigh-bourhood cats, doing weird cat voices like Johnny Morris. It's boring. One of the main reasons I'm having a kid is to eat up all that spare time. I won't be telling Dave this, though. He loves spare time. It would break his heart to know my feelings on the matter.

I drain my pint and put my hand on his shoulder. 'Don't worry, Dave,' I say softly, 'I'm gonna spend the next fortnight getting absolutely twatted.'

He looks up, doe-eyed. 'Thanks, mate,' he says. 'That means a lot.'

9

QUINCY

I'm pulling some blue surgical scrubs over my Levis and thinking that I look a bit like Doogie Howser MD. I am in a tiny side-room off the main corridor in the maternity ward. It seems that this is where the doctors and nurses leave their personal belongings and civilian clothes during the working day. I am surrounded by their handbags and wallets. There are iPods and mobile phones strewn about the place. They're not very security conscious, these people. This being Britain's poshest NHS hospital, maybe they're confident that no one is likely to thieve from them. They are wrong. 'If I stole those now, I'd get away with it easy,' I reason with myself. 'Nobody would ever suspect an expectant father whose wife has just been rushed into the emergency delivery room to have taken the time to go thieving. Even if they did suspect, they'd probably be too polite to actually bring it up. In the midst of a personal trauma like this, no one's gonna have the guts to accuse me of stealing a pink iPod mini from a trainee obstetrician.'

It's not usual for me to thieve, but extreme circum- stances can make you do strange things. Like those people trapped in car wreckages who start to have sex with each other amid the twisted metal and broken glass. It's a distraction technique to keep the mind from dwelling on the pain and fear. Maybe I'm subconsciously hoping to get caught and arrested and dragged down the nick, thus avoiding attendance at a birth that is rapidly spiralling out of control. Whatever my subliminal reasons are, it's definitely out of character for me to nick stuff – I'm simply too gutless.

A nurse pops her head around the door and says my wife has been asking for me. I drop the wallet and pull on the silly blue surgical hat they've given me. I feel like I'm about to start a shift on the deli counter at Morrison's. My hands are shaking a bit. I clock my reflection in the window and decide that, in this light, I look more like Quincy than Doogie Howser. Emboldened, I take a deep breath and stride out of the locker room to face my destiny.

We've already been here fourteen hours. Fourteen hours of labour. Sounds scary, doesn't it? Makes you imagine fourteen hours of incessant agony and screaming, hot towels, bucketloads of blood, legions of panicked midwives, shouty doctors, bleeping machines and stirrups. That's how they portray it on the box. That's also how other dads will describe it to you in a bid to make you shit yourself. Every dad I know has told me some sort of petrifying tale of delivery-room woe over the past nine months. Not one of them has tried to reassure me that some births actually do pass without notable incident. That's because messy-birth stories are the modern man's equivalent to war stories.

The modern man has generally led a life devoid of action, danger and peril. While his ancestors fought in the

Somme or spent five years in a Japanese POW camp getting repeatedly jabbed with a spiky piece of bamboo through the bars of his cage, the modern man just drifts through life moaning about the price of petrol and the inadequate speed of his broadband connection. Our lives are a pathetic series of namby-pamby concerns and rubbish, self-indulgent whinging. This book alone should have already given you an accurate impression of just how inconsequential the preoccupations of the twenty-first-century Western male truly are. The closest any of us ever gets to raw, undiluted terror is in the delivery room. So it's little wonder we milk those moments for anecdotes until they're bone-dry. It's the source of constant exaggeration and one-upmanship within inter-male conversations.

'We were in there for the best part of a week,' one might say to another over a pint. 'My missus was losing a litre of blood per minute. Two midwives dropped dead from exhaustion right in front of us. In the end they had to cut the baby out of my wife's bumhole. It was the only possible exit point apparently.'

'Well, that's nothing,' another will retort. 'They ran out of drugs in our hospital, so I had to nip out to Threshers and buy my missus a bottle of Teacher's whisky to swig while they amputated her legs, which had become infected with MRSA during the first of three abortive caesarean attempts. In the end she died.'

'But I saw her earlier this morning. She looked fine.'

'Oh yeah, she's alive now. But she was technically dead for eighteen minutes. They had to jump-start her heart using one of those special machines with the electric blasters.'

So late last night, after my wife had woken me up and explained that her waters had broken, I was expecting the worst. I drove bleary-eyed to the hospital and checked her in. They stuck us in a nice, softly lit maternity room and said the midwife would be in to see us soon. My wife popped herself up on the bed and we started to wait.

'What are you staring at?' she asked me after a few silent moments had passed.

'You,' I said. 'Are you sure your waters have broken?'

'Of course I'm sure,' she said. 'Why?'

'Well, you don't seem to have gone into labour yet.'

'Oh really? How can you tell?'

'Well, you should really be screaming by now. And sweating. And telling me to fuck off and that.'

'OK then: fuck off.'

'Yeah, like that but more shouty and mad . . .'

'No, I really mean it. Fuck off.'

So I fucked off. The lady from the ante-natal classes said I should do whatever my missus says during labour. Mind you, I was beginning to question the credibility of those ante-natal classes. I mean, they told me about the blood and the pain and the tears. They told me about the need to bring along light, nutritious snacks such as trail bars and dried fruit. (I forgot to buy these and so ended up throwing half a box of After Eights and a Babybel into the birthing bag on the way out the door.) They suggested I bring some iPod speakers through which to play the soothing sounds of Enya or Clannad. (Again I forgot these, but I am not averse to the idea of having a stab at 'Orinoco Flow' myself, should the situation demand it.) They even went as far as to warn me that my wife might actually shit herself before my very eyes. But they didn't say anything about the boredom, about the long, tedious hours in which you just sit around waiting for the real action to start.

'So, how are you finding labour so far?' I asked her as I re-entered the room, having had a little walk around the ward to let her calm down. This was supposed to show her that I'd now accepted that she really was in the early stage of childbirth. But I must have misjudged it in some way because she just told me to shut my 'fucking mouth'.

Which only reconfirmed to me that she was in labour. She had not yet got on to pushing, heaving, thrashing or crying. In fact, she still had her jeans on. There were certainly no signs of a baby – she hadn't so much as shat herself yet. But it was unlike her to be quite so sweary towards me, so I was prepared to take her word for it when she said she was experiencing regular contractions. She has always had an intimidatingly high pain threshold. I find it emasculating, if I'm honest. I'll get a paper cut from opening an envelope and yelp like I've been smashed in the face with a broken beer glass. She drops an iron on her foot and winces like she's just stubbed her toe.

'How regular are the contractions?' I asked her.

'About once every ten minutes,' she said. 'I'm actually having one right now.' Then she kind of flinched in the same way I do when I nick myself shaving.

The first few hours tick-tocked by without anything much happening. Occasionally someone came in and took her blood pressure. I kept asking questions about the 'diameter of the contraction' in a bid to sound knowledge-able and interested. I didn't really know what any of it meant: I was just regurgitating any old phrases I could remember from the gigantic *Guide to Childbirth* that I'd found next to our bed a few weeks earlier. Everyone ignored me anyway. I almost began to wish that I'd brought a book with me. Or some cards, a set of Travel Yahtzee, some felt tips and a colouring book. Once we ran out of conversation, the atmosphere became slightly awkward, to be honest. Mostly I just sat there holding my wife's hand and trying to adopt a sympathetic but calm facial expression. I'm no good at doing that sort of thing though; my face lacks the subtle nuance of the accomplished thespian. So I wound up sitting there with this weird furrowed brow and exaggerated pout, like Gary Coleman in *Diff'rent Strokes*.

In the end I actually fell asleep on the floor. One of the nurses, sensing that my slightly imbecilic demeanour might prove a liability during the lengthy birthing process, made me up a little bed on the floor with a camping mattress. I screwed the hood of my sweatshirt tight around my face and drifted quickly into a shallow sleep, punctuated by a series of horrifying apparitions. First I dreamed that the doctors were rummaging around my wife's innards unable to find the baby; then I dreamed that they found the baby, but that it had a dog's head. Next, I dreamed that the baby was born with my face, complete with stubble and receding hairline, and was pointing and laughing at me manically as it left the womb. Finally I dreamed that my mother was in the room, urging the doctors to have me ejected. 'Don't let clumsy watch,' she was saying. 'He'll only trip over one of the machines and ruin everything.'

My gangly lack of co-ordination is a source of constant amusement and concern to my mother. I once fell down the stairs in my dressing gown when I was about fifteen, exposing my flapping genitals to some friends she'd invited round for coffee. Another time, when I was babysitting for one of my nieces, I slipped on some wet grass in the park and kicked her face down into a paddling pool. Some other mums rushed over and fished her out, shooting me horrified scowls and refusing to let me have her back.

'She's my niece!' I explained. 'Give her to me!' They just ignored me.

'Don't worry,' they comforted the wailing child. 'We won't let the nasty man hurt you.' It was like a kidnapping. They only agreed to hand her over once I'd shown them ID to prove that I was a relative and not just a mad teenage bastard who walked round parks trying to drown toddlers.

These are the regrettable incidents around which my mother has chosen to define my entire persona. Trouble is, this cruel and superficial caricature she has created has started to govern my own sense of self. As I drifted in and out of consciousness on that hospital floor, my mother's disembodied cackling echoed through my mind and I began to fret uncontrollably about my physical ability to father a child. Never mind the question marks that still hung over my mental, emotional and spiritual capabilities – I was now questioning my body's ability to perform basic childcare tasks. Would I be able to even hold this infant without tripping over my own feet and dropping it down a flight of stairs? Would I squish its delicate innards with my ungainly and brutish hands? Maybe I was the sort of useless incompetent who ends up on the front page of the paper having accidentally trapped his baby's hands in the George Foreman Grilling Machine while trying to make a tuna melt. There I'd be, looking all guilty on the front page of *The Sun* below a headline that read 'Evil Twat Toasts Baby'. The humiliation of it! I mean, I don't think I'm that much of a twat, but nobody does until they actually wind up toasting a baby. Then they think, 'Oh no! I've accidentally toasted the baby! Hopefully people will realise that I'm not evil, just clumsy!' But by that stage it's too late; the papers have got hold of the story and the public are drawing their own conclusions. You're vilified across national news media, people call radio phone-ins to demand that the government have you chemically castrated and you end up hiring Max Clifford for a million quid that you haven't got. But not even he can save you, and you wind up having to live under an assumed name and get facial surgery like a former mob henchman turned FBI informant, only much less exciting and glamorous. The further this baby crept from the womb, the more pronounced my anxieties became.

I was suddenly awake but remained still on the floor with my eyes shut. My heart was pounding and my brain throbbed with worry. I sensed a commotion in the room. For just a few moments I considered continuing to feign sleep until the whole thing was over and done with. Perhaps I could pretend to be dead. Then the midwife accidentally kicked me in the shin and I sprang up like a meerkat.

'I think I nodded off!' I said, bewildered.

'You've been asleep for two hours,' my wife replied dismissively. I glanced outside and noticed that morning had broken. My wife was in a bumless gown and had tubes and wires attached to her.

'What's happening now?' I asked.

'We're about to administer the epidural,' said a male nurse clutching a massive syringe.

'I thought we were going to talk about that first . . . I mean, weren't you only gonna have that if it got unbearably painful?' I said.

'It is unbearably painful,' my wife deadpanned.

Then they shot a nuclear dose of painkilling drugs into her spine and everyone drifted out of the room.

At least we were now approaching the sort of heightened state of drama everyone had led me to expect. The midwife who had guided us calmly and sympathetically through the night finished her shift and was replaced by someone who seemed rather less smart and charming. She shambled into the room, barely introduced herself and tucked into a packet of Dairylea Dunkers beside the bed.

'I haven't had my breakfast,' she explained with her mouth full. She didn't instil much confidence in me. If she applied the same slapdash approach to midwifery as she did to her own personal nutrition then we were all in trouble. The contractions started to come quicker.

'PUSH! PUSH!' the midwife shouted in my wife's face, spitting crumbs of Dunker everywhere. Then, as soon as the pain receded, she would slump back into her chair, returning her attentions to the vacuous chit-chat she'd been sharing with a student doc who'd come along to watch.

'I always laugh when I hear about these celebrities who are too posh to push,' she droned. 'Like Merr-derna. Merr-derna has had all her kids with a caesarean. But what makes Merr-derna more special than anyone else?'

'Is she talking about Madonna? How could she not know how to say the name properly?' I thought to myself angrily. 'She must be doing it on purpose to annoy me.' I became fixated by the issue. Suddenly it was the only sound my brain could register: 'Merr-derna, Merr-derna, Merr-derna.' With the tension and the hot August sun shining in my face I eventually snapped.

'MADONNA!' I shouted. 'YOU MEAN MADONNA!'

'I know, that's what I said!' she barked back at me. 'Merr-derna. I know who I mean!'

'But why are you saying it like that?'

'Like what?'

'With "er"s instead of "a"s? How could you not know how to say her name properly? She's the most famous person on the planet! The pronunciation is commonly recognised to be MA-DONN-A! It's not like "potato" or "tomato" or "garage"! It's not open to debate!'

'I don't like your tone,' she said in a manner she'd clearly been trained to employ with problem patients.

'What's going on?' said an important-looking lady doctor striding through the door.

'You're a doctor – you'll know!' I said. 'Is it Merr-derna or Madonna?'

She ignored me and began to take a concerned look between my wife's thighs. 'Right, we've waited long enough for this baby,' she said. 'We're getting it out right now – take her into the delivery room.'

Nurses arrived and quickened their pace as they started to wheel my wife's bed out of the door and into a room across the hall full of elaborate Heath Robinson-style devices. The doctor explained that the baby might be starting to panic. And if the baby started to panic, it might shit itself. And if it shat itself, it might swallow its own shit and get brain-damaged. So they'd have to cut it out right away to prevent all that from happening. Then she sent me into that little side-room to put my scrubs on.

And now I'm in my scrubs and shuffling into the delivery room preparing to face my destiny. 'Life – funny old business really, isn't it?' I think to myself. 'You drift along getting born, learning to use the potty, going to school, then going to work, having a girlfriend, going for a nice walk in the park once in a while, sometimes getting the odd parking ticket. You have it off, you get a bit drunk, you watch telly. You get a stabbing pain in your chest and convince yourself it's a heart attack, then call NHS Direct and they tell you it's just wind. You think thoughts, you hear noises, you wonder where to go on holiday. Sometimes you inexplicably find yourself smelling your own hand. Yep, it might have its ups and downs but, generally speaking, it seems to jog along fairly predictably. You get to thirty-two and think you've seen it all. And then you're in a hospital and your wife, the person you've kind of based all your assumptions about the next sixty years of your life on, is lying on a bed with loads of doctors and nurses setting about her with machines, looking like she might easily cark it any minute now. Meanwhile, your unborn child is inside her tummy possibly bingeing on its own shit. Anything could happen in the next couple of minutes. *Anything.* My life could be turned on its head. I will not become a decent family man in a warm friendly house with a loving wife and child. I will be a heartbroken wreck living in a bed-sit drinking Malibu from a teacup and wishing I was dead. Up until this point the most dramatic thing that had ever happened to me was getting briefly stuck under a lilo at White City swimming baths in 1984. For a few seconds I thought I was drowning. Then I just kind of broke free and carried on playing. I guess I thought it'd never get any worse than that. If anything goes wrong now, I'm not sure I've got the strength to deal with it.'

I survey the room. The fussing medics. The bowls of what looks like offal but may well be my wife's pancreas and spleen. My wife looks up at me with an expression that seems to plead for reassurance. 'No good looking at me,' I think. 'I'm in a worse state than you. I mean, at least you've got all those lovely spine drugs numbing your brain. Me, I'm flying solo.' Nevertheless, I try to give her my best look of reassurance. I think it comes out like the Gary Coleman face again, but she doesn't seem to mind. She's battered.

'Push! Push!' the assembled maternity team shout in unison. They encourage me to join in. I feel all self-conscious and just mumble the words meekly. 'I can see its head!' shouts someone. 'Do you want to come down and look?' they ask.

'No thanks, if it's all the same to you,' I reply.

Everyone laughs. 'For fuck's sake, my wife and child are about to die!' I think to myself. 'Forgive me if I don't want to walk down there and watch the whole messy business up close, you unfeeling bastards!'

Suddenly a baby appears. Just like that. One minute the doc is looking panicked and hopeless; the next this slippery, wrinkled human being has flopped into her arms like a wet balloon. She places it directly on my wife's chest.

'Jesus Christ!' I say, gasping for air. Nobody is dead after all. The baby is looking a bit blue, but no one seems overly concerned about that. It's probably normal, so I just don't mention it.

The medical team are cooing like it's the first time any of them has ever seen this happen.

'Can you tell what it is?' one of them asks me.

'Yeah!' I say defensively. 'It's a girl, I think!'

'That's right!' they chorus. 'It's a little girl!' I start to cry. I gingerly take the baby in my arms and brandish her under my wife's nose.

'Look, we've had a little girl!' I squeak in weird, fluctuating octaves. She's so off her tits it's hard to know if any of this is actually registering. She smiles and nods, but for all I know she thinks I've just asked her if she'd like a Toblerone and some Skips for her tea.

As more tears spew down my face, I'm filled with an overwhelming sense of pride. Pride for producing this little baby. Pride for guessing the sex right when I was put on the spot by that nurse. And perhaps most of all pride for crying real, unforced tears of sincere emotion. I don't think I've had a good cry since I lost the Subbuteo World Cup Final on my mum's kitchen table in 1988. And even that was partly due to some cat litter getting in my eyes. I shed a few tears at my grandma's funeral ten years ago but, if I'm being entirely honest, I helped them along a bit by conjuring a few extra-sad thoughts and blinking a lot. I figured it would be a bit rude not to. But these tears are different; they are 100 per cent natural, unforced and involuntary. I call them organic tears, and, as they scorch my cheeks, they feel good. I wipe them from my face with my sleeve and look down at this little girl in my arms. A mop of black hair, wrinkled skin, a bluish-grey complexion and pretty, open eyes that dart around the room. You could call her scary and weird-looking, I suppose, but I quite like her. I kiss her putty-like forehead and tell her that daddy loves her very much. And d'you know what? I actually feel like I mean it.

10

SATAN

I suppose to anybody else she may still look a bit strange. She's still got that slightly corpse-like complexion, and there's a bit of scabby umbilical cord dangling from her belly button. Plus, there's blood still smeared here and there where that effing midwife didn't wash her properly. But to me she's beautiful. I know that sounds corny, like something I feel I'm supposed to say. But you'll just have to take my word for it: that's genuinely how I feel. I'm not trying to make myself out to be any more sensitive or caring than the next bastard. I mean, falling in love with your own offspring moments after it's born is actually quite egotistical. I helped make this thing. Her nose looks a bit like mine. Of course I think she's great. Becoming infatuated with your own spawn is just about the purest form of narcissism. Actually, make that the second purest form of narcissism. The purest form of narcissism is that practised by a leading Hollywood actor, who is rumoured to be having a homosexual affair with his own professional lookalike.

People worry about failing to form a bond with their own baby. They think there'll be no chemistry. That they'll perceive the child as nothing more than a wrinkly, wailing bundle of inconvenience. But sitting in this delivery room with her in my arms, watching her big, blue, useless eyes flitter about the place trying to consume the meaningless blurry shapes that surround her, I don't think I'm going to have that problem. Admittedly, her attitude towards me has been slightly indifferent so far. But then she's only about twenty minutes old, so she probably needs more time to get to know me. Once she's heard a few of my jokes, watched me dance, heard me tell a few brilliantly imaginative and off-the-cuff bedtime stories and seen some of those amusing facial expressions I've been developing for her, I feel certain that she'll warm to me.

And once we've got that blood off her and that scabby bit of cord removed, she'll look even more gorgeous and lovable than she does already. Not that aesthetics should matter. I mean, look at *Rosemary's Baby*. That child was the spawn of the devil and yet Rosemary still learned to love it soon enough. Mia Farrow shuffles into that room full of Satanists, sees the cot covered in black velvet sheets with an upside down crucifix hanging where a Winnie the Pooh would usually be and can immediately tell that something's not quite right. Then she peers inside at the terrifying infant and can't believe her eyes.

'What have you done to it?' she asks the assembled throng of devil lovers. 'What have you done to its eyes?'

An awkward silence falls over the room. The Satanists don't know where to look. In the end one of them clears his throat and says: 'Satan is his father . . . he came up from hell and begat a son of mortal woman.'

Personally, I always thought he could have phrased that a bit better. I mean, when you're breaking bad news, you should try to be a bit gentle. Say something like 'Look, luv, there's no easy way of putting this: we drugged you then summoned up Satan and got him to have it off with you while you were unconscious. I know it sounds stupid but it seemed like a laugh at the time. Anyway, that's his kid over there. Sorry.' Employing weird biblical terms like 'begat' was always likely to make a bad situation worse. Obviously Rosemary is furious to learn that she was date-raped by Satan. But anger soon gives way to mere annoyance, which in turn gives way to involuntary maternal instinct. Within minutes she's gently rocking the demented little bastard to sleep and singing him a nice lullaby. Not that he'd probably appreciate that sort of thing, but it's the thought that counts. The point is, it doesn't matter how your child turns out, you're genetically programmed to think it's brilliant and want to take care of it and all that. Even if it has demonic eyes and a set of hoofs where its hands and feet should be. All my baby's got is an iffy complexion which in any case will probably start to look a bit healthier within the next hour or so.

Someone takes the baby from me and injects it in the foot. I don't like to ask why – I'm sure it's for the best. I'm so awestruck by what these people have just done that they could start dangling her upside down and slapping her on the arse right now and I wouldn't question them. In fact, that was the sort of thing the *Carry On* films had half-led me to expect anyway. That, and a scenario in which I accidentally slip on some afterbirth, go skating the length of the corridor and get my head stuck between the cleavage of an overbearing matron. If there's one element of disappointment to this otherwise magnificent day, it's that none of those things have actually happened.

One thing's for sure: special bonds were formed in this room today. These heroic few were the architects of my fledgling family. In fact, I now consider them to be unofficial family members themselves. I imagine that we will occasionally holiday with the obstetrician in years to come. Perhaps the anaesthetist and her husband will come over for lunch once in a while. I can't see myself getting too matey with that midwife but even she might pop round sometimes to see how we're getting on. I'll just make sure I'm out those days. None of us will ever forget this moment.

At least, that's what I'd like to think. But a few of the nurses have just ambled out of the room carrying a pile of bloodied debris. And the doctor who seemed to be in charge is now rushing into the adjacent room, where another emergency delivery seems to be under way. 'Hang on a minute,' I think to myself. 'We were the centre of everyone's universe a minute ago! I thought we were special! But we were obviously just another faceless family on your baby conveyor belt. I feel so used.'

We're moved on to a ward with loads of other mums, babies and gormless-looking dads who are standing around awkwardly, not really knowing what to do next. The uniformity of it makes me feel even less special. On reflection, ours was a fairly unexceptional birthing experience. A load of boring waiting, a sudden flurry of activity, then a strange sense of anti-climax. A great allegory for all of life's important moments really.

I am suddenly overcome with a very particular feeling and can't quite put my finger on what you might call it. A sort of yearning inside. A strangely familiar ache; a feeling of emptiness. Is it post-natal shock perhaps? Or sorrow? Regret? Panic? No, it's none of those things. Ah, that's it: it's hunger.

'I'm nipping out for a sandwich,' I tell my wife. She half-ignores me while casually breast-feeding the new-born and reading a copy of *Heat* at the same time. This starting-a-family business: it's as easy as breathing.

I swagger down the hospital corridor still dressed in my scrubs. I am so excited about everything. I carry myself like a father: with confidence, purposefulness and a touch of self-importance. I am half-hoping that, in this get-up, I may be mistaken for an actual doctor. Perhaps someone will approach me in the lift and ask my advice on their thrombosis. 'Ah yes,' I could say, stroking away at my chin. 'Thrombosis . . . tricky . . . verrrrrrry tricky.' Then, hopefully, the lift door would ping and I could just run off. Perhaps someone else might even invite me to take part in a surgical procedure. Nothing serious, like a heart bypass: that would be too dangerous. But maybe I could just help recast someone's broken arm. Or assist in a vasectomy. I could probably get away with that if I kept my mouth shut and passed the forceps whenever anyone asked.

But none of this happens. In fact, once I'm out on the street in this silly blue uniform, people just swerve to avoid me on the assumption that I'm a lunatic. I stop at a flower stall to pick up some celebratory daffs for my wife.

'New dad?' asks the burly, shaven-headed florist as he wraps them up for me.

'Yes!' I say, delighted that someone has bothered to acknowledge my new lofty status in the human race. 'I've just had a little girl!'

He looks a good fifteen years older than me. I figure he's probably got three or four littluns of his own at home. Certainly he's got a nice big gut that's befitting of a proper dad. My stomach is flat in a puny, as opposed to a cover of *Men's Health*, sort of way. How can I expect a child to respect me, looking as weak and callow as this? I'm waiting for this florist to hand me my change with a complimentary nugget of parenting advice. Maybe a tip on how to cultivate a gut something like his. What's his secret? Suet for breakfast? One of those beer hats with the straws attached? Come on, man, furnish me with your wisdom!

'Welcome to eighteen years of hell,' is all he says as he hands over the flowers and the change.

'Oh,' I say, a little confused. 'Thanks.'

He does a little shake of his head as he turns to the next customer, no doubt seeking a way in which to spoil their mood and crush their dreams in similar fashion.

'Someone's anniversary is it?' he'll say. 'Yeah, well, what's the point in celebrating another year spent ensnared in a joyless and debilitating relationship? Monogamy is unnatural, human relationships are futile and we all die in the end anyway. That'll be four pound fifty for the tulips, cheers.' Hardly bloody service with a smile, is it?

Still, it'll take more than that miserable harbinger of doom and chrysanthemums to piss on my disco. I've become well used to the jaded attitudes of parents like him over the past few months. When you first tell them you've got a baby on the way, they're all 'It's the best thing you'll ever do!' But that soon gives way to a patronising tirade of warnings about how shitty your life is about to become. 'Now you'll find out what life's really about, you naive, lazy bastard!' they seem to say. Having spent years resenting your carefree lifestyle of late nights, lie-ins and puke-free clothing, they shiver with excitement about you finally joining the ranks of baggy-eyed, moaning, knackered shitheads like them. Honestly, to listen to them you'd have thought no one had ever had to change a couple of nappies, knock up a bit of mashed banana and sing the odd nursery rhyme five or six times a day. The way they grumble about parenthood, you'd have thought it was like working in a Stalinist gulag. Something tells me it's rather less taxing than that. But what do I know? Maybe I'll see what they're on about in a couple of months' time and regret my irritatingly positive attitude to the whole thing. But for now I'm not going to let Mr Chuckles the flower man or his ilk knock me off my stride.

When I get back on to the maternity ward, I can hear another delivery turning ugly in the theatre.

'Fuuuuuckkkk! Nnnnnnoooooo!!' I can hear some poor woman screaming.

'See,' I say excitedly, nudging my wife as I hand over the daffs. 'That's the sort of thing I was expecting from you! Screaming and shouting and all that!'

She ignores me and continues to read a story about Mischa Barton's underarm sweat marks. I am suddenly overcome by a strange urge to go and interfere with what's going on in that delivery room. I creep over and try and peer through the gap in the door. A harassed-looking dad steps outside to catch his breath. It's all got too much for him. Lucky for him, I'm on hand with a comforting word or two.

'See your missus is having a bit of trouble over there,

pal,' I wink at him knowingly. He looks up at me, eyes wild and bloodshot, mouth too dry to speak.

'Shame, innit?' I continue. 'Don't worry, it'll all work itself out in a minute. What's probably happening is that your nipper's trying to eat its own shit. But they're very good this lot, they'll sort it all out for you in a jiffy.' He just keeps staring, his mouth now wide open. Poor bloke doesn't know how to thank me.

'Shame your wife's the squeamish type, mind you,' I conclude. 'Don't know if you noticed, but mine barely made a peep.' He is now walking back into the delivery room where things seem to be coming to a head.

'Anyway, be lucky!' I call after him.

That's me: wise, helpful and interfering. I'm starting to feel like a dad already.

II

BRAIN

I walk up the garden path, open the gate, put one foot on to the street and then stop. I blink. I turn my head around slowly and look back at the house. Then I turn back again and look at the street. My mouth falls open like a stupid fish. I look both ways, furrow my brow and think to myself: 'What was it I was supposed to do next?'

My brain doesn't respond. It just slouches lazily inside my skull with its feet up, smoking a fag, reading *The Sun* and occasionally lifting its right buttock to release a fart. Damn that useless bastard. Still, I'm partly to blame for its flabby, slothful condition, having spent years feeding it a diet of sweary cartoons, SAS memoirs and booze. I strain to think harder – or at least furrow my brow a bit harder, which pretty much amounts to the same thing these days. No, it's no use, I haven't got a clue what I'm doing right now or what I'm supposed to do next. Or even what it was I was doing just a few seconds ago. It's a bit like walking into a room and forgetting what you went in there for – but applied to your entire life.

I became a dad roughly twenty-two hours ago. But I think it may only have sunk into my consciousness during the four hours of sleep I managed overnight. Maybe it was spending a night alone in the house without my wife and the regimental sense of order she brings to things. Maybe it's the crushing weight of expectation and responsibility that fatherhood has suddenly placed on my delicate psyche. But something's malfunctioning up in my head and, no matter what special thinking face I pull, it's showing no signs of righting itself any time soon.

I feel like Sam Beckett in *Quantum Leap*. You know, where he suddenly woke up each week in a different person's body, unsure of where he was or what the hell was going on? But at least he had that bloke played by Dean Stockwell helping him to make sense of the situation with his little hand-held computer. Plus, he was invariably being chased by members of the Ku-Klux-Klan or taking part in a rodeo or engulfed in some other set of self-evident circumstances. Me? All I'm doing is standing in a nondescript residential street looking at my own wrist. I do this sometimes while loitering to make myself look less ridiculous to passers-by. Instead of looking at me and thinking, 'Look at that gormless imbecile standing around blinking into space like the fella out of *Quantum Leap*, only less handsome, brave and resourceful,' I imagine that they'll think: 'Wow, look at that dynamic and thrusting individual looking at his watch! He's the sort of guy for whom time is money and money is time! I wish I was as on the ball as him!' Unless they get close enough to realise that I'm not actually wearing a watch and am, in fact, just staring at my naked wrist.

Someone does come up the street. It's an old woman wearing a sleeveless jacket. I don't think it's the one I mistook for a gypsy confidence trickster, but it's so hard to tell. The only people who ever seem to wander past our house are elderly women in sleeveless jackets. Never a child in a duffel coat. Never a builder in a string vest. Never a coterie of topless young ladies wearing cycling helmets and running at top speed. Just elderly women, ambling slowly in sensible, sleeve-free outerwear.

At our old place loads of different people used to walk by. Once, I was skipping down the front steps en route to my weekly five-a-side match, all dressed up in my shorts and shin pads.

'Where are you playing, mate?' a nosey parker asked me as I made towards my Fiat Panda. When I turned round, guess who it was? Only Robbie Williams!

'Erm, just round the corner, under the flyover,' I said, trying to act all casual as if I didn't really know who he was.

'Need any spares?' he asked. He was with a couple of mates. I did a quick piece of mental arithmetic and realised that three extra players would unbalance the sides. I worried I'd look a bit of a prick in front of my mates if I turned our well-organised game of five versus five into a shambolic game of seven versus six just because I'd got star-struck by a former member of Take That. So I said: 'We've got even sides, I'm afraid.' Bear in mind, this wasn't recently. This was years back, when *Angels* had just come out and Williams was probably the most famous bloke in the country. It counted as a genuinely jaw-dropping celebrity encounter. But all I could say to him was, 'We've got even sides, I'm afraid.' Mind you, I think he respected me for it. Not that I require the respect of Robbie Williams to feel important or anything. He kind of grinned and shrugged at the strange nostalgic sensation that the word 'no' must have evoked. Then, probably just to emphasise the nature of the dynamic that prevails between celebrities and normals, he demanded that I give him and his mates a lift to the pub on my way to the game. Even though the pub was completely out of my way. Reader, I succumbed to that dynamic. They all crammed into my little Fiat and told me funny stories about their recently completed tour of Germany while I chauffeured them to their trendy gastro-boozer. And I ended up being ten minutes late for the game.

As I trotted on to the pitch and took up my position to defend a corner, one of my team-mates asked where I'd been.

'Just giving Robbie Williams a lift to the pub,' I replied. Unsure of how best to respond, he jabbed his knee firmly into the small of my back. And do you know what the strangest thing about that story is? It's not even a lie.

This old woman is staring at me funny. I don't think it's that she's spotted I'm not wearing a watch; it's a much more hostile stare than that realisation would demand. She's suspicious. I'm standing outside this rather twee, respectable little cottage with its tree in the front garden and flowers up the wall and what-have-you, and she's thinking something's not quite right. My face doesn't fit. I'm scruffy, I'm stupid-looking and I'm wearing shorts. And trainers. And a hooded top with two full-length sleeves. I can hardly blame her for thinking I'm a burglar really, can I?

'Can I help you?' she says all snootily, giving me the once-over.

Part of me enjoys this sort of situation. I like to confront people's prejudices and embrace the opportunity to ram them down their throats. I half-want this woman to just come out and accuse me of robbing so I can hit back with something cutting and witty like: 'What? You think just because I'm sporting sleeves and sports casuals that I can't be a property owner? That my snotty nose and dropped vowels have no place in your leafy hamlet? Well, I've got news for you! Have a little look at my driver's licence! That's right – this is my address! I'll show you the deeds if you want! Hard work bought me this. No hand-outs. No charity. Hard graft! Good, honest graft! Look at these hands! Feel them! Ravaged by hours of typing facetious nonsense for left-of-centre broadsheets, they are! Behold my worn larynx and dried-out tongue! Battered and bruised through years of broadcasting assignments for obscure digital TV channels, local radio stations and lamentable television advertising campaigns! That's right, madam, mine is the sooty, wind-battered face of the old-school working man who pulled himself up by the bootstraps! And I'll be damned if I'm to stand here on my own doorstep and be judged by the likes of you! I paid for every last brick of this house. Well, the bank helped. To be honest, I've got an interest-only mortgage that's stretching me pretty much to the limit. I mean, it'd probably make more sense to keep on renting, with prices what they are, but whaddaya gonna do? You've got to get your foot on the ladder sooner or later, ain't you?'

And maybe in the past that's exactly the sort of thing I would have said. Back when I was an angry young man with something to prove to the world. Before the wondrous epiphany of fatherhood showed me that the world is a harsh enough place already without the likes of me shouting the odds at every second person who gives them a funny look in the street. In other words, if this had happened to me about thirty-six hours ago, before I'd seen my first child born, endured a fitful night's sleep, gone home on my own, got all confused and emotional and wound up standing outside my house feeling vulnerable and in need of a reassuring cuddle.

'Erm, this is my house . . .' I tell the old woman.

'Yeessss,' she says slowly, suddenly switching her tone from one of suspicion to sympathy.

'But the thing is . . . my wife's just given birth.'

'What, in there?' she says pointing at the house.

'No, at the hospital . . .'

'Yeesssss . . .'

'And, well, I've got to go to the hospital now and bring her things. But I don't know what things, and I don't know how to get there, and I'm not sure what time visiting starts . . .'

She's already halfway up the alley by the time I've realised that I'm saying all this out loud.

'Well, good luck,' she says with a wave. 'I'm sure you'll be fine.'

Easy for her to say, the condescending old cow. Still, that little exchange did at least help jog my memory as to some of the matters in hand. I need to get back to the hospital, that much is clear. My wife and daughter need me. What for? Hard to say. Maybe I could change a nappy or read it a story or say something helpful to my missus about her emotions or her stitches or something. My role will become apparent with time, I'm sure. But how to get there? And when? And what was it that I was supposed to take with me? Something about a towel and some pants maybe. And some loose-fitting trousers? For the baby or the wife? Or me? Impossible to say. I shuffle up and down the garden path trying to decide what to do. This isn't like *Quantum Leap* at all. It's like *EastEnders* when Arthur Fowler nicked the Christmas Club money and went bananas on the allotment. I've got to get a grip.

The best thing to do in a situation like this is retrace one's steps. I remember the hours that followed the birth. I remember nipping outside the hospital to ring round the grandparents. As both sets of our parents are divorced, it was necessary for me to make four separate phone calls rather than two. One of the lesser-discussed side-effects of broken homes is the inflated phone bills incurred by the children in later years. My new daughter has four different grandparents all living separately from each other. This will make maintaining a relationship with each of them more difficult from a practical point of view. In an ideal world both couples would still be married and all living together in a tiny attic, like in *Charlie and The Chocolate Factory*. Even better, all of us − grandparents, parents, uncles, aunties and cousins − would live en masse in a gigantic shoe. That really would provide my little girl with the perfect support system in which to grow up. But modern society would doubtlessly label such a set-up as 'fanciful', 'outmoded' or 'a bit noncey'.

I call my mum first, knowing that she'll be the one who's fretting hardest. This is what I hear when she answers the phone:

'OHMYGOD   CHRISTINHEAVEN!   IKNEW
SOMETHINGHADGONEWRONG! IJUSTFELTIT!
AMOTHERKNOWS! IREMEMBER WHENIHAD
YOURBROTHER HECAMEOUT WITHISCORD
ROUNDHISNECK   LIKEHEWAS   BEING
STRANGLED ANDOFCOURSE YOURFATHER
WASN'TTHERE. *HE* WAS PROBABLYOFF ATONE
OFHIS FUCKINGPARTIES! IWASSOSCARED ...
ARRRRRRGGGH ... sob ... sob ... Hello? Are
you still there?'

'Yes.'

'Well, come on then, is it a boy or a girl?'

'It's a girl, and everyone's fine.'

'ARRRRRGHHHHH ... IKNEWIT! IKNEWIT
WOULDBEAGIRL! AMOTHERKNOWS! I'MSO
HAPPYNOBODYDIED!   IHAVEN'TSTOPPED
CRYING ALLMORNING ...'

I put the phone down and called my father-in-law. He
too is the emotional sort. But then he's from Hungary,
where being the emotional sort is the law.

'Oh, thank God!' he said shakily in his thick Hungarian
accent. 'I am pleased about that.' Hungarians speak in very
literal sentences, I've noticed.

'I'm sure,' I said, speaking quickly enough to suggest
that I didn't have much time to talk. In fact, I was just
trying to get off the phone before he started crying. But it
was too late.

'I'm actually crying a bit right now', he said matter-of-
factly, with a disconcerting tremble running through his
central European twang.

'Oh, um ... well ... that's a shame,' I spluttered.

There's something about talking to foreigners that makes me come over all English.

'There's no shame in it,' he said soberly, sniffing up some rogue tears.

'No, of course, I just meant . . .'

'I cried when each of my own children was born. I cried when my parents died. I admit it to you without shame . . .'

'Crikey,' I thought to myself. 'He's off on the list of occasions on which he's cried. We could be here all day.'

'I cried in 1969, when I was still exiled from my homeland by the Communists and I received news via telegram from Budapest that . . .'

There are two things my father-in-law likes to do during everyday conversation. One is cite the precise year when a particular event took place. You might ask him if he fancies a cup of tea, and he will look into the middle distance, as if picturing a terrible battle or a majestic eagle in flight, and respond: '1957. That was the first time I was offered a cup of tea by an Englishman. . .' and then launch into a detailed anecdote surrounding the incident. Which I don't mind as long as I've got the time to listen. I mean it's a generally more lyrical and interesting way to respond than simply grumbling 'milk no sugar', like most English people do. The other thing he likes to chuck into everyday chatter is a nice bit of crying. I would say, in all the years I've known him, he's been crying about 20 per cent of the time. Not that I think he's any more miserable than the next bloke. In fact, once you get behind the strange accent and bouts of sobbing, you begin to realise that, relatively speaking, he's a pretty jolly fella. He's just not afraid to wear his heart on his sleeve. Johnny Hungarian is like that. Probably something to do with all those years of war and trauma, the Commies, the Nazis, all that other stuff.

What other stuff? I don't know. I suppose I should know having been involved with this Hungarian family for the past twelve years, but I've never been that attentive when it comes to listening to family history. Whenever dinnertime conversation turns to Hungary's long history of persecution, war and injustice (if, indeed, that is what's been going on over there throughout history – as I say, I have no way of knowing), I just sort of drift off into my own, imagined idea of Hungary. My imaginary Hungary features moustachioed men in colourful, billowing trousers, jaunty waistcoats and curly shoes who fight with giant sabres atop magical flying carpets while dusky ladies dressed in silks perform sexy dance routines with snakes wrapped around them. And yes, I am aware that my imaginary Hungary is not only misinformed and a bit racist but probably based more closely on Turkish stereotypes than Hungarian ones. But what are Hungarian stereotypes? There are none! And for that they've only got themselves to blame. What do you think of when you think of Hungary? Shut your eyes and think of it right now. See? Nothing! Now perhaps you can appreciate my attitude towards the whole place. I mean, I've been to Hungary a few times, and I still can't think of much I'd associate with the place. Other than my father–in–law. And men crying.

'I cried a bit myself,' I told him, partly to distract him from crying and partly because I wanted him to know that I too have some semblance of human emotion hidden somewhere deep beneath my galvanised exterior of trite cynicism, muddled irony, English reserve and juvenile half-wittery.

'What? You? Really?' he said.

'Yes, 'fraid so. Couldn't help myself,' I said proudly.

There was a silence. I chose to interpret the silence as happiness. Perhaps a bit of pride. And maybe a bit of relief that his son-in-law was not necessarily the immature berk he'd taken him for over the past twelve years.

'Well done,' he said, his endorsement filling me with pride.

'I suppose I could do with being just a tiny bit more Hungarian myself in certain ways,' I thought to myself. 'Show some emotion once in a while. Take things more seriously. Begin each anecdote with an announcement of the year in which it took place. One thing is for sure – I'll definitely be investing in a jaunty waistcoat.'

Next I had to call my mother-in-law, then my dad. I figured they could wait a bit longer to get the good news on account of them being so unemotional. They care not for the flim-flam and frippery of emotional jabber and sentimental discourse. They deal in hard facts and rigour. I called them last, because I knew they would be less concerned about anything going wrong during the birth. It's not that they don't care. Their brains are just too relentlessly rational to let them worry about much. Both of them are a bit like Rain Man, I suppose. Give them cold hard information, and they're as good as gold. Start trying to engage them in the stuff of human heartache and they'll start bashing themselves about the head and shouting, 'Qantas never crashed!' or something.

With this in mind, I took care to deliver the good news to my mother-in-law in a cold, flat monotone – as if I were working on a checkout at Tesco and requesting a price check on six-packs of Club biscuits. I wasn't about to insult the woman by dressing the news up in needless ceremony or frivolous hoop-la: I've got more respect for her than that. She responded with the words 'I thought so', which made me feel ever so slightly stupid for even bothering to give her the news. Of course you've had the baby! Isn't it obvious? Don't you know that all statistics on childbirth over the past ten years among women of a similar age, weight and socio-economic background pointed towards this precise outcome, you blithering idiot?! Well, anyway, that's my mother-in-law for you. Steely and stern. Like Clint Eastwood but with a computer for a brain and a predilection for pottery. I knew she was feeling mushy and gleeful on the inside, she just wouldn't let me see it. As a son-in-law, I am a disappointment to her. But if she's Clint, then I hope she at least sees me as that orang-utan he starred alongside in *Any Which Way But Loose.*

Finally I contacted my dad. 'Sorry to bother you, I just didn't want you to worry,' I say, immediately realising I'd chosen the wrong tack.

'Why would I be worrying?' he demanded.

'Erm, I dunno, I didn't mean worry. I meant "wonder". I didn't want you to wonder what might be happening with the baby and all that.'

'In what sense?' he persisted sternly.

'Ey?'

'In what sense didn't you want me to wonder about the baby *and all that?*'

'Er, well, you know, I thought you might be sat at home thinking something like "I wonder if that baby has been born yet".'

'No. I wasn't thinking that. I knew perfectly well that you would call once the baby had been born, so what would be the point of wondering about it in the meantime?'

Remember Mr Logic out of *Viz*? That's what my dad acts like sometimes.

'Yes. Quite right,' I venture with a gulp. 'Well, you were right. The baby was born and I have called you. Just as you envisaged.'

'I know.'

'I know you know.'

'Good. Well. Congratulations.'

'Thanks.'

Luckily for both him and me, I know full well that my dad is a big, cuddly pussycat inside. The trick is to not let him know that you know he's a big, cuddly pussycat. If you do, he will only overcompensate by starting to act like Mr Spock. I can ignore it because I have seen his softer side on countless unguarded occasions.

One of my favourites was on a cold winter's afternoon in Brighton about twelve years ago. It was the first time he had met my girlfriend and future wife. 'He's a bit gruff at first but just a big cuddly pussycat inside,' I'd warned her, hoping to Christ that he did something pussycat-ish at some stage to back up my claims. He didn't let me down. After a lunch throughout which he'd been mildly gruff, we were walking along the busy high street when our attentions turned to a distressed young lady screaming at the top of her voice at no one in particular, 'HELP ME! HELP ME! I CAN'T TAKE THIS! I'M SO SAD!' Possibly the only way of describing her would be as a crack whore. Mangled teeth, grubby hair, skeletal features, and bulgy, psychotic eyes. You know the type. This being a cold winter's afternoon on an English high street, it goes without saying that nobody stopped to help her. Why would they? She was probably just shouting at an imaginary voice in her head that taunted her with persistent renditions of Brotherhood of Man's back catalogue whenever the drug supplies ran low in her veins. Fearing that any sort of encounter with her might ruin my delicately balanced afternoon, I quickened my step. Then, suddenly, I noticed my old man walking towards her.

'Dad! What the fuck are you doing?!' I squealed like a big, soppy girl. But it was too late. He already had a comforting arm around the crack whore's shoulder.

'What's the matter?' he asked gently.

'Oh Christ!' I muttered under my breath in sulky, adolescent despair. The crack whore began to explain her predicament to him. I can't remember the exact details, but it was something to do with an absentee boyfriend, an unscrupulous landlord and a dealer who steadfastly refused to entertain the notion of credit. She actually made it sound quite convincing and poignant. As soon as my dad started talking to her, she stopped screaming like a mentalist and just sobbed gently. I stood there with my mouth open, my idiotic brain convincing itself that my girlfriend would probably call off our relationship on the basis of my dad being a crack whore botherer.

'I'm really sorry about this,' I told her.

'Why? I think it's really nice. No one else bothered to help her,' she replied, which made me feel a bit stupid for apologising.

My dad talked for about twenty minutes with the crack whore, asking her about the specifics of her problems, offering nuggets of sympathy and pearls of advice. God knows what he knew about the tribulations of being a crack whore, but he looked as if he was doing his best to understand. Throughout the conversation he kept a comforting arm wrapped around her, unconcerned by the visible muck that caked her entire person. She seemed so touched and appreciative. My girlfriend looked awestruck by his compassion. I just stood there feeling like a flimsy, unsympathetic drip for reacting in the way I had. Eventually he gave her some money to get herself a room for the night. That was probably the bit that resonated most strongly in my mind. The lessons I should have learned from my father that day were: have the courage to help other people, however alien and intimidating they may appear; show some humanity and try to empathise with those less fortunate than yourself; listen to their problems, understand their plight and lend a helping hand wherever you can. But the only lesson I chose to learn was: 'If someone's crying, give them twenty quid. That'll shut them up.'

Unfortunately I have relied on cash hand-outs as a substitute for genuine compassion ever since. Made your niece cry in an over-exuberant play fight? Bung her a tenner. Uncle weeping over recently deceased aunt? That'd probably take more like fifty or sixty quid. You can imagine how much I've spent on my father-in-law over the years.

Of course my dad has taught me loads of other valuable lessons over the years, too. But I can't say I've always been a receptive pupil. He tried to teach me chess once, but it never worked out. I only saw him on the odd Saturday, so I'd always forget what he'd already taught me in between lessons. Plus, on that particular day of the week I always had half a mind on what time *Dukes of Hazzard* was starting. I mean, how the fuck could I have maintained interest in him going on about castling when the Dukes were gearing up to make a mockery once again of Boss Hogg's ludicrous brand of redneck law enforcement?

Right, so where was I? Oh yeah, I rang round the grandparents, went back to the hospital and hung around in a woozy, faintly surreal state of family bliss. The baby, much tinier than I could possibly have imagined it would be, lay there sleeping. My wife and I gazed wordlessly at each other, trying to absorb everything that had happened and what the rest of our lives were going to be about. We also shared a large bag of Mini Cheddars. When the baby woke up, my wife fed her and then I tried to change her nappy. It was terrifying: her tiny limbs seemed so delicate and fragile that I dithered as hesitantly as an ill-qualified bomb-disposal expert. She cried throughout the whole distressing experience, and in the end a nurse had to come over and help. I felt inadequate and a bit sad. Then it was time to leave.

But before I left, my wife gave me a list. Yes! That's it, the precious list! She scrawled it on a napkin with her shaky hand, which was still covered in dressing and bits of tube. In a tiny red bookie's biro that I found in my pocket. And now I'm standing on my garden path, patting all of my pockets to check if the list is hiding in one of them. I go back into the house. I spend a few pointless moments opening drawers full of junk and phone bills and bank statements, throwing them around and making a strange frustrated growl. I run up and down the stairs a few times, opening doors, scanning rooms for the list.

I left that hospital with so much information. Important, precious information. Information that my brain immediately flushed out the moment I walked out through the doors. Perhaps I'm being harsh on my brain: perhaps it's not lazy, just full: full with all the earth-shattering events of yesterday; all the concerns and fears about the future; all those images of my wife and daughter lying in the hospital bed together; so many thoughts, ideas, colours, shapes, smells and things. Damned, relentless things. Ordinarily my brain has about a dozen or so things to compute on an average day. Suddenly it's being overloaded to a million times its usual capacity. It's close to collapse. Trying to recall the details of what I'm supposed to be doing this morning could be the wafer-thin mint that finally causes it to explode and dribble out of my nostrils in liquid form.

If only I could find this list. The list will tell me what I need to bring to the hospital. The list will tell me what time visiting hours start. The list will tell me how to get there, where to park, what to say to my wife and how to change the baby's nappy without more humiliating interventions by the nurses. The list will probably even come with handy illustrations. Yes, the precious, precious list will make everything all right.

Only the list isn't here. Deep down, I think I always knew it wasn't here. Even before I lost my temper with myself and started turning over the mattress on our bed, pulling open kitchen drawers and turning waste paper baskets upside down. Where did it go? Discarded on my way out of the maternity ward? Dropped on the floor of my brother's car when he gave me a lift home from the hozzy last night? Accidentally eaten in my sleep? Who knows? It's probably just gone the same way as all the other lists, receipts, airline tickets and sundry important bits of paper I've lost over the years. Consigned to the vast dustbin of forgetfulness, disorganisation and inefficiency that has hindered my everyday life since childhood. Oh, it may seem funny and charming and quirky when you're twelve or twenty or even thirty-one. When the worst thing that can happen is that you forget to switch off your own gas oven and accidentally kill yourself and the cat. But I am now responsible for another human being. I have to get sane. I need to whip my brain into shape and start making sense of what the hell it is I'm supposed to be doing. It's no longer enough to flick on my mental lights once or twice a day. They need to be on constantly: I must be focused, diligent and sharp at all times. Like a sniper, or the bloke who does my book-keeping.

I make a mental note to lose fewer notes. Then I grab a giant hold-all, fill it with half the contents of my wife's wardrobe, chuck in a couple of towels and some wet wipes for good measure and call a cab to take me to the hospital.

12

TUPPERWEAR

That sound. Why won't it stop? It's been going on for ages. What is it? It can't be crying. I'm pretty sure it's not screaming either. Those sounds are like old friends to me now, I'd recognise them anywhere. This is different. Is someone talking to me again? I wish people would stop doing that. Can't they see I'm tired? Their words are only making things worse.

But hang on, I don't think it's words I can hear. It's something else, something just as familiar but twice as irritating. It's a knock at the door. Again. I snarl and hunch my shoulders like a wildcat primed for attack. Only I am woozy and tired and feel a bit sick – like one of those lions in the zoo which has just been shot in the arse with a tranquilliser dart after trying to savage a tourist. I am dressed in some nylon football shorts and a vest. I am unshaven. The last time I looked at my face in the mirror (something I'm generally trying to avoid), I looked about eighty years old. Suffice to say, I'm not really in the mood to receive visitors right now. But what can I do? They just keep coming. I used to pride myself on keeping the borders of my home tightly secured against unwanted guests, but what can I tell you? I'm just too dazed and disorientated to resist. One week into fatherhood, and I've already surrendered at least 50 per cent of the principles I've always held dear.

I open the door and in they traipse. No 'Hello's, no 'How you doing?'s. No 'Hey, you look great in those shorts!' They just push past me and start looking for the baby. This must have been what Joseph felt like when all the wise men and shepherds starting tipping up at the stable door that night. But at least that lot brought precious gifts. All I've got is a gaggle of grim-faced Hungarians carrying Tupperware boxes filled with a brown substance that I'm assuming passes for one of their national dishes.

'Vhere is she?' one of them asks as they pass through the front room.

'She's asleep upstairs,' I say, trying to conjure some merriment in my voice.

They silently trundle upstairs and surround the cot. I just hope they don't wake her up. I mean, imagine coming round from a nice kip to be confronted by three strange Hungarians wearing unruly beards, maroon polo necks and stony, expressionless faces. Thank God, her eyes aren't working properly yet or she might be emotionally scarred for life.

I leave them to it. It's pointless to resist. It's best just to smile, stick the kettle on and try to take advantage of the fact that someone else is keeping an eye on the baby by sneaking off to the toilet for a fifteen-minute kip on the floor.

It's only been a week, and I'm already obsessing over where my next nap is coming from. I tell my wife I'm going to make her a sandwich so I can sleep for five minutes while leaning against the fridge. I nipped out to the shops for some milk and stole twenty minutes on a park bench. I am trying to master the art of sleeping with my eyes open, so nobody will be able to tell. Failing that, I may just draw eyeballs on to my eyelids.

I know what you're thinking: how tired can you possibly get in just one week? Well, you have to understand that, until very recently, I was used to a great deal of sleep. I ordinarily liked to get ten hours, even on a school night. The constant interruptions I've had to my deep, peaceful slumbers over the past seven days are more than my body can handle. Basically, I've spoiled myself. That's one of the problems with having your first child in your thirties. By that stage you're already a bit set in your ways: you've spent too many years becoming accustomed to a self-indulgent lifestyle. I mean, my parents started having kids when they were in their early twenties, when they hadn't yet had a chance to cultivate a lifestyle defined by lazy TV marathons, binge-drinking and expensive convenience food from the Sainsbury's Taste The Difference range (or whatever the luxury equivalents were in their day: Radio Luxembourg and a beef-dripping sandwich, I suppose). They had no idea that there was any sort of life beyond sleep deprivation, shit and tears. They had no problem with it. As George Michael once so rightly pointed out: ignorance is kind to the heart and mind. I think he was talking about someone having it off with a floozy behind their girlfriend's back, but, like so many of his songs (with the possible exception of 'Wake Me Up Before You Go Go'), the sentiment was universally applicable.

But of course, none of this is really surprising. I knew I'd be tired. One of the appeals of fatherhood was that it would force me to be a less lazy person. If I come out of the next few months feeling like a Maggie Thatcher-type automaton who only requires four hours of sleep per day in order to function properly, then it'll all have been worthwhile.

The non-stop merry-go-round of visitors doesn't make things any less confusing. An aunt leaves as an old schoolfriend arrives. They disappear, to be replaced by a second cousin. She sticks around for three hours and only pushes off once two of your wife's former colleagues show up. Next thing you know, some mate of a mate who you're almost certain you've never actually met before but who works nearby has appeared on the doorstep clutching a bunch of tatty-looking tulips and wondering if it'd be all right if she came in and just stared at the baby for half an hour. The weirdo. I don't mean to sound cruel, but I'm struggling to see what the attraction is anyway. Obviously, to my eyes the baby's great. But she's my baby. I can stare at her for ages and not get bored. When I say 'ages', I mean about thirty minutes. She doesn't actually do much in the way of comic turns or diverting conversation, so half an hour is pretty much my limit. Still, that's a good fifteen minutes more than I'm usually able to concentrate on anything else without getting distracted and checking to see if there's anything good on telly.

How do they even know about the baby? I blame Facebook. I knew I shouldn't have uploaded all those pictures when I got in from the hospital on the day of the birth. I wasn't thinking straight. It didn't really dawn on me how inappropriate the pictures were for public consumption until my wife got home and saw what I'd done.

'What the fuck?!' was all she was able to say once she'd logged on. Nothing says 'Home Sweet Home' quite like your missus breastfeeding the baby while fiddling about on Facebook with her spare hand.

'Oh, yeah,' I said, glancing over her shoulder at the pictures. 'I put them up the other night – I thought people would like to see.'

I'd called the album 'Our New Arrival'. As she clicked through the images, it was like her mouth was struggling to keep up with her brain. She just kept saying, 'What . . . the . . . fuck?' like a mantra.

One of the baby all covered in goo. One of me holding her in my cool surgical scrubs. One of my wife covered in sweat and blood and looking as if a little part of her soul had just died. Another of her splayed out on the bed in exhaustion with her boobies showing. I'd thought they were the very epitome of heart-warming family snaps when I uploaded them. I wanted all those friends, relatives, obscure work colleagues from yesteryear and completely random strangers who had befriended me on Facebook to share in my joy. But, on reflection, I maybe should have been a bit more selective about how much joy I shared. I mean, I think my wife is the most gorgeous woman in the world. But I'll be honest, she didn't look her best in those pictures. Who does look their best forty minutes after boshing a seven-and-a-half-pound human being out of their arse? I could have at least left the topless pics out, I suppose.

'What were you thinking?' she eventually asked, once she'd stopped spluttering in astonishment.

'Come on, it's not like they're all porny or anything, is

it?' I pleaded. 'These are your breasts in their most natural state. No one would look at them in a pervy way, if that's what you're thinking.'

'No, that's not what I'm thinking,' she said.

Which was weird. Because as I said the words I was secretly thinking about how I might react if one of my Facebook friends had posted a similar picture of their wife. In all honesty, I don't think I would have thought that it was natural and touching and motherly. I think I would have thought something like: 'Wow-wee, it's my mate's wife's boobies! Yeee-ha! I never thought I'd get a butcher's at those! I think I'll download them to my hard disk immediately for future reference.' Still, she's not to know that.

'It's not about people perving over them,' she reiterated.

'What's it about then?' I asked.

'It's about . . . just not wanting people to see them at all.'

'Exactly, in case they perv over them.'

'No. I just don't exactly look at my best, do I?'

'I think naked breasts are naked breasts,' I said, not quite sure where I was going. 'I mean, they don't have to be covered in baby oil or have tassels on them to look nice.'

'You're a fucking dick, d'you know that?' she said calmly. 'Think of it this way: would you want me to take a picture of you just after an operation with your knob dangling about and post it on the internet?'

'Depends,' I mused. 'Would the operation have actually been on my knob? Because I remember I had an operation on my balls once, and they turned all the colours of the rainbow.'

She didn't answer.

'Anyway, it's a moot point,' I said, somewhat boldly considering I wasn't quite sure what 'moot point' actually meant. 'They didn't operate on your boobs. They didn't even touch your boobs, did they? Or did they?'

There was a silence. She clicked on the final picture. It was an uncompromising close-up of her right breast with our daughter blindly trying to locate the nipple with her mouth. She looked up from the screen and glared at me awaiting explanation.

'You look like a, what d'you call it, an earth mother?' I smiled reassuringly.

'A what?'

'You know, like one of them African women out of the documentaries with the dangling boobs and the plates in their mouths.'

'You're not making this any better,' she explained.

I deleted the pictures. Later I decided to shut down my Facebook account altogether to avoid similar mishaps. But by that stage it was too late. The word was out, and well-wishers were already banging at the door like the zombies from *Night of the Living Dead*. Before the Hungarians have even left, one of the neighbours knocks round with a bottle of red wine. She's the posh sort you get round here: no sleeves, plenty of pearls and a dead nice cut-glass accent.

'It's not for the baby,' she quips as she hands me the booze, 'but I thought you might be in need of a glass or two this evening once you've got her off to sleep . . . oh, I see, you're opening it now. Well, fair enough, I suppose.'

Judging by her reaction, I'm guessing it's still early.

How am I supposed to know? My existence is no longer fashioned around the narrow-minded conventions of twenty-four-hour time-keeping. I answer not to Greenwich Mean Time but to the whimsical sleeping patterns of a tiny baby. This being the height of summer, there's almost constant daylight, which makes it even easier to lose sight of what time it is in the real world. I learned days ago that looking at clocks only crushes your will to carry on. So you ignore time, you sleep when you can and drink whenever circumstances allow. That's why I am currently in the kitchen pouring myself a tumblerful of this plonk. I knock it back in two healthy gulps. There, that's better. I've never really been a daytime drinker, but right now it feels like all the usual rules of decency have been temporarily suspended. It's like you imagine it might be after a nuclear attack on London: the survivors could just race down to the nearest PC World and nick whatever they like, then have sex with a stranger on the way home. I mean, who'd be asking questions, right?

As I use my arm to wipe the red wine from my mouth, the neighbour eyes me with pity and a tiny bit of fear.

'Sorry,' I say. 'My manners! D'you want a bit?'

Rather than pour her a fresh glass, I find myself just offering her the dregs of what's left in mine. She politely declines and asks to see the baby. I direct her upstairs to join the Hungarians. Then I reload my tumbler.

I catch sight of my reflection in the kitchen window. It's not pretty. The gradual hair loss I've been experiencing over the past five years seems to have accelerated in recent days. It's thinner than ever on top. Combined with my vest-and-shorts get-up, I look like I'm going to a fancy dress party as a badly out-of-shape Steve Ovett. I thought fatherhood would make me look more respectable. Turn me into the sort of bloke who shaves every morning, stands upright at all times and wears a tie even when he hasn't got a meeting that day. But instead I am the sort of bloke who stands in his kitchen at 11 a.m. in a vest slurping mid-priced Shiraz and wondering if any of his visitors would think it was weird if he crawled under the table for a fifteen-minute snooze.

Before I get a chance to do so, they've all come back downstairs.

'Is she still sleeping?' I ask.

'No, of course not,' says my father-in-law. 'She's crying. Can't you hear her?'

I concentrate for a few seconds, willing my brain to register what my ears are telling it. Yep, I suppose he might be right – that does sound like a baby crying.

'Oh yeah, sorry, I though that was the bathroom fan,' I mutter, then shuffle upstairs to comfort the baby. By 'comfort' I mean get her out of her cot and hand her to my wife for a feed. I discover my wife sprawled out in the bedroom with her legs in the bed but her hands and face on the floor. She must have been so tired that she fell asleep before she could actually manage to get herself into position. We've both been doing a bit of that lately. I suddenly lost consciousness while trying to fit a Scart lead into the back of the telly the other day. She found me on one knee with my eyes shut and a long stream of dribble protruding from my lower lip. Right now she looks like one of those fossilised victims of ancient volcano eruptions who were encased in molten lava while in the middle of an everyday chore. I prod her shoulder with my foot. She doesn't move.

'Shit . . . are you . . . are you dead?' I mumble. My foggy, delirious brain finds it difficult to panic in the way you might have thought it would. I just think: 'How will we stop the baby crying if she's dead? We won't be able to feed it. I'll have to get one of the Hungarians to nip out for some SMA.'

Suddenly her eyes blink open, and she assumes a more conventional position. I hand her the crying child, and we exchange a wordless glance of baggy-eyed bewilderment as she fastens it to her breast. This is pretty much how we've been communicating for days now. This is a war, and we are soldiers on the front line. We just have to get through it as best we can; no words could possibly make things any easier. Verbal communication just seems like pointless and indulgent showmanship now, mere noise used to dress up crude human experience as something more poetic than it actually is. Our challenges are self-evident: keep the baby warm, happy and fed, and try to sleep whenever and wherever we can. It's a case of just switching off and letting The Force guide us from there.

Downstairs the Hungarians are getting on well with the posh neighbour. They're all saying things like 'Doesn't she look like her mother?' and 'Yes, but I also think there's a hint of her father'. I've noticed everyone's been saying this sort of stuff over the past few days. It's like a default language that people automatically slip into when they are in the presence of a new-born baby. I play along, chipping in with remarks like 'Yes, she has the same shaped jaw-line as my mother, but she definitely has Uncle Tom's ears!'

Everyone nods. But, as they gaze upon her in her cot, I suspect their thoughts are just as prosaic as my own: 'Yep, that's a baby all right. Isn't it small? Not doing much, is it? Better think of something to say. Maybe I'll say it looks a bit like its mother.'

Most of the thoughts that float through your brain when you're looking at a baby are meaningless. They're not really even thoughts at all, more like strange, formless reactions you feel in the gut and the heart. What do they call them again? That's it: 'emotions'. Staring at a baby is a hypnotic experience that most of us seem to find sooth-ing and curiously uplifting. But some people claim to derive insight from staring at this fledgling being as it lies there doing sod all. They say things like 'She's going to be a joker, this one', while nodding their head knowingly. Or 'She's got such intelligent eyes', even though her eyes are almost permanently shut. Which, if you want to be pedantic about it, is almost the opposite of intelligent eyes. Shut eyes are stupid eyes. But all of that's neither here nor there really, because the people saying this stuff are just saying it to pass the time while they sip tea and eat biscuits and prepare to have one last look at the baby before naffing off.

'Would you like more tea, anyone?' I ask the Anglo-Hungarian throng.

Everyone shakes their head, because they still haven't finished the cups I gave them five minutes ago. 'How about more biscuits?' More head-shakes. 'Oh well,' I say, 'the baby will have finished feeding in about ten minutes. I'll bring her down so you can have another stare before you go.'

Everyone seems to perk up when I say this, and they start to chatter among themselves again.

'Of course, it's perfectly clear that she is going to be extremely artistic,' I hear someone say as I wander into the kitchen looking for something to eat.

I may sound a bit moany and resentful toward these house guests, but they're not all bad. These Hungarians are not the first people to have turned up bearing Tupperware boxes containing home-cooked meals. People also bring flowers, fruit and magazines. My mum even brought some Berocca soluble vitamins the other day. We are being treated like invalids who are slowly dying. Frankly, I could get used to it. I pour the brown Hungarian matter into a pan, let it simmer for five minutes, then spread some between two pieces of Hovis with some ketchup. I feel instantly energised.

'Does anyone want any of this . . . stuff?' I say, lumbering back into the front room with a mouthful of sandwich. But the neighbour has gone, and the remaining Hungarians are busily saying goodbye to my wife. One of them is claiming that the baby has a 'wise face' and 'unusually dexterous hands'.

'Bye then!' I cheer, firing crumbs across the hallway as they make towards the exit. I don't know whether it's the breakfast wine or the Hungarian sandwich or the fact that the house is about to be guest-free for the first time in days, but I am overwhelmed with a fleeting sense of euphoria. The door shuts, and I look at my wife and daughter. Unusually, none of us are sleeping or crying. I sigh a contented sigh. Here we are, cocooned in a fuzzy-headed little netherworld where days are spelt out by cups of tea, slices of cake, nappy changes, naps and unsolicited visitors. I may not have shaved, worked or exercised in days. I may feel entirely cut off from the real, civilised world that is presumably still turning outside the front door. I may be wearing a vest and feeling so tired I could puke. But I like it. It feels strangely blissful. I'm just not quite sure you could call this living.

13

POKER

I am lying on my bed trapped somewhere between asleep and awake, with the baby splayed out on my chest. I have dribbled all over her head. We are both snapped back to consciousness by the sound of someone complaining about the inadequacy of local parking facilities.

'Your granddad's here,' I tell the baby, gently wiping some of my drool from her hair.

Gently I pick her up and softly pad downstairs with her cradled in my arms. I emerge into the living room brandishing her at my dad. He frowns at me.

'Oh my God! What are you holding her like that for?' he says. I look down at the baby who looks quite happy. But what do I know?

'Give her to me,' he says, holding out his arms and shaking his head wearily. 'The poor little thing will get crippled lying there like that.'

My brain is tired and disorientated enough to take his word for it. In the SAS they weaken prisoners' minds for interrogation by keeping them awake for days on end, stood on one leg in a cold room with the crackle of an untuned radio pumped loudly into their ears – which doesn't sound a million miles away from the circumstances

I've been living under for the past couple of weeks. So if my dad tells me I'm holding the baby wrong, then I'm in no fit state to disagree. Right now he could tell me that there was no baby at all and that I'd actually been cradling a large bag of brown sugar with a baby's face Sellotaped to it for the past few hours. I'd just smile, nod, squish the baby into the kitchen cupboard above the kettle and curl up on the sofa for a nice kip.

'Jesus, careful! You nearly dropped her!' he shrieks as I hand her to him.

I smile apologetically.

'Did I?' I say, looking around the room for confirmation. But the only other person there is my wife, who is so tired that she's starting to look like that snake out of *The Jungle Book* with the weird, spinning eyes. I won't get any sense out of her.

'Yes, I think I did nearly drop her,' I say to my dad with a slight, inexplicable giggle in my voice. 'Sorry.'

He holds her in his arms and talks soothingly to her. 'What are we going to do about your stupid daddy?' he says. 'We'll have to report him to social services, won't we? It's not safe for you here. He's an idiot.'

I stand beside them, listening, nodding and slouching in a gormless sort of a way. He may be slagging me off, but he's doing it in a special baby voice that I actually find quite comforting. Anyway, what do I care if he thinks I'm an incompetent idiot? It's better than him thinking I'm in total control – then he'd never offer to help. Maybe if I actually had dropped the baby when I was coming down the stairs, he might have agreed to take her off our hands for a night or two while we caught up on some sleep and got our heads together.

'What's this they've got you dressed in?' he says, regarding the West Ham pyjamas I bought her with abject disgust. 'How revolting! You poor thing – being dressed up like a clown in this tasteless crap.' I just grin and nod some more.

When my dad was in his early twenties, he ran a rock 'n' roll club with his brothers called The Big Beat. It was in Harrow, north London, and they managed to attract some of the top bands of the time: The Animals, The Yardbirds, The Moody Blues – even The High Numbers, who went on to become The Who. Pretty cool, huh?

Kids would come from all over London to watch bands at The Big Beat. Sometimes different gangs would end up fighting on the dance floor, so my dad hired a couple of meatheads to keep the peace. Trouble was, they had such an uncompromising approach to their work that they ended up causing more aggro than the clientele themselves. Once they chased a gang of bike-chain-wielding hoodlums out of the club and all the way down the street outside. After twenty minutes they still hadn't come back, and my dad started to worry that they might have been nicked or something. Eventually one of the meatheads reappeared over the horizon, puffing, wheezing and chuckling all at once.

'What happened?' asked my dad.

'Well, I managed to catch up with one lad outside the train station,' panted the goon.

'And?' said Dad.

'And I whacked him over the head with me cosh. Laid him spark out!'

'So what's the joke?' Dad enquired.

'The joke was, he weren't one of the kids we'd been chasing. Everyone got muddled up in the crowds. Turns out he was just some poor bastard running for a train!'

I like it when my dad tells me stories about The Big Beat. Then again, I like it when anyone tells me lightly comedic tales of calamitous street violence. But the stories surrounding that club have particular relevance in my mind because it's where my parents met.

When my mum was sixteen, she dreamed of hanging out at The Big Beat. It may have been housed in the sleepy, civic environs of the Harrow Weald Memorial Hall, but it was still the hottest spot for miles around. Problem was, she was too young. Then she got pally with a girl called Michelle Delaney, who said she could get her in no problem, because her brothers ran the place. So one Friday night my mum put on her best clobber, did her hair up in a gigantic beehive and snuck out of the house behind her parents' back. True to her word, Michelle managed to get both of them past the burly doormen with ease.

It was while she was waiting to check her coat in at the cloakroom that she first clocked my dad, standing there in his fancy suit with a fag on the go. As their eyes met, she reckons it was one of those spine-tingling romantic moments. You know, like there was some sort of instant magnetism between them. It sounds corny, I suppose, but I like to suspend my cynicism whenever she recounts the story. After all, that was the precise moment that I came into being, in some kind of faraway, notional sense at least. It's better than your mum telling you that your dad got hold of her at the work's Christmas do after failing to cop off with her better-looking mate.

They then fell in love and started courting. My mum's parents, who were a bit prim and aspirational, didn't approve. They probably dreamed of mum one day marrying a dreary accountant from a slightly better-off family who would eventually buy her a semi-detached house in Hertfordshire and condemn her to a life of domesticity and Valium abuse. They certainly didn't envisage her taking up with a wannabe rock 'n' roll impresario who lived on the estate up the road.

My dad's family was huge. They all lived together on a council estate in Stanmore. His Irish father and Scouse mum churned out kids at the prolific rate that only Roman Catholics can muster. I suppose it was something to do with the inherently lairy mix of Irish, Scouse and London cultures that may have lent my dad, the oldest of eight kids, a certain cocksure swagger.

If there was one thing my mum's mum didn't like, it was cocksure swagger. She objected to anyone with even the faintest whiff of self-confidence about them. She thought people like that were show-offs. My dad would turn up at their little home in Harrow in his old man's car, wearing his flashy clothes, talking his flashy talk and having the audacity to look my grandma in the eye when he spoke to her. The flaming cheek of the man! She generally preferred people to be painfully inhibited. She saw a certain sort of warped dignity in it, I suppose. Suffice to say, my dad was her living, breathing nightmare. He epitomised a post-war generation that wanted more out of life than retarded, buttoned-down conformity. They wanted to be treated as equals! They wanted to wear nice clothes and drive fast cars just like the posh kids! They wanted to dance to loud rock 'n' roll music and cast off the suffocating social conventions of yesteryear! And most of all they wanted to get your sixteen-year-old daughter pregnant! Well, maybe that last bit wasn't an explicit part of my dad's manifesto, but it was nevertheless what he did.

Mum's parents weren't the sorts to come over all Claire Rayner in that sort of situation. There was no 'Never mind, luv, let's all sit down and talk about what we should do'. It was more a case of 'Your father and I have decided that you'll have the baby in secret, then give it up for adoption to the nuns'. What was my mum supposed to do? Or my dad, for that matter? I mean, he'd got a girl five years his junior up the spout. They'd only been going out six months. He was lucky my granddad didn't come round the estate with a shotgun.

So off they sent her to some grim hospital, where she gave birth to a baby daughter in the most unspeakably painful and heartbreaking circumstances. She named it Caroline. My dad was forbidden from seeing them, but he managed to creep in behind everyone's back and briefly meet his little daughter soon after she was born. A few days later she was taken away from my poor mum, who, of course, never really got over it. The laws back then stopped her from trying to contact Caroline directly, but over the years she wrote tons of letters to her and sent them to the adoption society. The adoption society weren't allowed to notify Caroline of the letters, but Mum hoped she might one day get curious and come looking for them. And years later Caroline did get in touch. Only she was no longer

Caroline. She had grown up, with the help of a little operation, to be none other than the actor Ross Kemp!

No, not really. Would have been a nice twist though, wouldn't it?

So, just to be clear: everything so far is true other than the bit about Ross Kemp being my long-lost sister. Got it? Good. Right, anyway, in spite of all this messy business, Mum and Dad eventually got together. When mum's parents found out that she was still knocking about with dad, they went ballistic and threw her out of the house.

They finally got married in 1964, when she was twenty and he was twenty-five. They had my three brothers within the first three years of their marriage. They lived in a succession of council houses for the next ten years or so, my dad scraping together a few quid however he could, first as a road manager for rock bands like The Searchers and later as a film extra. In the early 1970s he went all radical and got involved in the Workers' Revolutionary Party. During the three-day week, when civil unrest simmered and tanks took to the streets of London, the government even bugged my parents' phone. But I don't think he was really ready to blow anyone up or commandeer the apparatus of the state. He was basically a hippy who'd read too many books. While he banged on about Trotsky and social injustice and how all property was theft, Mum would just smile, nod, carry on doing the dishes and wonder how they were going to pay the gas bill. Then in 1975 they had me – the youngest by seven years. And about three years after that they split up. My dad got a proper job, remarried and a few years later had my younger sister with his new wife.

One day, when I was nineteen, Mum told me to come

into the living room and sit down because she had something to tell me. Her unusually formal, melodramatic tone made me come over all queasy. It didn't help that I had been smoking skunk weed all afternoon in my bedroom and she had managed to catch me just as I'd briefly crept out in search of a sandwich. As my head started to swim with nausea, she suddenly burst out crying. I stared through bloodshot eyes at her demented, blubbering features and tried to tune in to what she was saying, thinking to myself: 'What? You and my dad? Something about some nuns? And a baby? What baby? Slow down, Mum, can't you see I'm stoned? Pete Townshend? What's he got to do with anything? Seriously, if you don't slow down, I think I'm gonna spew. I wonder if we've got any Yop in the fridge? That'd make everything seem better, some lovely Yop. And maybe a Twix.'

I shuffled off to the kitchen to check the fridge. There was no Yop. Then, all of a sudden, her mad flurry of words distilled in my head. I shuffled back into the living room and said, 'Sorry, did you just say that you had a baby with my dad when you were sixteen and then had it adopted?'

'Yes,' she whimpered.

It was the most earth-shattering news I'd ever heard. Remember, this was years before that whole John Major and Edwina Currie story broke.

I gave my mum a cuddle, and we talked about it for a bit longer. She filled me in on the salient details and explained that she'd never found the right time to tell me before. My brothers had found out a few years beforehand, when one of them had discovered Caroline's birth certificate among my mum's personal papers.

As you can imagine, my head was full of all sorts of thoughts after that. It wasn't dissimilar to how I felt after watching the revelatory denouement of *The Usual Suspects*, when my brain started racing back through every scene in the film, looking at it from a fresh perspective. Suddenly certain things made sense. Like the strange sense of sadness that always seemed to simmer beneath my mum's veneer of claptrap-spouting joviality. But mostly it intensified my sense of life's chaotic nature. This feeling had already been cultivated over the past nineteen years by all the cat-killing, loan sharks, stolen *Star Wars* figures, Gat-gun shoot-outs and other pathetic little incidents that had somehow impacted on my worldview. I looked on my mum and dad's story as impossibly romantic, terrifying, complicated and preposterous all at once. I kind of loved it and hated it at the same time. One thing was for sure: I didn't want to go through anything similar.

So about a year later I got together with the girl I'd had a crush on since I was at school. We fell in love, went to university together, then moved back to London, got jobs, got a mortgage, got married and had a baby. No adoptions, no nuns, no rock 'n' roll clubs and no involvements in speculative leftist *coups d'état*. The High Numbers never even made so much as a cameo appearance. Sure, there was the time we briefly got to party backstage with short-lived Liverpudlian Britpop sensations Space, but, other than that, we played life with a comparatively straight bat. I'd like to think I could raise my daughter in a more controlled environment than I was raised in. I've not got too many complaints about the way my parents treated me. My dad may have done the off, but at least he was a good bloke. Better a good dad that's absent than a shit one who sticks around. And at least I got to go to McDonald's more than the average kid. An estranged father will never turn down his kid's request for a Big Mac and fries. Back then a meal deal would have only cost about two pounds fifty – which is a small price to pay if you're a dad looking to ease a tiny part of his conscience. This is why kids from broken homes tend to be chubbier than those who live with both parents.

In short, living in a single-parent family isn't all bad. But had my dad been around more then I suppose there's a chance I'd have grown up to be less of a dumbo. He would have had a better chance of teaching me chess for starters. Not to mention the other stuff he would have liked to teach me. Like when he bought me a book on birdwatching and took me up Richmond Park with some binoculars. I liked the idea of doing that sort of stuff, I really did. I could envisage myself being one of those swotty kids who actually choose to do clever stuff outside school hours. But cultivating that sort of personality in a child is a full-time job. The odd weekend of cerebral pursuits here and there was never going to make a lasting impact on my fledgling brain. There was no way I was going to go home and crib up on the lesser spotted whitethroat during my own time when there was no one there hassling me to do so. With my mum at work, I was left to my own devices most of the time. If I wasn't trying to avoid being locked in the airing cupboard by my brothers, I liked to relax with a bowl of Instant Whip in front of the box. Or just while away a few hours melting polystyrene in the bathroom sink. I was very much a boy of simple pleasures.

As a result of my sedentary lifestyle, my worldview was largely shaped by whatever crap the TV or cinema served up. Fatherly role models were provided by Australian soaps or the teenage comedies of John Hughes. And king among all screen fathers was always, to my mind, Teen Wolf's dad. Still is. What wasn't there to love about him? For starters, he was a wolf. Second, he was a widower who managed to raise a troubled son single-handedly while simultaneously running his own small business. He was warm, dependable and cuddly. That scene where he appears at the bathroom door in wolf form to gently comfort his son, Michael J. Fox, is one of the most poignant moments of cinematic fatherliness ever committed to celluloid. Teen Wolf's dad is the dad I want to be. In fact, if I was even half the man Teen Wolf's dad was, then I'd be happy. But of course, *Teen Wolf* was just a film. And not a very realistic one if you think about it: I mean, why would being a werewolf necessarily make you better at playing basketball?

In real life I had no one remotely like Teen Wolf's dad serving as a role model. What I had were my older brothers. You've already heard enough about them to get the idea that they weren't exactly dedicated mentors. That said, they did once teach me how to play poker.

'Sam, d'you want us to teach you how to play our special card game?' they asked one evening with uncharacteristic enthusiasm. Even at the age of ten I was wily enough to know they must be up to something. And I knew what: they figured they could teach me the rudiments, get me hooked then clean out the contents of the Natwest Young Savers piggy bank that sat atop my bedroom cabinet containing about £7.80 in loose change. To me that represented a year's worth of saving towards my mum's Christmas present. To them it represented a sixteenth of an ounce of low-grade Lebanese hashish as sold by a bloke outside the Wimpy in Chiswick. Doesn't sound like much, but if they smoked it through a chillum, it could have put their brains out of action for a whole school week. Suffice to say, the stakes were pretty high.

My poker lesson amounted to little more than five minutes of them impatiently explaining how the hands worked. I tried to ask questions to clarify a few points, but it was too late: they were already dealing the cards and telling me that I'd pick it up as I went along. The first couple of hands went up to about 20 pence. Those were losses I could sustain. Soon there was a knock at the door, and some of their mates began to drift in. The living room filled up with cigarette smoke and the stench of budget lager. I felt slightly scared in a grown-up sort of a way. I lost another couple of hands, but the rules gradually started to make sense. Soon I was getting the hang of things. More importantly, I was getting dealt the right cards. I won a couple of hands for small change, and my brothers laughed it off. They probably told themselves it was all part of the hustle. But as the stakes grew, so did my confidence. I won a couple of quid. Then a fiver. I was beginning seriously to jeopardise my brothers' sixteenth of Leb and, even worse, was embarrassing them in front of their mates. Just to escalate matters, I decided to get a bit flashy.

'Come on, you wankers, this is getting a bit too easy,' I said as I flamboyantly lobbed another handful of change into the middle of the table, leaning back on my chair like I was Johnny Big Bucks. If this had been a western, they would have warned me about getting too sure of myself and gently implied that I should watch my smart mouth if I wanted to get out of there alive. But they were more blunt than that.

'Sam, here's the deal,' they said as I sat there taking an ostentatious swig from my celebratory glass of Vimto. 'If you win another hand like that, we're gonna kick your head in.'

Experience should have told me to take the threat seriously. But I was high on my own success. For a brief moment on that smoky evening in 1985 I thought I was immortal. So instead of saying 'Fair enough, chaps, that's perfectly understandable. Why don't you just take all the money back and I'll pop off to bed?' I fixed my oldest brother's stare with my best Clint Eastwood and said, 'Deal.'

I remember the exact moment I got dealt the fourth queen.

'Wait a minute, that's four of a kind!' I thought to myself gleefully. In fact, I think I may have actually muttered it out loud – I hadn't quite got to grips with the idea of a poker face yet. Luckily they were too drunk to hear me. Everyone had folded bar me and one of their mates.

'What's he got?' asked an onlooker nervously as I was forced to show my hand.

'Well,' slurred a brother as I reached to turn my final card over. 'He's got two queens showing. And I haven't seen any others so far. But I doubt he's got . . .'

'FOUR QUEENS!' I blurted before he could finish speculating. 'FOUR QUEENS! FOUR QUEENS! I've got four queens!'

My hands reached for the pile of cash sitting in the centre of the table. In the interests of dramatic effect I'd like to pretend there was a brief moment of silence as it dawned on me what was about to happen. But the truth is I didn't have time to think before the first shoe hit me. I remember hearing someone shout, 'Right, we fucking warned you,' and the rest is a blur of vintage '80s trainers descending on me as I lay curled up in the corner, clutching whatever winnings I had managed to grab and giggling with adrenalised fear.

So they did at least teach me some important lessons that day. They taught me to understand the consequences of my actions, never to get too cocky and that success brings its own challenges.

It may be unfair to say that that was the only lesson I ever received from them. My middle brother went through a brief boxing phase when he was in his teens. One day he came home and said that I needed toughening up. He dragged me upstairs to my mum's bedroom, where he turned the double bed into a makeshift ring. He spent a good hour teaching me how to jab, dodge and weave, followed by a futile ten minutes trying to teach me how to skip. Once that was over with, he announced it was time to put all I'd learned into action. We climbed on to the mattress – me on my feet, him on his knees to even things up.

'Right,' he said, 'remember everything I've told you. Keep your guard up and keep moving.'

'Is he serious?' I thought to myself. 'I haven't understood a word he's said for the past hour. I was happily sat in front of *Sunday Sunday* with Gloria Hunniford a minute ago, now I'm wobbling about on a mattress being made to fight a bloke twice my size.'

'Ding ding!' shouted my brother. Then he punched me in the mouth and I cried. That was the end of the lesson. He said I just wasn't cut out for boxing like he was.

The only other bloke who ever spent a prolonged period living at our place was Rab the milkman, whom my mum took up with when I was about nine. He was a gangly Scottish fella with a stupid bubble perm and a moustache, like a cross between the footballer Terry McDermott and Ronald McDonald. I found the fact that he was a milkman quite glamorous, and he would often let me join him on his morning rounds, when I would gain thrilling access to his Unigate Dairies float and all the precious bounty it carried. Among the dozens of silver- and gold-topped bottles there was always two crates of cartoned milk we carried especially for delivery to Feltham Young Offenders Institute.

'Why don't they get bottles like everyone else?' I asked Rab.

'Because they'd use the glass to try and kill themselves or each other,' he replied flatly. Suddenly the job seemed so dangerous and edgy, it was like I was doing work experience with Delta Force. There were other things that made Rab seem cool too, like the fact that he claimed to have once played professional football for Hibernian. Although now, of course, I realise that most of what he said was complete lies, and Rab was, in fact, a bit of a twat.

My brothers were old enough to appreciate this at the time. He generally made their lives a nightmare. Once he stumbled into the local pub where my oldest brother was having a drink with some mates. Rab slumped drunkenly beside them and, by means of an intro, sunk his teeth into one of their legs, drawing blood. When the others objected, Rab offered to fight them all. Eventually he grabbed my brother by the shoulder and insisted he return home to see his mum immediately.

Once home, Rab perked up.

'I'm home, hon!' he called out to my mum. 'And I've brought you your favourite.' He produced a thin carrier bag that he'd had stuffed down the front of his coat and emptied it on the coffee table. Out flopped two greasy, stone-cold doner kebabs.

My mum regarded them for a few seconds and asked, 'Are you drunk?'

Rab chuckled.

'Me? Drunk? I dunno what you're talking about, hon! I'm away upstairs for a quick pish. You get stuck into your kebab.'

And with that he staggered upstairs, vomited in the toilet and didn't emerge again for the rest of the evening. Shortly afterwards, my brother moved out and went to live with my dad.

'I was a semi-pro golfer, ya bastards!' Rab announced one night after another lengthy session down the local. We were sat watching telly and failing to treat his latest boast with sufficient respect. Before we knew it he had gone off to fetch his 9-iron from the cupboard under the stairs and was stood in front of the TV demonstrating his swing.

'I could be making a fortune on the tour if I wanted!' he insisted.

We shifted position to try and view the screen behind him. Eventually he snapped.

'Right, ya bastards! You're all coming with me to the park right now.'

He fetched a ball and a tee, and we were all marched reluctantly down to the local square. The fact that it was dark didn't seem to bother him; he assured us that he could make his golfing prowess apparent with just a single shot. He shakily pressed the tee into the grass, placed the ball on top and instructed us all to stand back. He spent a few minutes carefully positioning himself, then let fly. Only nothing really flew at all. He just skimmed the top of the ball, which trickled lamely about a yard in front of the tee. But Rab was oblivious: he stood with his hand to his brow like a ship's captain looking out to sea and cooed loudly: 'Jesus Christ! Did you see that, ya bastards? Must have sailed straight over those trees and outta the park!' With his vicious attack on my brother's mate's calf still fresh in our memories, we all thought it safer to gently applaud, then quickly head home.

He may have acted the hard man with us kids, but he was strangely petrified of my dad. Whenever my old man came round to pick me up at weekends, Rab would scuttle upstairs and hide in one of the bedrooms. Which was weird, because my dad didn't seem to have much of a problem with him at all. One Saturday afternoon Dad was dropping me off when I spotted Rab coming up the street the other way.

'Hey, look Dad, there's Rab!' I shouted, naively certain that the two men would be thrilled to see each other.

'Where? What are you talking about?' said my dad

irritably, looking around. I looked back, and Rab had disappeared.

'He was there a minute ago,' I insisted. Then I saw a movement beside a Ford Cortina parked at the side of the road. Squatting down beside it was Rab.

'There he is!' I said, assuming he must have dropped something. It didn't occur to me for a moment that Rab was hiding.

'Don't be ridiculous,' grumped my father. 'You're seeing things!'

I walked right up to the car and tried to address Rab but found him shuffling on his haunches around the other side.

'Rab, what are you doing?' I asked as he tried to shoo me away with a wave of his arm.

'Piss off!' he hissed, ducking his head. Looking back, I think my dad had cottoned on to what was happening but just couldn't bring himself to acknowledge the absurdity of the situation.

'Come on, there's nobody under the car, let's go inside,' he said. I left Rab, crouched and humiliated beside that Cortina, wondering to myself why he had told me to piss off.

Things came to a head for Rab a few months later. My middle brother was sixteen by now and had left school to become a postman. He worked shifts and would come home at strange hours of the day, tired, irritable and hungry. One afternoon he turned up to find Rab sprawled lazily on the sofa with an empty tub of raspberry ripple ice-cream beside him.

'I bought that ice-cream specially for my pudding when I got in from work!' my brother exploded.

'Well, don't blame me, son,' grinned Rab. 'That tub was sitting there empty when I got home from my round. Must've been someone else who ate it.' But my brother knew otherwise.

'You've still got bits of it in your stupid fucking moustache, you thieving cunt!' he spat, pointing an accusatory finger at the tell-tale drips around Rab's mouth. The row escalated quickly, and Rab jumped to his feet, taking a swing at my brother's head. My brother made off to the kitchen and came back waving my mum's biggest carving knife and telling him to get out of the house. Which he did. A few days after that he came back to collect his things, and then we never saw him again. We took ice-cream seriously in our house.

I'm changing the baby's nappy on the living-room floor.

'You're not doing that right,' says my dad, peering over me.

'In what way?' I ask.

'In every way,' he replies.

'This is the way I always do it,' I insist. 'It seems to work fine.'

'Well, why is she crying her eyes out then?'

'Because babies cry their eyes out. Don't they?'

'They do if you change their nappy like that.'

I wait for him to tell me how I should be changing the nappy. But he just looks at his watch and says, 'Shit, my pay-and-display is about to run out. I've got to go.'

I decide to remove the nappy I had already stuck on her arse and start again. There is a short interim period between the old nappy being removed and the new one being fitted, during which she fires a yellowish projectile shit across the room like a rocket. It hits the wall next to the plasma and starts to drip down apologetically. It looks a bit like chicken korma. I quickly wipe her up and attach the new nappy. Then I start to scrub the shit from the wall. And d'you know what? I don't really stop to think how my dad, my brothers, Rab or even Teen Wolf's dad would approach the situation. I just keep scrubbing until the shit has disappeared. Only it never does. But it does at least fade to a faint stain, which I reckon will be almost unnoticeable in dim lighting.

14

TWAT

My wife hears me calling the baby a twat on the baby monitor.

'You can't call the baby a twat!' she says through the speaker from downstairs.

'But she's acting like one!' I explain. 'She keeps pretending to be asleep, then waking up and screaming when I try to put her down. She's playing mind games.'

My wife comes upstairs. She looks disappointed. Stupid baby monitor.

'Look, I wouldn't have called her a twat, had I known you were listening,' I reason.

'What kind of excuse is that?'

'Well, it's only you who's offended by it. To her ears it's just a noise.'

'That's not the point.'

'Yes it is. She can't even understand her own name yet – how's she supposed to know that "twat" is a rude word?'

'I'm not worried about you offending her. I'm worried about her first word being "twat".'

I look down at the baby's tiny, scrunched-up face. She doesn't look anywhere near ready to talk yet. Whenever she does open her mouth, all that comes out is a croaky sort of belch and a splat of thin, white puke.

'Are you asking me to stop swearing in front of the baby?' I ask in disbelief.

'That's exactly what I'm asking you to do,' she says.

'But swearing is my release!' I protest. 'Think yourself lucky. For some blokes it's glue.'

She takes the baby from my arms, giving me a dirty look as if I was some sort of abusive father. Next thing I know, she's announced a blanket ban on all potty mouthing. I'm not allowed to swear at or in front of the baby. It's like Mao's fucking China round here. Ha! Can't stop me writing my precious swear words down, can you? No baby monitor to spy on me while I write, is there?

In the night the baby cries and cries and cries. My wife feeds her, and she shuts up for, like, ten minutes. Then, just as we're drifting back towards sleep, she starts up again. Maybe she needs burping? Maybe she's too hot? Maybe she's had a bad dream? Maybe she's worried about the situation in Gaza? I don't bloody know. There's no way of knowing. She is less communicative than a pot plant. You'd have more luck asking a cactus what the matter was.

But we can at least try to find a way of making it stop. In the depths of the night we blearily sing her songs, walk her round, put a finger in her mouth for her to suck on.

'Maybe she needs winding?' one of us mumbles.

We try an elaborate succession of methods to elicit a burp. First we lay her over our shoulders and stroke her back. That doesn't work, so we hold her to our chest, facing outwards, with the palm of our hands resting on her stomach. Still no dice. My wife doesn't let me try the more elaborate ones that require above-average dexterity. 'You'll gouge out her eyeball or something,' she reasons.

Every parent we know has a different winding method that they claim is fail-safe. A sister-in-law teaches us one where you sit the baby upright on your knee, grab her by the face and rotate her head in vigorous circles. It proves the most effective so far. She burps twice after about thirty seconds. It's also funny to watch. I film it on my mobile phone and show it to my dad when he comes round.

'Jesus, it looks like you're . . . you're strangling her,' he says in horror. I look back at the footage, sniggering. It really does look like she's being strangled. I stop sniggering. It reminds me of those dehumanising torture rituals you see US troops subjecting Iraqi prisoners to. We decide not to ever do it again, however effective it seems.

In the night she sleeps in a basket next to our bed. She wakes up needing a feed every two hours. I have no real role to play in this but feel I ought at least to wake up and give some moral support. Over the past few weeks I have trained myself to sit upright and blurt out 'Do you need any help? Sure? OK, goodnight' without actually waking up.

Sometimes, only occasionally, she goes straight back to sleep after her feed. I lie in bed listening out for her breathing. I am unsettled by the eerie silence. I have to get out of bed, creep over to her basket and rest my hand on her chest to check her lungs are moving.

'What are you doing?' my wife asks, waking up with a start.

'I'm checking that she's still breathing,' I say. 'I thought she might be dead.' The baby wakes up and starts to cry.

I pick her up and walk her round the bedroom. She keeps on crying. I walk her up and down the stairs. She keeps on crying. I stick a badger-shaped glove puppet on my hand and start saying 'Barry Badger doesn't like it when you cry' in what I consider to be a hilarious badger voice. She cries even louder. My wife calls out from the bedroom: 'Stop doing the badger voice. She doesn't like it.'

I walk into the bathroom and switch on the light. The fan starts to make a whirring sound. She stops crying! She likes the sound of the fan. Maybe it reminds her of being inside the womb. It's not what I imagined it would sound like inside a woman. I'd always thought their innards echoed with the sexy whine of a jazz saxophonist. This is more of a mechanical, monotonous drone. But who cares? I have found a way of stopping the crying. I have broken the Enigma code of my baby's tear ducts.

The next night I am lying in bed, unable to sleep again. I get up and check that she is breathing again. She wakes up again.

'For fuck's sake!' says my wife.

'Don't swear in front of the baby!' I say.

She chucks the badger puppet at me. I pick the baby up and head for the bathroom.

'I'll have this sorted in a jiffy,' I announce confidently. I walk into the bathroom and switch on the light. She keeps on crying. The fan starts to whirr. She keeps on crying.

'Can't you hear the fan?' I ask her. 'It's nice, isn't it? It's like being inside Mummy's tummy.' She keeps on crying. She makes out she doesn't know what I'm on about. See what I mean? Twat.

This carries on for weeks. Time and time again she fools me into thinking I've found the magic formula to stop her crying. Time and time again my hopes are dashed. In the dead of night I take her downstairs and switch on the TV. She keeps crying while I surf through the channels. When I get to Price Drop TV, she stops suddenly. She is captivated by a young female presenter eulogising about a vegetable steamer. Maybe it's the soothing tones of the presenter's sales patter. Or the orangey glow of her complexion. Perhaps it's the steamer itself that has caught her eye. Certainly, £18.99 for a device that cooks a whole family meal at that speed seems like exceptional value. Price Drop TV appears to be the answer to my prayers. I hit the Sky Plus button so I can show her the same bit again the next night. But of course she's gone off the orangey host and her vegetable steamer by then. She's gone off Price Drop TV altogether. So I surf some more. Eventually we land on Muslim TV. Her jaw drops, and she falls silent. After ten minutes of watching she nods off to sleep. I say a little prayer of thanks to Allah.

By the next night she's so over Islam. She's fickle. Her attention span makes mine look positively vast. Soon she's gone off the idea of telly altogether. Within a week I'm standing in the kitchen at half-past three in the morning repeatedly flicking the lights on and off like a strobe while jumping up and down on the spot. It's a bit like being at a rave, only really quiet and lonely and depressing. But it's what seems to work today.

'Please stop crying,' I plead with her in a whisper on one of the nights when none of the tricks seems to be working. I have reached breaking point. I feel like sobbing. All I want is a sleep. In fact, a sleep would be an indulgence. A nap would do. A snooze would be luxury. I'd sell both my kidneys for a humble doze. I am practically on my knees begging her to give it a rest.

'I'll buy you a pony if you just stop crying,' I whimper. She just looks straight through me like I wasn't even there.

Her pious resistance to bribery is starting to irritate me. And it's not just bribery either: all of the techniques I usually employ to get my own way with people just don't wash with her.

First I try rational appeals.

'You're only crying because you're tired,' I explain gently. 'And the more you cry, the more tired you'll get. Can't you see? It's all just a vicious circle.' She screams until snot comes out of her nose. She's not ready to listen to reason. So I start to pull out a few dirty tricks.

'Oh, you're crying!' I sneer at her. 'How very mature of you. What a constructive course of action!'

But sarcasm is pointless. So I give mockery a go.

'Waaahh! Waaahh! Ooh, I'm a big baby! I can't stop crying! My life's so hard! Coz all I do all day is sit around drinking milk and having my arse wiped!' It's all like water off a duck's back to her.

As a final throw of the dice I become aggressive.

'Are you gonna stop crying, or is daddy going to have to get very angry with you?' I ask menacingly.

'Remember what we said about threatening the baby?' says my wife. I didn't even know she was listening. Stupid baby monitor.

★

These nightly exchanges are bringing my limited interpersonal skills into sharp focus. These techniques are pretty much all I've ever used to get my own way with people. I try to be reasonable, but that doesn't work with everyone. Sometimes I patronise. Occasionally I condescend. From time to time I do that thing of just repeating whatever someone says back to them. But, you know, in a silly voice. And once in a while I just put my hands over my ears, turn around and walk away. I use these tricks at work; I use them against my wife; I've even used them to hurry up waiters with my dessert. They are tried and tested. They work.

In fact, they're wasted on the trivial conflicts thrown up by everyday life. Imagine the impact they could have in a court of law or on the diplomatic circuit. Palestine? I'd turn up and do a load of quite cruel yet funny impressions of delegates from both sides. It'd lighten the mood and put the senselessness of all that bloodshed into sudden perspective. Northern Ireland? I'd probably use a bit of light sarcasm to lampoon the folly of sectarianism. Tibet? I'd patronise the Chinese into submission. If that didn't work, I might turn aggressive. I'd find a way somehow. I'm a persuasive person.

That's what I always thought anyway. But this baby is impervious to my powers. I just can't break her down. No amount of words will help. It's unnerving, because words are all I have. Flannel and chatter are usually my answer to everything. Without them I am helpless.

She's not trying to point-score. There's no argument to win here. She's got no agenda for me to expose and belittle. She is just genuinely distressed. And I have to find a way of making her better. It's intimidating. So I pick her up, I cuddle her, I let her suck my finger and I go into the kitchen and start flicking the lights on and off. And I learn to keep my mouth shut. Most of the time.

I also learn this: babies just cry. I can sometimes hear the one from two doors down wailing its guts up in the night. I see loads of the little bastards in their pushchairs up the high street bawling away. They're all at it. It comes naturally to them. There doesn't have to be a reason, beyond the fact that they've suddenly been awakened from a peaceful nine-month slumber, dragged out of the comfort of a nice warm womb and chucked unceremoniously into the noisy, col-ourful, stinking world. It's disorientating and scary. In adult terms it'd be like being snatched from your comfy bed in the dead of night, blindfolded, slung in a van, driven up to Hartlepool and booted through the doors of a Yates Wine Lodge into the middle of a local hen night's lock-in. You couldn't run away, because your legs wouldn't work. You couldn't call for help, because you wouldn't know how to speak. So you'd just sit there and cry and cry and cry. And not even Price Drop TV could make you stop. That's what being born must feel like. Being born is rubbish.

So where's my motivation? If you don't have kids of your own, you may be wondering why I'm putting up with all this. Why I didn't just grab my toothbrush, hot-foot it to Heathrow and catch the first flight to Fiji after the first few nights of torture? Well, listen to this: eventually she nods off. I mean, she has to in the end, doesn't she? And then, just before I do the same, I find myself staring at her face. It has quickly turned from red and tear-stained to delicate and peaceful. Her nose is tiny and perfect. Her skin is smooth like ivory. Her soft, dark hair frames her tiny, beautiful features. Can you see what's happening here? I'm turning all poetic and soppy. That's what happens every single night. All the pain and suffering she's put me through are just washed away in seconds. Everything inside my body is pleading with me to shut my eyes and go to sleep, but I can't. I just keep staring. And I feel all proud and warm and happy inside. It's like the worst sort of all-consuming crush. Don't worry, I'm not actually going to write a poem; it's not that bad.

I don't suppose there's anything exceptional about this response. God must have made us this way. Only I don't believe in God, so I suppose it must be the upshot of some complex process of evolution that you could trace back to the paternal conduct of giant turtles on the Galapagos or something.

The days are a walk in the park by comparison. Some babies seem to keep the crying up 24/7, but we've been lucky. Ours just sleeps, feeds and occasionally opens her eyes really wide and stares into space for fifteen minutes or so. That's what passes for a moment of genuine excitement in our household these days. If we're lucky, she'll even contort her little mouth into an amusing 'O' shape while she's staring. That's when you have to cry out in excitement to whoever else is in the house: 'Come quickly! You'll never fucking believe what's happening! She's staring into space while pulling an unusual facial expression! Get the camera!'

'Do we really have to be one of those twee families who go around saying stuff like "sugar" and "fiddlesticks"?' I ask my wife during the baby's afternoon nap. This swearing issue has been playing on my mind. 'What are you going to do next? Ban us from watching ITV? Make us eat brown bread?'

'If you swear in front of her all the time, she'll grow up foul-mouthed,' she says.

'Don't be stupid. There were no swearing restrictions in my family and look at us – dead eloquent.'

'Sam, you're niece's first word was "cunt".'

That shuts me up.

My wife doesn't mind a good swear herself, but she's not as committed as I am. There was no swearing in her house when she was growing up. She was too busy having piano lessons and playing with wooden, educational toys to be bothered with foul-mouthed experimentation. It wasn't that her parents were particularly strict. I suppose her household was just so pleasant that there was never any call to resort to nasty words. I imagine that she might have let the occasional 'flipping hell' slip out during heated games of Pictionary. Other than that, it was all pretty polite.

Round my house it was total foul-mouthed anarchy. My mum would never use one swear word when five of them strung together into a hybrid super-swear word would do. 'Shitfuckingwankfacetosser!' we'd hear her scream to herself after we'd displeased her in some way. 'Fuck it all! Fuck it all!' she would squawk in a kind of demented sing-song while clearing up the mess from another unsanctioned party. Sometimes these wild-eyed sing-songs would be mostly swearless but rich in berserk sarcasm: 'I luuuuuurve my life!' she'd warble or, bizarrely,

'You're the creeeaam in my cofffeeeee!' To be fair, she rarely swore directly at us. Usually she seemed to be screaming at the heavens, angrily holding God to account for the unmanageable predicament he'd landed her in.

I've got to admit, there was a certain eloquence to mum's mental outbursts. She laces words together – sweary or otherwise – with a poetic vim.

Once, when I was about eleven, my mate Joe was round playing with *Star Wars* figures in the living room. My brother came back from his shift at the post office and started rowing with my mum in the kitchen about unpaid housekeeping or something. Joe started to look a bit concerned, so I tried to distract him by zooming my replica Millennium Falcon round his head, making laser-gun noises. Suddenly there was a loud smash, and the pair of us ran into the hallway to see what was happening. My brother had lobbed his baked spud and beans against the kitchen wall. Between them they had wrecked the place. There was orange tomato sauce and bits of broken plate everywhere.

'Shit fire!' screeched my mother, which was a trademark phrase of hers. 'You fucking little shit arse!'

Poor old Joe's face went all pale and disturbed. It wasn't like he hadn't heard swearing before. I don't suppose he'd heard it come out of a mum's gob before, though. She ran screaming out of the house. My brother kicked a chair over, punched a dent in the door and stormed off in the opposite direction. I was dead embarrassed. When Joe's mum came round to pick him up, she politely asked where the adults were and why there were baked beans everywhere. Joe said he'd explain on the way home.

It got so I was barely able to distinguish between polite and impolite language. I knew the 'F' and 'C' words were not to be used in civilised company but, beyond that, I didn't have a clue. There was teacher at primary school who coached the football team who was often willing to indulge us in a bit of matey footballing banter. One day, in a misjudged bit of dressing-room larking, I told him to 'bugger off'. I had no idea what it meant, but it struck me as quite a grown-up, old-fashioned sort of a phrase, the sort of thing a teacher would almost admire you for using. I was wrong. The bastard whacked me round the back of the head with his clipboard. 'But "bugger" isn't swearing, sir!' I insisted. I never made the first team after that.

My dad was similarly perturbed by my foul effing and jeffing whenever I visited his home on weekends. Once, when I was about seven, I upset him by casually commenting that it was 'pissing down' outside. I didn't have a clue that he was objecting to the word 'pissing'. I thought he was just upset about the weather. Even when he explained it to me, I chose to argue the toss with him. 'Piss? Ha! That's not swearing!' I insisted. Which only made things worse. No one likes a seven-year-old trying to outwit them in a semantic debate.

In the summer, he would usually take us on holiday, where he would learn, over the course of a fortnight in our company, the full extent of his offspring's unsavoury manners. He seemed ever so disappointed. We were all in a hire car in Portugal once when I whimsically enquired from the back seat: 'What's a poofter?' My dad and his missus exchanged uncomfortable glances, and my brothers started to grin.

'It's a derogatory term for a homosexual', my dad explained in terms I had no chance of understanding.

One of my brothers ill-advisedly tried to alleviate the awkward atmosphere that ensued by piping up: 'Yes, like "turd burglar".' He later told me that he wasn't quite sure what 'turd burglar' actually meant, but he'd recently heard a mate use it and saw that moment in the car as the perfect opportunity to give it a run-out. It was an error of judgement.

My dad stopped the car and clipped him round the ear, barking, 'That's enough of that!' I was nonplussed. The lexicon of homophobia remained a mystery to me. A few months later an old family friend came round for lunch with his boyfriend, and I thought nothing of referring to them as 'turd burglars' to their faces. Which just goes to show the pitfalls of brushing swear words under the carpet.

'A kid should understand that swear words are very powerful. And that with great power comes great responsibility,' I suggest to my wife hopefully.

'That's from *Spiderman*,' she points out.

'What I'm saying is, kids will hear swear words whether you like it or not,' I continue. 'The best you can do is tell them what they mean and let them make their own mind up.'

'Oh really? And what are you going to tell our daughter when she asks you what "twat" means?'

'Not sure. It means "fanny", doesn't it? Or does it?'

None of this tackles the sticky business of my niece and the 'C' word. I'd only been going out with my wife for a few months when I convinced her to come on a family holiday to Ireland with my mum and my brothers and their wives. My youngest brother had his daughter in tow, who was just walking. It was an ugly fortnight, characterised by violent rows and heavy drinking. It was no place for a new girlfriend, let alone a child. My wife spent the whole time looking a bit shell-shocked by the general hullabaloo and antagonism that permeated those long days spent in quaint fishing village boozers. We argued constantly over the sort of stuff that I suppose all brothers argue about: long-disputed Subbuteo matches mostly. Occasionally my mum would burst into tears. Maddy, my tiny, cherubic niece, would merrily totter around the place, seemingly oblivious to the menacing climate. One day my wife turned to me, looking even more ashen-faced than usual.

'What is it?' I slurred.

'Maddy just said "cunt",' she replied.

'What?' I said, looking all confused and patting Maddy on her little blonde head. 'Naaah! She can't even talk, can you darling?'

'Cunt!' squeaked Maddy back at me.

It sounds funny written down, but it didn't seem so nice when you actually witnessed it. That ugly word spilling out of a face so angelic was a disconcerting thing to behold, I can tell you. Maddy had no sense of the power wielded by this exciting new term. But she'd been exposed to its persistent usage for over a week and was now repeating it back like a parrot. Which I guess makes my missus the winner of our argument. If I keep calling the baby a twat, it'll only be a matter of time before she calls me one back. Which will be justified but nonetheless distressing.

'OK, you're right, I suppose,' I concede to my wife. 'But that wasn't Maddy's first word. She was about three years old,' I add, making sure I at least scored some sort of pathetic consolation point.

I go upstairs and stand over the baby's cot watching her sleep. I stare at her gorgeous, innocent little face and try to imagine it saying the 'C' word. I don't like it. I find it much easier to imagine her waking up suddenly, looking me straight in the eye and saying 'Daddy!' Or perhaps 'Morning!' Or even 'Rosebud!' in a weird, drawn-out croak. But, please, not 'cunt'. Never 'cunt'.

It's the next morning.

'Mummy,' I say, holding the baby in front of my face and doing the special baby voice. My wife carries on reading her posh-looking book. Something about a blind woman's plight in a prisoner-of-war camp, I shouldn't wonder.

'Muuuuummmy!' I persist.

'What is it?' she finally relents with a sigh.

'Daddy broke the swearing ban . . .'

A long pause.

'What did he say?'

'He called you a wanker. I think you should divorce him.' I keep the baby suspended in front of my grinning face.

'Maybe I will,' says my wife.

15

WORK

I peep through the blinds at the world outside. As the sun-light hits my eyes, I flinch and make a strange hissing sound. Resentfully, I peer at the birds, the trees, the litter. And the people. All those bastard people. 'Look at them with their routines and their jobs and their . . . lives,' I think to myself. 'I was once like them.' It's all just a distant memory now. I've been cocooned in this house for weeks. Or is it months? Hard to say. I know the baby has already outgrown certain items of clothing. This is what I've been reduced to: working out the passing of time by reference to clothing labels. Calendars are pretty much pointless to me. If someone asked me what the date was, I'd tell them it was roughly three to six months.

My chin is stubbly, and my eyes are drooping. I've worn tracksuit bottoms to the shops eight days running. I live off a diet of cake and tea. At first this lifestyle seemed novel. Then it became frustrating. But lately I've entered into the strangest phase of all: I'm actually starting to enjoy it. I've been institutionalised. I can barely imagine going back to civvy street now. From my vantage point at the bedroom window it all seems so hectic. Why is everyone in such a hurry? Feed time isn't for another hour and three-quarters.

But of course, those people – 'the others', I call them – don't care about feed time. What do they care about? What matters in the outside world? My mind strains to remember, but it's no use. All that matters to it now are the simple routines that prevail between these four walls. It really is like prison, just as I had envisaged: we spend long periods confined to our sleeping quarters (although, like Cat A prisoners on suicide watch, we are rarely allowed to actually sleep). There are regimented mealtimes. We slop out eight or nine times a day. I feel like 'fresh fish', a naive and petrified new inmate struggling to survive. My wife is a firm but fair warden. Which makes my daughter 'the daddy', calling the shots from inside her well-appointed cell.

Yes, it's so much simpler in here. Meanwhile, 'the others' continue to scurry around with implausible urgency outside. What *is* it that they're so preoccupied with? Slowly it starts to drift back to me. That look of concentration and mild panic in their eyes. The way they look at their precious 'watches' to see what 'time' it is. The fact that they've bothered to shave and put on proper clothes. Yes, that's it, they're going to work. I remember work. It once seemed so important. I had ambitions. I had five-year plans. I had places to go, people to see, meetings to doze through and colleagues to secretly despise. Those colleagues probably wouldn't recognise me if they saw me now, standing at the window with a baby in one hand and a slice of lemon drizzle cake in the other, naked but for a pair of loose-fitting karate pants. In their narrow-minded perceptions I may seem like a drop-out, a failure or a tramp. But the truth is, I am liberated. I have stepped back, seen the bigger picture and chosen to say 'no' to the social conventions that dictate the way they live. Why should I hit deadlines and change my pants every day just because that's what 'The Man' says I should do? Screw The Man! I refuse to line his pockets any longer. I am happy here with my wife, my daughter and my prison fantasy. Today I shall spend my afternoon hand-washing shit-stained baby-grows using a bar of Vanish in the bathroom sink. I'm living the dream.

'Have you seen this American Express bill?' says my wife, wandering into the room. She has been doing paper-work downstairs. She said she wanted to keep her mind active. I knew it would end in tears. Opening the mail always does. And once you actually start to read it, you're just asking for trouble.

'Bills? Ha! They're of no relevance to us any more!' I want to tell her. 'Leave those to the squares and the bread heads! I do not recognise mainstream society's oppressive "billing system". From now on we shall get by using a simple bartering process with other like-minded parents from the local area. Either that or eBay. Either way, shut up about the bill.'

But I don't say any of that stuff. I just stand and gawp while she starts to read out some choice highlights of my expenditure in the months leading up to the birth.

'A hundred and fifty quid on a lunch ... what the fuck?'

'It was important. It was to do with work. Or some-thing.'

'A grand at Harvey Nichols? What for?'

'Erm, trousers. And some speciality cheeses.'

'Five hundred quid cash withdrawal from a service station in Chesterfield.'

'That was a bet that went wrong.'

She looks concerned. I'm a bit shaken up. That piece of paper is like a portal into the past life that I'd all but forgotten. A life of foolish decadence in which I spent money as a means of passing time. It became a hobby, like crochet or bridge. Only much more expensive and destructive to the soul.

I don't want you to think that that was my full-time lifestyle. I don't ordinarily prance about like the King of Siam, dining on swan flesh sandwiches, swigging thirstily from bejewelled goblets of monkey blood and buying socks fashioned from puppy-dog hair. But a few months before the baby came along my cousin Bruce gave me a bit of advice.

'Being a dad takes away the spontaneity from your life,' he said. 'You can't just go out and get spannered on a whim any more. And you have to start thinking twice about spending sprees. So make sure you cram a bit of that in before it's too late.'

Which correlated well with the advice Dave had given me less articulately a week or two beforehand. You know, about going out and getting twatted.

Well, I didn't need telling three times. On Bruce and Dave's recommendations I went berserk with my credit card, descending quickly into a horrific cesspit of greed and excess. I took myself out to lunch at nice restaurants while my wife was at work. I'd sit there alone like some weirdo scoffing starters, desserts, glasses of wine – the lot. Even coffee. I don't even like wine or coffee. I spent an afternoon in the Apple store splurging on attachments, some of which I still haven't opened. Scriptwriting software for my laptop? Like I'm going to write a flipping script. Who was I trying to kid? A device that claims to make you run faster if you plug it into your iPod? A printer that fits in your inside pocket? Most of it got lost in the move, still in their wrappers. That wasn't even the worst of it: I became the sort of bloke who, when buying a round of drinks in the pub, came back with loads of bags of crisps that nobody had even asked for. Yes, it really was that insane. As the memories of gargantuan bar bills and three-figure taxi meters start to stack up in my mind, I begin to feel dizzy.

'How much does it all come to?' I ask hesitantly.

'A few grand,' she says casually. 'Plus there's this month's mortgage and your VAT bill to pay. We've got all that covered, right?'

'Hahaha!' I blurt as a delaying tactic.

'Pardon?'

'I mean, yes! Of course! No problem!' I've sat down on the bed now and placed the sleeping baby beside me. I put the remains of the lemon drizzle cake on her tummy. I've suddenly lost my appetite.

'By the way,' I say in my best la-di-da, it-doesn't-really-matter-but-I-just-thought-I'd-ask-anyway sort of voice, 'you're still on full pay from work, right?'

'Only for another month,' she says. 'Then it drops to half.' Rubbish, stupid, useless maternity cover.

I give her the baby and go off to the toilet to clutch my head and make a high-pitched whining sound in panic. All of my idealistic notions about opting out of the rat race disintegrate in seconds. I need to get back to work. What was I thinking, just hanging around the house for weeks on end whistling 'Baa Baa Black Sheep'? Since when did responsible fathers act like that? It's like I just forgot to earn a living. Like I became some sort of . . . of . . . *hippy*. Thank Christ for that AmEx bill! I've been snapped back into a state of moral decency and capitalist gusto as fast as you could say 'repayment deferrals'.

I know, I know. My wife should probably be more keenly aware of our financial predicament. But it's impossible for me to keep her abreast of my earnings, because it's impossible for me to keep abreast of them myself. I haven't had a proper salary in almost ten years. I am 'self-employed'. To you, that may just sound like code for 'I get to masturbate about six or seven times a day', but it's more complicated than that. I call myself a journalist, but there's all sorts of things I do to earn money. Maybe the best way to illustrate my professional life is to outline my working week in the lead-up to the birth of my daughter.

On the Monday I was booked to appear on a weekly news review show on ITV. I would be part of a three-person panel of 'experts' who discussed the week's biggest news stories from a moral perspective. I know: I didn't have a clue what that meant either. But if you're a self-employed person, you can't afford to be too sniffy about what sort of employment you undertake. My policy is: if the people offering to pay me think I'm able to do it, then I might as well take their word for it. Only on this occasion I was probably wrong to do so. I'd got accidentally drunk the night before. Really drunk. The sort of drunk that makes you wake up the next morning feeling like you've been raped by a gorilla. I'm not usually so unprofessional as to get that twatted the night before a job, but we weren't supposed to be filming until two in the afternoon. Anyone can sober up and get themselves shipshape by that time of day, right? Wrong. I woke up bleary-eyed at midday. I cursed my cousin Bruce for setting me along this path of incessant revelry. I got a call from the TV producers saying my cab would be arriving at one. I checked through my e-mails to remind myself what the topics of discussion would be on the show. 'Let's hope for something nice and easy,' I thought to myself. 'A story about shortening hem-lines or obese children or the weather . . . something that I can just wing my way through.' Finally I stumbled on an e-mail headed 'Zimbabwe Special'. My head throbbed. My temples spewed out a sudden projection of sweat. I went to the toilet and threw up. Zimbabwe? In this state? I wasn't sure it was possible. I skimmed the BBC website. I cribbed some background on Wikipedia. I considered calling the producers and making something up about the death of a relative – probably Bruce, seeing as it's him I choose to blame for all of this. I went back to the toilet and threw up again. Then my cab arrived.

It wasn't so bad in the end. I stuck a tie on in the car. The make-up lady worked wonders with my complex-ion. Once we started filming, I nodded in the right places, stroked my chin where necessary, regurgitated a few opinions I'd read online at what I assumed were the cor-rect junctures and managed to squeeze in a facetious remark at the end to lighten the mood a little. All in all, a decent day's work done under difficult circumstances. I came away with a few hundred quid in my pocket, not sure whether to curse or thank silly old Robert Mugabe for the indirect part he had played in the afternoon's proceedings.

The next day I found myself alone in a tiny, darkened room saying these words over and over again in a really loud, stupid voice: 'This summer, find fun . . . find friendship . . . find family!' On the screen a cartoon fish danced about to the rhythm of some sort of underwater calypso party. In my headphones a voice kept saying, 'Could you try that again with more warmth this time please?' I sat up straight, clutched my script with added purpose and tried again. 'Fffffind ffffun . . . ffffinf ffffriendship . . . ffffind ffffamily.' I stared through the glass window at the producer.

'How's that? Any warmer?' I asked.

'Erm, it just sounded like you dragged out the 'F's more, to be honest,' he said, not unreasonably. 'Can we go again one more time? Remember, this is for kids, so let's really try to ramp up the fun, yeah?'

I was doing a voice-over to help promote a film about an animated family of dancing fish. I think the producer and I both knew he'd booked the wrong voice-over artist. I don't really do warmth. Or fun. I'm not sure what I do. My voice sounds a bit like a cat being savaged by a fox. Or, at best, like the sort of fifteen-year-old schoolboy who shouts 'Fuck off, mister' at you for no reason from the top window of a double-decker bus when you're trying to mind your own business on a provincial high street somewhere in the south-east of England. People close to me have described my voice variously as 'idiotic', 'grating', 'obnoxious' and 'fucking annoying'. But in the TV voice-over business it's considered 'urban' apparently, and that seems to be all the rage right now. The producer eventually decided that we'd achieved something in the vicinity of 'warmth' and let me go home.

On the Wednesday I went to interview Girls Aloud for a magazine at a photo studio in east London. They were dead nice. At the end of the day I asked if we could all have a picture taken together.

'Where are you off to now?' asked Cheryl Cole as we lined up for the snapper.

'Off home to check on my missus. She's due to give birth any day now,' I said.

'Oh, that's lovely, congratulations!' she said in her lovely Geordie voice. The others joined in the cooing. I felt proud.

'Just think, if it happens tonight, I'll always be able to tell my kid that I was with Girls Aloud on the day it was born!' I said.

I don't know why I said that. It was just a foolish moment of excited reverie, I suppose. As soon as the words left my mouth, a weird, awkward atmosphere fell over the room. A minute beforehand I'd had the sense we might all stay in touch and become friends. Now I could see them all exchanging funny glances like I'd weirded them out a bit. I suppose it did sound a bit nerdy and stalkerish. I felt embarrassed and went home.

The next day I took part in a documentary for BBC Three about the history of the word 'cunt'.

And on the Friday I went to Birmingham to film a series I was supposed to be fronting about crime in the UK. I was interviewing a young drug dealer called Carl when I received a text from my wife telling me that her waters had broken. I told Carl what had happened and explained that I had to go home right away. He wasn't happy that I was cutting short his fleeting moment of fame.

'What the fuck are you saying, blood?' he said. 'Finish the interview first. You're being disrespectful.' His hand kept fishing inside his jacket as if he had a knife or something in there. I was conflicted. On the one hand I knew I should really get home to be with my wife. On the other hand I didn't want to upset Carl in case he stabbed me. I could see the headlines flashing though my brain: 'Obscure television reporter stabbed to death after prematurely ending interview with drug lord.' Wouldn't have made much of an epitaph, would it? In the end, a producer stepped in and distracted Carl with some fancy TV double-speak while I snuck off to the station.

So there you have it: five days that give a pretty fair reflection of a working life that could be politely described as 'portfolio', less politely described as 'louche' and more accurately described as 'irresponsible and stupid'. I mean, I love my work. It's good fun. I don't have to go into an office very often, I rarely do the same thing two days running, and I don't have a boss telling me what to do. Sometimes, if I really feel like it, I can cancel stuff and spend a whole day watching my box set of *Dick Turpin* DVDs, starring Richard O'Sullivan. Who could complain about a life like that? The fact that I have no pension, no sick pay, no paid holidays, little in the way of savings and absolutely nothing in the way of security never really bothered me before. I was sticking it to the system. And if things ever really did go tits up, then what did I stand to lose? My home maybe. But I'd thought long and hard about life as a hobo, and I reckoned I could handle it. Those long nights stood round a burning oil drum. The all-day, guilt-free drinking binges. It actually seemed like good fun. I'd grow a beard and learn to play the harmonica. I think my marriage is solid enough to survive a few years of vagrancy. My wife would stick by me and become a she-tramp with leaves wrapped round her feet and pants made from a Tesco carrier bag. We'd be the couple you saw fighting over a can of Special Brew in the park. It'd be romantic. And from time to time I'm sure people would still give me the odd day's work. I might not get so much of the on-camera stuff, but I'm sure I could still write the odd book review or perform the occasional voice-over. I mean, you don't get much more 'urban' than a tramp, do you?

But things are different now. I have a daughter to look after. The overheads are low at the moment – she feeds for free from her mother's boobies and dresses mostly in hand-me-down all-in-ones. But I expect it won't be long before she's demanding sweeties or a Stretch Armstrong or a deposit on a studio flat in Shoreditch. I can't allow her to fall into vagrancy in the meantime. No one likes to see a tramp-baby, do they? Mind you, the thought of her growing up as some sort of cheeky Dickensian street urchin is not entirely unappealing. Scurrying up chimneys, shining the shoes of the upper classes, performing the Lambeth Walk in her raggedy trousers in return for a shiny ha'penny piece. They say economic meltdown is just around the corner. The return of the traditional English guttersnipe may well be one of the few consolations.

Nevertheless, a dad shouldn't tit about interviewing pop bands for a living. A dad should be out on the seven o'clock train doing the *Times* crossword. He should have a brolly under his arm and a big promotion on his mind. I'm thirty-two – I should have a personal assistant and one of those intercom boxes on my desk by now. As it is, I don't even have a desk. I've got a dining table covered in unopened mail and old newspapers that I balance my laptop on whenever I have to write. The other day I tried to type an article one-handed while holding the baby in my other arm. Every time I tried to hit the space bar I banged her head on the table. This confronted me with a tricky conundrum: complete the article and give the baby concussion or stop and set in motion a sequence of events that could ultimately let her starve. In the end I just dumped her on the floor and let her scream for ten minutes while I finished the article very quickly to a below-par standard. Which was probably the worst of all worlds.

Yes, dad-work should either involve a desk and a secretary or a hammer and a helmet. A helmet with a lamp on it. You know, outdoorsy work in freezing cold temperatures that leaves you with rough, grizzled hands and recurring lumbago. That's the respectable way for a father to earn a crust. Either way, dads should come home grumpy and tired and difficult to talk to. They should exude a certain misery that underlines just how much they've sacrificed to put food on their family's table. But a dad who ponces about from one media engagement to the next, coming home at reasonable hours with a skip in his step and a twinkle in his eye? There's something a bit undignified about that, isn't there? It's the sort of thing my grandma would have probably thought of as more than a bit 'queer'.

'We're joined now by journalist Sam Delaney, who's going to give us his sideways glance at the day's newspapers. Welcome to the studio, Sam!'

I frown. I hesitate. I do all the things I know I'm not supposed to do on a live radio station. I open my mouth to speak, but all that comes out is a noise halfway between a cough and a gurgle. It's like the death rattle signalling the sad demise of my broadcasting career.

The presenter, who has been busy staring at her computer screen and hasn't yet bothered to actually look me in the eye, suddenly looks up with an expression of concern.

'Anything, ha ha, anything, erm, caught your eye this morning, Sam?'

'Grrrrhhhuuuh,' I say. It's supposed to mean 'yes', but my larynx doesn't seem to be responding to basic instructions. This aspect of my work shouldn't really be that taxing. A radio station sends a cab to your home. You get in, you go the studio, you shake someone's hand, you walk into the little room, you wait for the presenter to give you the nod and you just start talking. You can say pretty much anything as long as you don't swear, blaspheme, offend the Islamic faith or insult the memory of Princess Diana, Queen of Hearts.

It's hardly a professional skill to rank up there alongside heart surgery or glass-blowing or even hairdressing. But it's something I can do. Occasionally I even do it quite well. But this is my first day back in the saddle after a long and life-changing break. I think I've lost my edge. Most of the talking I've been doing over the past couple of months has been in special cuddly-toy voices. And something tells me that the listening public don't want to hear the Sunday papers reviewed by Barry the Badger. His views would sound even less credible than my own.

'Erm, yes, well. There's some news here,' I eventually manage to splutter while pointing at the front page of a broadsheet.

'What about?' asks the increasingly worried-looking presenter.

'You know, the government have announced a thing about crime, but the other lot have hit back with something else. Hard to say how it will all end up really, isn't it?'

There's a pause.

'OK, that's great. More of Sam's musings coming up after the travel with Laura!'

The sound of beeping horns and clattering trains rumbles in my headphones over a galloping travel news soundtrack. Then the producer's voice drifts above it. 'That was great Sam, thanks,' it says. 'Actually, we're really running out of time, so I think we can let you go now. There's a cab waiting outside for you.'

I thank the host, who doesn't even bother to look up as she says goodbye. I don't blame her. The producer gives me an insincere smile of gratitude as I leave; the eighteen-year-old runner shoots me a look of sympathy. It's a bit humiliating, I suppose. I'm being unceremoniously booted out after just forty seconds back at work. This should have been a nice and easy way to reacclimatise myself to professional life. I made an effort. I even put some proper trousers on and everything. But I flailed about like an amateur. It wasn't as if I just forgot how to speak with fluency or wit. I forgot how to speak altogether. Which, along with stringing the odd nifty sentence together on a keyboard, is one half of my entire skill set down the drain.

My mind may not ever have been as sharp as a razor, but it had its moments. Now it is as blunt and useless as a rusty butter knife. My tongue, once quick and nimble and always ready with a puerile remark or brilliantly idiotic *bon mot*, is now fat and bloated and cumbersome. There is no edge or urgency left inside me. It seems domestic life and fatherhood have sucked it all away and replaced it with a cosy sense of complacent indifference. I haven't felt as content in years. Or as useless.

Even my dad had knuckled down and got a proper job by the time he was my age. And I've always looked on him as some sort of maverick Kerouac figure in comparison to me.

It's not like I have any other career options to fall back on either. I don't have a trade up my sleeve. My 65-year-old neighbour knocked round the other day and asked me to change the cartridge in her Glade Air Freshener. I managed to break it, cut my hand and drop the cup of tea she'd made me all over her carpet. Suffice to say, I'm unlikely to find much work as an odd-job man. Spouting shit on air and in print is pretty much all I've ever known. What else could I possibly do? I did that milk round with Rab but Unigate would never take me back now; he took off suddenly with his uniform and a crate of Ski yoghurts – tainting me by association. It's only a matter of weeks before my daughter comes off the breast and goes on to bottles of uncompetitively priced SMA formula milk. If I don't remember how to earn a living by then, we're all doomed.

As Richard Gere once said in *An Officer and a Gentleman*: 'I've got no place left to go.'

16

PERSPEX

I arrive uncharacteristically early. I have shaved and am wearing a suit and tie. I order a cappuccino, then pick up a copy of *The Times*, neatly fold it and purse my lips thoughtfully as though examining an interesting news story about Darfur. I am acting like a grown-up.

That's because I am here to meet my financial adviser. That's right, my financial bloody adviser. Idiots like me can have them too, you know. I can't pretend I am constantly on the phone telling him to shift assets between various hedge funds or buy kumquats and sell pork bellies. I just bung him a few quid to invest every time I'm feeling flush in order to stop myself from blowing it all on a puppy or some magic beans.

He arrives after five minutes, and I shoot to my feet extending my hand warmly. He settles into the sumptuous leather armchair opposite my own. My suit, this swanky setting, the armchairs and the cappuccinos: it's all a pointless charade really. I suppose I think it will impress him. But what the hell does he care? He's not my bank manager. This isn't a job interview. He works for me. I wouldn't treat my cleaner like this – and that's not me being snobby either. It's just that she's Polish and shy and has a rubbish grasp of the English language, despite having lived here for over two years. The other day I asked her if she enjoyed her summer trip back to Warsaw and she replied, 'Sixteen pounds.' If I took her out for a posh coffee at a fancy West End bar every time I wanted to brief her on the laundry or the dusting, she'd just feel uncomfortable.

But this financial bloke carries a briefcase and chucks about terms like 'tax redemption', 'yield spread premium' and 'self-amortising loan' with casual aplomb. He's serious and intimidating. Something in my subconscious tells me I have to impress him. In reality, I might be better off going for the sympathy vote by arranging to meet him by some swings then turning up in a pair of wee-stained pyjamas and offering him a sip from my plastic bottle of economy cider. At least that way he might leave the meeting feeling a moral responsibility to manage my financial investments with renewed vigour.

As it is, I'm showing him that I'm just about rich enough for him not really to bother about my welfare but not quite rich enough for him to consider me one of his top-class clients who might one day help him retire to a big house made out of jewels in the Caribbean.

I order him a cappuccino. 'Is it as bad as they're all saying?' I ask.

'What?' he says.

'The, erm, what d'you call it? Credit card crunch?'

'The what?' he says angrily.

'I mean the credit crunch. Not credit card. Just credit in general. It's all getting crushed, isn't it?'

There is a silence.

'I suppose you've seen what's been happening in the markets,' he finally says, motioning at my folded copy of *The Times*. I nod thoughtfully, like I was just immersed in a scrupulous analysis of the financial pages before he arrived. Then I shift the paper casually aside, so he won't see that I was actually perusing the TV listings to check what time this afternoon's screening of *The Karate Kid 2* starts on Sky Movies.

'Now's not the time to do anything hasty,' he says. 'The last thing you should do is panic-sell.'

'Sell what?' I think to myself. At the height of its value my investment portfolio would have struggled to finance a trip to Londis to purchase a packet of wine gums and some bin bags.

I have made little progress since my early days as a NatWest Young Saver. Back then I dreamed of one day laying my hands on a sacred porcelain rendition of Sir Nathaniel Westminster. Sir Nathaniel was the piggy bank that NatWest sent you when your savings balance reached a hundred quid. He was an imperious fellow dressed in a three-piece pinstripe suit and red bow-tie, with a pair of half-moon spectacles. Maybe, had my brothers not mugged me out of that money during the ill-fated poker game of 1985, I might have a Sir Nathaniel by now. Perhaps I might have gone beyond Sir Nathaniel and graduated to a giant piggy bank called something like Lord Sebastian Oinkworthy the Third, whom NatWest store in their deepest underground vaults for the real fat cat customers. But, for whatever reason, my finances have pretty much always been a shambles ever since I was wrongly deprived of that winning pot back when I was ten. I think it probably instilled in me an 'easy come, easy go' philosophy which has discouraged me from ever putting much aside for a rainy day.

'I'm afraid your investments are likely to fall in value before they rise,' says the adviser in the same tone of voice that a vet once used to inform me of my dog's pancreatic cancer.

'Oh well,' I say jovially. 'What's nothing take away nothing anyway?'

He doesn't respond.

'That's right: nothing!' I continue.

Still no answer.

'Or is it, in fact, something? Don't two minuses make a plus?'

He ignores me and stirs his coffee with a weary look on his face.

Of course, all I was really hoping to get from him was some advice on scraping together some extra dough. A tax loophole or a benefit scam or something. I've got a kid now: shouldn't that qualify me for some kind of governmental reward scheme? I mean, I voted for Labour. What's the point of putting the pinkos in charge, if you don't get a hand-out when you need one? When we were kids, my mum used to get the family allowance (or 'The Fam', as she called it) once a month. It was a nice little bonus on top of her measly wages, which, on a month when she hadn't been caning the Dorothy Perkins store card too hard, we could spend on little treats like a takeaway or 'a binge'.

'Sod it, I've just got The Fam – let's all have a binge,'

she'd say. We'd cheer with excitement at the prospect of a night in front of the box with a wild array of confectionery, fizzy pop and booze. One of my brothers would be dispatched down the offy to buy my mum a bottle of Martini Extra Dry and a large box of Maltesers. They'd get beers and crisps for themselves, and I'd ordinarily go for some Rolos, a Marathon and a two-litre bottle of R Whites. We were always Labour supporters in our house, but on binge nights I think we may all have said a secret inner thank-you to Mrs Thatcher's government for The Fam and all the wonderful spoils it brought us. 'She may have raped society, sunk the *Belgrano* and stitched them miners up, but she's not all bad,' I'd quietly think as I sank my teeth into the rich caramel centre of another Rolo. Of course, it probably wasn't Thatcher who actually introduced the Fam but at least she hadn't got round to abolishing it yet. Which was nice of her.

My mum worked as a secretary at a Perspex sign company opposite my primary school. She was based in the offices upstairs, but it was down to the basement that I would head once I'd finished my school day and nipped across the road to meet her. It was down where they actually made the signs. I became mates with the staff of West Indian machinists, who would let me watch them at work and occasionally give me a go on the lethal-looking Perspex-cutting contraptions. I loved Perspex. When I was nine years old, it was like a full-blown obsession. Maybe it was all the bright colours it came in; maybe it was the fact it was so flexible and strong; or maybe it was just that it smelt a bit like petrol. Other kids' rooms were full of *Star Wars* figures, Lego or Meccano, but there was a time when mine was filled almost exclusively with Perspex. It was so versatile: I could fight with it. I could use it as a pretend gun, a sword or a dagger. I could get a long, bendy bit, tie a piece of string between each end and fire a shorter, spikier bit from it like a bow and arrow. Also, I could melt it with a Clipper lighter and inhale the toxic fumes. Aesthetically, it lent my room a touch of post-industrial cool, a bit like The Hacienda but with a West Ham bedspread and a torn-out *Smash Hits* poster of Five Star stuck to the wall.

'A kid like that shouldn't be running around down here,' said Bill, the humourless hunchback supervisor whenever he saw me frolicking amid the dangerous tools and plastics. Of course, he was right. Looking back, I think most of the factory workers were too pissed or stoned at that time of day to monitor me properly. As I slashed and jabbed at an imaginary adversary with my length of green plastic across the factory floor, it was a miracle I didn't at least once trip and cut my own head off in one of the machines. But we didn't appreciate the danger at the time. We thought Bill was just a miserable old bastard who was trying to ruin our fun.

Once, one of the younger workers called Tony got me one of those fake rusty nails from the joke shop that you slip on your finger. We covered it in a generous amount of tomato ketchup, and Tony picked me up and started running around the factory floor like a madman shouting, 'Help! Help! Call an ambulance! The boy's got a nail tru his hand! Jesus Christ! Somebody do something!' I screamed my head off in a brilliantly real portrayal of agony and terror. Within seconds Bill came hobbling round the corner shouting, 'I fucking told you about letting him play down here! You wouldn't listen!'

I screamed some more. Tony stifled his giggles.

'Take me upstairs to where my mum sits,' I whispered out of the side of my mouth. He barged up the stairs still holding me and shouting, 'Get Brenda! Get Brenda! Her boy's mangled his hand!'

In the more refined environs of the upstairs offices all hell broke loose as this giant Jamaican in overalls rampaged about the place clutching a screaming child with blood apparently streaming from his hand. My mum rushed out of her office, grabbed my hand, took one look and said, 'Very funny, you couple of stupid bastards.' She wasn't even being sarcastic. She thought the whole stunt was hilarious. (Mind you, she was an office prankster herself. She used to sneak into the blokes' loos and stretch cling film over the toilet bowls so it was almost invisible. The bosses would go in to take a leak, and all the wee would splash back up all over their trousers.) Anyway, I wasn't allowed back in the factory after that, and Tony got an official warning from Bill. See what I mean? Miserable old bastard.

Another time my mum got an unexpected tax rebate from the Inland Revenue. Once she'd paid off a few outstanding debts, she took me and my brothers up to Wembley Market, each with a roll of notes in our pockets. I bought a fluorescent orange cable-knit jumper, a black bomber jacket and a chunky neck chain in fake silver. I'd actually gone there with the intention of getting a Soda Stream and some records but, during the course of the morning, had developed a strange admiration for the rough-looking blokes who ran the stalls and decided to waste my dough on trying to mimic their dress sense.

In any case, there always seemed to be some way of stumbling on the odd cash injection in times of need when my mum was skint. I was hoping this adviser fellow might scheme up something similar. Times are tough. I couldn't have predicted that the arrival of my first dependant would coincide with a total loss of faith in my own professional capabilities. I haven't managed to complete a decent day's work in weeks. I feel like a cat that's been neutered. My mind is filled with nursery rhymes and shitty nappies and is steadfastly refusing to be cajoled into anything approaching focused, disciplined, work-like thinking. Meanwhile, the baby is due to come off the breast in a matter of weeks, and all that SMA formula milk isn't going to pay for itself.

The crime show I was working on ended in tears, by the way. After my little period at home playing a full-time dad, I just didn't feel ready to go back to the front line of criminality. My first day back on the project was with the drug squad in Reading. A cameraman and myself were to accompany a team of armoured officers on a drug raid on a house being used as a marijuana farm by a Vietnamese gang. Sounds brilliant, right? And it was. The lead officer smashed the door in with a battering ram at 7 o'clock in the morning. As everyone piled into the house, I was in the thick of things, yelping with excitement and trepidation. I anticipated a shoot-out or at least a minor scuffle in which the gang members might try to employ elaborate kung-fu manoeuvres against the cops. But all we found was a timid nineteen-year-old Vietnamese stooge huddled in the corner of the front room amid an impressive forest of skunk weed. They nicked him and threw him in the back of a van. I just stood there taking pictures of the drugs on my mobile and sending them to my mates. Admittedly, it was hardly the sort of journalistic conduct that marks you out for a Pulitzer Prize. My producer encouraged me to confront the prisoner with a hard-nosed line of questioning about the venomous effect his dirty foreign drug-harvesting had on decent British society.

'Give him both barrels,' I was told as I climbed inside the van to confront him. But I just half-heartedly wafted the microphone in his face and said, 'How do you feel, mate?' He tried to answer then started to sob. I found myself giving him an awkward hug and my own eyes unexpectedly welled up with tears. It wasn't what you'd call Paxman-esque.

People had warned me that this would happen once I became a dad. Inexplicable emotion and girlish sentimentality keep washing over me when I least expect it. Maybe it's because fatherhood encourages you to see the world in a broader sense and interpret all the pain and sadness and wrong-doing through the prism of your child's young life. Maybe it's because some tiny part of your heart breaks on the day you see that child come into the world. Or maybe it's because you just turn into a big soppy tart from all that time changing nappies and playing with cuddly badgers and that. Whatever the reason, I just felt too soft and mushy to play the part of a cut-price Roger Cook.

It was just unfortunate timing that my first few months of fatherhood should coincide with a job that entailed long days spent in the company of Yardies, Triads and other assorted ne'er-do-wells in the murkiest quarters of Britain's underworld. My existence became an improbable mix of drug raids and nappies, firearms and blankies, garrotting wires and num-nums.

And, for the uninitiated, 'num-num' is not a new breed of vicious drug criminal from Sri Lanka but baby slang for a dummy. Furthermore, if there are any parenting fascists tut-tutting as they read this, then, no, I don't give my baby a num-num. I just like to use the word because it sounds cute. It's just one of many words and phrases that have found a new appeal since I became a father. 'Snuggle', 'bum-bum', 'nip-nap-noo' and indeed 'booby' are all terms that now spill from my mouth as easily as expletives. Holding a baby in my arms has made me, for some reason, speak in a babyish manner. Which presented the odd communicative faux pas when trying to interact with hard-nosed villains. Things reached their nadir when I accidentally slipped the term 'cheeky-chops' into a chat with a member of the Turkish heroin mafia. You should have seen the look he gave me! A few days later I got the call from my agent: the producers were taking me off the job. The words made it sound like I was a maverick New York cop having his gun and badge taken away because of his cavalier approach to law enforcement. But the truth was almost the complete opposite: I was having my principal source of income removed because fatherhood had turned me into a big soppy idiot.

Things were starting to look bleak. That's why I called the financial adviser.

But what good is he doing me? He's been sitting before me in that armchair speaking in a series of incomprehensible financial terms for almost forty minutes. Eventually he stops and pulls some forms out of his briefcase. Ah, the forms! Those special bits of paper that signal the fact that the meeting's nearly over and everything's going to be OK. All I need to do is sign each of them in three different places and say something like 'That all seems to be in order'. Then he goes away. And I pay for the coffees, which, owing to the needlessly posh location, cost almost as much as a monthly mortgage repayment. I hope this bloke knows what he's doing with my cash.

17

MASTERCHEF

'*Carmella, who the fuck did you think I was when you married me?*' Tony Soprano asks his wife. They are in the pool house. He is wearing a dressing gown. '*You knew my father. You grew up around Dickie Moltisanti and your Uncle Eddie. Where do you get off acting all surprised when there are women on the side? You knew the deal.*'

'*The deal?*' says Carmella in disbelief.

'Yeah, the deal!' I think angrily to myself, glancing at my wife. We are in the bedroom. I am wearing a dressing gown. She is eating a tangerine 'Where do you get off acting all surprised when we end up spending every night watching DVDs in our dressing gowns?'

She's not really surprised. She seems to be enjoying these sedentary evenings in front of the box as much as I am. It could start to get a bit boring and repetitive, I suppose, but I find that pretending in my mind that I am Tony Soprano really helps.

'Stop staring at me like that,' says my wife. I look back at the screen. Tony has just punched a hole in the pool-house wall. I'll probably do that next time we have a row. I start to work out which is the weakest, most flimsy wall in the house.

Not that there's been any rows for a while now. The air of tension and hysteria that prevailed during those first couple of months of sleepless parenthood has finally subsided. Peace and quiet have broken out. Systems have been implemented and routines put in place. The baby's Tet Offensive is over. And it's all thanks to *The Sopranos*. God bless those rotund New Jersey sociopaths.

Our daughter lies sleeping at the end of the bed like a loyal and obedient puppy. The mind games are over. This is how it works every night: we take her into the bedroom, shove a bottle of formula milk in her gob and slap on a *Sopranos* DVD. She is transfixed by it. Maybe it's the tragicomic dialogue or the nuanced meditation on the human condition that permeates every show. Or maybe it's all the fighting and swearing and that. Who knows? Either way, I don't think she could get off to sleep each night without the soothing sounds of Tony pistol-whipping a henchman or Paulie Walnuts hastily digging a grave underneath a flyover. Certainly I'm not about to find out. I've found a night-time routine that works, and I'm sticking to it in every last detail. It's become a superstition – like always wearing the same lucky clothes to the football. The world probably wouldn't cave in if I stopped doing it, but I'd better carry on just in case.

She usually starts to nod off toward the end of the evening's first episode. We leave her lying there on the bed while we sit through another episode, by the end of which she's usually sleeping deeply enough for us to transfer her gently to her cot. After that, if we're both feeling dead saucy and adventurous, we may even watch a third episode. What the hell, we're still relatively young. Who says having kids takes the magic out of a relationship?

If politicians and clergymen really want to find a way of preserving the traditional family unit, then they need look no further than the DVD box set. When your social life has died a slow, painful death, it's cold outside and there's a baby confining you to your house every night of the week, gathering round the telly and watching three hours' worth of high-end American drama is all you've got. It provides an experience that the whole family can share in and bond over. I know it's brought my missus and me closer together. For months we communicated in little more than grunts and sighs. But the other night, as we watched Tony strangle an FBI informant to death with a length of wire, we held each other's hands softly and exchanged a look that seemed to say, 'I'm glad I married you. I'm glad we had our gorgeous daughter. And most of all, I'm glad we invested in seasons 4, 5 and 6 in the HMV sale, because I don't think life can get any better than this.'

Everyone's at it. And it's not just *The Sopranos* either. *The Wire*, *The West Wing*, *Deadwood*: these are the shows that are saving a whole generation of kids from growing up in broken homes. Why would dad stay at the pub for one more drink with the girl from bought ledger when he could be at home, snuggled up with the woman he loves, watching Larry David getting himself embroiled in another calamitous predicament? And how could she ever get bored with a man with whom she's sat through every last episode of *Nip Tuck*? She couldn't. That kind of shared experience runs too deep. It entwines your souls.

No wonder our parents split up. The best they had back in the '70s was *The Sweeney*. And when an episode of that ended, you had to wait an entire week to see what happened next. The frustration must have driven them mad.

Yep, DVDs have made staying in every night of the week actually seem like fun. And somehow more glamorous and cerebral than just sitting there slack-jawed in front of normal, rubbishy, British TV. Soap operas that make you so sick with sadness you feel like ringing up your mum and telling her you need a cuddle; sitcoms so mirthless you'd get more laughs out of contracting the Ebola virus on holiday. TV makes you feel old and fat and bored and pointless. DVD box sets make you feel cool, clever and sexy. Besides, you haven't got the energy to do much else. Parenthood seems to instil in you a unique form of deep-impact fatigue that, older dads tell me, never goes away. There's no light at the end of the tunnel. You've got a life sentence of listlessness. When the day is over and the baby is asleep, you don't have the energy to do anything worthwhile like build a matchstick *Cutty Sark* or play Guess Who? with your partner. It takes pretty much all you've got left just to shove that silver disc in the DVD player and press 'play'.

We did try and go out together a few Fridays ago. My father-in-law was visiting from Hungary, so he agreed to baby-sit. My wife put on a dress, and I even wore a pair of leather shoes with laces. It was as though we were Richard Burton and Elizabeth Taylor on their way to the 1963 Academy Awards ceremony. Only we were just nipping out to the local cinema for the 6.30 showing of *American Gangster,* starring Denzel Washington. We were just too nervous to do anything more daring. What if the baby woke up and started to cry? What if the house exploded? What if she got hungry and Hungarian granddad started feeding her raw onions in pig fat or pickled fish guts or whatever the hell it is they eat over there? No, it was best we made this a speed date and got back to the house before anyone died.

'Seems a bit of a shame to not . . . you know . . . get a little bit out of it. Seeing as it's the first time we've been out in ages,' my wife ventured as we hurried out the front door.

'What? Are you mental? There's not time for that!' I said in disgust. 'If you want, I'll get you a can of gin and tonic and you can drink it on the bus.'

She ignored me and doubled back up the stairs. I stared at my watch frantically. What was she doing up there? I started calculating that we might actually have to sacrifice watching the last hour or so of *American Gangster* if we were to make it back in reasonable time. It wouldn't matter too much. I mean, the last hour of most films is usually just padding, isn't it?

'Right, let's go,' said my wife, skipping back down the stairs and out the front door with an unusual amount of bonhomie.

'What did you go upstairs for?' I asked once the door had shut behind us.

'This!' she announced, producing a polythene bag of weed from her pocket.

Nothing confirms that you're approaching middle age quite like a bag of stale weed kept in a box on the mantelpiece, does it?

Still, she loves smoking that stuff. And, what with trying to get pregnant, then being pregnant, then breast-feeding, she hasn't been able to touch it for nearly two years. As she sat on the back seat of the bus rolling a spliff, her eyes twinkled with a look that said, 'It's good to see you again, old friend!' I felt happy for her.

Personally, I hate the stuff. It brings on my epilepsy something rotten. When I was seventeen, I walked into an Amsterdam coffee shop with four mates and, trying to act the big man, asked the owner what the strongest gear they had was. He told me it was a special type of hashish called Temple Balls. I boldly slapped my guilders on the counter and told him to serve me up a big fat lump. It was 10 a.m. One of us rolled the biggest, dirtiest spliff I'd ever seen in my life, crammed full of my hash plus the assortment of toxic weeds the others had bought. I had a couple of tokes and immediately started to feel peculiar. But we had a busy itinerary of smoking lined up for the day, and there was no time to hang around. Everyone wanted to go and tick the next coffee shop off the list. As I stood up at the table to follow my mates out of the door, my vision suddenly went blank. All I could see was blackness. I remember frantically waving my own hands in front of my face, to no avail. My last words were 'Hold up, lads!' and a split second later I was on the floor, flapping about like a dying fish. The eyewitness reports weren't pretty: I kicked chairs and tables, I foamed at the mouth and, of course, I pissed my pants. Two of my friends tried to hold me down, but I clawed at their faces and ripped out handfuls of their hair. When I came to, covered in sweat and urine, the first thing I saw was a group of petrified adolescent Germans huddled in the corner with a look of sheer terror on their faces. The poor stoned bastards were probably paranoid enough without some English dingbat performing an incontinent break-dance routine by their feet. The coffee shop proprietor came over and handed me a cup of water.

'Sorry about the mess, mate,' I said croakily.

'Hey, no worriesh!' he smiled. 'Temple Ballsh getsh them every time!'

'Do what?'

'Hey, when five English guysh come in and one of them ordersh a bag of that shtuff, I know for sure only four of them are walking out on two legsh!'

Then he started to laugh. Glad he found it funny, the blood-sucking, drug-pushing Dutch bastard.

Once I got back to England, I started to see a neurologist. He ran a load of tests and brain scans and eventually concluded that my epilepsy was reactive. I was unlikely just to have a fit out of the blue while walking along the street. I had to stimulate it in some way by making myself pass out.

'So what are you trying to say?' I asked him.

'Well, for starters, I'd suggest you never go near another marijuana cigarette again,' said the doc. Well, he would say that, wouldn't he?

Foolhardy and idiotic as I was, I ignored his advice and, as a result, was plagued by similar undignified episodes throughout my late teens and early twenties. The worst was probably the morning I woke up on the fifteenth floor of a hospital twenty miles from home with stitches in my head, blood on my face and wires stuck all over my chest.

I looked around the room and saw about half a dozen elderly men attached to machines lying all around me.

'Where am I?' I asked.

'Cardiac ward, son,' piped up one of the codgers with a slightly irritating smirk.

'Cardiac ward? Which hospital?'

'Kingston,' he replied.

Kingston? What was I doing in Kingston? I didn't even know where Kingston was. I still don't.

'Shit. What happened?' I muttered.

'Well, by the looks of you, you've lost a fight and had a heart attack!' he chuckled. The others joined in. If I'd had the energy, I would have got up and switched their machines off.

I rang my eldest brother.

'You'd better come and get me.'

'Where are you?'

'Kingston Hospital.'

'Why?'

'I've lost a fight and had a heart attack.'

'Oh. Where's Kingston Hospital?'

'I've no idea. Gotta go, there's a doctor coming.'

I put the phone down and scampered up to the doctor with my bumless gown blowing all around me. 'What the fuck?' was all I could say.

According to what they'd been able to piece together from the people who accompanied me in the ambulance, I had been to a football match, got a bit tipsy, travelled across town with some mates, smoked a few moody spliffs, fallen over in a driveway, cut my head on a wall, had a series of seizures and been ferried to the only hospital within a 10-mile radius to have a spare bed on a Saturday night. It just so happened that that spare bed was in the cardiac ward at Kingston. I was relieved. I felt like going up to that old codger who'd laughed at me and saying, 'Guess what? I haven't had a heart attack after all! And you have! IN YOUR FACE GRANDAD!'

Anyway, it wasn't any of those incidents that eventually made me give up smoking gear. It was just the sudden realisation, when I was about twenty-five, that I really didn't like it. I don't think I ever did. It made me feel slow-witted, tired, nauseous and really, really nervous. Nervous about having another fit. Nervous about the other people in the room not liking me. Nervous about how I was going to get home. Nervous that someone might be hiding under the bed. Nervous about North Korea. Just nervous about whatever happened to cross my mind, really. I'd only been smoking it all those years because that was what everyone else around me did. And I didn't have much else on: when your days are filled with nothing but video games, *Home and Away* and Penguin biscuits, then smoking something that induces anxiety and paranoia can actually seem like an amusing distraction. But not when you've got a job or any other sort of preoccupation that requires you to converse with other adults or walk near busy traffic.

We were walking near some busy traffic towards the cinema when my wife offered me the spliff. She knows I don't touch the stuff but still makes the gesture out of habit.

'Fuck it,' I thought. 'We're out on the town! Just like when we were students! It's like the mid-'90s all over again! Come on everyone, let's get battered and dance to

Oasis! Later on we can watch *Trainspotting*! Woo hoo! Girl Power!'

I took two tokes, went a bit dizzy and, just as we were walking into the foyer to collect our tickets, announced that I wanted to go home. Apparently, *American Gangster* was pretty average anyway.

Who needs going out when staying in is so brilliant anyway? The secret to true domestic happiness, I have discovered, is just to give in to it. Buy yourself some loose-fitting cotton trousers with an elasticated waist and embrace the glories of the quiet life. The beauty of it is that my wife can't possibly lose respect for me when she's complicit in the whole thing. Or so I thought.

'I'm going out on Saturday night,' she casually mentions one night during *Masterchef*. (Some British TV shows are OK to watch – specifically the ones designed to reassure you that the humdrum mechanics of domestic life are some kind of exhilarating art form. It helps cultivate a state of false consciousness among the stay-at-home parenting community that rustling up a bit of dinner is a sexy and glamorous experience. Even if, like me, all you usually do is heat up a couple of fish fingers and slap them between two end-slices of Hovis with a bit of ketchup.)

'You're going out? Where? Who with? Is this some sort of joke?' I blurt.

'No. I'm going out with the girls for a few drinks. It won't be a late one.'

Rejection. Hurt. Betrayal. Confusion. I give her a stare that expresses all of these emotions plus some brand new, as yet unnamed ones that I didn't even know I was capable of feeling.

'So, you're breaking ranks, are you?' I say, shaking my head in lament.

'From what?'

'From DVD club! I thought things were going so well!'

'Eh? What difference does it make to you? You can still watch DVDs.'

'No I can't! If I watch any new episodes, you'll be behind! We won't be able to watch them together any more. The system will break! Don't break the system!'

She thinks about this. She knows I've got a point.

'Can't you just watch some episodes and not tell me that you've watched them. Then just sit through them again until I've caught up?'

I am alarmed and appalled by this suggestion.

'No, I most certainly cannot! I will not subvert the system like that. And anyway, you'll be able to tell I've already seen them and get irritated when I'm not as into them as you are.'

'Well, whatever, I'm going out, so you'll have to just find something else to do on Saturday night.'

'I will!' I say petulantly. 'Maybe I'll go out with the boys. And get drunk. And sing songs and . . . that.'

'No. You'll be here, looking after the baby.'

Oh yeah, the baby. Just me and her, left to our own devices. It could be interesting. I feel emboldened by the responsibility that's suddenly been handed to me.

Also, I'm quite glad that my wife is getting to go out. There's a part of me that's been worrying that she might get bored of this cosy life of ours and end up killing herself or cuckolding me with a gardener or a fireman or, worse, a slightly more successful voice-over artist. Then again, I also worry that once she's back out on the town, living a normal, decent, socially interactive life, I will strike her as even more stupid and slothful than I do already. All I can hope is that she comes home so paralytic that she can't even see me sprawled out on the sofa in my tracksuit and slippers covered in Wotsit crumbs. Then wake up with such a bad hangover the next morning that she vows never to go out again. I'll probably be welcoming her back into DVD club with open arms by Sunday night at the latest.

18
BED

I can't believe she's going through with this. Look at her with her make-up and her clothes and her perfume. Putting on her ear-rings. Looking in her mirror. What's she trying to prove? That's she's a better person than me, just because she smells nice and looks nice and generally treats herself with self-respect? Well, she can keep her self-respect. And her dignity. Let her run into the arms of the outside world with its pubs and people and fun and shapes and colours. I'm happy here with my glass of Ribena, my baby and my curiously engaging episode of *In The Night Garden*.

'There's two bottles of formula milk in the fridge,' she says. 'One for bedtime and one in case she wakes up.'

'Hrghuugh,' I say indifferently.

'And she's due a bath.'

'Nnnghn,' I nod.

'And if her gums start to play up, the Calpol is on the shelf in her room.'

'Calpol,' I say perking up. 'Now there's a delicious medicine.'

She glances at the TV screen, then at the baby, then at me.

'Don't watch telly right up until bedtime, will you? She's got that new book you could read her.'

She has now stood in front of the telly in order to command my attention. I lean sideways to see round her. The baby starts to whine half-heartedly.

'Are you listening?' she asks.

'Yes I am listening,' I say. 'Book, bath, bottle, bed. Fun to say, fun to do! Don't worry about us. Go out and have a good time.'

She starts to leave.

'Oh, just one last thing,' I say, just like Colombo.

'What?'

'I was thinking of taking a crap later and I'm not quite sure how to go about wiping my arse afterwards. Could you do me a little diagram?'

She kisses the baby and struts out into her precious, outdoor world.

We go back to *In The Night Garden*. The dim-witted, sponge-like characters tit about in their brightly coloured, hypnotic netherworld. The plot is unfathomable. And yet it's still so compelling. The baby is spellbound. I am too: maybe it's the music; maybe it's the funny gobbledygook they talk. Or maybe it's the gentle, soothing tones of the Derek Jacobi voice-over. Now there's a bloke who knows how to talk out loud. I'd make a real hash out of this: every time I talk it comes out too noisy and squawky and offensive. Fine for the moronic 'urban' masses but terrifying for kids. Even my own daughter, with her tiny ears and rubbish baby brain, cringes when I try to communicate with her verbally. But who needs words when we've got *In The Night Garden*? Somehow, the devilish masterminds behind this show have managed to tap into the fledgling psyche of children who are still too young even to understand their own names. It's sinister in a way, but I'm not complaining. She seems to like the fact that I'm as engaged in it as she is. Every now and again she looks up at my face to check I'm still watching, then smiles, snuggles up and grips my finger in her tiny hand. Then I well up a tiny bit. This show's almost as good as *The Sopranos*.

I'll tell you what: it's better than any of the crap they served up when I was a kid. *The Moomins*, *Willo the Wisp*, *Ivor the Engine*, *Chockablock*: what a load of dreary, depressing old toss. Conceived and executed by a load of stinking old hippies who'd taken too much acid in the '60s and thought it was a good idea to impose their 'far out' ideas on a generation of kids by means of crappy, cheapo animation. Oh, I'd watch it: what choice did I have? But I didn't enjoy it. It made me sad. And don't talk to me about *Bagpuss*. It was a load of rubbishly animated, meaningless bullshit that people who grew up in the '70s and '80s now think is ironic and clever to harp on about. Professor Yaffle: what a pompous know-it-all. If he came round my way shouting the odds, I'd set fire to the stupid wooden fucker.

The programme finishes. The baby looks at me. I look at the Nintendo Wii. 'Would now be an appropriate time for me to have a quick session on Super Mario Kart?' I ask myself. 'Maybe she's ready to join in on a two-player time trial? It could be fun. And educational.'

I switch on the console, start up the game and hand her a controller. She starts to lick it like a Cornetto. The race starts. I'm off to a flyer. She seems content enough. Then

'Bump!' She falls over backwards and smacks her head on the floorboards. I suppose the ability to sit upright for more than ten seconds at a time is a prerequisite for this sort of thing. She's rubbish at video games.

'So, what shall we do now?' I ask her once she's stopped crying. My wife had made mention of a book, but I'm not in the mood. She's got years of enforced reading at school ahead of her – the last thing she needs is me imposing a load of boring books on her prematurely. Besides, it's Saturday night and Mum's out. 'Let's go wild! Raid the Malibu! Order an extra-large meat-free pizza delivery and don't bother with a side salad! Invite some older kids round and try to skin up using oregano and dried banana skins!' She blinks back at me, with a distinct lack of enthusiasm.

I rummage through the cupboard and find her toy *du jour*: the electro drum. Her face lights up at the first glimpse of it. Personally, I find it a monotonous and rudimentary device, especially in comparison to the Wii. You whack it, it bleeps. You whack it again, it bleeps again. It's like R2-D2 without the mechanical expertise, computer hacking abilities or cheeky banter. Still, there's a certain thrill to be had from just watching the baby's excitable responses to it, I suppose. She likes it even more when I join in. Whack! Bleep. Whack! Bleep. Whack, whack, whack! Bleepety bleep blop. Whack, tap, whack, whack, kerpow!

Wait a minute! What's this? My random sequence of freestyle jazz whacking seems to have unlocked the hidden abilities of the electro drum! Suddenly, it's launched into a high-octane calypso freakdown. I sweep the baby up in my arms and we dance into the kitchen. I shuffle soulfully across the tiles, nimbly tiptoeing between the cat's litter tray and biscuit bowl. She whoops with glee, shimmies her shoulders, then, lost in all the excitement, tries to shove her index finger into my eye. It feels like being at Studio 54. Or at least a really good Billy Ocean concert. It's a special moment. And then she starts to giggle. It starts as a smirk, turns into a titter and suddenly she's laughing out loud like a big, silly idiot. It may sound a bit corny, but there really is nothing quite as brilliant and fulfilling as making her laugh. Not just because it sounds nice. And not just because it proves that you're beginning to bond and communicate in some meaningful way. Mainly, it's a competitive thing. My wife and I are locked in a constant, niggling contest to see who can elicit the most laughter out of our child. And while she's out neglecting her parental duties and having a so-called 'good time', I've stolen a march on her.

This battle has been intensifying with each passing week. Yesterday I was locked away in the front room trying to work when the captivating sound of her giggles drifted under the crack in the door and wafted round my head like Bisto fumes.

'What's going on in there?' I called out, dead jealous of all the merriment. There was a pause.

'Nothing,' my wife said, all shifty.

We lust after baby laughter like desperate junkies, trying ever more ludicrous ways to elicit the tiniest bit of precious giggling from her tiny larynx. She's no easy audience either. Standard tactics like the raspberry on the tummy don't wash with her. Games of peek-a-boo are an insult – she sighs and gives me her 'Try again, you tiresome little prick' look. Her sneering attitude makes the occasional chuckle seem even more precious. Whenever her little face opens up into beaming frivolity, I go dizzy with euphoria.

And if laughter is the commodity, then jokes are the currency. I covet them with a raging obsession.

'You're making her laugh!' I called out to my wife in an accusatory tone. 'I heard you! How did you do it? Was it the thing with her toes? Was it the monkey face? TELL ME, DAMN YOU!'

But she didn't tell me, just as I wouldn't tell her if the tables were turned. Like I say, this pursuit of laughter is turning ugly. It's only a matter of time before one of us dresses up as a clown and starts careering round the front room on a unicycle. And no one will be laughing then, will they?

After all the laughter and electro drumming she's in no mood for bed. I stick her in the bath, which she immediately pisses into, causing further hysteria.

We're on the bed in the established manner: me in my dressing gown, her in her jim-jams. She has a bottle in her gob and, it being Saturday night and everything, I am drinking a can of Kronenbourg. I can see her eyes twitching around suspiciously as she drinks her milk. She knows something's not quite right. She misses *The Sopranos*.

'*Family Fortunes*?' she seems to be saying as I flick through the channels. '*Family fucking Fortunes*? Are you having a laugh or what?'

I keep flicking. *Midsomer Murders*, *The National Lottery*, the news?

'Come off it, Dad,' her eyes tell me. 'This is just insulting.'

'But *CBeebies* finishes at seven! What am I supposed to do? I can't mess with the system!' I tell her, pointlessly.

She looks at me with what I can only interpret as disgust.

Then I stumble on the rugby. Apparently it's the world cup final. Just an excuse for public school boys to feel each other up, if you ask me, but to my surprise she actually seems to like it. She's snuggled back up and clutched my finger in that tear-inducing way again.

'What the hell,' I think to myself. 'It's a big event, and England are playing. No one need ever know that I've watched it. Let's give it a go.'

I crack open another lukewarm can from the four-pack that's sat beside the bed.

By the time she's finished the bottle, the game seems to be reaching its conclusion. I've not really managed to make much sense of it, but England are definitely losing. She's straining to keep her eyelids open, clearly more engrossed in the match than I am. Eventually she gives in and drifts off.

'I'll give it till full time, then I'll stick her in the cot,' I think to myself.

But by full time I've fallen asleep too. I wake up in a fug about an hour and a half later. She is lying on my chest, face down, dribbling on to my throat. The remote has got jammed under my arse and the telly screen has gone all fuzzy. I flick back to BBC 1, where *Match of the Day* is starting. The baby doesn't flinch. She's deep under. Really I should put her in the cot, but we're too cosy like this. I wonder how my wife could possibly be having a better time than me right now. I've propped myself up on a pillow, the baby is all warm on top of me like a living, breathing electric blanket and the football's just started.

By the way, I understand that this whole scenario sounds like a lamentable and contrived depiction of what some doofus might perceive to be a laddish fantasy, but what can I tell you? I like European cinema with subtitles, I eat salad most days, I moisturise, I exercise, I've even been known to read a bit of poetry in my time. I'm as modern as the next poncey metrosexual dickhead. But sometimes you can forget how enjoyable the most obvious and clichéd things can be. It's like 'Don't You Want Me', by The Human League. It's become such a staple at weddings and naff office parties that you start to think it's just some sort of stupid novelty track. You relegate it in your brain to the status of 'I'm Too Sexy' by Right Said Fred or 'Mr Blobby' or something. But then, one day, when you've managed to avoid hearing it for about five years and you're driving along in the car on your own in an above-average mood, that magnificent, seductive, twinkling synth intro kicks in and you think to yourself: 'I LOVE this song. What is it again? Shit! It's "Don't You Want Me"! "Don't You Want Me" is in fact one of my all-time favourite songs! It's only artificial cultural connotations that have somehow stigmatised it and altered my perceptions of what is actually the quintessential British pop classic. Damn those artificial cultural connotations. Always getting in the way of my fun.'

That's what having a beer in front of the football feels like. You realise that before it became a cliché it was actually really good. In fact, it became a cliché because it was so good.

Also, I am aware that boshing four cans of strongish continental lager while in charge of an infant is probably not in the parenting handbook or anything. But she's pretty much immobile, so she can't really escape my clutches and start jamming her fingers in electric sockets, no matter how drunk I get. Plus, my mild tipsiness has ushered a nice, relaxed atmosphere into the house this evening. That's why she's drifted off so peacefully. She's very receptive to the prevailing vibe. And anyway, it's not like I'm legless and have been knocking back chasers or anything. I may be merry, but I am in control.

I hear a key in the door. This should be interesting. Just wait till she sees how well things have gone in her absence. So much for going out being the new staying in. Staying in is the new staying in! Reclining comfortably on the bed, cushioned by a gigantic maternity pillow, I smile smugly.

'I am a natural father', I think to myself for the first time. I look out of the bedroom window, see the comforting orange light of the street lamp reflecting in the glass and inhale that comforting, autumnal whiff of burning leaves. Everything is right with the world. Only, those burning leaves don't smell too healthy. In fact, they smell more like . . . what is it? Burning hair? Where exactly is it coming from?

'Fuck!' exclaims my wife as she enters the room. 'The bed's on fire, the bed's on fire! You're burning the fucking baby, you fuckwit!'

I chuckle condescendingly and briefly protest.

'I'm not burning anythi . . .' But then I glance to my left and realise she is quite right. The corner of the maternity pillow has caught fire on the wall-mounted bedside lamp.

My wife wrenches the baby from my grasp. As I frantically beat down the flames, I surreptitiously sweep the empty beer cans under the bed with my foot so she won't see them.

Later, once the baby's safely asleep in her cot and we've had a chance to take stock, we have a full and frank discussion about what happened. Or rather I slouch, head in hands, bemoaning my own pathetic failings as a father and human being.

'I hate myself,' I say for about the fortieth time in the past hour.

'Shit happens,' shrugs my wife.

'Not that kind of shit. We could have died,' I insist, shaking my head.

'It wasn't that bad!' she says. It's nice of her to comfort me. But I'm not sure anyone can help me now. I thought I might not have what it takes to be a dad, and now I know I was right. I haven't quite toasted the baby's hand in a sandwich-maker, but I wasn't far off. What scant self-respect I ever possessed has dissolved into a sorry puddle of self-loathing.

'Did you have a nice time, at least?' I snivel.

'Yes I did,' she says. 'It was a nice change, you should try it.'

'What?' I say, raising my head slowly. 'Going . . . out?'

'I think it'd do you good,' she smiles.

'You just want me away from the baby for a while, don't you? You think I'm a liability, is that it?'

'No. It's not that. It's just . . .'

'Yes?'

'Well, you have been acting a bit . . . mental lately.'

'Oh.'

'You may need to go out. Do the things you used to do. See your mates. Remind yourself that you're a good bloke.'

'How is seeing my mates going to remind me that I'm a good bloke? All my mates call me a wanker,' I blub.

'They don't mean it. They're just being funny,' she smiles.

'Yeah, they are funny, aren't they?' I say, allowing a tiny grin to bleed slowly across my mournful face. I picture my mates standing round in the pub, listening to the story of me accidentally burning the bed, slapping me on the back and calling me a wanker. 'Really funny,' I reiterate.

'Right then, next Saturday is your day,' my wife insists. 'And we shall never speak of this shameful incident ever again.'

19
DRUGS

'Wanker.'
'Wanker.'
'Dickhead.'
'Wanker.'
'Mug.'

I have just told my mates about setting the bed on fire. It's not a bad response, I suppose. I didn't exactly expect a round of applause. But I had thought they might at least chuckle a bit while they insulted me. Maybe even slap me on the back, reassure me that they've all made similar mistakes in the past and tell me not to be so hard on myself. But they don't. They just shake their heads in judgemental disgust and carry on calling me names for a few more minutes. This isn't helping me to feel better about myself at all.

These are the men with whom I've been going to football for the past seventeen years. We have travelled the UK and beyond together to watch our team lose. We have drunk together, we have laughed together and we have fallen over together. In case you're wondering, no, we have never cried together – we're not that bloody close. But we've shared some of life's most poignant, coming-of-age moments. We have grown up in each other's idiotic company. These are my mates. Yes, they may be the sort of mates who will call you a wanker, who will mock everything you say and do, who will put sweet wrappers and fag-ends in your mouth when you fall asleep on the train, who will steal your shoes and throw them in a river and who will sometimes question the very point of your existence. But they are mates nonetheless. Mates who, when push comes to shove, would be there for you when you really needed them. As long as they weren't busy with other, more important stuff.

Among them is one of my brothers. He was the one who got me into all this in the first place. When I was a kid, each of my three older brothers supported a different London team. Each of them tried to lobby and harangue me into following their respective sides. It was my middle brother who proved successful. He was the same one who would later 'teach' me boxing and pull a knife on Rab the milkman. Suffice to say, he had always been the one with the most persuasive personality. So I ended up going to West Ham like him.

I look at him. He's the only one yet to pass comment on the bed incident. He's keeping his counsel. I should imagine he's feeling a bit sorry for me. Protective even. He'll probably say something to make me feel a bit better in a minute. He drains his drink and fixes me with fiery eyes full of . . . what is it? Hate? No, it's gentler than that. Disappointment? No, not that either. Disdain. That's the word for it.

'Silly bastard,' he says. At least he has the decency to fix me in the eye sincerely when he says it. The others earnestly nod in agreement. They all turn their backs and talk among themselves.

We are in a pub in a village somewhere in Berkshire. We are on our way to watch West Ham play at Reading. Whenever we leave London, we like to get off the train a few stops before our final destination, pick out a secluded pub and get a bit drunk before heading off to the game. It's a routine, a tradition, a method of having fun. I can't remember why it's fun. Written down here in black and white, it doesn't sound like fun at all. But then, the ins and outs of what objectively constitutes a fun experience are neither here nor there. My brain has been trained for many years to categorise these cold, uncomfortable, inebriated afternoons as 'fun experiences', and who am I to argue with my own brain? This is just what I do at the weekend.

At least, it's what I used to do. Right now, I am feeling badly out of practice. Frankly, I'm struggling to keep up, like a little kitten thrown into a lion's den. Although I wouldn't really say this lot are like lions – more like a collection of rancid strays. The point is, I've known them most of my life, but after my leave of absence they seem like strangers to me now. They speak so quickly; their language is so lewd and coarse; they drink, they smoke and they pull these scary faces while they talk. It's all so confusing. Can't we all just sit down and have some quiet time for five minutes? I need a wee. I feel sick. I can't hear what any of them are saying. I don't think I've had a conversation with more than one adult at a time for about six months. I have to keep reminding myself not to lapse into my Barry Badger voice. I wonder how my brother would react if I asked him for a cuddle.

'I knew you weren't cut out for fatherhood,' snarls one of the throng.

'Why not?' I respond, all stuttery and high-pitched.

'Coz you barely know how to wipe your own arse, let alone someone else's. Setting fire to a baby? That's a bit off really, isn't it? Let's be honest – it's borderline noncing.'

I pause. I croak. I try to think of an appropriate comeback.

'Yeah, well, at least I'm not . . . a bloody . . . gay,' is the best I can muster.

'What?'

'That's what you are,' I say with a fake chuckle, hoping some of the others will join in with my rubbishy line of mockery. 'You're like a big gay!'

I point a limp, accusatory finger at him to emphasise my point. It doesn't matter. Everyone's shaking their heads and looking at me pitifully. They go back to talking among themselves.

I used to be good at this. I could take the banter and dish it back out. Now all I can come up with is a mumbled chunk of embarrassing playground homophobia that even a real-life playground homophobe would probably consider too witless and ineloquent to employ.

I have let my mates down, the gay community down and, most of all, myself down. You know you've hit rock bottom when you struggle to match the beer-sodden rep-artee of a bar load of West Ham fans. I mean, this isn't exactly *the Oxford Union Debating Society*. All you really have to do is swear loudly and with venom and they'll accept you as one of their own. But I haven't had what you might call a right proper swear-up in ages. At best, I've been limited to a bit of light 'domestic swearing' around the house. You know, nothing major, just the odd angry exclamation after stubbing a toe on the coffee table or injuring a knuckle on the cheese-grater. The other day I shouted 'Fuck you!' at our gas-fuelled open fire after singeing my eyebrows while lighting it. It felt briefly liberating until I heard my wife shouting 'Stop swearing at the fire' from upstairs. Stupid baby monitor.

It's not just the dialogue I'm struggling to keep up with either. It's the drinking too. The speed with which they're sinking pints is preposterous. They're making them disappear like magicians. I'm having trouble getting the first down my throat. It's freezing outside, and the cold, fizzy lager feels like it's solidified into a gigantic iceberg halfway down my gullet, forming a ballast against any more liquid entering the body. Inside my lungs lurks a painful burp that can't be expended and which is causing a stabbing sensation to spread across my entire chest. Perhaps I'm having a heart attack? Best not to mention it: they'll only take the piss. I secretly spill half of my remaining pint into a pot plant and hope no one notices.

I thought drinking less would be a natural benefit of fatherhood. But I was wrong. All I have done is spread my boozing out more thinly across the week. Whereas I used to avoid drink all week long and binge at weekends, I now drink small amounts on a daily basis. I find a can of Foster's at about half-seven every night – just after I've got home from work, bathed the baby, put her to bed, done a bit of housework, caught up on some e-mails and contemplated the fact that all of this will start over again at about 6 o'clock the next morning – helps stave off the nagging suspicion that I may be losing the will to live.

But binge-drinking is out of the question. It's hard enough waking up at 4 a.m. to wipe shit off another human being's arse at the best of times. But with a pounding headache, a mouth like Chernobyl and a stomach full of acid and regret, it's simply unthinkable. So I have now learned to stop drinking after a maximum of two alcoholic units per night.

Now, after a long spell on the sidelines, I have been unceremoniously thrust back on to the front line of binge-drinking. It's been a terrifying, high-speed booze assault from the moment I arrived at Paddington Station at 10 o'clock this morning and found them guzzling cans from their Thresher's carrier bags. There is no mercy, no retreat and no surrender in this sort of drinking environment. I want to go home.

'Another pint?' someone asks.

'Erm, I might just have a ha . . .'

But it's too late. They have handed me a large, gassy glass of freezing-cold continental lager and a small glass of unsolicited whisky to go with it. And they are watching me. They smell blood. They sense my powers have been weakened. But they will not see me fail today. I know how to do this. Pathetic, pointless, macho drinking habits were what I was brought up with. Now is the time for me to call upon all that experience and show them what I'm made of. I slam the whisky down my throat with a wince. I immediately bring the beer to my lips and begin to guzzle hungrily, my eyes shut and my toes secretly curled inside my shoes. There, that showed them.

'Sam, Sam, wake up you bell-end.'

I can feel a hand on my shoulder. Where am I? I open my eyes and see a shiny, wet, *faux* mahogany table-top staring back at me. I can smell stale fag ash and chip fat. I look up. My friends are standing around looking quizzical. They are shaking their heads again.

'What happened? Did I have a fit?' I ask.

'No.'

'Did one of you knock me out?'

'No. You fell asleep, you twat.'

'Shit. How long was I out for?'

'I dunno. Forty seconds.'

I try to shake the fuzziness from my head.

'Look, I didn't get much sleep last night. The baby's teething and . . .'

I look at their stupid faces and detect a softening of attitude. A few of this lot are dads themselves. They know what it's like.

'Mate, you'll get used to it,' someone says, putting an arm round me.

'I remember the first time I went to football after my first was born,' says another, wistfully. 'Arsenal away, it was. Spewed all over a steward's shoes. Cunt threw me out.'

There's a silence as everyone contemplates this moving anecdote.

Eventually Frank comes over and puts an arm round me. He's the youngest of the group and always has a grin on his face and an ill-thought-out plan for misadventure hovering perilously on his lips. He starts leading me towards the pub's back door.

'Come on, I'll sort you right out,' he says.

He leads me into the beer garden and towards a concrete out–house.

'Where are we going?' I ask.

'The kitchens,' he smiles.

'What for?'

'To see the chef.'

'Are you buying me a bacon sandwich?'

'No. Even better. I'm going to buy you some lovely drugs.'

'What? No, I don't want any lovely drugs. Thanks all the same.'

'How else are you going to wake up?' he asks incredulously.

'Trust me, they won't make me wake up. They'll make me go all epileptic. Don't make me take the lovely drugs, Frank.'

But there's no stopping him. I am being forced towards the kitchen door.

'How are we going to get drugs in here?' I ask.

He looks incredulous again, as though I'm the one being stupid.

'Every village pub chef in Britain sells coke on the side,' he explains. 'Didn't you know that?'

'No. I did not know that,' I say.

'Trust me, I used to live in a village. Think about it: how else are they making their money?' he asks almost rhetorically.

Before I have a chance to make sense of the question, we are inside the kitchen. There is a fat man in his forties microwaving a plastic jug full of baked beans. There is also a spotty-faced teenager fetching something from the freezer and a rotund, smiley-faced waitress arranging things on a tray. Their heads turn, and they regard the pair of us with sullen indifference. I blink and try to look apologetic. Frank grins confidently and sways around a bit in the doorway.

'Hello pal,' he barks at the chef, who, to my untrained eye, makes for an unlikely-looking drug-dealer. 'We're looking for Charlie.'

The chef exchanges a confused glance with his two underlings, then looks back at us and says in a timid, bumpkinish voice:

'I beg your pardon?'

'You know, a bit of gear?' Frank elaborates with a wink.

Again, the kitchen staff just gawp at us in bafflement.

'Look, mate,' says Frank, a hint of exasperation creeping into his voice, 'all we're looking for is a bit of chop, right?'

Even I'm losing track of the euphemisms now. I don't like this. It doesn't feel like a dad thing to be doing on a Saturday afternoon. I should really be at Homebase buying Rawlplugs.

'I'm sorry, but I really don't know what you mean,' says the chef politely.

'SNIFF!' shouts Frank, the beer and frustration getting to him. 'WE'RE LOOKING FOR SNIFF!'

'Steph?' says the chef. 'Sorry mate, Steph doesn't work here any more. She got a job at the Bell and Crown up the road, you'll have to go up there I'm afraid.'

Frank is furious. 'Come on, we're going,' he says, tugging me by the arm and stomping out petulantly.

'OK, thanks, we'll try the Bell and Crown then,' I say needlessly over my shoulder.

We walk briskly through the bar, telling the others it's time to go.

Later, inside the ground, the drinking continues. My mate Noel shoves his hands down his pants and pulls out two miniature bottles of brandy which he had stashed next to his genitals so as to get past the stewards on the turnstile.

'Here you go,' he says, twisting the cap from one and tipping a few glugs into my beer. I say 'thanks' in a semi-disgusted sort of a way. Things are getting more boisterous. People all around are singing and throwing beer over each other's heads. A stranger lobs a plastic pint glass across the concourse. It clips me on the shoulder and splashes lager on to my face. I'm briefly annoyed before I remember that, in the current context, this counts as fun. It's his way of extending a hand of friendship. I cheer and join with his song about hating Frank Lampard. He seems happy. At least he's helped wake me up a bit.

Up in the stands I doze off again. Midway through the first half I wake up and hear laughter ringing in my ears. Dozens of fans are pointing and laughing at me. It appears they have also been taking pictures on their mobile phones.

'It's not that boring, mate,' people shout.

'You could have woken me up!' I say to my mates, only to notice that they too have been taking pictures on their mobiles. Noel has texted one to my wife with the word 'mug' written beneath it.

'She won't find that funny at all,' I say to Noel grumpily. 'She'll find that hilarious,' I think to myself bitterly.

We either win the game or lose it. Or possibly draw. It's impossible to tell. My vision has gone blurry, and I've lost track of time, space and reason. The one benefit of this is that the notion of 'tiredness' no longer makes any sense. The combination of fatigue and drunkenness has somehow broken the space–time continuum. I feel like I am now operating in some sort of fourth dimension, where normal rules don't apply. A flurry of episodes unfold in a bizarre, jumbled sequence. There are six of us huddled in the back of a stinking mini-cab. We are pulling up at some services off the M4.

'Where are we? What are we doing here?' I am asking.

'We are getting the lovely drugs,' grins Frank from the front seat. 'This man is getting them for us. Then you will feel all right.'

He gestures at the young Asian bloke behind the wheel. There is loud bass thumping out of his speakers. He has sparkly earrings and a hair-do so modern and spiky it's starting to scare me.

'Are you a chef?' I ask him.

'No,' says Frank. 'He's not a chef. He's a driver who knows how to get the lovely drugs.'

A tiny part of my mind is still working well enough to feel anxious about what may happen if they really do get the drugs. I can't be too careful. Once, when we were driving back from the FA Cup Final in 2006 in a big, fancy limo, they dipped cocktail sausages in cocaine and shoved them up a mate's nose while he was sleeping. And took pictures. They like taking pictures of things.

I notice my brother in the corner of the car. Thank God he's here. At least he'll protect me.

'What do you think I should do about the lovely drugs?' I ask him hoping for a bit of fraternal concern or guidance.

He shrugs and says, 'I dunno. Just keep taking them until you start to feel weird. Then go home.'

It doesn't make me feel any better.

A train station. A train. A mass altercation with a ticket inspector. I lock myself in a toilet and try to sleep. But the stench inside makes me want to gag. I stumble back out and fall asleep curled up on a seat. Someone stuffs an empty packet of Maltesers in my mouth and sticks a fag-end on my ear. Back in London they don't let me go home. We get in a taxi and go to another pub. Everyone buys more alcohol. I stumble into the toilet to have a wee. It is full of loud, drunken men talking in shouty, sweary voices. They are like us but perhaps even more so. I don't know why they are all in the toilets. It seems strange. Frank appears beside me at the urinal.

'Why are we here?' I ask him.

'The drugs, the lovely drugs,' he says again.

'But what about the man in the taxi?' I say.

'Forget about him. I'm meeting a friend here who will help us.'

I drunkenly step back from the urinal and knock into a group of the loud, sweary strangers.

'Mind out, mate,' one of them says. He has wide, aggressive, bloodshot eyes. He looks like he's on drugs. Maybe he's Frank's drug friend.

'Are you Frank's drug friend?' I slur.

'You what?' he snarls back at me.

'Have you got the stuff?' I smirk. His friends seem to be encircling me.

Frank steps towards me and grabs my shoulder.

'No, Sam, this isn't my mate,' he says.

'No, that's right, I'm not your fucking mate', says the angry man.

'These aren't the droids you're looking for!' I laugh, pointing at all the men who have surrounded me. It's all starting to feel a bit rum. Frank starts to shout at them aggressively, and I sort of dance in and out of a few people, feeling strangely playful. 'I know how to sort this situation out,' I think to myself. 'I'll just lie on my back and invite everyone to tickle my tummy. That'll lighten the mood.' Someone pushes my face. I push theirs back. The shouting and swearing gets louder, and the gang of toilet buddies suggest we should leave their toilet. They are impolite. We are outnumbered, so we leave, shouting half-hearted insults as we do so. Back at the bar my pals have started to drift away to their homes anyway. Frank is still going on about his friend and the lovely drugs. He vows never to give up on them. I walk out of the pub into the cold night air. A bus pulls up, and I stumble on without saying goodbye.

When I wake up, all I can see are trees. Trees as far as the eyes can see. Their branches cut bleak, creepy figures against the dark winter sky. I blink three times and hope to see something that looks more like home. I don't. I am in a bus garage somewhere quiet and dimly lit and rural-looking. I stand up suddenly, and my right leg, numbed with pins and needles, gives way beneath me. I stumble towards the door and roll down the steps on to the pavement. I feel humiliated. A mother and her young son step over me as they dismount the bus.

'Where are we?' I ask them from the ground. 'What time is it?'

The mother looks scared, grabs her son and hurries away. To all intents and purposes I am now a vagrant.

I climb back to my feet and try to shake some feeling into my leg. I try to find my bearings. It's not good. It all looks like stupid countryside. How far do London buses actually go? This is like a terrible dream. There is no one around apart from the bus driver, who is still sat in his little driving compartment. I approach him, but he quickly presses a button and the doors shut with an unfriendly hiss.

'Shit,' I think to myself. 'I'm that guy. The one covered in dirt and stinking of beer that everyone wants to avoid eye contact with on the bus. How did this happen?'

I start to walk. It's impossible to tell where. I stick to the road. If I keep walking, I will eventually find a road sign or a landmark. Or a welcoming inn that will offer me food and a bed for the night while I attempt to work out what's happened. But the farther I walk, the narrower the road becomes. It grows darker, and the trees start to encroach on me. I panic and decide to cut across the woodland. I think I can hear traffic in the distance. I trip on a root, twist my ankle and tumble to the floor. I think to myself: 'This has not been a good day out. Not in the least.' I feel ready to give up. I begin to doubt that I will ever find my way home again. I contemplate a new life spent here in the woods, surviving on leaves and pine kernels and slowly developing special squirrel-like climbing abilities. Maybe it wouldn't be so bad. Then I throw up in some bracken.

My phone rings. It's my mate Dave.

'Do you fancy a pint?' he asks.

'A pint? A pint? No, there'll be no more pints,' I mumble.

'You sound pissed. Where are you?' he says.

'No idea', I say.

There is a long pause. Eventually Dave says, 'I'm in the car on the way back from the shops. Stay where you are, work out your bearings and I'll come and pick you up.'

It's a touching gesture, which I throw back in his face. 'It's best you forgot I ever existed!' I say and put the phone down.

I rub my ankle and climb to my feet. I start to limp back up the road I came down. Eventually a light glimmers in the distance. It's coming towards me and getting larger. It's a taxi, right out here in the middle of nowhere. I didn't even know they had black cabs in the countryside. I tell the driver my address and ask him to take me to whatever train station will help me get there quickest. He shrugs, and I get in.

Five minutes later we are pulling up outside my home, and he is asking me for four pounds fifty. 'But, how?' I ask in amazement.

'You were only at the common at the top of the road,' he says. 'Go home and get some sleep, young man.'

He is easily the kindest person I've encountered all day.

I stumble through the front door and make my way to the living room. A fire is glowing, and my wife is watching telly. I stand dramatically in the doorway, clutching its frame and panting. There is dirt on my face and trousers. I probably smell.

'You're still awake,' I say.

'Of course I'm still awake,' she says casually. 'It's only eight o'clock. Did you have a nice time?'

'I had a . . . a . . .' I begin, but it all gets too much. I slump on to the sofa and embrace her. For a moment I feel like I'm going to sob. The cold air and fear have snapped me back to sobriety. The day's varied indignities are rattling through my brain like a slide show. I have not behaved in an adult manner. I have been a dick.

'I'm sorry,' I blurt, my face pressed to her shoulder.

'What for?' she asks.

'For everything. For being a rubbish dad and a rubbish husband.'

'You're not rubbish,' she says.

'I am,' I say, breaking into a remorseful, incoherent monologue. 'All the beer . . . the wankers . . . lovely drugs . . . he was just a chef . . . ticket inspector . . . I thought Frank knew them . . . special squirrel-climbing abilities . . . and it only cost me four pound fifty. Anyway, sorry. I'm useless.'

'Slow down,' my wife says, clutching my face. 'You've been out with your mates. You've got a bit drunk. You've all acted like idiots for a few hours. That was the plan, wasn't it?'

I think about this for a moment.

'S'pose so,' I say meekly.

'Did you take any drugs?'

'No.'

'Did you hurt anyone or get nicked or have a fit?'

'No.'

'You didn't snog some girl or anything, did you?'

'No.'

'Well then, what's the problem?' she concludes. 'The curry delivery man will be here in a minute. *Strictly Come Dancing*'s about to start. Shut up and sit down.'

I fall asleep and, this time, don't wake up for eleven hours.

20

ROCKY IV

'. . . So Chimpy McGhee told all the other animals that they could now live in the forest without fear of disease, famine or short-sighted planning permissions issued by the local council.' The baby sits in my arms slowly drifting towards sleep. 'And all the other animals cheered Chimpy's name and thanked him for his bravery. The end.'

As I finish my story, she stretches her arms out across my chest in what I choose to interpret as a cuddle. I nuzzle the top of her head and inhale the comforting whiff of Johnson's Baby Shampoo.

'It's time for bed,' I whisper. She wriggles up closer as I carry her through to her bedroom. I place her softly in her cot and begin to bury her in three cuddly monkeys, two bunnies, a tortoise, a penguin, Iggle Piggle out of *In The Night Garden* and a soft toy of indeterminate species which I reckon is probably a mouse but my wife insists is a really skinny pig. The baby shuts her eyes and smiles. I lean down and kiss her lightly on the forehead.

'Daddy loves you,' I say.

'Erurkh,' she croaks with her eyes shut tight, as if to say, 'Shut up and get out, you soppy tart.'

If tonight is like any of the last fifteen or sixteen nights, she won't be bothering us again for another twelve hours. We'll have time for a nice dinner, a film and perhaps even some hanky-panky. Yep, parenthood is an absolute piece of piss. And it's pretty much all down to my excellent storytelling abilities.

We're approaching Christmas: the business end of the year. I used to sneer at Yuletide merriment. Now, immersed in some sort of Jimmy Stewart fantasy, I am about the most Christmassy bastard you could ever hope to meet. For weeks now I've been telling my little girl Christmas-themed bedtime stories so rich in compelling narrative and heart-warming sentiment that they can only be described as magical. All off the top of my head too. I could be as rich as J. K. Rowling if I remembered to jot any of it down. The details are probably wasted on the baby. She just stares through me vacantly, totally oblivious to the gripping plot lines and life-affirming character arcs. But I think she somehow imbibes the general sentiment. There is a comforting rhythm to the way I speak, which she absorbs through osmosis. It sends her into an almost hypnotic state of sleepy contentment.

I prove this to myself by sometimes reading her chapters from whatever book I happen to have lying next to the bed at the time. The other night I read her six pages from the autobiography of Guildford Four member Gerry Conlon. By applying the same gentle vocal stylings to his tales of police torture and judicial miscarriage as I would to one of Chimpy McGhee's tales of forestry adventure, I had her completely captivated. I pulled off the same trick while reading her an extract from Simon Napier-Bell's *I'm Coming to Take You to Lunch – A Tale of Boys, Booze and*

How Wham! Were Sold to China. It may have been an at times startling account of the gay music impresario's hedonistic romp through 1980s' pop Babylon, but to the baby's ears it was as compelling as any stupid Beatrix Potter classic.

The point is, I get to lie on my bed reading my own book for half an hour every evening and dress it up as an act of studious childcare. Everyone's happy, and absolutely no one gets hurt. Successful fatherhood, I am discovering, is based on a simple system of compromises, deceptions and confidence tricks such as this.

This is just one of the discoveries I have made since my unfortunate day out at the football. I lost it for a moment back then. I mean, all I'd really done was gone out, had a few beers and fallen asleep on a bus. Nothing unusual or particularly regrettable about that, I don't suppose. But it was my reaction to it that was the big problem: I let it get to me. I found myself on the verge of tears, contemplating life as a squirrel. It wasn't pretty, was it? In retrospect, I perhaps judged myself a bit too harshly. I've been doing that a lot lately. Ordinary day-to-day acts of stupidity that would have gone without mention in the past have suddenly taken on vast significance in my mind. Setting fire to the bed, starting a fight in a pub toilet, getting lost in some woods: that sort of stuff comes as naturally as breathing or eating or going to the toilet to an imbecile like me. I've been doing things like that all my life. No point sweating these things: for every stupid thing I do there's usually an act of mild cleverness to balance it out. For instance, I am pretty decent at reverse parking. Focusing on stuff like that usually helps whenever I've felt my self-esteem dip below standard levels. I am an old hand at letting myself down. I know how to handle it. But letting my daughter down is a different matter. What has she done to deserve me?

Now I'm learning not to worry so much. I'll probably always be an idiot on the inside. As long as I act like a decent and responsible adult on the outside, that's all that matters. And that's what I've been doing lately.

And the baby is doing OK. In fact, she seems pretty happy to me. My missus tells me she is generally happy with my all-round fatherly performance too.

'How happy, out of ten, with ten being Teen Wolf's Dad and one being Fred West?' I ask her.

'I'm not getting into that sort of discussion,' she insists.

But I can tell by her eyes that she is giving me a seven and a half – which I am categorising as Jim Robinson from *Neighbours*.

Not bad, but I could do better. I have resolved that staying in watching *The Sopranos* all the time is not necessarily the way forward. It makes me sad, dull and depressed. It was that sort of indolent lifestyle that briefly made me forget how to earn a living, speak to strangers or do up the buttons on a shirt. Equally, acting like a drunken adolescent is unlikely to engender respect from my wife and daughter or make me much happier in the long run either. This is why I am searching for a middle way. Now, Buddhists will tell you that the 'middle way' is the practice of non-extremism, a path of moderation away from the extremes of self-indulgence or self-mortification. For me that means making sure I get home from work in time to do bath-time and trying not to get battered on a school night too often. Make a up a few bedtime stories, get a bit of exercise in, remember to wash my hands after pissing. Grown-up stuff. As long as I tick these boxes, I can feel good about myself as a bloke and as a father. For now anyway: who knows what progress I may make in the future? This time next year I may be an eight and a half (John Peel) or even a nine (God, the father of Jesus).

I know what you're thinking – how come The Almighty comes just below Teen Wolf's dad in the league table of fathers? Well, they're similar characters. They're both single parents, they both possess special powers and they're both entirely fictional. But God loses points for not intervening with a lightning bolt when the Romans crucified his son. The Resurrection was too little too late.

I hope that I will eventually be able to achieve Buddhist-like levels of enlightenment and spiritual balance. Mind you, it'll probably take a bit more research. So far, all I've done is quickly scan Buddhism's Wikipedia entry and find something about striving to awaken the true inner self. I'm not sure I'm ready for that. Disappointingly, there's no mention of how one goes about learning to levitate or break metal bars over your head like those Buddhist monks do. I interviewed one of them once when they came over to do a show at Hammersmith Apollo. He told me about this special 'vibrating hand technique', where you hold your hand an inch from an adversary's forehead and use it to communicate spiritual energy into him through vibrations. It's like a sort of curse. After you've done it, you can kill him any time you want, using brainwaves. You can do it right there and then or leave it for another five years and strike him down when he's least expecting it. I liked this idea a great deal, although I wasn't quite sure how it fitted in with the whole Buddhist ethos of peace and harmony. Mind you, I was conducting the interview through a dodgy translator, who may have skipped some of the pertinent details. Plus, I'm not altogether sure I didn't dream the whole thing.

My point is that if I can manage to be a little bit more like Buddha and a little less of a dick, then I will be a much happier person. Which will probably make my daughter a much happier person too. I'm not sure if it'll make my wife a much happier person, mind you: she seems to prefer it when I am halfway between happy and sad. When I'm proper sad, I mope and moan. But when I'm happy, I mean really happy, I tend to shout and swagger a bit too much. My self-confidence can sometimes sky-rocket, and I'll wake her up in the night with stupid ideas for a film about a talking hat or my designs for a new type of automatic tennis racket. It drives her round the bend. When I finish writing this book, I'll probably send her mental with my own sense of relief and self-congratulation. She's probably planning a holiday with her mum already. I don't blame her.

Anyway, like I say, physical exercise is forming a central plank of my new design for life. And here I am, on a cold winter's morning, running alongside the riverbank with a thin layer of frost forming atop my woolly West Ham hat. I feel brave to be out here this early in the morning. Heroic even. Globules of sweat form on my temples, then squirm into the corners of my eyes. Steam blows from my mouth. John Cafferty's theme to *Rocky IV* pumps into my ears through my headphones.

I thunder past the ducks, the trees and the rowers.

I focus on my breathing: it's smooth, controlled and steady. Not those spluttering, chitty-chitty-bang-bang gasps I used to do whenever I exercised in the old days.

I skip over a dog turd and flob clumsily into the river as John Cafferty sings about the moment of truth drawing near.

My own destination, or moment of truth as Cafferty puts it, is the railway bridge beside my house, where I like to finish my run. I feel like Rocky training for his show-down with Ivan Drago in the wilds of Communist Russia. I don't need Drago's state-of-the-art exercise machines and computerised fitness monitors. All I need is an open track, some running shoes and a bucketload of guts. And a small bottle of Evian, in case I begin to feel dehydrated. This is the only way for a man to train. While Rocky was pursued constantly by KGB agents in old-fashioned Mercedes saloons (a crappy choice of vehicle for an off-road pursuit really – no wonder Communism fell), I am pursued for a 100-metre stretch by two exuberant border terriers, one of which jumps up and tries to bite my penis before I shoo him away and begin to climb the steps of the bridge. When I reach the top, I gaze out across the majestic, winding Thames and the rows of houses and trees that constitute my neighbourhood and try to think of something celebratory and poignant to shout. A bit like when Rocky climbed to the top of that mountain and jeered in defiance at the whole Soviet Union. But I am too exhausted to think of anything decent, so I just shout 'Adrian!' because it seems like a funny thing to do. I notice two teenagers cycling past on their way home from a big night out. One of them flicks me the 'V's. I stretch down, then wander home.

I shower, I shave, I give the baby her milk and put her down for her mid-morning nap.

Then I receive a strange voice mail message on my mobile phone.

'I'm a friend of your grandmother's,' it says. 'She has something for you. Please call immediately.'

Usually, my gran calls me herself and spends twenty minutes shouting 'I can't bloody hear you' down the phone until I just have to hang up (after which I'm certain she continues to shout the same phrase for a further twenty minutes before dropping the receiver and falling into a deep sleep). Nowadays she lives in a home and has a phone-bitch who, when I call back, tells me to visit on Saturday to collect my long-overdue birthday present. I know, I know; it shouldn't take the promise of a gift to make me want to visit my own gran. But what can I tell you? It does.

On Saturday I forgo my trip to the football to take the baby on a day trip to see her great-grandmother at the old people's home (my nan calls it 'the coffin-dodgers'). Day trips with the baby are just one of the things I am doing more of, to make myself feel like a proper, functioning, reliable adult. I fasten her up in her car seat and hit the M4. This is a journey I have done a hundred times before, at high speeds, listening to loud music while simultaneously texting people from my mobile and steering with my knees. But today I drive like a dad. My hands are on the wheel in the ten-to-two position. I stick to the slow lane, driving so cautiously that even old women in Ford Fiestas occasionally ride right up to my bumper and flash their lights. And I sing nursery rhymes all the way. The baby just eyes me with a look of befuddlement from the back seat and occasionally cries.

I arrive at the home and stride excitedly into my gran's room in eager anticipation of what, if past experience has taught me anything, is likely to be at least twenty quid's worth of W.H. Smith's vouchers. She is sat in the corner, looking grumpy and not very pleased to see me.

'Happy Birthday,' she says in her croaky Liverpudlian squawk. Then she throws me this knot of tangled wool and a crumpled sheet of knitting instructions.

'It's a hat for the baby,' she explains. 'You'll have to finish it yourself, I'm too tired.'

Now, I've had some crap presents in my time. Once, when I was ten, my brother gave me a Mars bar which he'd pre-soaked in four-star petrol. But even that didn't compare to this unfinished hat, meant not for me but my child. There's not even a card. She could at least have wrapped it.

'Is this some sort of fucking joke?' I ask.

'I can't bloody hear you,' she replies.

It is immediately apparent that she has only summoned me here to show how annoyed with me she is. She gets like this when I haven't visited her for a while. It's supposed to be a form of corrective punishment. The irony is, it only makes me less likely ever to visit again. What she doesn't realise is that I have a trump card up my sleeve in the form of the baby, whom I have kept hidden beneath a blanket in her pushchair.

'Look who I've brought!' I announce, lifting the blanket with a theatrical flourish to reveal my sleeping offspring.

Gran's head turns slowly like a tortoise. She peers over her spectacles at this tiny, cherubic child. It's a sight of peaceful beauty that could surely melt even the coldest of hearts and combat the most curmudgeonly of moods.

'Fat hands,' says Gran.

'Pardon?' I say.

'The baby. It's got fat hands,' she enunciates in staccato as though I'm the deaf one.

I look down at my daughter's admittedly chubby, almost entirely wristless, hands.

'Yes, I suppose they are a bit fat,' I say.

I suspect this wasn't the sort of response she was looking for. So she tries again.

'And fat legs too. What do you feed her?'

'Lard mainly', I smile, squeezing the baby's voluminous thighs and realising they feel like one of those executive stress gizmos you keep on your desk. 'You look lovely, by the way,' I tell Gran. She turns her face to the window, rolls her eyes and tuts.

The baby wakes up and cries.

'Probably wants her nappy changing,' says Gran. 'I'm not doing it.'

In her mind it probably only seems like last week that I was born. That's probably why she seems so shocked that I am trying to change the baby's nappy myself.

'Bloody hell! What are you doing?' she says, her eyes bulging out of her skull.

'I'm changing its nappy,' I smile, laying the baby on its mat and grabbing the wet wipes from the bag.

'Well, ehm, d'you want me . . .' she is stuttering and muttering in panic. She can't believe her eyes. She thinks the Alzheimer's has taken hold once and for all. 'Do you want me to call a nurse? They'll have the equipment,' she says.

'Don't worry,' I say. 'I do this all the time. I've got all the stuff I need here in the bag,' I say.

'You do it all the time?' says Gran. 'What, really?'

'Yeah. Wait a minute. You do realise that this is my baby, right?'

'Of course I do,' she says, narrowing her eyes and glaring at us both suspiciously. She watches me change the nappy for a while, seemingly deep in thought.

'Your grandfather never changed a nappy in his life,' she eventually says. 'Too lazy.'

'Well, it was different back then, wasn't it?' I say. 'We're more resourceful these days.'

'Oh, listen to him. "Resourceful", is he?' she says, presumably to an imaginary friend in her head. I can detect a tiny glint of respect somewhere in her ordinarily disdainful eyes. I have momentarily impressed her, and she feels slightly ashamed by it.

'Probably quite difficult to change a nappy on a baby that fat,' she says, just to balance things out a bit.

'Yeah, that's right,' I say. 'Impressive, isn't it?'

'They're bringing my lunch in a minute,' she says. 'You'd better go.'

So I leave – feeling just a little more concerned about her than usual. It's not like her to give up so easily on pissing me off. She really is getting on.

Later that evening I am sat with my wife in front of *Nigella Express* eating tea. We are having baked potato with beans and cheese. Nigella is proposing to make a three-course 'supper' for guests in less than half an hour.

'I'm about to beat a 240 millilitre tub of cream with a teaspoon of vanilla!' she beams at us. I haven't got a fucking clue what she's on about. But I know I like it.

'Why can't I be more like Nigella?' I find myself thinking. Then I spill a forkload of baked beans down myself, some of which manage to crawl into the crevices between the cushions of our sofa.

'This is ridiculous!' I unexpectedly announce to my wife. 'We're supposed to be a family, and we should eat like a family! From now on, we'll eat every meal at the dining table!'

She's taken aback by my assertiveness. In my mind she finds it sexually attractive. She certainly seems to be winking at me, but that may just be because I spat a small amount of baked potato in her eye.

The dining table has been playing on my mind for a while now. It seems to symbolise the sort of traditional, almost Victorian, family environment I'd like my daughter to grow up in.

When I was growing up, all we used the dining table for was playing Subbuteo on. Also, our dog Bella used to sleep under there. She was usually good-natured, but she found that fact that we liked to stage table football tournaments on the roof of her home irritating. As an act of revenge she would seize on any Subbuteo equipment we foolishly left out overnight and eat it. She gnawed her way through floodlights, corner flags and, on one disastrous occasion, even players. Midway through our 1987/8 season Bella consumed a whole Atletico Bilbao starting eleven, plus substitutes. It was a massacre that derailed the league season. We wouldn't have minded, but we used Atletico Bilbao to double as Sunderland and even sometimes – at a stretch – Man U.

I want a dining table to mean more to my little girl than flick-to-kick football. I want it to give her a warm sense of belonging and security every time she sits down at it. I want her to exchange witty remarks, intelligent insights and TV viewing suggestions across our table while she eats balanced, heart-healthy meals on a nightly basis.

That's why I have put my foot down. That's also why I have spent a whole hour clearing all the unopened mail and newspapers off it this evening. So we can sit down together and eat. And talk. And experience the sort of moment that bonds a proper family. The table is round and made out of glass. I bought it when I was feeling a bit flush. It's about time we got our money's worth. I sit on one side; my wife sits opposite. The baby is balanced precariously in her high chair between us. We are having omelette with chips and peas followed by Muller Fruit Corners with a glass of Appletiser on the side and no telly or anything.

'So,' I say to my wife, all seriously, 'how was your day?'

'What?' she says with a curl of the lip.

'Your day. How was it?'

'I told you already when I came in. It was shit.' She is back at work.

'Ah yes, of course. Shit, yes.'

'Why are you talking like it was Victorian times?' she asks. It is true that I have affected a posh accent and deep, gravelly burr with which to conduct dining-room conversation. It just seems right.

'Did you happen to read about this business with the economy and what-have-you? Terrible,' I say, ignoring her question about the voice.

'No, I did not,' she says, rolling her eyes at the baby and stabbing a McCain oven chip with her fork.

'No, nor did I,' I say.

There is an awkward silence. We munch our food and stare at the door. The door that leads to the room with the sofas and the telly and the scatter cushions. And then the baby starts to wimper.

'Oh dear, she's crying!' I say. 'Do you think it's this room?'

'Yes, definitely,' says my wife. 'I think she'd be much more comfy next door.'

'Righto, you grab the baby, I'll grab the plates,' I say standing up. 'At least we tried, right?'

'Yep, we tried,' she says, already scuttling off with the infant under her arm.

We're sat down in front of *Hell's Kitchen* just in time to see Jim Davidson booted out. Evenings in don't get much better than this.

21

SPLEEN

A grim, yellow light flickers from the ceiling. A sickly, surgical smell permeates the room. I stare down at the torn fabric on the seat of my swivel chair and pick idly at the foam inside. My other hand is squeezing my mum's shoulder. Above the monotonous buzz of the light fitting I can hear the voice of the doctor – sad but friendly, encouraging but serious – reading out some medical terms and conditions like they are the small print from the bottom of a dodgy insurance advert.

'There is a reasonably significant risk that your spleen could be ruptured during this procedure,' he deadpans.

My mum nods and smiles nervously. My oldest brother, who is sitting to my left, stares at the wall and looks like he's going to puke. The doctor looks like he's waiting for some sort of response.

'That's shouldn't be a problem,' I say encouragingly. I don't want anyone getting too worried. I think it's best to respond to all of the doc's warnings with a matter-of-fact smile and a shrug. But the fact is, I have no idea what a spleen is. For all I know, it could be the thing that navigates our arms or makes sure our eyes don't pop out of our faces every time we sneeze. Still, I figure you can probably get computerised spleen replacements from Japan now if you're willing to fork out enough dough. Easy for me to act all cavalier, mind you. It's not my spleen he's on about.

My mum keeps nodding and smiling. My brother keeps staring at the wall. The doc goes back to his list.

'There is a significant chance that the colon itself may get damaged, in which case we'll have to fit a colostomy bag,' he says.

My mum looks concerned.

'But that would only be a temporary thing,' I tell her – as though I've got a flaming clue.

'No,' interrupts the doc. 'I'm afraid it would be permanent.'

'Why did he have to go and tell her that?' I think. 'I almost had the poor cow convinced.' Sometimes there's nothing worse than an honest doctor.

I put my arm right round my mum's shoulders and squeeze her tight, as though that might make up in some small way for the fact that she could be shitting into a bag for the rest of her life. She offers me a weak smile of thanks but, for once in her life, is completely lost for words.

'Well, that's about it then,' I say with inappropriate merriment. I half-rise to my feet in a bid to bring an end to the whole unsavoury discussion. I see no point in sitting here listening to the sort of demented, miserable stuff that may or may not happen to my mum when she goes under the knife tomorrow.

But the doc's not finished. He can't finish. He's like a runaway train of bad tidings. He is spewing out worst-case scenarios like he's got bad-news Tourette's. I suppose he's obliged to. If he doesn't outline every last possible eventuality, then one day someone will only lose a spleen and sue the whole NHS on the grounds that they weren't warned about it.

'Hang on a minute! No one ever mentioned anything about losing my spleen! I wouldn't have agreed to the operation had I known!'

'But you'd just been knocked down by a bus. If we hadn't operated, you would have died.'

'That's not the point. That spleen was very dear to me. It was my favourite internal organ. I'm not sure life will be worth living without it. But hand over ten grand of taxpayers' money and we'll call it quits.'

The doctor shifts position, straightens his back and tries to fix my mum's wobbly gaze. I can tell he's gearing up for something major.

'Lastly, I must warn you that there is a risk of death.'

I look at my mum, my mum looks at me, we both look at my brother, my brother looks at the wall. I'm beginning to think he might actually be dead. We look at the doc. The doc doesn't know where to look. What I'm trying to say is, it's awkward.

'They have to say that to everyone,' I tell my mum with what's supposed to be a reassuring wrinkle of the nose.

'No, actually,' says the doc. I can sense that he's starting to find my constant attempts to undermine him slightly irritating. 'This is a major operation. It's likely to last around five hours. Taking into account your age, it poses an above-average risk, I'm afraid.'

My mouth has gone dry, and my head's gone all tingly. My annoyingly upbeat commentary on the whole situation has come to an abrupt halt. I've run out of material. My well of emptily comforting platitudes has run dry. I just sit there and gulp. Now it's my mum putting her arm around me. The doctor breaks the brief silence by smiling warmly and telling my mum with sincerity, 'But we'll do our best to make sure that doesn't happen.'

Then the three of us all have to sign some forms, and the meeting draws to a close. I've been in some rubbish meetings in my time. Budget meetings, marketing meetings, meetings where phrases like 'We'll no longer be needing your services' are used. I've even been in one of those meetings where someone starts throwing an 'ideas ball' around. But however bad those meetings were, at least no one ever informed me that my mother might be about to die. I mean, that really is the mark of a crappy meeting, isn't it? It kind of puts all of the other crappy meetings into context. I'd chuck as many bloody ideas balls around a conference room as I was asked to, as long as no one caught one and said, 'Here's an idea – let's kill Sam's mum.'

But the last half-hour was so much more than just a rubbish meeting. It probably ranks as one of the rubbishest episodes in my entire life. I know she isn't dead yet, but inside my naturally pessimistic mind I am already compiling a funeral playlist and fighting back the tears. Not just at the thought of her death but at the extra misery that will be heaped on if, as would probably be the case, her dying wish was to have songs from the musical *Mamma Mia* played as we enter the chapel of rest.

Yep, this is easily worse than the time I got caught under a lilo at White City swimming baths in 1984. And definitely scarier than the brief moment I thought my wife and child were going to die during the birth all those months ago. That fear came and went in a matter of seconds – it didn't have time to ferment and intensify to this brain-mangling level.

We step out into the waiting room, where other grim-faced patients sit around anticipating similarly bad news, passing the time with two-year-old copies of *Take a Break* magazine. Like that's going to make them feel any better. The gastro-enterology unit is where people go to kiss goodbye to large chunks of their bowels. It's not the jolliest part of the hospital.

The three of us – my brother, my mum and I – shuffle about and mutter. It's weird. We're not usually short of words, my mum and I. My brother hates hospitals, so I half-expected him to go a bit weird. I give him an awkward brotherly hug. He pulls a face that makes him look like he's having a stroke. He's specifically hated this hospital ever since he had to spend three nights here in the late '80s after a jogger smashed his jaw to pieces outside our local boozer. My brother had the drunken audacity to mock his running style and shout the words, 'Go on, my son,' as he ran past, so the jogger turned back and punched him in the face. Then the gutless bastard just ran off in his soppy tracksuit. They rushed my bro to A&E and ended up having to wire up his jaw. He couldn't open his gob more than half an inch for the next six weeks. My mum had to liquidise his meals and serve them to him through a straw. The only minor upside of the whole thing was that he had to grow a beard, which, some people commented, made him look a tiny bit like Jeremy Irons.

No wonder he's looking queasy. My mum, meanwhile, is trying to put a brave face on things.

'I just don't want you boys worrying about me,' she says. This has been her position ever since she broke the news about her cancer a few weeks ago. She was ready to face it; she just didn't want her condition to bother her sons. I could see what she meant. If she died, she'd have nothing left to worry about. We'd be the mugs left sitting around crying our tits off, moaning on about how we miss our mum and boring everyone with tedious, self-indulgent memories of how great she was, like we were living out some sort of Violet Kray fantasy.

Still, this isn't the time to start thinking that sort of thought. This is the time to say inspirational and defiant things like 'You'll get through this!' and 'I know you're strong enough to fight this bastard cancer, goddammit!' But I'm too confused, saddened and tired. I've been here waiting for that stupid, miserable meeting with the doc for the past seven hours. I need some sleep. She needs a bed on the ward, which they say could take another couple of hours to materialise. Other relatives arrive. I hug my mum, tell her I love her, then decide to walk all the way home along the river and have a think. Which is probably the last thing I need.

I should have seen all this coming. Whenever things start to go a bit too well, I get suspicious. I start to think that something rubbish must be lurking for me round the next corner. And I'm quite often right. It's about yin and yang, or whatever you want to call it. The balance of the universe. For every good thing there must be an equal and opposite rubbishy thing. I've got a perfect wife, a gorgeous daughter, a nice home, a decent career, a ginger cat and high-speed wi-fi access in every room. I was approaching content. I was almost happy. I was verging perilously on the edge of smugness. And then my Old Dear calls me at work to say she's got stupid bloody cancer of the colon. Of course she has. It's all so predictable.

I amble along the Thames and try to force my brain to focus on the positives. Like the baby. The way she makes me feel when I see her in the morning. Her little giggles. Her toothy grin. The way she's learned to say 'dada'. Does it help me feel any better? Does it fuck.

Don't get me wrong, that baby is the best thing that ever happened to me. She makes my life seem fulfilling and altogether less pointless than it used to. I miss her every second we're apart. But I can't say her existence has managed to negate the impact of all of life's other irritations. I don't tread in dog shit and think to myself: 'Never mind! Who cares about this new pair of Nike Airs getting ruined when I have been blessed with the wondrous gift of a child?' No, I still think, 'Shit, I'm going to have to go home and scrape that off with a knife.' I hoped fatherhood would give me a broader, more sober perspective on life. It hasn't. If anything, it makes day-to-day problems seem more severe, because I now worry about how they may impact on the baby.

Mind you, she does at least provide a useful distraction from all the other stuff. She is mobile these days. She crawls and climbs and rolls and throws things around. She is able to chuck food at us, pour water over electrical appliances and heave herself across the living-room floor on her arse in the direction of the open fire. This means that I can never relax or take my eye off her for a second. I have had to quickly train my previously flabby and indifferent brain into a focused, attentive and diligent machine. There simply isn't enough time for me to sit around worrying about my mum's cancer or the dog shit on my trainers as much as I'd like to. I am too busy trying to stop her from eating cat food or bursting into flames.

I wake up on the morning of my mum's operation. It's ten to seven. I wonder how I'm going to get through the day without a terrifying mental picture of my mum laid out on an operating table plaguing my every thought. Wondering if the procedure will be successful. Wondering if she's even still *alive*.

My maternal grandma used to tell me, 'Always get out of bed the moment the alarm goes off. No point just lying there. You'll only end up "thinking".' She'd say the word 'thinking' with the sort of disgusted sneer most of us would reserve for the word 'felching'. I always wanted to ask her what her problem was with the notion of thought. Where she thought civilisation might be today if everyone had her sneering attitude towards the use of one's brain. But I never picked her up on it because I was too scared. And now I realise that she may have been right anyway. The world keeps turning, whether you think about it or not, doesn't it? What good does it do to sit around thinking a load of stupid, pointless, egotistical thoughts in the meantime? You'll only get yourself all het up and anxious.

In any case, I've got no choice in the matter these days: when the baby wakes up, I wake up. I stagger into her room, pull open the blinds and approach her cot. She is

standing up, clinging on to the bars. She blurts out something that I think is supposed to mean 'hello' and chucks a
cuddly penguin at me. I get her up, take her back into our
bedroom and dump her on top of my sleeping wife. I go
downstairs, make her up a bottle of milk, fix two cups of
tea and feed the cat. I get the baby dressed and give her
some breakfast. I make myself a bowl of porridge, then see
my wife out the door so she can catch the early train to
work. I clean the baby's face, which is covered in banana
and oats, get her out of her chair and spend fifteen minutes
reading her a pop-up book about a renegade farmer with a
talking tractor. While I do this, she methodically tears the
book to pieces. I make her some pasta with vegetables for
her lunch while she sits on the kitchen floor playing with,
and occasionally eating, some colourful dough. I pack the
pasta into a Tupperware box and stuff it in her change bag
along with an apple, a yoghurt, a small tub of raisins, five
clean nappies, some wet wipes, some nappy bags, a change
of clothes, an emergency bottle of Calpol, a couple of
cuddly monkeys and some cream for her arse. I put on her
jacket and shoes, put on my jacket and shoes, stick her
in her pushchair and wheel her out of the house. Then I
walk her to Sophie's house.

With my wife and me back at work, Sophie looks after
the baby three days a week. She is brilliant and warm and
diligent. She is all the things I should be. She also has an
array of toys far more vast, interesting and educational than
anything we've got in our house. For this reason, among
others, the baby loves going to Sophie's. Very occasionally, she may whimper slightly when I kiss her goodbye.
This makes me feel sad. But most days she reaches out to

Sophie with a big smile and ignores me when I kiss her goodbye. This makes me even sadder. Still, I reckon it's better for her to get used to being out and about with other people at an early age. If she hung around the house with me the whole time, she'd just end up like Sloth from *The Goonies*.

I go home. I get changed. I run six miles by the river. I come back, I shower, I shave, I pack my bag for work. And as I make my way towards my nearby office, I realise that it's only ten o' clock and I've already achieved something worthwhile today. I've worked, I've exercised, I've put a smile on my little girl's face. I've helped my wife get off to work and I've tidied the kitchen. I've even steamed some broccoli. I have been a family man. A dad. Not quite Teen Wolf's dad, admittedly. But a dad all the same.

I have less time to get all of my work done because the day is squeezed at either end by childcare responsibilities. There's no time to sit around looking at narcoleptic puppies falling off chairs on YouTube or e-mailing abuse to friends and former colleagues. I have to work with a level of concentration and intensity that is completely unfamiliar to me. I actually quite like it. I get stuff done. I hit deadlines and earn money. It's strangely exhilarating. And best of all, it helps to distract my mind from whatever ghastly predicament my mum is currently in.

In the afternoon I pick up the baby a few hours early and walk her down to the park. It's the first proper sunny day of the year. We walk along the side of the railway tracks with her jabbering inconsequential nonsense at me from the pushchair. I nod and say things like, 'Yes, quite right,' and 'Oh really? Well I never.' It strikes me that this is good conversational practice for when my wife and I are deranged geriatrics with nothing much left to say to each other.

We get to the park and head for the swings and slides. Of course, she's still a bit too young and useless to make proper use of the facilities, but she can sit on my lap while I muck about on the swing, clutching her tightly to my front and listening to her giggle with excitement. It's pretty quiet here. Just three or four people walking dogs in the grassy bit and a smattering of mums pissing about on the see-saws and roundabouts with their kids. I'm the only dad here. I make a big show of having fun with the baby. I encourage her to call me 'dada' as loudly as possible. I'm not trying to show off: in situations like this I just lapse into a form of mental anxiety that I like to call 'nonceanoia'. It's that feeling that dads get when they find themselves in kid-friendly environments like this. You're very often the only bloke around. You feel conspicuous. You feel shifty. You're not so much 'standing around and playing with your child' as 'lurking creepily near other people's children'. Hey, don't blame me for thinking this way – blame *The News of the World*; they're the ones who planted the seeds of paedo-obsessivism in the minds of me and the rest of the nation. I may know that I'm not a nonce, but I'm afraid I can't blame the other mums for giving me suspicious sideways glances. The papers have pumped our minds full of fear. The spectre of predatory paedos hangs over each and every one of us every time we leave the house. For all they know, my baby isn't a real baby at all but a prop fashioned from latex and beads to gain me access to this playground. This is why I'm trying my best to demonstrate loudly the fact that she can speak. 'Who am

I?' I shout gaily at her, loud enough for the other mums to hear. The baby just looks at me blankly, befuddled by my line of questioning.

'Who am I? Am I your dada? That's right! Say "dada"!' Still no response. My insistent tone is making me look even more suspicious and weird. The baby makes an un-usual quacking noise that sounds nothing like the word 'dada', then frowns and points urgently at the rocking horse on the other side of the playground. I pick her up and skip over to the horse in a manner that I hope demonstrates my authentic fatherly credentials.

It's one of those long, red horses with six or seven seats along it. I sit the baby on the front one and climb on the seat behind to hold her in place. I'm about to start rocking the contraption when I hear a voice from behind me saying, 'Room for a couple more?' It's a male voice. 'Must be a nonce,' I think to myself casually.

I don't look round. I hear the man's voice conversing with a small boy. I feel them climbing on the seats behind me. I half-turn around and say to the boy, 'Ready?' He nods and I use my feet to start gyrating the horse back and forth. The baby starts to giggle. The boy starts to cheer.

'Do the noise, granddad! Do the noise!' he says. And I hear the man start to make a clippety-clop noise.

I am impressed by the man's horse impersonation. It verges on the uncanny. 'It must be Johnny Morris,' I think. 'But I thought he was dead?' I turn around. It is not Johnny Morris. But I do recognise the face from somewhere. I narrow my eyes and stare at him. He keeps on doing the horsey noise, only slightly more nervously. Then I work it out.

'Mr Martin!' I exclaim.

'Yes,' he says, looking surprised and concerned.

'It's me! Sam! You remember! I was one of your pupils!'

He blinks back at me, trying to register a face he last saw twenty-two years ago, when he was my headmaster at primary school. I beam at him with a strange sense of excited anticipation. I want him to be impressed. I want him to feel proud. Proud that I have grown into a normal, fully limbed human adult with trousers and shoes and coherent words coming out of his mouth. Not some loser degenerate lying in the gutter completely naked but for a thick layer of grime and a dead pigeon strapped around his groin with string, throwing cider everywhere and shouting abuse at him for never giving him the chance to succeed when he was younger. Which, to be fair, is what he might reasonably have expected from me. I want to say, 'Look at me, Mr Martin! Aren't you proud I'm not drunk and mad! Here I am in the park at four in the afternoon, with my daughter, completely sober, being an adult! You helped make this impressive individual you see before you today! How do you feel?'

He eventually says, 'Oh yes, Stuart.'

'No. Sam. My name is Sam.'

'Of course. Sam. I remember.' He eyes me suspiciously. He glances at the baby. He's probably thinking I'm a nonce. Can't blame him for that, I suppose. Still, I'd better clear the matter up.

'This is my daughter!' I say, all pleased with myself. Then I turn to the baby and say, 'This is Mr Martin. He's the big boss man. You must do whatever he tells you!'

I laugh a little too loudly at my own joke. He chuckles awkwardly. I am excited to be exchanging matey yet suitably reverential banter with a man I used to call 'Sir'. It makes me feel grown up, confident and charming. Although I must say he doesn't seem quite up to speed with the whole knockabout nature of the chat. He looks a bit uncomfortable really. Maybe I should stop rocking the horse so vigorously.

'I never thought I'd see the day,' I laugh.

'Hmmm?' he says, not catching my drift.

'That I'd be rocking Mr Martin on a horse. Funny, innit?'

He laughs hesitantly. Perhaps he's beginning to think I'm mad. I suppose I am acting a little bit too over-enthusiastic about what is, after all, a fairly prosaic encounter in the park. Maybe I'm coming across as a bit needy. Maybe I am a bit needy. It's like I've suddenly made a new friend. I must admit I haven't acquired many new mates since I've been living around here. Dave is the only bloke I socialise with locally, but he doesn't count because I'd known him for years. It'd be nice to have a few blokes who I could bump into on my way down the shops and go for a spontaneous pint with. Or someone round the corner with whom I could arrange a Sunday afternoon game of three-and-in down the rec. Ideally, these friends would be of a similar age to me and in possession of hilarious personalities and glamorous yet unintimidating lifestyles. But Mr Martin will do for now.

'Who's this?' I say, looking at the two-year-old lad sat in front of him.

'This is my grandson, James,' he replies.

'Hello, James!' I say, ruffling the boy's hair chummily.

There's still something stiff about his manner. I'm not really sure we're at the stage of having pints or games of three-and-in with each other quite yet. I wonder what I'm doing wrong? Fatherhood seems to have deprived me of what few socialising skills I once possessed.

Mr Martin and James are getting off the horse. As a final throw of the dice I blurt out, 'Remember sports day?'

'Which sports day?' he asks.

'Erm. Any of them?' I say, desperately.

'Well, yes. I remember the sports days.'

'Good, weren't they?' I mumble.

'Yes,' he says with a touch of sympathy creeping into his voice now. 'Yes, they were good.'

There is an awkward silence. He fastens the buttons on James's coat.

'Anyway, nice to see you again, we must be off,' he says.

'Bye then,' I mutter. And then I watch as Mr Martin and James disappear out of the park gates.

The baby looks at me. I can detect a touch of patronising condolence in her eyes. It doesn't feel nice to have been mugged off in front of my own daughter like that. Especially not by my old headmaster. I thought that moment could have been more poetic. It should have verified my passage from youthful tyke to bona fide adult. I don't quite know what I expected from him. Maybe a manly bear hug. Or a short dizzy spell of excitement at the mere sight of my face. Or for him to have instantly confessed: 'I have followed your career closely, Sam Delaney, and I am impressed. I was a particular fan of your fleeting appearance on that documentary about the history of the C word.' Then he might have walked off thinking to himself, 'That one boy vindicates my entire teaching career.'

Who knows why he reacted like he did? Maybe he doesn't read the papers I write for. Maybe he doesn't have access to the obscure digital TV channels I sometimes appear on. Maybe he just gets nervous around former pupils and thinks they're going to head-butt him or something. Personally, I never had much of a problem with the bloke. He was firm but fair really. He also had an impressive way of clicking his fingers while pointing and shouting 'You boy!' during assembly when he spotted me acting the goat. It got to the stage where I acted the goat on purpose just to see his technique in action.

I text my mate Olly in Dubai, saying, 'I just saw Mr Martin.' He texts back immediately, asking, 'Did he do that finger-pointing thing where he clicks his fingers?' I tell him that he didn't. I regret not asking him to do it when I had the chance. I may never see Mr Martin again. And if I do, I get the sense he may avoid me. Olly texts me again.

'Where did you see him?'

'At the swings and slides,' I reply.

'Swing and slides?' Olly texts back. 'What are you? Some sort of nonce?'

I put the baby back in the pushchair and hastily wheel her home.

22

DICKHEAD

Steam hisses from cappuccino machines, and the scent of roasted coffee beans wafts through the air and up my nose. I briefly gag, then sip from my plastic cup of tap water. The baby slurps some babychino from her plastic spoon. My eyes dart across the day's newspaper headlines.

'Global Warming To "Drown Britain" by 2020, Warn Scientists.'

'Terror Threat Set To Intensify, Says Security Chief.'

'Iranian Nuclear Strike "Unavoidable", Claims Diplomat.'

'Mini-Me Beds Chanelle! He Was Like A Jack Russell On Heat, Says Source.'

This is Planet Earth in 2009. The world my daughter will grow up in. A world of environmental catastrophe, terrorism, nuclear war and reality TV stars having it off with dwarfs. A world of 'babychinos'. For the moment I feel safe laughing from the sidelines, assuming I'll be safely dead from natural causes by the time Britain sinks into the North Sea or the Iranians invent a rocket powerful enough to shoot their nukes at whitey. But what of the baby? She'll be reaching maturity just as all of these ugly issues really start to ripen. She'll be on the front line of a world where religious extremists blow up school buses on a daily basis and where one in every two people is a reality TV star willing to have sex not only with dwarfs but with animals and robots and bin bags and slabs of concrete, just to get their picture in the paper. Perhaps the reality TV stars will be having sex with the terrorists. Perhaps there will even be reality TV shows based on becoming a terrorist. *Make Me A Suicide Bomber*. Or even worse, *Bum Me Then Bomb Me!*, in which twelve wannabe Terror WAGs compete to get sodomised then blown up by a Basque separatist. One thing's for sure: the world is spiralling out of control fast. How could I have brought a child into this stinking grotesquery of evil? I am a bad man.

I look at my little angel sitting there, blissfully oblivious of the despicable future she is destined to grow up in, guzzling her babychino like she hasn't a care in the world. The idiot. I mean, there's more air than milk in that tiny cardboard cup. They still charged me a quid for it, mind you. I might just as well have blown in her face for thirty seconds for all the nutrition she's getting from it.

She sticks her nose in the cup, clamps her teeth around the rim, lifts her head up and spills the dregs of watery white liquid down her top. I'm not sure if she's got the wherewithal to survive the apocalypse that is gradually unfurling before her.

I feel a bit guilty and indulgent for not considering all this in the first place. When we decided to have a baby, all we thought about was ourselves. About whether we had enough money, enough space in the house, enough time on our hands and enough love in our hearts. But really, how relevant is that sort of stuff in the long term? The baby is only a baby for a few short months. Before long she'll be a proper human being with her own shit to deal with in the big wide world. By the time she's beginning to face up to the reality of a new life under the sea, I could be dead – having left her with what is likely to be a paltry inheritance and a head load of crappy life advice that will be of even less use to her than it was to me. What do I know about sub-aqua living? I can barely swim.

Shame really, innit?

I rummage through the rest of the paper in search of light relief. Ah, the family section, this ought to lift my spirits. Look, there's a picture of a friendly little tyke with his face painted like a tiger. Sweet.

'Parent Groups Raise Fears Over Toxic Face Paints,' reads the headline.

Bloody hell. Even the family section is intent on souring my mood.

'Salt And Your Baby's Kidneys: The Truth,' shouts another headline on the opposite page.

It gets worse.

'Are You Giving Your Baby Too Much Fluid?'

'How Ethical Are Your Wet Wipes?'

'Who Is Watching The Person Who's Watching Your Child?'

'Macrobiotic Babyfoods: Has The Bubble Burst?'

'How Do You Come To Terms With The Revelation That Your Mother Is A Murderer?'

I involuntarily answer each of the questions inside my head in quick-fire succession.

'Yes! No! Pass! No! I mean yes! I mean, I don't know. Just leave me alone!'

They give you a lot to think about in these newspapers, don't they? No wonder I usually stick to the sport. Some wanker in a rugby shirt nicked that section before I got here. I suppose I could have bought my own paper instead of relying on the coffee shop's complimentary copy, but, at a pound a babychino, I feel morally obliged to make the most of all of the facilities this place has to offer.

The family section is even more disconcerting than the proper news bit. At least I can pretend all that stuff that's going on in the Middle East or the North Pole or wherever doesn't really exist. None of it really affects me directly. I can just skim those stories, stroke my chin, look a little bit concerned and try to crib enough pertinent facts to look knowledgeable if it ever comes up in conversation with friends. Which it probably won't, seeing as I specifically seek out complacent and idiotic friends in order to avoid those sorts of conversation.

But this parental stuff is worrying. Or rather, it suggests there is stuff worth worrying about that I haven't ever bothered to worry about. Which is, in itself, quite worrying, if you see what I mean. Perhaps I should read the stories and make my own mind up? No, that would be ridiculous. There's no time. And I have no interest. My advice? If the baby's crying, give it a Milky Bar.

I look around the coffee shop on this fine Saturday morning. It's jam-packed with happy-looking, well-heeled families feeding their kids expensive milky foam and eating pastries. They haven't got a bleeding care in the world. Good luck to them. They are living in a Utopia where food and sanitation are plentiful and the worst real anxiety you ever experience is suddenly realising on the way into work that you forgot to leave any food out for the cat. We are living in a pampered, Western, conflict-free Nirvana. We have literally run out of things to worry about. But this has left a gaping void in the part of the human brain reserved for fear. It needs to be filled with something. So we invent stuff to shit ourselves about. (I sound like Michael Moore or Noam Chomsky or David Icke, don't I? But there is a crucial difference. Whereas they say these sorts of things because they are passionate believers in them, I say these sorts of things because I'm looking to justify my own lazy ignorance.)

It's probably the same deal with the real news too. None of it's as bad as it seems. I mean, my parents had to raise kids under the very real spectre of the Cold War and the possibility of full-blown nuclear Armageddon. It wasn't a case of 'Iran *may* have a bomb that they *may* one day work out how to let off'. It was more a case of 'Russia *really* have got *loads* of bombs that they are *really* going to fire at us any moment now'.

And as for the environment, they didn't even know about the environment back in the '70s. The word hadn't been invented yet. They were all breezing about doing mad anti-environmental stuff without even realising it was wrong. They'd have Tupperware parties where they all burned the Tupperware and giggled as they watched the poisonous fumes drift into the earth's atmosphere and slowly murder the ozone layer. They would get drunk and spray aerosols at the sun for kicks. Americans would blow up petrol stations on the 4th of July using government funding just to see the pretty colours. Millionaires would pay through the nose to chase polar bears around glaciers in four-wheel-drive gas-guzzlers, firing bullets at them made out of elephant tusks and dangerous chemicals. They were wantonly destroying the planet, and no one was even telling them to stop it.

These days we're still wantonly destroying the planet, but at least there are loads of people making us feel guilty about it. This guilt has even managed to get idiots like me separating their plastics from their glass in the recycling bins. And while it's likely that small acts like this won't make a blind bit of difference in the scheme of things, it's all a step in the right direction. By the time my daughter is grown up, the entire population of the world will be on board. Her generation will be raised to feel guilty about the environment every single second of every single day of their lives. Recycling stuff and remembering to switch off the TV at night will be second nature to them. Saving the planet will no longer be seen as the preserve of stinking hippies and peace freaks but of perfectly ordinary slobs like us. As a result, the planet will probably be saved by the time my daughter is eighteen. Long before Britain gets anywhere near sinking into the sea anyway.

I fold up the paper and put it back on the communal paper rack. Ah, that's better. I have been wholly convinced by my own garbled line of reasoning. Everything is right in the world, and no one has got anything to worry about – all thanks to my brilliant brain. The baby seems to sense this fact and screams with excitement, then tips what's left of my water over my lap. It looks like I've pissed myself. I don't care, not with the future looking this rosy.

The door opens, and in walks Dave pushing his little girl in a buggy. They come over. My daughter and his daughter eye each other suspiciously.

'You look like you've pissed yourself,' remarks Dave.

This is where Dave and I now meet on weekend afternoons. Not the pub. Not the rec for a game of three-and-in. Not even round one of our houses for a session on the Xbox. Here in a coffee shop, like a couple of big girls.

'What are you drinking?' I say, rising to my feet.

'I dunno, what are you drinking?' asks Dave.

'Tap water.'

'But it's a coffee shop,' he says nervously. 'Shouldn't we have a coffee?'

'Hey! They can't tell us what to drink! I hate coffee, and I've given up pretending otherwise.'

'You're right!' he says, visibly inspired by my rhetoric. 'I hate coffee too! It tastes like poison and makes me feel ill. Fuck them. Get me a tap water.'

'Anything for the littlun?'

'She'll have a babychino.'

That's what Dave and I are like these days. We are assertive. We will not just roll over and drink whichever hot beverages 'The Man' says we should drink. We drink our own beverages on our own terms. And sometimes they may not even be hot. Why? Because we're men, that's why. More than that: we are dads. We have grown into our roles. We have learned that you don't become that sort of bloke overnight. You can't force it. You can't make yourself become more decisive or sensible. You don't automatically start choosing to meet up at the coffee shop rather than the boozer. But it happens gradually, because time teaches you that doing these things just makes life easier. We don't even feel like we're sacrificing anything by being here sipping water instead of in the pub guzzling sambuca and gin. We choose to be here of our own free will. It just seems simpler and more pleasant not to be drunk in charge of the babies. It sounds weird, I know, but there it is.

We even look better. Fresher, more rested, less confused and red in the face. We have slowly harnessed our new lives as semi-responsible adults. Dave's eye no longer twitches. I am a bit balder than I was a year ago, but even that's not so bad: it makes me feel more daddish.

'We're having a second,' says Dave.

'A second what?' I ask.

'A second kid.'

'Brilliant,' I say. Actually, it comes out more like '*Brilliant?*' just to be on the safe side.

'Yeah,' he nods earnestly. 'It is brilliant.'

He pauses and pretends to be thinking serious thoughts.

'Becoming a dad is . . .'

'A journey?' I interrupt.

'Yeah. How did you know I was going to say that?'

'Because that's what you told me about eighteen months ago. About two months before you told me that becoming a dad ruins your life.'

'Yeah, well, I've gone back to thinking of it as a journey now.'

'What sort of a journey?'

'Well, it's got its ups and downs,' he says. 'There are moments where you think it's ruined your life. And other moments where you think it's the best thing ever.

And mostly moments where you think it's all right really and not half as much of a hassle as you thought it'd be.'

'I agree,' I say – because I do. 'So what made you decide to have a second?'

'Well, the missus wants to, and my attitude is "In for a penny, in for a pound". Know what I mean?'

'Fair dos,' I say. Then we drain our waters and stroll out of the coffee shop.

I've bought a chocolate brownie to share with the baby when we get home. I decide to text my mum to tell her about this. My mum is obsessed like a demented addict with baked goods of all forms. I use it as a way of tormenting her.

'I've got a chocolate brownie to have with my tea,' I write.

Just as I'm approaching my front door, my phone beeps with her response.

'Well, I'm round my cousin's house having a slice of date and walnut cake,' it reads. 'So up yours, you cunt! Xxx'

Suffice to say, my mum is better. The doctor managed to cut the cancerous growth out of her intestines without rupturing her spleen, damaging her bowels or killing her. He did a nice clean job of it, and she was out of the hozzy after four days. She didn't even have to have chemo or anything. In fact, it all culminated in such an implausibly happy outcome that, if it were the plot to a thriller, you'd be half-expecting a last-minute twist in which her spleen suddenly bursts out of her stomach at a family gathering and bounces round the room infecting the rest of us with a fatal form of cancer. Or something. But nothing like that happened. And I have put a ban on my brain thinking those sort of paranoid, pessimistic thoughts from now on.

I feel like I've learned to cherish the good times. When mum was ill, all I did was yearn for those moments when there was nothing serious to worry about. From now on I've resolved not to sully those carefree moments by inventing stupid, imaginary worries. Not just for my sake but for my daughter's too. She doesn't want to grow up with a father who's riddled with self-doubt and worry. Dads shouldn't spend their time fretting. They should accept themselves and get on with it. They should be pillars of certainty and calm. From this point forward that's the sort of man I'm going to be. Or at least, that's how I'm going to act.

Anyway, you can tell my mum's better by the way she's swearing and eating cake again. These are her two favourite pastimes. The idea of her cramming slices of home-baked date and walnut into her gob while calling me a cunt via text message reminds me how lucky I am to have her around.

That evening she has a party to celebrate the fact she didn't die. It's in a room above a boozer in Hammersmith. The evening sun shines brightly through the windows as friends and family start to gather. There's sandwiches, chicken legs, the lot. There's even a few quid behind the bar. My mum's insisted on playing songs from *Mamma Mia* on the pub stereo, but I suppose you can't have everything.

My older sister is there. That's right, the one they had adopted all those years ago. She ended up getting in touch about a year after my mum told me about her existence.

Her name's not Caroline any more; it's Annie. She's married with two kids of her own, and they're all part of the family. That was another thing that turned out suspiciously well. I assumed she'd turn out to be a drug addict or a thief or a killer or, I dunno, a racist or something. But no, she's lovely. You couldn't hope for a better big sister. Interestingly, despite having not grown up with us or been subject to the same cultural influences, she is very similar in personality to my brothers and me. Only, you know, kinder, smarter and less of a dick.

'Come on, everyone, let's have a toast! Mum hasn't got arse cancer any more!' shouts one of my brothers just as Abba's 'Gimme Gimme Gimme (A Man After Midnight)' has drawn to a close on the stereo. Everyone looks round at him, drunkenly swaying about with his plastic glass of champagne held aloft. See what I mean? Dick.

Mind you, he's a lovable dick. Which, when it comes down to it, is the best you can hope for in a relative. At least, it's the best I can hope for. A good honest bunch of lovable dicks: that's what all the people who surround me tonight are. I look around at them all: half-cut and swaying, talking bollocks, eating cake and generally feeling happy about Mum not being dead. I'm lucky to have them, I suppose. I think about the baby at home being looked after by a friend. And I hope that one day she'll grow up to think of me as a lovable dick. Maybe just lovable and not a dick at all. But either way is fine really. I hug my wife – about the only non-dick I know. And I say a little thanks in her ear for not minding that I can be such a dick sometimes. I don't think she hears me properly because she responds by saying, 'Quarter to nine, I think.' I kiss her and contemplate a future of more little babies, all of whom will hopefully see me as a lovable dick.

The next day I'm having lunch with my wife and daughter. I say lunch: it's only midday. But the days start earlier when you're a dad. You have elevenses at nine, lunch at twelve, dinner at six and sometimes even have breakfast before you go to bed at night. I am a bit hungover in a silly, slightly euphoric way. We are in one of those restaurants we avoided like the plague before we had a kid: it's packed with screaming children, the menu is made up entirely of things you can dip in ketchup and the tablecloths double as painting canvases.

A little girl of about three is giving her dad grief on the next table.

'I don't want this,' she grumbles, regarding her bowl of pasta with a disgusted sneer.

'But it's what you ordered, darling,' he says kindly.

'It looks funny.'

'It's just how you have it at home,' he pleads.

'No it's not. I want something else. I want chips,' she insists.

The dad looks at his wife. The wife shrugs in resignation. He calls the waiter over and orders a bowl of chips.

'That's what we've got ahead of us,' I tell my wife.

'Not if we nip that kind of thing in the bud early,' she says.

'Quite right,' I say, gazing sternly at our daughter, who is looking worryingly toddler-like these days. 'If this one gives me any of that crap, I won't stand for it.'

'Exactly,' my wife agrees. 'It's just a matter of telling her she eats what she's given or nothing at all.'

'Yeah!' I say, warming to the theme. 'You've got to lay it on the line. I'll tell her straight: "I am prepared to let you starve to death if necessary."'

My wife narrows her eyes in thought.

'I'm not sure that's the right way to put it,' she says.

'Of course it is!' I say. 'You need to show them that their destiny is in their own hands.'

'Is that out of *Spiderman*?' she asks.

'No!' I protest before realising it might be. 'Hang on, maybe. Either that or *Star Wars*. I'm not sure.'

She goes back to examining the menu. I go back to surveying the restaurant. The level of behaviour is nothing short of despicable. Worse than anything I've ever seen in a boozer or at the football. Kids are fighting and puking and weeing. It's like the last days of the Roman empire. The funny thing is, I find it strangely relaxing. These sorts of restaurant are the only places you can take your kid without fear of upsetting or disturbing anyone. Our daughter can cry and shout and lob chips across the room with gay abandon, and no one will bat an eyelid. For once I can sit back and let her wreak havoc from her high chair without giving a flying fuck.

Who knew I'd find so much happiness in a high-street burger chain? That's the thing about fatherhood: you discover a whole new set of ways to be happy. Plus, you get to pretty much keep all your old ways of being happy too. As long as you manage to get the balance right, you can effectively treble your daily fun quota. And by extension, make yourself at least four times happier in real terms. And that's not just my personal opinion: that is mathematical fact. I think you'll find my numbers add up.

Some people may deem this new life a sell-out, but how can I be a sell-out when I am enjoying the company of my family over a plate of microwaved onion rings while simultaneously sporting a pair of box-fresh, rare Nike Air Pegasus 89s? See, I'm getting the best of both worlds! I'm living the dream! In your face, rest of the world!

ACKNOWLEDGEMENTS

Huge thanks to everyone who helped me with this book: my agent Matthew Hamilton, my editor Bernard Dive, Rowan Yapp, who first approached me about the idea, and everyone else at John Murray including Roland Philipps, James Spackman, Shona Abhyankar, Mandi Jones, Polly Ho-Yen, Nikki Barrow, Caroline Westmore and Caroline Lotinga.

Thanks also to Mark Law and everyone at the *First Post* who first gave me a forum in which to harp on about the trivialities of my day-to-day existence.

Special mentions to Kevin Curtis for the film, Ian Prytherch for the needles and Andy Friedlander for the tea and biscuits.

I would also like to express my immense respect for the good people of Hungary, a beautiful land rich in noble culture and history. Since completing this book I have learned much of your proud people and the great contributions they have made to the human race.

Finally, I am massively grateful to everyone who helped Coco and I through our first year together, especially: Bren, Baz, Chris Payne, Peter Pallai, Maddy, Mopsy (you're too nice to possibly be mentioned anywhere else in this book), Coach Pete, Sophie Wright, Joseph, Frankie and Ella.

Biggest thanks of all, as always, to the love of my life, Anna.

SAM DELANEY

Sam Delaney is a writer and broadcaster whose journalism has appeared in the *Guardian* and the *Sunday Telegraph* and who has written and presented documentaries for the BBC and Channel Four. This is his second book. He lives in London with his wife and daughter.

WILL GRAYSON,
WILL GRAYSON

Other Books by John Green

LOOKING FOR ALASKA

AN ABUNDANCE OF KATHERINES

PAPER TOWNS

THE FAULT IN OUR STARS

Other Books by David Levithan

ARE WE THERE YET?

NICK AND NORAH'S INIFINITE PLAYLIST (*with Rachel Cohn*)

DASH & LILY'S BOOK OF DARES (*with Rachel Cohn*)

THE LOVER'S DICTIONARY: A NOVEL

EVERY YOU, EVERY ME (*with Jonathan Farmer*)

Reviews for *Will Grayson, Will Grayson*

"A BRILLIANT novel."   *— Seattle Times*

"A WINNING combination infused with wit,
sarcasm, and plenty of musical references."
                                        — Chicago Tribune

"A MOVING novel when it comes to the matters of
the heart."   *— San Diego Union Tribune*

"This novel has SERIOUS BUZZ."
                            — EntertainmentWeekly.com

"One of the best books of the year."   *— Bookpage*

"A HILARIOUS collaboration between SUPER-
STAR AUTHORS."   *— The Daily Beast*

"Original idea, well-written, humorous, touching ...
A GREAT READ."   *— OutSmart*

"John Green and David Levithan have an easy
familiarity."   *— The San Francisco Chronicle*

★ "[A] terrific high-energy tale of teen love, lust,
intrigue, anger, pain, and friendship."   *— Booklist*

★ "Complete with honest language, interesting
characters, and a heartfelt, gritty edge, this quirky
yet down-to-earth collaboration by two master YA
storytellers will keep readers turning pages."   *— SLJ*

★ "An intellectually existential, electrically ebullient
love story that brilliantly melds the ridiculous with the
realistic."   *— Kirkus Reviews*

"Funny, rude and original."
                            — New York Times Book Review

John Green (www.johngreenbooks.com) is an award-winning, *New York Times*–bestselling author whose many accolades include the Printz Medal, a Printz Honor and the Edgar Award. He has twice been a finalist for the LA Times Book Prize. With his brother, Hank, John is one half of the Vlogbrothers (youtube.com/vlogbrothers), one of the most popular online video projects in the world. You can join the millions who follow John on Twitter (@realjohngreen) and tumblr (fishingboatproceeds.tumblr.com). John lives with his family in Indianapolis, Indiana.

David Levithan (www.davidlevithan.com) is a *New York Times*–bestselling and award-winning author of many books for teens, including *Boy Meets Boy* and (with Rachel Cohn) *Nick and Norah's Infinite Playlist*. He is also an editorial director/VP at Scholastic, where he founded their Push imprint. David lives in New Jersey.

WILL GRAYSON, WILL GRAYSON

JOHN GREEN
DAVID LEVITHAN

PENGUIN BOOKS

PENGUIN BOOKS

Published by the Penguin Group
Penguin Books Ltd, 80 Strand, London WC2R 0RL, England
Penguin Group (USA) Inc., 375 Hudson Street, New York, New York 10014, USA
Penguin Group (Canada), 90 Eglinton Avenue East, Suite 700, Toronto, Ontario,
Canada M4P 2Y3 (a division of Pearson Penguin Canada Inc.)
Penguin Ireland, 25 St Stephen's Green, Dublin 2, Ireland (a division of Penguin Books Ltd)
Penguin Group (Australia), 707 Collins Street, Melbourne, Victoria 3008, Australia
(a division of Pearson Australia Group Pty Ltd)
Penguin Books India Pvt Ltd, 11 Community Centre, Panchsheel Park,
New Delhi – 110 017, India
Penguin Group (NZ), 67 Apollo Drive, Rosedale, Auckland 0632, New Zealand
(a division of Pearson New Zealand Ltd)
Penguin Books (South Africa) (Pty) Ltd, Block D, Rosebank Office Park,
181 Jan Smuts Avenue, Parktown North, Gauteng 2193, South Africa

Penguin Books Ltd, Registered Offices: 80 Strand, London WC2R 0RL, England

www.penguin.com

First published in the USA by Dutton Books, a member of Penguin Group (USA) Inc., 2010
This edition published in Great Britain by Penguin Books Ltd 2013
045

Set in 11.4/15.44pt Carre Noir
Printed in Great Britain by Clays Ltd, Elcograf S.p.A.

British Library Cataloguing in Publication Data
A CIP catalogue record for this book is available from the British Library

ISBN: 978-0-141-34611-3

www.greenpenguin.co.uk

MIX
Paper from
responsible sources
FSC   FSC™ C018179
www.fsc.org

Penguin Books is committed to a sustainable
future for our business, our readers and our planet.
This book is made from Forest Stewardship
Council™ certified paper.

To David Leventhal
(for being so close)
– DL

To Tobias Huisman
–JG

chapter one

When I was little, my dad used to tell me, "Will, you can pick your friends, and you can pick your nose, but you can't pick your friend's nose." This seemed like a reasonably astute observation to me when I was eight, but it turns out to be incorrect on a few levels. To begin with, you cannot possibly pick your friends, or else I never would have ended up with Tiny Cooper.

Tiny Cooper is not the world's gayest person, and he is not the world's largest person, but I believe he may be the world's largest person who is really, really gay, and also the world's gayest person who is really, really large. Tiny has been my best friend since fifth grade, except for all last semester, when he was busy discovering the sheer scope of his own gayness, and I was busy having an actual honest-to-God Group of Friends for the first time in my life, who ended up Never Talking to Me Again due to two slight transgressions:

1. After some school-board member got all upset about gays in the locker room, I defended Tiny Cooper's right to be both gigantic (and, therefore,

the best member of our shitty football team's offen- sive line) and gay in a letter to the school newspaper that I, stupidly, signed.

2. This guy in the Group of Friends named Clint was talking about the letter at lunch, and in the pro- cess of talking about it, he called me a bitchsquealer, and I didn't know what a bitchsquealer was, so I was like, "What do you mean?" And then he called me a bitchsquealer again, at which point I told Clint to fuck off and then took my tray and left.

Which I guess means that technically *I* left the Group of Friends, although it felt the other way around. Honestly, none of them ever seemed to like me, but they were *around*, which isn't nothing. And now they aren't around, leaving me utterly bereft of social peers.

Unless you count Tiny, that is. Which I suppose I must.

Andbutso a few weeks after we get back from Christmas break our junior year, I'm sitting in my Assigned Seat in precalc when Tiny waltzes in wearing his jersey tucked into his chinos, even though football season is long over. Every day, Tiny miraculously manages to wedge himself into the chair-desk beside mine in precalc, and every day, I am amazed he can do it.

So Tiny squeezes into his chair, I am duly amazed, and then he turns to me and he whispers really loudly because secretly he wants other people to hear, "I'm in *love*." I roll my eyes, because he falls in love every hour on the hour with some poor new boy. They all look the same: skinny and sweaty and tan, the last an abomination, because all February tans in Chicago are fake, and boys who fake tan—I don't care whether they're gay—are ridiculous.

"You're so cynical," Tiny says, waving his hand at me.

"I'm not cynical, Tiny," I answer. "I'm practical."

"You're a robot," he says. Tiny thinks that I am incapable of what humans call emotion because I have not cried since my seventh birthday, when I saw the movie *All Dogs Go to Heaven*. I suppose I should have known from the title that it wouldn't end merrily, but in my defense, I was seven. Anyway, I haven't cried since then. I don't really understand the *point* of crying. Also, I feel that crying is almost—like, aside from deaths of relatives or whatever—totally avoidable if you follow two very simple rules: 1. Don't care too much. 2. Shut up. Everything unfortunate that has ever happened to me has stemmed from failure to follow one of the rules.

"I know love is real because I *feel* it," Tiny says.

Apparently, class has started without our knowing, because Mr. Applebaum, who is ostensibly teaching us precalculus but is mostly teaching me that pain and suffering must be endured stoically, says, "You feel what, Tiny?"

"Love!" says Tiny. "I feel love." And everyone turns around and either laughs or groans at Tiny, and because I'm sitting next to him and he's my best and only friend, they're laughing and groaning at me, too, which is precisely why I would not choose Tiny Cooper as my friend. He draws too much attention. Also, he has a pathological inability to follow either of my two rules. And so he waltzes around, caring too much and ceaselessly talking, and then he's baffled when the world craps on him. And, of course, due to sheer proximity, this means the world craps on me, too.

After class, I'm staring into my locker, wondering how I managed to leave *The Scarlet Letter* at home, when Tiny comes up with his Gay-Straight Alliance friends Gary (who is gay) and Jane (who may or may not be—I've never asked), and Tiny says to me, "Apparently, everyone thinks I professed my love for you in precalc. Me in love with Will Grayson. Isn't that the silliest crap you ever heard?"

"Great," I say.

"People are just such idiots," Tiny says. "As if there's something wrong with being in love."

Gary groans then. If you could pick your friends, I'd consider Gary. Tiny got close with Gary and Jane and Gary's boyfriend, Nick, when he joined the GSA during my tenure as a member of the Group of Friends. I barely know Gary, since I've only been hanging around Tiny again for about two weeks, but he seems like the normalest person Tiny has ever befriended.

"There's a difference," Gary points out, "between being in love and announcing it in precalc." Tiny starts to talk and Gary cuts him off. "I mean, don't get me wrong. You have every right to love Zach."

"Billy," says Tiny.

"Wait, what happened to Zach?" I ask, because I could have sworn Tiny was in love with a Zach during precalc. But forty-seven minutes have passed since his proclamation, so maybe he's changed gears. Tiny has had about 3,900 boyfriends—half of them Internet-only.

Gary, who seems as flummoxed by the emergence of Billy as I am, leans against the lockers and bangs his head softly against the steel. "Tiny, you being a makeout whore is *so* not good for the cause."

I look way up at Tiny and say, "Can we quell the rumors of our love? It hurts my chances with the ladies."

"Calling them 'the ladies' doesn't help either," Jane tells me.

Tiny laughs. "But seriously," I tell him, "I always catch shit about it." Tiny looks at me seriously for once and nods a little.

"Although for the record," Gary says, "you could do worse than Will Grayson."

"And he has," I note.

Tiny spins in a balletic pirouette out into the middle of the hallway and, laughing, shouts, "Dear World, I am not hot for Will Grayson. But world, there's something else you should know about Will Grayson." And then he begins to sing, a Broadway baritone as big as his waist, "I can't live without him!"

People laugh and whoop and clap as Tiny continues the serenade while I walk off to English. It's a long walk, and it only gets longer when someone stops you and asks how it feels to be sodomized by Tiny Cooper, and how you find Tiny Cooper's "gay little pencil prick" behind his fat belly. I respond the way I always do: by looking down and walking straight and fast. I know they're kidding. I know part of knowing someone is being mean to them or whatever. Tiny always has some brilliant thing to say back, like, "For someone who theoretically doesn't want me, you sure spend a lot of time thinking and talking about my penis." Maybe that works for Tiny, but it never works for me. Shutting up works. Following the rules works. So I shut up, and I don't care, and I keep walking, and soon it's over.

The last time I said anything of note was the time I wrote the fricking letter to the editor about fricking Tiny Cooper and his fricking right to be a fricking star on our horrible football team. I don't regret writing the letter in the least, but I regret signing it. Signing it was a clear violation of the rule about shutting up, and look where it got me: alone on a Tuesday afternoon, staring at my black Chuck Taylors.

That night, not long after I order pizza for me and my parents, who are—as always—late at the hospital, Tiny Cooper calls me and, real quiet and fast, he blurts out, "Neutral Milk Hotel is supposedly playing a reunion show at the Hideout and it's totally not advertised and no one even knows about it and holy shit, Grayson, holy shit!"

"Holy shit!" I shout. One thing you can say for Tiny: whenever something awesome happens, Tiny is always the first to hear.

Now, I am not generally given over to excitement, but Neutral Milk Hotel sort of changed my life. They released this absolutely fantastic album called *In the Aeroplane Over the Sea* in 1998 and haven't been heard from since, purportedly because their lead singer lives in a cave in New Zealand. But anyway, he's a genius. "When?"

"Dunno. I just heard. I'm gonna call Jane, too. She likes them almost as much as you do. Okay, so now. Now. Let's go to the Hideout now."

"I'm literally on my way," I answer, opening the door to the garage.

I call my mom from the car. I tell her Neutral Milk Hotel is playing at the Hideout and she says, "Who? What? You're hiding out?" And then I hum a few bars of one of their songs and Mom says, "Oh, I know that song. It's on the mix you made me," and I say, "Right," and she says, "Well you have to be back by eleven," and I say, "Mom this is a historical event. History doesn't have a curfew," and she says, "Back by eleven," and I say, "Fine. Jesus," and then she has to go cut cancer out of someone.

Tiny Cooper lives in a mansion with the world's richest parents. I don't think either of his parents have jobs, but they are so disgustingly rich that Tiny Cooper doesn't even live *in* the mansion; he lives in the mansion's *coach house*, all by himself. He has three bedrooms in that motherfucker and a fridge that always has beer in it and his parents never bother him, and so we can sit there all day and play video game football and drink Miller Lite, except in point of fact Tiny hates video games and I hate drinking beer, so mostly all we ever do is play darts (he has a dartboard) and listen to music and talk and study. I've just started to say the *T* in Tiny when he comes running out of his room, one black leather loafer on and the other in his hand, shouting, "Go, Grayson, go go."

And everything goes perfectly on the way there. Traffic's not too bad on Sheridan, and I'm cornering the car like it's the Indy 500, and we're listening to my favorite NMH song, "Holland, 1945," and then onto Lake Shore Drive, the waves of Lake Michigan crashing against the boulders by the Drive, the windows cracked to get the car to defrost, the dirty, bracing, cold air rushing in, and I love the way Chicago smells—Chicago is brackish lake water and soot and sweat and grease and I love it, and I love this song, and Tiny's saying *I love this song*, and he's got the visor down so he can muss up his hair a little more expertly. That gets me to thinking that Neutral Milk Hotel is going to *see me* just as surely as I'm going to see them, so I give myself a once-over in the rearview. My face seems too square and my eyes too big, like I'm perpetually surprised, but there's nothing wrong with me that I can fix.

The Hideout is a dive bar made of wooden planks that's nestled between a factory and some Department of Transportation building. There's nothing swank about it, but there's a line out the door even though it's only seven. So I huddle in line for a while with Tiny until Gary and Possibly Gay Jane show up.

Jane's wearing a hand-scrawled Neutral Milk Hotel v-neck T-shirt under her open coat. Jane showed up in Tiny's life around the time I dropped out of it, so we don't really know each other. Still, I'd say she's currently about my fourth-best friend, and apparently she has good taste in music.

Waiting outside the Hideout in the face-scrunching cold, she says hi without looking at me, and I say hi back, and then she says, "This band is so completely brilliant," and I say, "I know."

This marks possibly the longest conversation I've ever had with Jane. I kick at the gravelly dirt a little and watch a miniature dust cloud encircle my foot and then I tell Jane how much I like "Holland, 1945," and she says, "I like their less accessible stuff. The polyphonic, noisy stuff." I just nod, in hopes that it appears I know what *polyphonic* means.

One thing about Tiny Cooper is that you can't whisper in his ear, even if you're reasonably tall like myself, because the motherfucker is six six, and so you have to tap his giant shoulder and then sort of motion with your head that you'd like to whisper into his ear, and then he leans down and you say, "Hey, is Jane the gay part of the Gay-Straight Alliance or the straight part?"

And Tiny leans down to my ear and whispers back, "Dunno. I think she had a boyfriend freshman year." I point out that Tiny Cooper had about 11,542 girlfriends freshman year, and then Tiny punches me in the arm in a way that he thinks is playful but actually causes permanent nerve damage.

Gary is rubbing Jane's arms up and down to keep her warm when *finally* the line starts to move. Then about five seconds later, we see this kid looking heartbroken, and he's precisely the kind of small-blond-tan guy Tiny Cooper would like, and so Tiny says, "What's wrong?" And then the kid answers, "It's over twenty-one only."

"You," I tell Tiny, stammering. "You *bitchsquealer*." I still don't know what it means, but it seems appropriate.

Tiny Cooper purses his lips and furrows his brow. He turns to Jane. "You got a fake ID?" Jane nods. Gary pipes up, "Me too," and I'm tensing my fists, my jaw locked, and I just want to scream, but instead I say, "Whatever, I'm going home," because *I* don't have a fake ID.

But then Tiny says real fast and real quiet, "Gary, hit me as hard as you can in the face when I'm showing my ID, and then, Grayson, you just walk behind me like you belong in the joint," and then no one says anything for a while, until Gary says, too loud, "Um, I don't really know how to *hit*." We're getting close to the bouncer, who has a large tattoo on his bald head, so Tiny just mumbles, "Yes you do. Just hit me hard."

I lag back a little, watching. Jane gives her ID to the bouncer. He shines a flashlight on it, glances up at her, and hands it back. Then it's Tiny's turn. I take a series of very quick, short breaths, because I read once that people with a lot of oxygen in their blood look calmer, and then I watch as Gary gets on his tiptoes and rears his arm back and wallops Tiny in the right eye. Tiny's head jerks back, and Gary screams, "Oh my God, *ow ow*, shit my hand," and the bouncer jumps up to grab Gary, and then Tiny Cooper turns his body to block the bouncer's view of me, and as Tiny turns, I walk into the bar like Tiny Cooper is my re-volving door.

Once inside, I look back and see the bouncer holding Gary by the shoulders, and Gary grimacing while staring at his hand. Then Tiny puts a hand on the bouncer and says, "Dude, we were just fucking around. Good one though, Dwight." It takes me a minute to figure out that Gary is Dwight. Or Dwight is Gary.

The bouncer says, "He fucking hit you in the eye," and

then Tiny says, "He owed me one," and then Tiny explains to the bouncer that both he and Gary/Dwight are members of the DePaul University football team, and that earlier in the weight room Tiny had spotted poorly or something. The bouncer says he played O-Line in high school, and then suddenly they're having a nice little chat while the bouncer glances at Gary's extrarordinarily fake ID, and then we are all four of us inside the Hideout, alone with Neutral Milk Hotel and a hundred strangers.

The people-sea surrounding the bar parts and Tiny gets a couple of beers and offers me one. I decline. "Why Dwight?" I ask. And Tiny says, "On his ID, he's Dwight David Eisenhower IV." And I say, "Where the frak did everyone get a fake ID anyway?" and then Tiny says, "There are places." I resolve to get one.

I say, "Actually, I will have a beer," mostly because I want something in my hand. Tiny hands me the one he's already started in on, and then I make my way up close to the stage without Tiny and without Gary and without Possibly Gay Jane. It's just me and the stage, which is only raised up about two feet in this joint, so if the lead singer of Neutral Milk Hotel is particularly short—like if he is three feet ten inches tall—I will soon be looking him straight in the eye. Other people move up to the stage, and soon the place is packed. I've been here before for all-ages shows, but it's never been like this—the beer that I haven't sipped and don't intend to sweating in my hand, the well-pierced, tattooed strangers all around me. Every last soul in the Hideout right now is cooler than anyone in the Group of Friends. These people don't think there's anything wrong with me—they don't even *notice* me. They assume I am one of them, which feels like the very summit of my high school career. Here I am, standing on an over-twenty-one night at the best bar in America's second city, getting ready to be among a couple hundred people who see the reunion show of the greatest no-name band of the last decade.

These four guys come out onstage, and while they don't bear a *striking* resemblance to the members of Neutral Milk Hotel, I tell myself that, whatever, I've only seen pictures on the web. But then they start playing. I'm not quite sure how to describe this band's music, except to say that it sounds like a hundred thousand weasels being dropped into a boiling ocean. And then the guy starts singing:

> *She used to love me, yeah*
> *But now she hates*
> *She used to screw me, bro*
> *But now she dates*
> *Other guys*
> *Other guys*

Barring a prefrontal lobotomy, there's absolutely no way that the lead singer of Neutral Milk Hotel would ever *think*, let alone *write*, let alone *sing*, such lyrics. And then I realize: I have waited outside in the cold gray-lit car-exhausted frigidity and caused the possible broken bones in Gary's hand to hear a band that is, manifestly, *not* Neutral Milk Hotel. And although he is nowhere amid the crowd of hushed and stunned NMH fans surrounding me, I immediately shout, "Damn you, Tiny Cooper!"

At the end of the song, my suspicions are confirmed when the lead singer says, to a reception of absolute silence, "Thank you! Thanks very much. NMH couldn't make it, but we're Ashland Avenue, and we're here to rock!" *No*, I think. *You're Ashland Avenue and you're here to suck.* Someone taps me on the shoulder then and I turn around and find myself staring at this unspeakably hot twenty-something girl with a labret piercing, flaming red hair, and boots up her calves. She says, askingly, "We thought Neutral Milk Hotel was playing?" and I look down and say, "Me—" I stammer for a second, and then say "too. I'm here for them, too."

The girl leans into my ear to shout above the atonal arrhythmic affront to decency that is Ashland Avenue. "Ashland Avenue is no Neutral Milk Hotel."

Something about the fullness of the room, or the strangeness of the stranger, has made me talkative, and I shout back, "Ashland Avenue is what they play to terrorists to make them talk." The girl smiles, and it's only now that I realize that she's conscious of the age difference. She asks me where I'm in school, and I say "Evanston," and she says, "*High* school?" And I say, "Yeah but don't tell the bartender," and she says, "I feel like a real pervert right now," and I say, "Why?" and she just laughs. I know the girl isn't really into me, but I still feel marginally pimping.

And then this huge hand settles on my shoulder, and I look down and see the middle school graduation ring he's worn on his pinkie ever since eighth grade and know immediately that it's Tiny. And to think, some idiots claim that the gays have fashion sense.

I turn around and Tiny Cooper is crying huge tears. One of Tiny Cooper's tears could drown a kitten. And I mouth

WHAT'S WRONG because Ashland Avenue is sucking too loudly for him to hear me, and Tiny Cooper just hands me his phone and walks away. It's showing me Tiny's Facebook feed, zoomed in on a status update.

Zach is like the more i think about it the more i think y ruin a gr8 frendship? i still think tiny's awesum tho.

I push my way through a couple people to Tiny, and I pull down his shoulder and scream into his ear, "THAT'S PRETTY FUCKING BAD," and Tiny shouts back, "I GOT DUMPED BY STATUS UPDATE," and I answer, "YEAH, I NOTICED. I MEAN, HE COULD HAVE AT LEAST TEXTED. OR E-MAILED. OR SENT A PASSENGER PIGEON."

"WHAT AM I GOING TO *DO*?" Tiny shouts in my ear, and I want to say, "Hopefully, go find a guy who knows there is no u in *awesome*," but I just shrug my shoulders and pat him firmly on the back, and guide him away from Ashland Avenue and toward the bar.

Which, as it turns out, is something of a mistake. Just before we get to the bar, I see Possibly Gay Jane hovering by a tall table. She tells me Gary has left in disgust. "It was a publicity ploy by Ashland Avenue, apparently," she says.

I say, "But no NMH fan would *ever* listen to this drivel."

Then Jane looks up at me all pouty and big-eyed and says, "My brother is the guitarist."

I feel like a total asshole and say, "Oh, sorry, dude."

And she says, "Christ, I'm kidding. If he were, I'd disown him." At some point during our four-second conversation I have managed to completely lose Tiny, which is no easy task, so I tell Jane about Tiny's great Facebook wall of dumpage, and she is still laughing when Tiny appears at our table with a round tray holding six shot glasses full of a greenish liquid. "I don't really drink," I remind Tiny, and he nods. He pushes a shot toward Jane, and Jane just shakes her head.

Tiny takes a shot, grimaces, and exhales. "Tastes like Satan's fire cock," Tiny says, and then pushes another shot in my direction. "Sounds delightful," I say, "but I'll pass."

"How can he just," Tiny yells, and then he takes a shot, "dump me," and another shot, "on his STATUS after I say I LOVE him," and another. "What is the goddamned world coming to?" Another. "I really do, Grayson. I know you think I'm full of shit, but I knew I loved him the moment we kissed. Goddamn it. What am I going to *do*?" And then he stifles a sob with the last shot.

Jane tugs on my shirtsleeve and leans in to me. I can feel her breath warm against my neck, and she says, "We're going to have a big frickin' problem when he starts feeling those shots," and I decide that Jane is right, and anyway, Ashland Avenue is terrible, so we need to leave the Hideout posthaste.

I turn to tell Tiny it's time to go, but he has disappeared. I glance back at Jane, who's looking toward the bar with a look of profound concern on her face. Shortly thereafter, Tiny Cooper returns. Only two shots this time, thank God.

"Drink with me," he says, and I shake my head, but then Jane pokes me in the back, and I realize that I have to take a bullet for Tiny. I dig into my pocket and hand Jane my car keys. The only sure way to prevent him from drinking the rest of the plutonium-green booze is to down one myself. So I grab the shot glass and Tiny says, "Aw, fuck him, anyway, Grayson. Fuck everybody," and I say, "I'll drink to that," and I do, and then it hits my tongue and it's like a burning Molotov cocktail—glass and all. I involuntarily spit the entire shot out onto Tiny Cooper's shirt.

"A monochrome Jackson Pollock," Jane says, and then tells Tiny, "We gotta bolt. This band is like a root canal *sans* painkiller."

Jane and I walk out together, figuring (correctly, as it turns out) that Tiny, wearing my shot of nuclear fallout, will follow us. Since I've failed at drinking both the alcoholic beverages Tiny bought me, Jane tosses the keys back to me in a high arc. I grab them and get behind the wheel after Jane climbs into the back. Tiny tumbles into the passenger seat. I start the car, and my date with massive aural disappointment comes to an end. But I hardly think about it on the way home because Tiny keeps going on about Zach. That's the thing about Tiny: his problems are so huge that yours can hide behind them.

"How can you just be so *wrong* about something?" Tiny is asking over the noisy screechiness of Jane's favorite (and my least favorite) NMH song. I'm cruising up Lake Shore and can hear Jane singing along in the back, a little off-key but closer than I'd be if I sang in front of people, which I don't, due to the Shutting Up Rule. And Tiny is saying, "If you can't trust your gut then what can you trust?" And I say, "You can trust that caring, as a rule, ends poorly," which is true. Caring doesn't sometimes lead to misery. It always does.

"My *heart* is broken," Tiny says, as if the thing has never happened before to him, as if it has never happened before to anyone. And maybe that's the problem: maybe each new breakup feels so radically new to Tiny that, in some way, it *hasn't* happened before. "And Yaw naht helping," he adds, which is when I notice he's slurring his words. Ten minutes from his house if we don't catch traffic, and then straight to bed.

But I can't drive as fast as Tiny can deteriorate. By the time I exit Lake Shore—six minutes to go—he's slurring his words *and* bawling, going on and on about Facebook and the death of polite society and whatever. Jane's got her hands, with fingernails painted black, kneading Tiny's elephantine shoulders, but he can't seem to stop crying, and I'm missing all the lights as Sheridan slowly unwinds before us, and the snot and tears mix until Tiny's T-shirt is just a wet mess. "How far?" Jane asks, and I say, "He lives off Central," and she says, "Jesus. Stay calm, Tiny. You just need to go to sleep, baby. Tomorrow makes everything a little better."

Finally, I turn into the alley and steer around the potholes until we get behind Tiny's coach house. I jump out of the car and push my seat forward so Jane can get out behind me. Then we walk around to the passenger seat. Jane opens the door, reaches across Tiny, manages through a miracle of dexterity to unfasten his seat belt, and then says, "All right, Tiny. Time for bed," and Tiny says, "I'm a fool," and then unleashes a sob that probably registers on the Richter scale in Kansas. But he gets up and weaves toward his back door. I follow, just to make sure he gets to bed all right, which turns out to be a good idea, because he doesn't get to bed all right.

Instead, about three steps into the living room, he stops dead in his tracks. He turns around and stares at me, his eyes squinting as if he's never seen me before and can't figure out why I'm in his house. Then he takes off his shirt. He's still looking at me quizzically when, sounding stone sober, he says, "Grayson, something needs to happen," and I say, "Huh?" And Tiny says, "Because otherwise what if we just end up like everybody at the Hideout?" And I'm about to say *huh* again, because those people were far cooler than our classmates and also far cooler than us, but then I know what he means. He means, What if we become grown-ups waiting for a band that's never coming back? I notice Tiny looking blankly at me, swaying back and forth like a skyscraper in the wind. And then he falls facefirst.

"Oh boy," Jane says behind me, and only then do I realize she's here. Tiny, his face buried in carpet, has taken to crying again. I look at Jane for a long time and a slow smile creeps over her face. Her whole face changes when she smiles—this eyebrow-lifting, perfect-teeth-showing, eye-crinkling smile I've either never seen or never noticed. She becomes pretty so suddenly that it's almost like a magic trick—but it's not like I want her or anything. Not to sound like a jerk, but Jane isn't really my type. Her hair's kinda disastrously curly and she mostly hangs out with guys. My type's a little girlier. And honestly, I don't even like my type of girl that much, let alone other types. Not that I'm asexual—I just find Romance Drama unbearable.

"Let's get him in bed," she says finally. "Can't have his parents find this in the morning."

I kneel down and tell Tiny to get up, but he just keeps crying and crying, so finally Jane and I get on his left side and roll him over onto his back. I step over him, and then reach down, getting a good grip under his armpit. Jane mimics me on his other side.

"One," says Jane, and I say, "Two," and she says, "Three," and grunts. But nothing happens. Jane is small—I can see her upper arm narrow as she flexes her muscles. And I can't lift my half of Tiny either, so we resolve to leave him there. By the time Jane places a blanket on top of Tiny and a pillow beneath his head, he's snoring.

We're about to leave when all of Tiny's snotting finally catches up with him, and he begins to make these hideous noises that sound like snoring, except more sinister, and also more wet. I lean down to his face and see that he's inhaling and exhaling these disgusting bubbly strands of snot from the last throes of his cryathon. There's so much of the stuff that I worry he'll choke.

"Tiny," I say. "You gotta get the snot outta your nose, man," but he doesn't stir. So I get down right by his eardrum and shout, "Tiny!" Nothing. Then Jane smacks him across the face, really rather hard. Nada. Just the awful, drowning-in-snot snoring.

And that is when I realize that Tiny Cooper cannot pick his nose, countering the second part of my dad's theorem. And shortly thereafter, with Jane looking on, I disprove the theorem entirely when I reach down and clear Tiny's airways of snot. In short: I cannot pick my friend; he cannot pick his nose; and I can—nay, I *must*—pick it for him.

chapter two

i am constantly torn between killing myself and killing everyone around me.

those seem to be the two choices. everything else is just killing time.

right now i'm walking through the kitchen to get to the back door.

mom: have some breakfast.

i do not eat breakfast. i never eat breakfast. i haven't eaten breakfast since i was able to walk out the back door without eating breakfast first.

mom: where are you going?

school, mom. you should try it some time.

mom: don't let your hair fall in your face like that — i can't see your eyes.

but you see, mom, that's *the whole fucking point*.

i feel bad for her — i do. a damn shame, really, that i had to have a mother. it can't be easy having me for a son. nothing can prepare someone for that kind of disappointment.

me: bye

i do not say 'good-bye.' i believe that's one of the bullshittiest words ever invented. it's not like you're given the choice to say 'bad-bye' or 'awful-bye' or 'couldn't-care-less-about-you-bye.' every time you leave, it's supposed to be a good one. well, i don't believe in that. i believe *against* that.

mom: have a good d—

the door kinda closes in the middle of her sentence, but it's not like i can't guess where it's going. she used to say 'see you!' until one morning i was so sick of it i told her, 'no, you don't.'

she tries, and that's what makes it so pathetic. i just want to say, 'i feel sorry for you, really i do.' but that might start a conversation, and a conversation might start a fight, and then i'd feel so guilty i might have to move away to portland or something.

i need coffee.

every morning i pray that the school bus will crash and we'll all die in a fiery wreck. then my mom will be able to sue the school bus company for never making school buses with seat belts, and she'll be able to get more money for my tragic death than i would've ever made in my tragic life. unless the lawyers from the school bus company can prove to the jury that i was guaranteed to be a fuckup. then they'd get away with buying my mom a used ford fiesta and calling it even.

maura isn't exactly waiting for me before school, but i know, and she knows i'll look for her where she is. we usually fall back on that so we can smirk at each other or something before we're marched off. it's like those people who become friends in prison even though they would never really talk to each other if they weren't in prison. that's what maura and i are like, i think.

me: give me some coffee.
maura: get your own fucking coffee.

then she hands me her XXL dunkin donuts crappaccino and i treat it like it's a big gulp. if i could afford my own coffee i swear i'd get it, but the way i see it is: her bladder isn't thinking i'm an asshole even if the rest of her organs do. it's been like this with me and maura for as long as I can remember, which is about a year. i guess i've known her a little longer than that, but maybe not. at some point last year, her gloom met my doom and she thought it was a good match. i'm not so sure, but at least i get coffee out of it.

derek and simon are coming over now, which is good because it's going to save me some time at lunch.

me: give me your math homework.
simon: sure. here.

what a friend.

the first bell rings. like all the bells in our fine institution of lower learning, it's not a bell at all, it's a long beep, like you're about to leave a voicemail saying you're having the suckiest day ever. and nobody's ever going to listen to it.

i have no idea why anyone would want to become a teacher. i mean, you have to spend the day with a group of kids who either hate your guts or are kissing up to you to get a good grade. that has to get to you after a while, being surrounded by people who will never like you for any real reason. i'd feel bad for them if they weren't such sadists and losers. with the sadists, it's all about the power and the control. they teach so they can have an official reason to dominate other people. and the losers make up pretty much all the other teachers, from the ones who are too incompetent to do anything else to the ones who want to be their students' best friends because they never had friends when they were in high school. and there are the ones who honestly think we're going to remember a thing they say to us after final exams are over. right.

every now and then you get a teacher like mrs. grover, who's a sadistic loser. i mean, it can't be easy being a french teacher, because nobody really needs to know how to speak french anymore. and while she kisses the honors kids' *derrieres*, with standard kids she resents the fact that we're taking up her time. so she responds by giving us quizzes every

23

day and giving us gay projects like 'design your own ride for euro disney' and then acting all surprised when i'm like 'yeah, my ride for euro disney is minnie using a baguette as a dildo to have some fun with mickey.' since i don't have any idea how to say 'dildo' in french (*dildot?*), i just say 'dildo' and she pretends to have no idea what i'm talking about and says that minnie and mickey eating baguettes isn't a ride. no doubt she gives me a check-minus for the day. i know i'm supposed to care, but really it's hard to imagine something i could care less about than my grade in french.

the only worthwhile thing i do all period — all morning, really — is write *isaac, isaac, isaac* in my notebook and then draw spider-man spelling it out in a web. which is completely lame, but whatever. it's not like i'm doing it to be cool.

i sit with derek and simon at lunch. the way it is with us, it's like we're sitting in a waiting room. every now and then we'll say something, but mostly we stick to our own chair-sized spaces. occasionally we'll read magazines. if someone comes over, we'll look up. but that doesn't happen often.

we ignore most of the people who walk by, even the ones we're supposed to lust after. it's not like derek and simon are into girls. basically, they like computers.

derek: do you think the X18 software will be released before summer?
simon: i read on trustmaster's blog that it might. that would be cool.
me: here's your homework back.

when i look at the guys and girls at the other tables, i wonder what they could possibly have to say to each other. they're all so boring and they're all trying to make up for it by talking louder. i'd rather just sit here and eat.

i have this ritual, that when it hits two o'clock i allow myself to get excited about leaving. it's like if i reach that point i can take the rest of the day off.

it happens in math, and maura is sitting next to me. she figured out in october what i was doing, so now every day at two she passes me a slip of paper with something on it. like 'congratulations' or 'can we go now?' or 'if this period doesn't end soon i am going to slit my own skull.' i know i should write her back, but mostly i nod. i think she wants us to go out on a date or something, and i don't know what to do about that.

everyone in our school has afterschool activities.

mine is going home.

sometimes i stop and board for a while in the park, but not in february, not in this witch-twat-frigid chicago suburb (known to locals as naperville). if i go out there now, i'll freeze my balls off. not that i'm putting them to any use whatsoever, but i still like to have them, just in case.

plus i've got better things to do than have the college dropouts tell me when i can ramp (usually about . . . never) and have the skatepunks from our school look down at me because i'm not cool enough to smoke and drink with them and i'm not cool enough to be straightedge. i'm no-edge as far as they're concerned. i stopped trying to be in their in-crowd-that-doesn't-admit-it's-an-in-crowd when i left ninth grade. it's not like boarding is my life or anything.

i like having the house to myself when i get home. i don't have to feel guilty about ignoring my mom if she's not around.

i head to the computer first and see if isaac's online. he's not, so i fix myself a cheese sandwich (i'm too lazy to grill it) and jerk off. it takes about ten minutes, but it's not like i'm timing it.

isaac's still not on when i get back. he's the only person on my 'buddy list,' which is the stupidest fucking name for a list. what are we, three years old?

me: hey, isaac, wanna be my buddy!?
isaac: sure, buddy! let's go *fishin'*!

isaac knows how stupid i find these things, and he finds them just as stupid as i do. like lol. now, if there's anything stupider than buddy lists, it's lol. if anyone ever uses lol with me, i rip my computer right out of the wall and smash it over the nearest head. i mean, it's not like anyone is laughing out loud about the things they lol. i think it should be spelled loll, like what a lobotomized person's tongue does. loll. loll. i can't think any more. loll. loll!

or ttyl. bitch, you're not actually *talking*. that would require actual *vocal contact*. or <3. you think that looks like a heart? if you do, that's only because you've never seen scrotum.

(rofl! what? are you really rolling on the floor laughing? well, please stay down there a sec while I KICK YOUR ASS.)

i had to tell maura that my mom made me get rid of my instant messenger in order for her to stop popping up whenever i was trying to do something.

gothblood4567: 'sup?
finalwill: i'm working.
gothblood4567: on what?
finalwill: my suicide note. i can't figure out how to end it.
gothblood4567: lol

so i killed my screenname and resurrected myself under another. isaac's the only person who knows it, and it's going to stay that way.

i check my email and it's mostly spam. what i want to know is this: is there really someone in the whole world who gets an email from hlyywkrrs@hothotmail.com, reads it, and says to himself, 'you know, what i really need to do is enlarge my penis 33%, and the way to do it would be to send $69.99 to that nice lady ilena at VIRILITY MAXI-MUS CORP via this handy internet link!' if people are actually falling for that, it's not their dicks they should be worried about.

i have a friend request from some stranger on facebook and i delete it without looking at the profile because that doesn't seem natural. 'cause friendship should not be as easy as that. it's like people believe all you need to do is like the same bands in order to be soulmates. or books. *omg . . . U like the outsiders 2 . . . it's like we're the same person!* no we're not. it's like we have the same english teacher. there's a difference.

it's almost four and isaac's usually on by now. i do that stupid reward thing with my homework — it's like *if i look up what date the mayans invented toothpicks, i can check to see if isaac's online yet.* then *if i read three more paragraphs about the importance of pottery in indigenous cultures, i can check my yahoo account.* and finally *if i finish answering all three of these questions and isaac isn't on yet, then i can jerk off again.*

i'm only halfway through answering the first question, some bullshit about why mayan pyramids are *so much cooler* than egyptian ones, when i cheat and look at my buddy list and see that isaac's name is there. i'm about to think *why hasn't he IM'ed me?* when the box appears on the screen. like he's read my mind.

boundbydad: u there?
grayscale: yes!
boundbydad: ☺
grayscale: ☺ x 100
boundbydad: i've been thinking about you all day
grayscale: ???
boundbydad: only good things
grayscale: that's too bad ☺
boundbydad: depends on what you think of as good
☺☺

it's been like this from the beginning. just being comfortable. i was a little freaked out at first by his screenname, but he quickly told me it was because his name was isaac, and ultimatelymydadchosetokillthegoatinsteadofme was too long to be a good screenname. he asked me about my old screenname, finalwill, and i told him my name was will, and that's how we started to get to know each other. we were in one of those lame chatrooms where it falls completely silent every ten seconds until someone goes 'anyone in here?' and other people are like 'yeah' 'yup' 'here!' without saying anything. we were supposed to be in a forum for this singer i used to like, but there wasn't much to say about him except which songs were better than the other songs. it was really boring, but it's how isaac and i met, so i guess we'll have to hire the singer to play at our wedding or something. (that is so not funny.)

soon we were swapping pictures and mp3s and telling each other about how everything pretty much sucked, but of course the ironic part was that while we were talking about it the world didn't suck as much. except, of course, for the part at the end when we had to return to the real world.

it is so unfair that he lives in ohio, because that should be close enough, but since neither of us drives and neither of us would ever in a million years say, 'hey, mom, do you want to drive me across indiana to see a boy?,' we're kind of stuck.

grayscale: i'm reading about the mayans.
boundbydad: angelou?
grayscale: ???
boundbydad: nevermind. we skipped the mayans. we
    only read 'american' history now.
grayscale: but aren't they in the americas?

boundbydad: not according to my school. **groans**

grayscale: so who did you almost kill today?

grayscale: and by 'kill,' i mean 'wish would disappear,' just in case this conversation is being monitored by administrators

boundbydad: potential body count of eleven. twelve if you count the cat.

grayscale: . . . or homeland security

grayscale: goddamn cat!

boundbydad: goddamn cat!

i haven't told anyone about isaac because it's none of their business. i love that he knows who everyone is but nobody knows who he is. if i had actual friends that i felt i could talk to, this might cause some conflict. but since right now there'd only need to be one car to take people to my funeral, i think it's okay.

eventually isaac has to go, because he isn't really supposed to be using the computer at the music store where he works. lucky for me that it doesn't seem to be a busy music store, and his boss is like a drug dealer or something and is always leaving isaac in charge while he goes out to 'meet some people.'

i step away from the computer and finish my homework quickly. then i go in the den and turn on law & order, since the only thing i can really count on in life is that whenever i turn on the tv there will be a law & order episode. this time it's the one with the guy who strangles blonde after blonde after blonde, and even though i'm pretty sure i've seen it like ten times already, i'm watching it like i don't know that the pretty reporter he's talking to is about to have the curtain cord around her neck. i don't watch that part, because it's really stupid, but once the police catch the guy and the trial's going on, they're all

> lawyer: dude, the cord knocked this microscopic piece of skin off your hand while you were strangling her, and we ran it under the microscope and found out that you're totally fucked.

you gotta know he wishes he'd worn gloves, although the gloves probably would've left fibers, and he would've been totally fucked anyway. when that's all over, there's another episode i don't think i've seen before, until this celebrity runs over a baby in his hummer and i'm like, oh, it's the one where the celebrity runs over the baby in his hummer. i watch it anyway, because it's not like i have anything better to do. then mom comes home and finds me there and it's like we're a rerun, too.

> mom: how was your day?
> me: mom, i'm watching tv.
> mom: will you be ready for dinner in fifteen minutes?
> me: *mom*, i'm watching tv!
> mom: well, set the table during the commercials.
> me: FINE.

i totally don't get this — is there anything more boring and pathetic than setting the table when there are only two of you? i mean, with place mats and salad forks and everything. who is she kidding? i would give anything not to have to spend the next twenty minutes sitting across from her, because she doesn't believe in letting silence go. no, she has to fill it up with talk. i want to tell her that's what the voices in your head are for, to get you through all the silent parts. but she doesn't want to be with her thoughts unless she's saying them out loud.

> mom: if i get lucky tonight, maybe we'll have a few
>   more dollars for the car fund.
> me: you really don't need to do that.
> mom: don't be silly. it gives me a reason to go to girls'
>   poker night.

i really wish she would stop it. she feels worse about me not having a car than i do. i mean, i'm not one of those jerks who thinks that as soon as you turn seventeen it's your god-given american right to have a brand-new chevrolet in the driveway. i know what our situation is, and i know she doesn't like that i have to work weekends at cvs in order to afford the things we need to pick up at cvs. having her constantly sad about it doesn't make me feel better. and of course there's another reason for her to go play poker besides the money. she needs more friends.

she asks me if i took my pills before i ran off this morning and i tell her, yeah, wouldn't i be drowning myself in the bathtub if i hadn't? she doesn't like that, so i'm all like 'joke, joke' and i make a mental note that moms aren't the best audience for medication humor. i decide not to get her that *world's greatest mom of a depressive fuckup* sweatshirt for mother's day like i'd been planning. (okay, there's not really a sweatshirt like that, but if there was, it would have kittens on it, putting their paws in sockets.) .

truth is, thinking about depression depresses the shit out of me, so i go back into the den and watch some more law & order. isaac's never back at his computer until eight, so i wait until then. maura calls me but i don't have the energy to say anything to her except what's happening on law & order, and she hates it when i do that. so i let the voicemail pick up.

> me: this is will. why the fuck are you calling me? leave
> a message and maybe i'll call you back. [BEEP]
> maura: hey, loser. i'm so bored i'm calling you. i figured
> if you weren't doing anything i could bear your
> children. oh, well. i guess i'll just go call joseph and
> ask him to do me in the manger and begat another
> holy child.

by the time i care, it's almost eight. and even then, i don't care enough to call her back. we have this thing about calling each other back, in that we don't do it very much. instead i head to the computer and it's like i turn into a little girl who's just seen her first rainbow. i get all giddy and nervous and hopeful and despairing and i tell myself not to look obsessively at my buddy list, but it might as well be projected onto the insides of my eyelids. at 8:05 his name pops up, and i start to count. i only get to twelve before his IM pops up.

> boundbydad: greetings!

grayscale: and salutations!

boundbydad: so glad u're here.

grayscale: so glad to be here

boundbydad: work today = lamest! day! ever! this girl tried to shoplift and wasn't even subtle about it. i used to have some sympathy for shoplifters

boundbydad: but now i just want to see them behind bars. i told her to put it back and she acted all 'put what back?' until i reached into her pocket and took the disc out. and what does she say to that? 'oh.'

grayscale: not even 'sorry'?

boundbydad: not even.

grayscale: girls suck.

boundbydad: and boys are angels? ☺

we go on like this for about an hour. i wish we could talk on the phone, but his parents won't let him have a cell and i know my mom sometimes checks my phone log when i'm in the shower. this is nice, though. it's the only part of my day when the time actually seems worth it.

we spend our usual ten minutes saying good-bye.

boundbydad: i really should go.

grayscale: me too.

boundbydad: but i don't want to.

grayscale: me neither.

boundbydad: tomorrow?

grayscale: tomorrow!

boundbydad: i wish you.

grayscale: i wish you, too.

this is dangerous because as a rule i don't let myself wish for things. too many times when i was a kid, i would put my hands together or squinch my eyes shut and i would devote myself fully to hoping for something. i even thought that there were some places in my room that were better for wishing than others — under the bed was okay, but on the bed wasn't; the bottom of the closet would do, as long as my shoebox of baseball cards was in my lap. never, ever at my desk, but always with the sock drawer open. nobody had told me these rules — i'd figured them out for myself. i could spend hours setting up a particular wish — and every single time, i'd be met with a resounding wall of complete indifference. whether it was for a pet hamster or for my mom to stop crying — the sock drawer would be open and i would be sitting behind my toy chest with three action figures in one hand and a matchbox car in the other. i never hoped for everything to get better — only for one thing to get better. and it never did. so eventually i gave up. i give up every single day.

but not with isaac. it scares me sometimes. wishing it to work.

later that night i get an email from him.

i feel like my life is so scattered right now. like it's all these small pieces of paper and someone's turned on the fan. but talking to you makes me feel like the fan's been turned off for a little bit. like things could actually make sense. you completely unscatter me, and i appreciate that so much.

GOD I AM SO IN LOVE.

chapter three

Nothing happens for a week. I don't mean this figuratively, like there is a shortage of significant events. I mean that no things occur. Total stasis. It's sort of heavenly, to tell you the truth.

There's the getting up, and the showering, and the school, and the miracle of Tiny Cooper and the desk, and the plaintive glancing at my Burger King Kids Meal Magic School Bus watch during each class, and the relief of the eighth period bell, and the bus home, and the homework, and the dinner, and the parents, and the locking the door, and the good music, and the Facebook, and the reading of people's status updates without writing my own because my policy on shutting up extends to textual communication, and then there's the bed and the waking and the shower and the school again. I don't mind it. As lives go, I'll take the quietly desperate over the radically bipolar.

And then on Thursday night, I go home and Tiny calls me, and some things start happening. I say hello, and then Tiny, by way of introduction, says, "You should come to the Gay-Straight Alliance meeting tomorrow."

And I say, "Nothing personal, Tiny, but I don't really go

in for alliances. Anyway, you know my policy on extracurricular activities."

"No, I don't," Tiny says.

"Well, I'm opposed to them," I say. "Just the curricular activities are plenty. Listen, Tiny. I gotta go. Mom's on the other line." I hang up. Mom's not on the other line, but I need to hang up, because I can't get talked into anything.

But then Tiny calls back. And he says, "Actually I *need* you to come because we have to get our membership numbers up. Our school funding is partly decided by meeting attendance."

"Why do you need money from the school? You've got your own *house*."

"We need money so that we can stage our production of *Tiny Dancer*."

"Oh. My. Sweet. Holy. God," I say, because *Tiny Dancer* is this musical, written by Tiny. It's basically Tiny's slightly fictionalized life story, except it is sung, and it is—I mean, I don't use this adjective lightly—the gayest single musical in all of human history. Which is really saying something. And by gay, I don't mean that it sucks. I just mean that it's gay. It is actually—as musicals go—quite good. The songs are catchy. I'm particularly fond of "The Nosetackle (Likes Tight Ends)," which includes the memorable couplet, "The locker room isn't porn for me / 'cause you're all too damned pimple-ey."

"*What?*" whines Tiny.

"I just worry it might be, uh—what did Gary say the other day—'bad for the team,'" I say.

"That's *exactly* the kind of thing that you can say

tomorrow!" Tiny answers, only a hint of disappointment in his voice.

"I'll go," I say, and hang up. He calls back, but I don't answer, because I'm on Facebook, looking at Tiny's profile, paging through his 1,532 friends, each cuter and trendier than the last. I'm trying to figure out who, precisely, is *in* the Gay-Straight Alliance, and whether they could develop into a suitably nonannoying Group of Friends. So far as I can tell, though, it's just Gary and Nick and Jane. I'm squinting at Jane's tiny profile pic in which she appears to have her arm around some kind of life-size mascot on ice skates.

And right then, I get a friend request from her. A couple seconds after I accept it, she IMs me.

Jane: Hey!
Me: Hey.
Jane: Sorry, that might have been inappropriate exclamation point use.
Me: Ha. All good.

I look at her profile. The list of favorite music and favorite books is obscenely long, and I can only get through the *A*'s of the music list before giving up. She looks cute in her pictures, but not quite like she looks in real life—her picture smile isn't her smile.

Jane: I hear Tiny's recruiting you to the GSA.
Me: Indeed.
Jane: You should come. We need members. It's kind of pathetic, actually.
Me: Yeah, I think I will.

Jane: Cool. I didn't know you had a Facebook. Your profile is funny. I like "ACTIVITIES: ought to involve sunglasses."

Me: You have more favorite bands than Tiny has exboyfriends.

Jane: Yeah, well. Some people have lives; some people have music.

Me: And some people have neither.

Jane: Cheer up, Will. You're about to be the hottest straight guy in the Gay-Straight Alliance.

I have the distinct feeling that flirting is occurring. Now, don't get me wrong. I enjoy flirting as much as the next guy, provided the next guy has repeatedly seen his best friend torn asunder by love. But nothing violates the rules of shutting up and not caring so much as flirting—except possibly for that enchantingly horrible moment when you act upon the flirting, that moment where you seal your heartbreak with a kiss. There should be a third rule, actually: 1. Shut up. 2. Don't care too much. And 3. Never kiss a girl you like.

Me, after a while: How many straight guys are there in the GSA?

Jane: You're it.

I lol, and feel like a fool for even thinking her a flirt. Jane's just a smart, snarky girl with too-curly hair.

And so it comes to this: At 3:30 the next afternoon, the eighth period bell rings, and for a nanosecond, I feel the endorphins sizzling through my body that usually indicate I have successfully survived another school day without anything happening, but then I remember: day ain't over yet.

I trudge upstairs while a flood of people race down, on their way to the weekend.

I get to Classroom 204A. I open the door. Jane is facing away from me with her butt on a desk and her feet on a chair. She's wearing a pale yellow T-shirt and the way she's leaned over, I can see a little of the small of her back.

Tiny Cooper is splayed out across the thin carpet, using his backpack as a pillow. He's wearing skinny jeans, which look very much like denim sausage casings. At this moment, the three of us constitute the Gay-Straight Alliance.

Tiny says, "Grayson!"

"This is the Homosexuality Is An Abomination Club, right?"

Tiny laughs. Jane just sits facing away from me, reading. My eyes return to Jane's back, because they have to go somewhere, and Tiny says, "Grayson, are you abandoning your asexuality?"

Jane turns around as I cut Tiny a look and mumble, "I'm not asexual. I'm arelationshipal."

And Tiny says to Jane, "I mean, it's such a tragedy, isn't it? The only thing Grayson has going for him is that he's adorable, and yet he refuses to date."

Tiny likes to hook me up. He does it for the pure-driven pleasure of pissing me off. And it works. "Shut up, Tiny."

"I mean, I don't see it," he says. "Nothing personal, Grayson, but you're not my type. A. You don't pay enough attention to *hygiene*, and B. All the crap you've got going for you is the crap I find totally uninteresting. I mean, Jane, I think we can agree that Grayson has nice arms."

Jane looks mildly panicked, and I jump in to save her from having to talk. "You have the oddest way of coming on to me, Tiny."

"I would never come on to you, because you're not gay. And, like, boys who like girls are *inherently* unhot. Why would you like someone who can't like you back?"

The question is rhetorical, but if I wasn't trying to shut up, I'd answer it: You like someone who can't like you back because unrequited love can be survived in a way that once-requited love cannot.

After a moment, Tiny says, "Straight girls think he's cute, that's all I'm saying." And then I realize the full extent of the insanity. Tiny Cooper has brought me to a Gay-Straight Alliance meeting to hook me up with a girl.

Which is of course idiotic in the kind of profound and multivalent way that only an English teacher could fully elucidate. At least Tiny finally shuts up, whereupon I begin staring at my watch and wondering whether this is what happens at a GSA meeting—maybe the three of us just sit here for an hour in silence with Tiny Cooper periodically rendering the room toxically uncomfortable with his un-subtle comments, and then at the end we go into a huddle and shout GO GAY! or something. But then Gary and Nick come in with some guys I vaguely recognize, a girl with a tomboy cut wearing a gigantic Rancid T-shirt that extends nearly to her knees, and this English teacher, Mr. Fortson, who has never taught me in English, which perhaps accounts for why he smiles at me.

"Mr. Grayson," says Mr. Fortson. "Nice to have you here. Enjoyed your letter to the editor a few weeks back."

"Biggest mistake of my life," I tell him.

"Why's that?"

Tiny Cooper jumps in then. "It's a long story involving shutting up and not caring." I just nod. "Oh my God, Grayson," Tiny stage-whispers. "Did I tell you what Nick said to me?" I'm thinking *nick nick nick, who the hell is nick?* And then I glance over at Nick, who is not sitting next to Gary, which is Clue A. He is also burying his head in his arms, which is Clue B. Tiny says, "He said he can see himself with me. Those words. I can see myself with you. Isn't that just the most fantastic thing you've ever heard?" From Tiny's inflection, I can't tell whether the thing is fantastically hilarious or fantastically wonderful, so I just shrug.

Nick sighs, his head against the desk, mumbles, "Tiny, not now." Gary runs his fingers through his hair and sighs. "Bad for the team, all your polyamory."

Mr. Fortson calls the meeting to order with a gavel. A real gavel. Poor bastard. I imagine that back in college or whatever, he did not imagine that gavel use would be part of his teaching career.

"Okay, so we've got eight people today. That's great, guys. I believe the first order of business is Tiny's musical, *Tiny Dancer*. We need to decide whether to ask the administration to fund this play, or if we'd like to focus on different things. Education, awareness, etc."

Tiny sits up and announces, "*Tiny Dancer* is all about education *and* awareness."

"Yeah," says Gary sarcastically. "Making sure everyone is aware of and educated about Tiny Cooper."

The two guys sitting with Gary snicker, and before I can think it through I say, "Hey, don't be a jerk, Gary," because I can't help but defend Tiny.

Jane says, "Look, are people going to make fun of it? Absuh-freakin'-lutely. But it's honest. It's funny, and it's accurate, and it's not full of crap. It shows gay people as whole and complicated—not just like 'oh my God I have to tell my daddy that I like boys and wah-wah it's so hard.'"

Gary rolls his eyes and exhales through pursed lips like he's smoking. "Right. You know how hard it is," he says to Jane, "since you're—oh, wait. Right. You're *not gay*."

"That's irrelevant," Jane responds. I glance over at Jane, who's giving Gary a look as Mr. Fortson starts talking about how you can't have Alliances within the Alliance or else there's no overarching Alliance. I'm wondering how many times he can possibly use the word *alliance* in one sentence when Tiny Cooper cuts Mr. Fortson off by saying, "Hey, wait, Jane, you're straight?"

And she nods without really looking up and then mumbles, "I mean, I think so, anyway."

"You should date Grayson," Tiny says. "He thinks you're super cute."

If I were to stand on a scale fully dressed, sopping wet, holding ten-pound dumbbells in each hand and balancing a stack of hardcover books on my head, I'd weigh about 180 pounds, which is approximately equal to the weight of Tiny Cooper's left tricep. But in this moment, I could beat the holy living shit out of Tiny Cooper. And I would, I swear to God, except I'm too busy trying to disappear.

I'm sitting here thinking, *God, I swear I will take a vow of silence and move to a monastery and worship you for all my days if you just this once provide me with an invisibility cloak, come on come on, please please invisibility cloak now now now.* It's very possible that Jane is thinking the same thing, but I have no idea, because she's not talking either, and I can't look at her on account of how I'm blinded by embarrassment.

The meeting lasts thirty more minutes, during which time I do not speak or move or in any way respond to stimuli. I gather that Nick gets Gary and Tiny to sort of make up, and the alliance agrees to seek money for both *Tiny Dancer* and a series of flyers aimed at education. There's some more talking, but I don't hear Jane's voice again.

And then it's over, and out of my peripheral vision I see everyone leaving, but I stay put. In the past half hour, I've collected a mental list of approximately 412 ways I might kill Tiny Cooper, and I'm not going to leave until I've settled on just the right one. I finally decide I'm going to just stab him a thousand times with a ballpoint pen. Jailhouse-style. I stand up ramrod straight and walk outside. Tiny Cooper's leaning against a row of lockers, waiting for me.

"Listen, Grayson," he says, and I walk up to him, and grab a fistful of his Polo, and I'm up on my tiptoes, and my eyes are about at his Adam's apple, and I say, "Of all the miserable things you've ever done, you cocksucker."

Tiny laughs, which only makes me madder, and he says, "You can't call me a cocksucker, Grayson, because A. It's not an insult, and B. You know I'm not one. Yet. Tragically."

I let go of his shirt. There's no physically intimidating Tiny. "Well, whatever," I say. "Shitbag. Dumbass. Vagina lover."

"Now *that's* an insult," he says, "But listen, dude. She likes you. When she walked out just now she came up to me and she was like, 'Did you really mean that or were you just joking?' and I was like, 'Why do you ask?' and she was like, 'Well, he's nice is all,' and then I told her I wasn't kidding, and then she smiled all goofy."

"Seriously?"

"Seriously."

I take a long, deep breath. "That's *terrible*. I'm not into her, Tiny."

He rolls his eyes. "And you think *I'm* crazy? She's adorable. I just totally made your life!"

I realize this is not, like, boyish. I realize that properly speaking guys should only think about sex and the acquisition of it, and that they should run crotch-first toward every girl who likes them and etc. But: The part I enjoy most is not the doing, but the noticing. Noticing the way she smells like oversugared coffee, and the difference between her smile and her photographed smile, and the way she bites her lower lip, and the pale skin of her back. I just want the pleasure of noticing these things at a safe distance—I don't want to have to acknowledge that I am noticing. I don't want to *talk* about it or *do stuff* about it.

I did think about it while we were there with unconscious, snot-crying Tiny below us. I thought about stepping over the fallen giant and kissing her and my hand on her face and her improbably warm breath, and having a girlfriend who gets mad at me for being so quiet and then only getting quieter because the thing I liked was one smile with a sleeping leviathan between us, and then I feel like crap for a while until finally we break up, at which point I reaffirm my vow to live by the rules.

I could do that.

Or I could just live by the rules.

"Trust me," I tell him. "You are not improving my life. Just stop interfering, okay?"

He answers with a shrug that I take for a nod. "So, listen," Tiny says. "About Nick. The thing is that he and Gary were together for a really long time and, like, they only broke up yesterday, but there's a real spark."

"Supremely bad idea," I say.

"But they broke up," says Tiny.

"Right, but what would happen if someone broke up with you and then the next day was flirting with one of your friends?"

"I'll think about it," says Tiny, but I know he can't possibly restrain himself from having another brief and failed romance. "Oh, hey." Tiny perks up. "You should go with us to the Storage Room on Friday. Nick and I are going to see this band, the uh—the Maybe Dead Cats. Intellectual pop punk. Dead Milkmen-ey, but less funny ha-ha."

"Thanks for inviting me before," I say, elbowing Tiny in the side. He pushes me back playfully, and I almost fall down the stairs. It's like being best friends with a fairy-tale giant: Tiny Cooper can't help but hurt you.

"I just figured you wouldn't want to come, after the disaster last week."

"Oh, wait, I can't. The Storage Room is over-twenty-one."

Tiny Cooper, walking ahead of me, reaches the door. He throws his hips against the metal bar, and the door flings open. Outside. The weekend. The brisk bare light of Chicago. The cold air floods over me, and the light rushes in, and Tiny Cooper is backlit by the sinking sun, so I can barely see him when he turns back around to me and pulls out his phone.

"Who are you calling?" I ask, but Tiny doesn't answer. He just holds the phone in his gigantic meaty hand and then he says, "Hey, Jane," and my eyes get wide, and I do the slit-the-throat motion, and Tiny smiles and says, "Listen, so Grayson wants to come with us to the Maybe Dead Cats on Friday. Maybe get some dinner first?"

" . . . "

"Well, the only problem is that he doesn't have an ID, and don't you know some guy?"

" . . . "

"You aren't home yet, are you? So just come back and pick his skinny ass up." Tiny hangs up and says to me, "She's on her way," and then I'm left standing in the doorway as Tiny races down the steps and starts skipping—yeah, skipping—toward the junior parking lot. "Tiny!" I shout, but he doesn't turn around; he just keeps skipping. I don't start to skip after his crazy ass or anything, but I do kinda smile. He may be a malevolent sorcerer, but Tiny Cooper is his own goddamned man, and if he wants to be a gigantic skipper, then that's his right as a huge American.

I figure I can't ditch Jane, so I'm sitting on the front steps when she shows up two minutes later behind the wheel of an ancient, hand-painted orange Volvo. I've seen the car before in the parking lot—you can't miss it—but I've never attached it to Jane. She seems quieter than the car implies. I walk down the steps, open the passenger door, and climb in, my feet landing in a pile of fast-food wrappers.

"Sorry. I realize it's disgusting."

"Don't worry," I say. This would be an excellent time to make a joke, but I'm thinking *shut up shut up shut up*. After a while the silence feels too weird, so I say, "Do you know this band, the uh, Maybe Dead Cats?"

"Yeah. They're not bad. They're sort of a poor man's early Mr. T Experience, but they've got one song I like—it's like fifty-five seconds long and it's called 'Annus Miribalis,' and it basically explains Einstein's theory of relativity."

"Cool," I say. She smiles, shifts into drive, and we jolt off toward the city.

Maybe a minute later, we come to a stop sign and Jane pulls over to the side of the road and looks at me. "I'm quite shy," she says.

"Huh?"

"I'm quite shy, so I understand. But don't hide behind Tiny."

"I'm not," I say.

And then she ducks beneath her seat belt and I'm wondering why she's doing that, and then she leans across the gearbox, and I realize what's happening, and she closes her eyes and tilts her head and I turn away, staring down at the fast-food bags on the floor of her car. She opens her eyes and jolts backward. Then I start talking to fill the silence. "I'm not really, uh, I think you're awesome and pretty but I'm not, like, I'm not, like, I guess I don't, um, really want a relationship right now."

After a second, very quietly, she says, "I think I might have gotten some unreliable information."

"Possible," I say.

"I'm really sorry."

"Me too. I mean, you really are—"

"No no no stop, that only makes it worse. Okay. Okay. Look at me." I look at her. "I can totally forget that ever happened if, and only if, you can totally forget it ever happened."

"Nothing happened," I say, and then correct myself. "Nothing didn't happen."

"Exactly," she says, and then our thirty-second stop at the stop sign ends, and my head is thrown back against the seat. Jane drives like Tiny dates.

We're exiting Lake Shore near downtown and talking about Neutral Milk Hotel and whether there might be some recordings out there that no one has heard, just demos, and how interesting it would be to hear what their songs sounded like before they were songs, how maybe we could break into their recording studio and copy every recorded moment of the band's existence. The Volvo's ancient heating system makes my lips feel dry and the leaning-in thing feels actually, literally forgotten—and it occurs to me that I am weirdly disappointed about how entirely un-upset Jane seems to feel, which in turn causes me to feel strangely rejected, which in turn causes me to think that perhaps a special wing at the Museum of Crazy should be erected in my honor.

We find a parking space on the street a couple blocks away from the place, and Jane leads me to a nondescript glass door next to a hot-dog restaurant. A sign on the door reads GOLD COAST COPY AND PRINT. We head up the stairs, the smell of delicious pork lips wafting through the air, and enter a tiny officelike shop. It is extremely sparsely decorated, which is to say that there are two folding chairs, a

49

HANG IN THERE kitten poster, a dead potted plant, a computer, and a fancy printer.

"Hey, Paulie," says Jane, to a heavily tattooed guy who appears to be the shop's sole employee. The hot-dog smell has dissipated, but only because Gold Coast Copy and Print stinks of pot. The guy comes around the counter and gives Jane a one-armed hug, and then she says, "This is my friend, Will," and the guy reaches out his hand, and as I shake his hand, I see that he has the letters, H–O–P–E tattooed on his knuckles. "Paulie and my brother are good friends. They went to Evanston together."

"Yeah, *went* together," Paulie says. "But we sure didn't graduate together, 'cause I still ain't graduated." Paulie laughs.

"Yeah, so, Paulie. Will lost his ID," explains Jane.

Paulie smiles at me. "That's a shame, kid." He hands me a blank sheet of computer paper and says, "I need your full name, your address, date of birth, social, height, weight, and eye color. And a hundred bucks."

"I, uh—" I say, because I don't happen to carry hundred dollar bills around with me. But before I can even form the words, Jane puts five twenties on the counter.

Jane and I sit down on the folding chairs, and together we invent my new identity: My name is Ishmael J. Biafra, my address is 1060 W. Addison Street, the location of Wrigley Field. I've got brown hair, blue eyes. I'm five ten, weigh 160 pounds, my social security number is nine randomly selected numbers, and I turned twenty-two last month. I hand the paper to Paulie, and then he points to a strip of duct tape and tells me to stand there. He holds a digital camera up to his eye and says, "Smile!" I didn't smile for my real driver's license picture, and I'm sure as hell not going to smile for this one.

"I'll just be a minute," Paulie says, and so I lean against the wall, and I feel nervous enough about the ID to forget being nervous about my proximity to Jane. Even though I know I'm about the three millionth person to get a fake ID, I'm still pretty sure it's a felony, and I'm generally opposed to committing felonies. "I don't even drink," I say out loud, half to myself and half to Jane.

"Mine's just for concerts," she says.

"Can I see it?" I ask. She grabs her backpack, which has been inked all over with band names and quotes, and fishes out her wallet.

"I keep it hidden back here," she says, unzipping a flap in the wallet, "because if I, like, die or something, I don't want the hospital trying to call Zora Thurston Moore's parents." Sure enough, that's her name, and the license looks completely real to me. Her picture is brilliant: Her mouth seems right on the edge of laughing, and this is exactly how she looked at Tiny's house, unlike all her Facebook pictures.

"This is a great picture of you. This is what you look like," I tell her. And it's true. That's the problem: so many things are true. It's true that I want to smother her with compliments and true that I want to keep my distance. True that I want her to like me and true that I don't. The stupid, endless truth speaking out of both sides of its big, stupid mouth. It's what keeps me, stupidly, talking. "Like, you can't know what you look like, right? Whenever you see yourself in the mirror, you know you're looking at you, so you can't help but pose a little. So you never *really* know. But this—that's what you look like."

Jane puts two fingers against the face on the license, which I'm holding against my leg, so her fingers are on my leg if you don't count the license, and I look at them for a moment and then look up to her and she says, "Paulie, for all his criminality, is actually kinda a good photographer."

Right then, Paulie comes out waving a driver's licenseish piece of plastic in the air. "Mr. Biafra, your identification."

He hands it to me. The knuckles on this hand read L-E-S-S.

It is perfect. All the holograms of a real Illinois license, all the same colors, the same thick, laminated plastic, the same organ donor info. I even look half okay in the picture. "Christ," I say. "It's magnificent. It's the *Mona Lisa* of IDs."

"No problem," says Paulie. "Ahright, kids, I gotta take care of some business." Paulie smiles and holds up a joint. I'm mystified as to how someone so pot-addled could be such a genius in the field of false identification. "See you later, Jane. Tell Phil to give me a call."

"Aye aye, cap'n," Jane says, and then we're walking down the stairs, and I can feel my fake ID in my front pocket, tight against my thigh, and it feels like I've got a ticket to the whole frakking world.

We get outside onto the street, the cold a permanent surprise. Jane takes off running ahead of me and I don't know whether I'm supposed to follow her or not, but then she turns around toward me and starts skipping backward. The wind in her face, I can barely hear her shout, "Come on, Will! Skip! After all, you're a *man* now."

And I'll be damned if I don't start skipping after her.

chapter four

i am shelving metamusil in aisle seven when maura stalks in. she knows my boss is an asshole about me standing around and talking while i'm working, so she pretends to look at vitamins while she's talking to me. she's telling me there's something really disturbing about the word 'chewable' and then all of a sudden the clock strikes 5:12 and she figures it's time to ask personal questions.

maura: are you gay?
me: what the fuck?
maura: it would be okay with me if you were.
me: oh, good, because the thing i'd be worried about
    the most is whether you were okay with it.
maura: i'm just saying.
me: noted. now will you just shut up and let me work,
    okay? or do you want me to use my employee
    discount to get you something for your cramps?

i think there really needs to be a rule against calling a guy's sexuality into question while he's working. and anyway, i really don't want to talk about it with maura no matter where we are. because, here's the thing — we're not that close. maura is the kind of friend i enjoy swapping dooms-day scenarios with. she's not, however, someone who makes me want to prevent doomsday from happening. for the year or so we've hung out, this has always been a problem. i know if i told her about liking guys, she'd probably stop wanting to date me, which would be a huge plus. but i also know i'd immediately become her gay pet, and that's the last kind of leash i want. and it's not like i'm really *that* gay. i fucking hate madonna.

> me: there should be a cereal for constipated people
>   called metamueslix.
> maura: i'm serious.
> me: and i'm seriously telling you to fuck off. you
>   shouldn't call me gay just because i don't want to
>   sleep with you. a lot of straight guys don't want to
>   sleep with you, either.
> maura: fuck you.
> me: ah, but the point is, you won't.

she comes over and messes up all the bottles that i've been putting in rows. i almost pick one up and throw it at the back of her head while she leaves, but the truth is if i brained her here, my manager would make me clean it up, and that would suck. the last thing i need is gray matter on my new shoes. do you know how hard that shit is to get out? anyway, i really need this job, which means i can't do things like yell or pin my stupid name tag upside down or wear jeans that have rips in them or sacrifice puppies in the toy aisle. i don't really mind it, except when my manager is around or when people i know come by and are all weird because i'm working and they don't have to.

i'm thinking maura will swing back into aisle seven, but she doesn't, and i know i'm going to have to act nice to her (or at least not act mean to her) for the next three days. i make a mental note to buy her coffee or something, but my mental noteboard is a joke, because as soon as i put something on there it disappears. and the truth is that the next time we talk, maura's going to pull her whole hurt routine, and that's only going to annoy me more. i mean, she's the one who opened her mouth. not my fault if she can't take the answer.

cvs closes at eight on saturdays, which means i'm out by nine. eric and mary and greta are all talking about parties they're going to, and even roger, our square-headed manager, is telling us that he and his wife are going to be 'having a night in' — wink wink, nudge nudge, hump hump, spew spew. i'd rather picture a festering wound with maggots crawling into it. roger is bald and fat and his wife is probably bald and fat, too, and the last thing i want to hear about is them having bald and fat sex. especially 'cause you know that he's making it sound all wink-nudge when the truth is he'll probably get home and the two of them will watch a tom hanks movie and then one of them will lie in bed listening to the other one pee and then they'll switch places and then when the second person is done in the bathroom, the lights will go off and they'll go to sleep.

greta asks me if i want to come along with her, but she's like twenty-three or something and her boyfriend vince acts like he'll disembowel me if i use any SAT words in his presence. so i just get a ride home, and mom is there, and isaac's not online, and i hate the way mom never has saturday night plans and isaac always has saturday night plans. i mean, i don't want him sitting at home waiting for me to get back and IM, because one of the cool things about him is that he has a life. there's an email from him saying he's going out to the movies for kara's birthday, and i tell him to wish her a happy birthday from me, but of course by the time he gets the message her birthday will be over and i don't know whether he's told kara about me, anyway.

mom is on our lime-green couch, watching the *pride & prejudice* miniseries for the seven-zillionth time, and i know i'll be totally girling out if i sit there and watch it with her. the weird thing is that she also really likes the *kill bill* movies, and i've never been able to sense a difference in her mood between when she's watching *pride & prejudice* and when she's watching *kill bill*. it's like she's the same person no matter what's happening. which can't be right.

i end up watching *pride & prejudice* because it's fifteen hours long, so i know that when it's over, isaac will probably be home. my phone keeps ringing and i keep not answering. that's one of the good things about knowing he can't call me — i never have to worry it's him.

the doorbell rings right when the guy's about to tell the girl all the shit he needs to tell her, and at first i ignore it the same way i'm ignoring my cellphone. the only problem is that people at the door don't go to voicemail, so there's another ring, and mom's about to get up, so i say i'll get it, figuring it must be the door equivalent of a wrong number.

only when i get there it's maura on the other side of the door, and she's heard my footsteps so she knows i'm here.

maura: i need to talk to you.
me: isn't it like midnight or something?
maura: just open the door.
me: are you going to huff and puff?
maura: c'mon, will. just open it.

it's always a little scary when she gets all direct with me. so while i'm opening the door i'm already trying to figure out how to dodge her. it's like some instinct kicks in.

mom: who is it?
me: it's only maura.

and, oh fuck, maura's taking the 'only' personally. I want her to just draw the teardrop under her eye and get it over with. she has enough black eyeliner on to outline a corpse, and her skin's so pale she looks like she's just broken dawn. only without the two dots of blood on her neck.

we're hovering there in the doorway because i don't really know where we should go. i don't think maura's ever really been inside my house before, except maybe the kitchen. she definitely hasn't been in my room, because that's where the computer is, and maura's the kind of girl who the moment you leave her alone will go right for the diary or the computer. plus, you know, asking someone to your room could be taken to mean something, and i definitely don't want maura to think i'm going to get all 'hey-why-

57

don't-we-sit-on-my-bed-and-hey-since-we're-sitting-on-my-
bed-how-'bout-i-put-my-dick-inside-you?' with her. but the
kitchen and the living room are off-limits now because of
mom, and mom's bedroom is off-limits because it's mom's
bedroom. which is how i find myself asking maura if she
wants to go into the garage.

maura: the garage?
me: look, it's not like i'm going to ask you to go down
    on a tailpipe, okay? if i wanted us to do a suicide
    pact, i'd opt for bathtub electrocution. you know,
    with a hair dryer. like poets do.
maura: fine.

mom's maxiseries hasn't come yet to its austen shitty lim-
its, so i know maura and i will be able to talk undisturbed.
or, at least, we'll be the only disturbed ones in the garage. it
seems really stupid to sit in the car, so i clear a space for us
by the things of dad's that mom never got around to throwing out.

me: so what's up?
maura: you're a prick.
me: this is a news flash?
maura: shut up for a second.
me: only if you shut up, too.
maura: stop it.
me: you started it.
maura: just stop it.

i decide, okay, i'll shut up. and what do i get? fifteen fucking seconds of silence. then it's all

> maura: i always tell myself that you don't mean to hurt
>   me, which makes it less hurtful, you know. but
>   today — i'm just so fucking sick of it. of you. just
>   so you know, i don't want to sleep with you, either.
>   i would never sleep with someone i can't even be
>   friends with.
> me: wait a second — now we're not friends?
> maura: i don't know what we are. you won't even tell
>   me that you're gay.

this is a classic maura maneuver. if she doesn't get an answer she wants, she will create a corner to back you into. like the time she went through my bag when i was in the bathroom and found my pills — i hadn't taken them in the morning, so i brought them along with me to school. she waited a good ten minutes before asking me if i was on any medication. this seemed a little random to me, and i didn't really want to talk about it, so i told her no. and then what does she do? she reaches into my bag and pulls out the pill bottles and asks me what they're for. she got her answer, but it didn't exactly inspire trust. she kept telling me i didn't need to be ashamed of my 'mental condition,' and i kept telling her i wasn't ashamed — i just didn't want to talk about it with her. she couldn't understand the difference.

so now we're back in another corner, and this time it's the gay thing.

me: whoa, wait a second. even if i was gay, wouldn't
    that be my decision? to tell you?
maura: who's isaac?
me: fuck.
maura: you think i can't see what you draw in your
    notebook?
me: you're kidding me. this is about *isaac*?
maura: just tell me who he is.

i fundamentally don't want to tell her. he's mine, not
hers. if i give her just a piece of the story, she'll want the
whole thing. i know in some twisted way she's doing this
because she thinks it's what i want — to talk about everything, to have her know everything about me. but that's not
what i want. that's not what she can have.

me: maura maura maura . . . isaac's a character. he
    doesn't actually exist. fuck! it's just this thing i'm
    working on. this — i don't know — *idea*. i have all
    these stories in my head. starring this character,
    isaac.

i don't know where this shit comes from. it's like it's just
being given to me by some divine force of fabrication.
    maura looks like she wants to believe it, but doesn't really.

me: like pogo dog. only he's not a dog, and he's not on
    a pogo stick.
maura: god, i forgot all about pogo dog.
me: are you kidding? he was going to make us rich!

and she's buying it. she's leaning against me and, i swear to god, if she was a guy i'd be able to see the boner in her pants.

maura: i know it's awful, but i'm kind of relieved that
    you're not hiding something that big from me.

i figure this would be a bad time to point out that i've never actually said i wasn't gay. i just told her to fuck off.

i don't know if there's anything more horrifying than a goth girl getting all cuddly. maura's not only leaning, but now she's examining my hand like somebody stamped it with the meaning of life. in braille.

me: i should probably get back to my mom.
maura: tell her we're hanging out.
me: i promised her i would watch this thing with her.

the key here is to blow off maura without her realizing i'm blowing her off. because i really don't want to hurt her, not when i just managed to bring her back from the brink of the last hurt i allegedly inflicted. i know as soon as maura gets home, she's going to dive right into her notebook of skull-blood poetry, and i'm doing my best not to get a bad review. maura once showed me one of her poems.

hang me
like a dead rose
preserve me
and my petals won't fall
until you touch them
and i dissolve

and i wrote her a poem back

> *i am like*
> *a dead begonia*
> *hanging upside down*
> *because*
> *like a dead begonia*
> *i don't give a fuck*

to which she replied

> *not all flowers*
> *depend on light*
> *to grow*

so now maybe tonight i'll inspire

> *i thought his soil was gay*
> *but maybe there's a chance*
> *i can get myself some play*
> *and get into his pants*

hopefully i'll never have to read it or know about it or even think about it ever again.

i stand up and open the garage door so maura can leave that way. i tell her i'll see her monday in school and she says 'not if i see you first' and i go har har har until she's a safe distance away and i can shut the garage door again.

the sick thing is, i'm sure that someday this is going to

come back to haunt me. that someday she's going to say i led her on, when the truth is i was only holding her off. i have to set her up with somebody else. soon. it's not me she wants — she just wants anybody who will make it all about her. and i can't be that guy.

when i get back to the living room, *pride & prejudice* is almost over, which means that everyone knows pretty much where they stand with everyone else. usually my mom is a crumpled-tissue mess at this point, but this time there's not a wet eye in the house. she pretty much confirms it when she turns the dvd off.

mom: i really have to stop doing this. i need to get a
     life.

i think she's directing this at herself, or the universe, not really at me. still, i can't help thinking that 'getting a life' is something only a complete idiot could believe. like you can just drive to a store and get a life. see it in its shiny box and look inside the plastic window and catch a glimpse of yourself in a new life and say, 'wow, i look much happier — i think this is the life i need to get!' take it to the counter, ring it up, put it on your credit card. if getting a life was that easy, we'd be one blissed-out race. but we're not. so it's like, mom, your life isn't out there waiting, so don't think all you have to do is find it and get it. no, your life is right here. and, yeah, it sucks. lives usually do. so if you want things to change, you don't need to get a life. you need to get off your ass.

of course i don't say any of these things to her. moms

don't need to hear that kind of shit from their kids, unless they're doing something really wrong, like smoking in bed, or doing heroin, or doing heroin while they're smoking in bed. if my mom were a jock guy in my school, all of her jock-guy friends would be saying, 'dude, you just need to get laid.' but sorry, geniuses, there's no such thing as a fuck cure. a fuck cure is like the adult version of santa claus.

it's kind of sick that my mind has gone from my mom to fucking, so i'm glad when she complains about herself a little more.

mom: it's getting old, isn't it? mom at home on a
    saturday night, waiting for darcy to show up.
me: there's not an actual answer to that question, is
    there?
mom: no. probably not.
me: have you actually asked this darcy guy out?
mom: no. i haven't actually found him.
me: well, he's not going to show up until you ask him
    out.

me giving my mom romantic advice is kind of like a goldfish giving a snail advice on how to fly. i could remind her that not all guys are dickheads like my dad, but she perversely hates it when i say bad things about him. she's probably just worried about the day i'll wake up and realize half my genes are so geared toward being a bastard that i'll wish i *was* a bastard. well, mom, guess what — that day came a long time ago. and i wish i could say that's where the pills come in, but the pills only deal with the side effects.

god bless the mood equalizers. *and all moods shall be created equal.* i am the fucking civil rights movement of moods.

it's late enough for isaac to be home, so i tell my mom i'm heading off to bed and then, to be nice, tell her that if i see any cute guys wearing, like, knickers and riding a horse sexily on the way to the mall, i'll be sure to slip 'em her number. she thanks me for that, and says it's a better idea than any of her friends at girls poker night have had. i wonder if she'll be asking the mailman for his opinion soon.

there's a dangling IM waiting for me when i banish my screen saver and check what's up.

boundbydad: u there?
boundbydad: i'm wishin'
boundbydad: and hopin'
boundbydad: and prayin'

all sorts of yayness floods my brain. love is such a drug.

grayscale: please be the one voice of sanity left in the
    world
boundbydad: you're there!
grayscale: just.
boundbydad: if you're relying on me for sanity, it must
    be pretty bad.
grayscale: yeah, well, maura stopped by cvs for a hag
    audition, then when i told her that tryouts were
    canceled, she decided she'd go for some
grayscale: nookie instead. and then my mom started

saying she had no life. oh, and i have homework to do. or not.

boundbydad: it's hard to be you, isn't it?

grayscale: clearly.

boundbydad: do you think maura knows the truth?

grayscale: i'm sure she thinks she does.

boundbydad: what a nosy bitch.

grayscale: not really. it's not her fault i don't really want to get into it. i'd rather share it with you.

boundbydad: and so you are. meanwhile, no big saturday night plans? more quality time with mom?

grayscale: you, my dear, are my saturday night plans.

boundbydad: i'm honored.

grayscale: you should be. how was the bday celebration?

boundbydad: small. kara just wanted to see a movie with me and janine. good time, lame movie. the one with the guy who learns that the girl he marries is a sucubus

boundbydad: sucubbus?

boundbydad: succubus?

grayscale: succubus

boundbydad: yeah, one of those. it was really stupid. then it was really boring. then it got loud and stupid. then there were about two minutes where it was so stupid it was funny. then it went back to being dumb, and finally ended lame.

boundbydad: good times, good times

grayscale: how's kara?

boundbydad: in recovery.

grayscale: meaning?

boundbydad: she talks a lot about her problems in the past tense as a way to convince us they're in the past. and maybe they are.

grayscale: did you say hi to her for me?

boundbydad: yeah. i think i phrased it as 'will says he wants you inside of him,' but the effect was the same. she said hi back.

grayscale: **sighs forlornly** i wish i could've been there.

boundbydad: i wish i was there with you right now.

grayscale: really? ☺

boundbydad: yessirreebob.

grayscale: and if you were here . . .

boundbydad: what would i do?

grayscale: ☺

boundbydad: let me tell you what i'd do.

this is a game we play. most of the time we're not serious. like, there are different ways it could go. the first is we basically make fun of people who have IM sex by inventing our own ridiculous scornographic dialogue.

grayscale: i want you to lick my clavicle.

boundbydad: i am licking your clavicle.

grayscale: ooh my clavicle feels so good.

boundbydad: naughty, naughty clavicle.

grayscale: mmmmmm

boundbydad: wwwwwwww

grayscale: rrrrrrrrrrrrrrrr

boundbydad: ttttttttttttttttttttt

other times we go for the romance novel approach. corn porn.

boundbydad: thrust your fierce quavering manpole at me, stud
grayscale: your dastardly appendage engorges me with hellfire
boundbydad: my search party is creeping into your no man's land
grayscale: baste me like a thanksgiving turkey!!!

and then there are nights like tonight, when the truth is what comes out, because it's what we need the most. or maybe just one of us needs it the most, but the other knows the right time to give it.

like now, when what i want most in the universe is to have him beside me. he knows this, and he says

boundbydad: if i was there, i would stand behind your chair and put my hands on your shoulders, lightly, and would rub them gently until you finished your last sentence
boundbydad: then i would lean forward and trace my hands down your arms and curve my neck into yours and let you turn into me and rest there for a while
boundbydad: rest
boundbydad: and when you were ready, i'd kiss you

once and lift myself away, sit back on your bed and
wait for you there, just so we could lie there, and
you could hold me, and i could hold you
boundbydad: and it would be so peaceful. completely
peaceful. like the feeling of sleep, but being awake
in it together.
grayscale: that would be so wonderful.
boundbydad: i know. i would love it, too.

i can't imagine us saying these things to each other out
loud. but even if i can't imagine hearing these words, i can
imagine living them. i don't even picture it. instead i'm in it.
how i would feel with him here. that peace. it would be so
happy, and it makes me sad because it only exists in words.

early on, isaac let me know that he always finds pauses
awkward — if too much time went by without me responding, he'd think i was typing something else in another window, or had left the computer, or was IMing twelve other
boys besides him. and i had to admit that i felt the same
fears. so now we do this thing whenever we're pausing. we
just type

grayscale: i'm here
boundbydad: i'm here
grayscale: i'm here
boundbydad: i'm here

until the next sentence comes.

grayscale: i'm here

boundbydad: i'm here

grayscale: i'm here

boundbydad: what are we doing?

grayscale: ???

boundbydad: i think it's time

boundbydad: time for us to meet

grayscale: !!!

grayscale: seriously?

boundbydad: deliriously

grayscale: you mean i would get a chance to see you

boundbydad: hold you for real

grayscale: for real

boundbydad: yes

grayscale: yes?

boundbydad: yes.

grayscale: yes!

boundbydad: am i crazy?

grayscale: yes! ☺

boundbydad: i'll go crazy if we don't.

grayscale: we should.

boundbydad: we should.

grayscale: ohmygodwow

boundbydad: it's going to happen, isn't it?

grayscale: we can't go back now.

boundbydad: i'm so excited . . .

grayscale: and terrified

boundbydad: . . . and terrified

grayscale: . . . but most of all excited?

boundbydad: but most of all excited.

it's going to happen. i know it's going to happen.

giddily, terrifyingly, we pick a date.

friday. six days away

only six days.

in six days, maybe my life will actually begin.

this is so insane.

and the most insane thing of all is that i'm so excited that i want to immediately tell isaac all about it, even though he's the one person who already knows it's happened. not maura, not simon, not derek, not my mom — nobody in this whole wide world but isaac. he is both the source of my happiness and the one i want to share it with.

i have to believe that's a sign.

chapter five

It's one of those weekends where I don't leave the house at all—literally—except briefly with Mom to go to the White Hen. Such weekends usually don't bother me, but I keep sort of hoping Tiny Cooper and/or Jane might call and give me an excuse to use the ID I've hidden in the pages of *Persuasion* on my bookshelf. But no one calls; neither Tiny nor Jane even shows up online; and it's colder than a witch's tit in a steel bra, so I just stay in the house and catch up on homework. I do my precalc homework, and then when I'm done I actually sit with the textbook for like three hours and try to understand what I just did. That's the kind of weekend it is—the kind where you have so much time you go past the answers and start looking into the ideas.

Then on Sunday night while I'm at the computer checking to see if anyone's online, my dad's head appears in my doorway. "Will," he says, "do you have a sec to talk in the living room?" I spin around in the desk chair and stand up. My stomach flips a bit because the living room is the room least likely to be lived in, the room where the nonexistence of Santa is revealed, where grandmothers die, where grades are frowned upon, and where one learns that a man's station wagon goes inside a woman's garage, and then exits the garage, and then enters again, and so on until an egg is fertilized, and etc.

My dad is very tall, and very thin, and very bald, and he has long thin fingers, which he taps against an arm of a floral-print couch. I sit across from him in an overstuffed, overgreen armchair. The finger tapping goes on for about thirty-four years, but he doesn't say anything, and then finally I say, "Hey, Dad."

He has a very formalized, intense way of talking, my dad. He always talks to you as if he's informing you that you have terminal cancer—which is actually a big part of his job, so it makes sense. He looks at me with those sad, intense you-have-cancer eyes, and he says, "Your mother and I are wondering about your plans."

And I say, "Uh, well. I thought I would, uh, go to bed pretty soon. And then, just go to school. I'm going to a concert on Friday. I already told Mom."

He nods. "Yes, but after that."

"Uh, after that? You mean, like, get into college and get a job and get married and give you grandchildren and stay off drugs and live happily ever after?"

He almost smiles. It is an exceedingly hard thing, to get my dad to smile. "There's one facet of that process in which your mother and I are particularly interested at this particular juncture in your life."

"College?"

"College," he says.

"Don't have to worry about it until next year," I point out.

"It's never too early to plan," he says. And then he starts talking about this program at Northwestern where you do both college and medical school in, like, six years so that you can be in residency by the time you're twenty-five, and you can stay close to home but of course live on campus and whatever whatever whatever, because after about eleven seconds, I realize he and Mom have decided I should go to this particular program, and that they are introducing me to the idea early, and that they will periodically bring this program up over the next year, pushing and pushing and pushing. And I realize, too, that if I can get in, I will probably go. There are worse ways to make a living.

You know how people are always saying your parents are always right? "Follow your parents' advice; they know what's good for you." And you know how no one ever listens to this advice, because even if it's true it's so annoying and condescending that it just makes you want to go, like, develop a meth addiction and have unprotected sex with eighty-seven thousand anonymous partners? Well, I listen to my parents. They know what's good for me. I'll listen to anyone, frankly. Almost everyone knows better than I do.

Andbutso little does my dad know, but all his explanation of this future is lost on me; I'm already fine with it. No, I'm thinking about how little I feel in this absurdly immense chair, and I'm thinking about the fake ID warming up Jane Austen's pages, and I'm thinking about whether I'm more mad at Tiny or in awe of him, and thinking about Friday, steering clear of Tiny in the mosh pit as he tries to dance like everyone else, and the heat turned on too high in the club and everyone sweating through their clothes and the music so uptempo and goose bumps that I don't even care what they're singing about.

And I say, "Yeah, it sounds really cool, Dad," and he's talking about how he knows people there, and I'm just nodding nodding nodding.

I'm at school Monday morning twenty minutes early because Mom has to get to the hospital by seven—I guess someone has an extralarge tumor or something. So I lean against the flagpole on the lawn in front of school waiting for Tiny Cooper, shivering in spite of the gloves and the hat and the coat and the hood. The wind tears across the lawn, and I can hear it whipping the flag above me, but I'll be damned if I'm going to enter that building a nanosecond before the first period bell rings.

The buses let off, and the lawn starts to fill up with freshmen, none of whom seems particularly impressed by me. And then I see Clint, a tenured member of my former Group of Friends, walking toward me from the junior parking lot, and I'm able to convince myself that he's not really walking toward *me* until his visible breath is blowing over me like a small, malodorous cloud. And I'm not going to lie: I kind of hope he's about to apologize for the small-mindedness of certain of his friends.

"Hey, fucker," he says. He calls everyone *fucker*. Is it a compliment? An insult? Or maybe it is both at once, which is precisely what makes it so useful.

I wince a little from the sourness of his breath, and then just say, "Hey." Equally noncommittal. Every conversation I ever had with Clint or any of the Group of Friends is identical: all the words we use are stripped bare, so that no one ever knows what anyone else is saying, so that all kindness is cruelty, all selfishness generous, all care callous.

And he says, "Got a call from Tiny this weekend about his musical. Wants student council to fund it." Clint is student council vice president. "He told me all the fuck about it. A musical about a big gay bastard and his best friend who uses tweezers to jack off 'cause his dick's so small." He's saying all this with a smile. He's not being mean. Not exactly.

And I want to say, *That's so incredibly original. Where do you come up with these zingers, Clint? Do you own some kind of joke factory in Indonesia where you've got eight-year-olds working ninety hours a week to deliver you that kind of top-quality witticism? There are boy bands with more original material.* But I say nothing.

"So yeah," Clint finally continues. "I think I might help Tiny out at the meeting tomorrow. Because that play sounds like a fantastic idea. I've only got one question: are you going to sing your own songs? Because I'd pay to see that."

I laugh a little, but not too much. "I'm not much for drama," I say, finally. Right then, I feel an enormous presence behind me. Clint raises his chin way the hell up to look at Tiny and then nods at him. He says, "'Sup, Tiny," and then walks away.

"He trying to steal you back?" Tiny asks.

I turn around, and *now* I can talk. "You go all weekend without logging on or calling me and yet you find time to call *him* in your continuing attempts to ruin my social life through the magic of song?"

"First off, *Tiny Dancer* isn't going to ruin your social life, because you don't have a social life. Second off, you didn't call me, either. Third off, I was so busy! Nick and I spent almost the entire weekend together."

"I thought I explained to you why you couldn't date Nick," I say, and Tiny's just starting to talk again when I see Jane, hunched forward, plowing through the wind. She's wearing a not-thick-enough hoodie and walking up to us.

I say hi, and she says hi, and she comes and stands next to me as if I'm a space heater or something, and she squints into the wind, and I say, "Hey, take my coat." I take it off and she buries herself in it. I'm still trying to think of a question to ask Jane when the bell goes off, and we all hustle inside.

I don't see Jane at all during the entire school day, which is a little frustrating, because it's even-the-hallways-are-freezing cold, and I keep worrying that after school I'm gonna freeze to death on the walk to Tiny's car. After my last class, I race downstairs and unlock my locker. My coat is stuffed inside it.

Now, it is possible to slip a note into a locked locker through the vents. Even, with some pushing, a pencil. Once, Tiny Cooper slipped a Happy Bunny book into my locker. But I find it extraordinarily difficult to imagine how Jane, who, after all, is not the world's strongest individual, managed to stuff an entire winter coat through the tiny slits in my locker.

But I'm not here to ask questions, so I put my coat on and walk out to the parking lot, where Tiny Cooper is sharing one of those hand-shake-followed-by-one-armed-hug things with none other than Clint. I open the passenger door and get into Tiny's Acura. He shows up soon afterward, and although I'm pissed at him, even I am able to appreciate the fascinating and complex geometry involved in Tiny Cooper inserting himself into a tiny car.

"I have a proposition," I tell him as he engages in another miracle of engineering—that of fastening his seat belt.

"I'm flattered, but I'm not gonna sleep with you," Tiny answers.

"Not funny. Listen, my proposition is that if you back off this *Tiny Dancer* business, I will—well, what do you want me to do? Because I'll do anything."

"Well, I want you to hook up with Jane. Or at least call her. After I so artfully arranged for you to be alone together, she seems to have gotten the impression that you don't want to date her."

"I don't," I say. Which is entirely true and entirely not. The stupid, all-encompassing truth.

"What do you think this is, eighteen thirty-two? When you like someone and they like you, you fucking put your lips against their lips and then you open your mouth a little, and then just a little hint of tongue to spice things up. I mean, *God*, Grayson. Everybody's always got their panties in a twist about how the youth of America are debaucherous, sex-crazed maniacs passing out handjobs like they were lollipops, and you can't even kiss a girl who *definitely likes you*?"

"I don't like her, Tiny. Not like that."

"She's *adorable*."

"How would you know?"

"I'm gay, not blind. Her hair's all poofy and she's got a great nose. I mean, a *great* nose. And, what? What do you people like? Boobs? She seems to have boobs. They seem to be of approximately normal boob size. What else do you want?"

"I don't want to talk about this."

He starts the car and then begins banging his tetherball of a head against the car's horn rhythmically. *Ahnnnk. Ahhhnk. Ahhhnk.*

"You're embarrassing us," I shout over the horn.

"I'm going to keep doing this until I get a concussion or you say you'll call her."

I jam my fingers into my ears, but Tiny keeps headbutting the horn. People are looking at us. Finally I just say, "Fine. Fine! FINE!" And the honking ceases.

"I'll call Jane. I'll be nice to her. But I still don't want to date her."

"That is your choice. Your stupid choice."

"So then," I say hopefully, "no production of *Tiny Dancer?*"

Tiny starts the car. "Sorry, Grayson, but I can't do it. *Tiny Dancer* is bigger than you or me, or any of us."

"Tiny, you have a really warped understanding of compromise."

He laughs. "Compromise is when you do what I tell you and I do what I want. Which reminds me: I'm gonna need you to be in the play."

I stifle a laugh, because this shit won't be funny anymore if it's staged in our goddamned auditorium. "Absolutely not. No. NO. Also, I insist that you write me out of it."

Tiny sighs. "You just don't get it, do you? Gil Wrayson isn't *you*; he's a fictional character. I can't just change my art because you're uncomfortable with it."

I try a different tack. "You're gonna humiliate yourself up there, Tiny."

"It's going to happen, Grayson. I've got the support on the student council for the money. So shut up and deal with it."

I shut up and deal with it, but I don't call Jane that night. I'm not Tiny's errand boy.

The next afternoon I take the bus home, because Tiny is busy at the student council meeting. He calls me as soon as it's over.

"Great news, Grayson!" he shouts.

"Great news for someone is always bad news for someone else," I answer.

And sure enough, the student council has approved a thousand dollars for the staging and production of the musical *Tiny Dancer*.

That night I'm waiting for my parents to come home so we can eat, and I'm trying to work on this essay about Emily Dickinson, but mostly I'm just downloading everything the Maybe Dead Cats have ever recorded. I kind of absolutely love them. And as I keep listening to them, I keep wanting to tell someone how good they are, and so I call Tiny, but he doesn't pick up, and so I do exactly what Tiny wants— just like always. I call Jane.

"Hey, Will," she says.

"I kind of absolutely love the Maybe Dead Cats," I say.

"They're not bad, yeah. A bit pseudointellectual but, hey, aren't we all?"

"I think their band name is a reference to, like, this physicist guy," I say. In fact, I *know* it. I've just looked the band up on Wikipedia.

"Yeah," she says. "Schrödinger. Except the band name is a total fail, because Schrödinger is famous for pointing out this paradox in quantum physics where, like, under certain circumstances, an unseen cat can be *both* alive *and* dead. Not *maybe* dead."

"Oh," I say, because I can't even pretend to have known that. I feel like a total dumbass, so I change the subject. "So I hear Tiny Cooper worked his Tiny Magic and the musical's on."

"Yeah. What's your problem with *Tiny Dancer*, anyway?"

"Have you ever *read* it?"

"Yeah. It's amazing, if he can pull it off."

"Well, I'm, like, the costar. Gil Wrayson. That's me, obviously. And it's just, it's embarrassing."

"Don't you think it's kind of awesome to be, like, the costar of Tiny's life?"

"I don't really want to be the costar of *anyone*'s life," I say. She doesn't say anything in response. "So how are you?" I ask after a second.

"I'm okay."

"Just okay?"

"Did you get the note in your coat pocket?"

"The what—no. There was a note?"

"Yeah."

"Oh. Hold on." I put the phone down on the desk and ransack my pockets. The thing about my coat pockets is that if I have a small amount of trash—like, say, a Snickers wrapper—but I don't see a garbage can, my pockets end up becoming the garbage can. And I'm not great when it comes to taking out the pocket trash. So it takes me a few minutes before I find a folded piece of notebook paper. On the outside it says:

To: Will Grayson

From: The Locker Houdini

I grab the phone and say, "Hey, I found it." I feel a little sick to my stomach, in a way that is both nice and not.

"Well, did you read it?"

"No," I say, and I wonder if maybe the note is not better left unread. I shouldn't have called her in the first place. "Hold on." I unfold the paper:

Mr. Grayson,
You should always make sure no one's watching when you unlock your locker. You never know (18) when someone (26) will memorize (4) your combination. Thanks for the coat. I guess chivalry isn't dead.

> yours,
> Jane

p.s. I like how you treat your pockets the way I treat my car.

Upon finishing the note, I read it again. It makes both truths more true. I want her. I don't. Maybe I am a robot after all. I have no idea what to say, so I go ahead and say the worst possible thing. "Very cute." This is why I should adhere to Rule 2.

In the ensuing silence, I have time to contemplate the word cute—how dismissive it is, how it's the equivalent of calling someone little, how it makes a person into a baby, how the word is a neon sign burning through the dark reading, "Feel Bad About Yourself."

And then finally she says, "Not my favorite adjective."

"Sorry. I mean, it's—"

"I know what you mean, Will," she says. "I'm sorry. I, uh, I don't know. I just got out of a relationship, and I think I'm, like, kind of just looking to fill that hole, and you're the most obvious candidate to fill the hole, and oh my God that sounds dirty. Oh, God. I'm just gonna hang up."

"I'm sorry about cute. It wasn't cute. It was—"

"Forget it. Forget the note, really. I don't even . . . Just don't worry about it, Grayson."

After an awkward hanging up, I realize the intended ending of the "I don't even . . ." sentence. "I don't even . . . like you, Grayson, because you're kind of how can I say this politely not that smart. Like, you had to look up that physicist on Wikipedia. I just miss my boyfriend, and you wouldn't kiss me, so I kind of want to just because you wouldn't, and it's really actually not a big deal but I can't find a way to tell you that without hurting your feelings, and since I'm far more compassionate and thoughtful than you with your *cutes*, I'm just going to stop the sentence at *I don't even*."

I call Tiny again, this time not about the Maybe Dead Cats, and he picks up on the first half-ring and says, "Good evening, Grayson."

I ask him if he agrees with me about what the end of

her sentence probably was, and then I ask him what short-circuited in my brain to call the note cute, and how is it even possible to be both attracted and not attracted to someone at the very same moment, and whether maybe I am a robot incapable of real feelings, and do you think that actually, like, trying to follow the rules about shutting up and not caring has made me into some kind of hideous monster whom no one will ever love or marry. I say it all, and Tiny says nothing, which is a basically unprecedented turn of events, and then when I finally stop, Tiny says *hrmm* in the little way that he has and then he says—and I am quoting him directly here—"Grayson, sometimes you are *such. a. girl.*" And then he hangs up on me.

The unfinished sentence stays with me all night. And then my robot heart decides to do something—the kind of something that would be enjoyed by a hypothetical girl-I-would-like.

At school on Friday, I eat lunch superfast, which is easy enough to do because Tiny and I are sitting with a table full of Drama People, and they are discussing *Tiny Dancer*, all of them speaking more words per minute than I speak in a day. The conversational curve follows a distinct pattern—the voices get louder and faster, crescendoing until Tiny, talking over everyone, makes a joke, and the table explodes in laughter and then things calm briefly, and then the voices start again, building and building into the coming Tiny eruption. Once I notice this pattern, it becomes difficult not to pay attention to it, but I try to focus on wolfing down my enchiladas. I chug a Coke and then stand up.

Tiny holds up his hand to quiet the chorus. "Where ya going, Grayson?"

"I gotta go check on something," I say.

I know the *approximate* location of her locker. It is approximately across from the hallway mural in which a poorly painted version of our school mascot, Willie the Wildkit, says in a speech bubble, "Wildkits Respect EVERYONE," which is hilarious on at least fourteen different levels, the fourteenth being that *there is no such thing as a wildkit.* Willie the Wildkit looks approximately like a mountain lion, though, and while I am admittedly not an expert in zoology, I'm reasonably sure that mountain lions do not, in fact, respect everyone.

So I'm leaning against the Willie the Wildkit mural in such a way that it appears that I'm the one saying that Wildkits Respect EVERYONE, and I have to wait like that for about ten minutes, just trying to look like I'm doing something and wishing I'd brought a book or whatever so I wouldn't look so aggressively stalkerish, and then finally the period bell rings and the hallway floods with people.

Jane gets to her locker, and I step into the middle of the hallway, and people make way for me, and I take a step to the left to get the angle just right, and I can see her hand reach up to the lock, and I squint, and 25-2-11. I turn into the flow of people and walk to history.

Seventh period, I take this video game—design class. It turns out that designing video games is incredibly hard and not nearly as fun as playing them, but the one advantage of the class is that I have Internet access and my monitor faces away from the teacher most of the time.

So I e-mail the Maybe Dead Cats.

From: williamgrayson@eths.il.us
To: thiscatmaybedead@gmail.com
Subject: Make My Life
Dear Maybe Dead Cats,
If you happen to play "Annus Miribalis" tonight,
could you possibly dedicate it to 25-2-11 (a certain
girl's locker combination)? That would be amazing.
Sorry about the short notice,
                                        Will Grayson

The reply comes before the period is even over.

Will,
Anything for love.
MDC

So after school on Friday, Jane and Tiny and I go to Frank's Franks, a hot-dog restaurant a few blocks away from the club. I sit in a small booth next to Jane, her hip against my hip. Our coats are all bunched up across from us along with Tiny. Her hair is falling in all these big curls on her shoulders, and she's wearing this non weather–appropriate top with thin straps and quite a lot of eye makeup.

Because this is a classy hot-dog joint, a waiter takes our order. Jane and I each want one hot dog and a soda. Tiny orders four hot dogs with buns, three hot dogs without buns, a bowl of chili, and a Diet Coke.

"A *Diet* Coke?" asks the waiter. "You want four hot dogs

with buns, three hot dogs without buns, a bowl of chili, and a *Diet* Coke?"

"That's correct," says Tiny, and then explains, "simple sugars don't really help me put on muscle mass." And the waiter just shakes his head and says, "Uh-huh."

"Your poor digestive system," I say. "One day your intestinal tract is going to revolt. It's going to reach up and strangle you."

"You know Coach says ideally I should put on thirty pounds for the start of next season. If I want to get scholarships from Division I schools? You gotta be *big*. And it's just so hard for me to put on weight. I try and I try, but it's a constant battle."

"You've got a real hard life, Tiny," says Jane. I laugh, and we exchange glances, and then Tiny says, "Oh my God, just *do* it already," which leads to an uncomfortable silence that lasts until Jane asks, "So where are Gary and Nick?"

"Probably getting back together," Tiny says. "I broke up with Nick last night."

"That was the right thing to do. It was doomed from the start."

"I know, right? I really think I want to be single for a while."

I turn to Jane and say, "I bet you five bucks he'll be in love within four hours."

She laughs. "Make it three and you're on."

"Deal."

We shake.

After dinner, we walk around the neighborhood for a little

while to kill time and then get in line outside the Storage Room. It's cold out, but up against the building, we're out of the wind at least. In line, I pull out my wallet, move the fake ID to the front picture window, and hide my real driver's license between a health insurance card and my dad's business card.

"Let me see it," says Tiny, and I hand him my wallet, and he says, "Damn, Grayson, for once in your life you don't look like a bitchsquealer in a picture."

Just before we get to the front of the line, Tiny pushes me in front of him—I guess so he can have the pleasure of watching me use the ID for the first time. The bouncer wears a T-shirt that doesn't quite extend over his belly.

"ID," he tells me. I pull my wallet from my back pocket, slide the ID out, and hand it to him. He shines a flashlight on it, then turns the flashlight onto my face, and then back to the ID, and then he says, "What, you think I can't add?"

And I say, "Huh?"

And the bouncer says, "Kid, you're twenty."

And I say, "No, I'm twenty-two." And he hands me my ID and says, "Well, your goddamned driver's license says you're twenty." I stare at it, and do the math. It says I turn twenty-one next January.

"Uh," I say. "Um, yeah. Sorry."

That stupid h-o-p-e-l-e-s-s stoner put the wrong fucking year on my ID. I step away from the club's entrance, and Tiny walks up to me, laughing his ass off. Jane is giggling, too. Tiny claps me too hard on the shoulder and says, "Only Grayson could get a fake ID that says he's twenty. It's totally worthless!"

And I say to Jane, "Your friend made it with the wrong year," and she says, "I'm sorry, Will," but she can't be *that* sorry, or else she'd stop laughing.

"We can try to get you in," Jane suggests, but I just shake my head.

"You guys just go," I say. "Just call me when it's over. I'll just hang out at Frank's Franks or something. And, like, call me if they play 'Annus Miribalis.'"

And here's the thing: they go. They just get back into line and then I watch them walk into the club, and neither of them even tries to say *no, no, we don't want to see the show without you.*

Don't get me wrong. The band is great. But being passed over for the band still sucks. Standing in line I hadn't felt cold, but now it's freezing. It's miserable out, the kind of cold where breathing through your nose gives you brain freeze. And I'm out here alone with my worthless fucking hundred-dollar ID.

I walk back to Frank's Franks, order a hot dog, and eat it slowly. But I know I can't possibly eat this one hot dog for the two or three hours they'll be gone—you can't savor a hot dog. My phone's on the table, and I just watch it, stupidly hoping Jane or Tiny might call. And sitting here, I only get more and more pissed. This is a hell of a way to leave someone—sitting alone in a restaurant—just staring straight ahead, not even a book to keep me company. It's not even just Tiny and Jane; I'm pissed at myself, for giving them an out, for not checking the date on the stupid ID, for sitting here waiting for the phone to ring even though I could be driving home.

And thinking about it, I realize the problem with going where you're pushed: sometimes you're pushed here.

I'm tired of going where I'm pushed. It's one thing to get pushed around by my parents. But Tiny Cooper pushing me toward Jane, and then pushing me toward a fake ID, and then laughing at the fuckup that resulted, and then leaving me here alone with a goddamned second-rate hot dog when I don't even particularly like first-rate hot dogs—that's bullshit.

I can see him in my mind, his fat head laughing. *It's totally worthless. It's totally worthless.* Not so! I can buy cigarettes, although I don't smoke. I can possibly illegally register to vote. I can—oh, hey. Huh. Now there's an idea.

See, across from the Storage Room, there's this place. A neon-sign-and-no-windows kind of place. Now, I don't particularly like or care about porn—or the "Adult Books" promised by the sign outside the door—but I'll be damned if I'm going to spend my entire night at Frank's Franks *not* using my fake ID. No. I'm going to the porn store. Tiny Cooper doesn't have the nuts to walk into a place like that. No way. I'm thinking about the story I'll have when Tiny and Jane get out of the concert. I put a five on the table—a 50 percent tip—and walk four blocks. As I get near the door, I start to feel anxious—but I tell myself that being outside in the dead of winter in downtown Chicago is much more dangerous than any business establishment could possibly be.

I pull the door open, and step into a room bright with fluorescent light. To my left, a guy with more piercings than a pincushion stands behind a counter, staring at me.

"You browsing or you want tokens?" he asks me. I don't have the first idea what tokens are, so I say, "Browsing?"

"Okay. Go on in," he tells me.

"What?"

"Go ahead."

"You're not going to ID me?"

The guy laughs. "What, are you sixteen or something?"

He nailed it exactly, but I say, "No, I'm twenty."

"Well, yeah. So that's what I figured. Go ahead."

And I'm thinking, *Oh, my God. How hard can it fucking be to successfully use a fake ID in this town?* This is ridiculous! I won't stand for it. "No," I say, forcefully. "ID me."

"All right, man. If that's what gets your maracas shakin'." And then, real dramatically, he asks, "Can I see some ID, please?"

"You may," I answer, and hand it to him. He glances at it, hands it back, and says, "Thanks, Ishmael."

"You're welcome," I say, exasperated. And then I'm in a porn store.

It's kinda boring, actually. It looks like a regular store—shelves of DVDs and old VHS tapes and a rack of magazines, all under this harsh fluorescent glow. I mean, there *are* some differences from a regular video store, I guess, like A. At the regular video store, very few of the DVDs have the words *guzzling* or *slut* in them, whereas here the opposite seems to be the case, and also B. I'm pretty sure the regular video store doesn't have any devices used for spanking, whereas this place has several. Also, C. There are very few items for sale at the regular video store that make you think, "I have no earthly idea what that is supposed to do or where it is supposed to do it."

Other than Señor Muy Pierced, the place is empty, and I very much want to leave because this is possibly the most uncomfortable and unpleasant portion of what has heretofore been a pretty uncomfortable and unpleasant day. But the whole trip is completely worthless if I don't get a memento to prove I was here. My goal is to find the item that will make for the funniest show-and-tell, the item that will make Tiny and Jane feel like I had a night of hilarity they can only glimpse, which is how I finally come to settle upon a Spanish-language magazine called *Mano a Mano*.

chapter six

at this moment, i want to jump ahead in time. or, if that doesn't work, i'll settle for traveling back in time.

i want to jump ahead in time because in twenty hours i will be with isaac in chicago, and i am willing to skip everything in between in order to get to him faster. i don't care if in ten hours i'm going to win the lottery, or if in twelve hours i'm going to get the chance to graduate early from high school. i don't care if in fourteen hours i am going to be jerking off and have the most life-altering orgasm in all of unrecorded history. i would fast-forward past it all to be with isaac instead of having to settle for thinking about him.

as for traveling back in time, it's really simple — i want to go back in time and kill the guy who invented math. why? because right now i'm at the lunch table and derek is saying

derek: aren't you psyched for mathletes tomorrow?

with that simple word — *mathletes* — it's like every ounce of anesthesia i've ever collected in my body wears off at once.

me: holy sweet f-ing a

there are four mathletes in our school. i am number four. derek and simon are numbers one and two, and in order to enter competitions they need at least four members. (number three is a freshman whose name i deliberately forget. his pencil has more personality than he does.)

simon: you do remember, right?

they've both put their meatburgers down (that's what the cafeteria menu calls them — meatburgers), and they're staring at me with looks so blank i swear i can see the computer screens reflected in their glasses.

me: i dunno. i'm not feeling very mathletic. maybe you
     should find a subset-stitute?
derek: that's not funny.
me: ha ha! wasn't meant to be!
simon: i've told you — you don't have to do anything.
     in a mathletic competition, you enter as a team,
     but are judged as individuals.
me: you guys know i'm your biggest mathletic
     supporter. but, um, i kind-of made other plans
     for tomorrow.
derek: you can't do that.
simon: you said you'd come.
derek: i promise it'll be fun.
simon: nobody else will do it.
derek: *we'll have a good time.*

i can tell derek's upset because it looks like he's considering having a slight emotional response to the informational stimuli being presented to him. maybe it's too much, because he puts down his meatburger, picks up his tray, murmurs something about library fines, and leaves the table.

there's no doubt in my mind that i'm going to bail on these guys. the only question is whether i can do it without feeling like shit. i guess it's a sign of desperation, but i decide to tell simon something remotely resembling the truth.

me: look, you know that ordinarily i'd be all over
      mathletes. but this is like an emergency. i made
      like a — i guess you could call it a date. and i
      really, really have to see this person, who's coming
      a long way to see me. and if there was any way to
      do it and go to the mathletic competition with you,
      i would. but i can't. it's like . . . if a train is traveling
      at ninety miles an hour and it needs to get from
      the mathletics competition to the middle of chicago
      in, like, two minutes for a date, it's never going to
      make it in time. so i have to jump on the express,
      because ultimately the tracks that lead to the date
      are only being laid down this one time, and if i get
      on the wrong train, i'm going to be more miserable
      than any equation could ever account for.

it feels so strange to be telling someone this, especially simon.

simon: i don't care. you said you'd be there and you
    have to be there. this is an instance where four
    minus one equals zero.
me: but simon . . .
simon: stop whining and find another warm body to
    get in mr. nadler's car with us. or even a cold body
    if it can stay propped up for an hour. it would be a
    change of pace to have someone who can actually
    add, but i swear i won't be choosy, *you fart*.

it's amazing how i usually make it through the day
without realizing i don't have that many friends. i mean,
once you get out of the top five you'll find a lot more of
the custodial staff than members of the student body. and
while janitor jim doesn't mind if i swipe a roll of toilet
paper every now and then for 'art projects,' i have a feeling
he wouldn't be willing to forfeit his friday night for a trip
with the calcsuckers and their faculty groupies.

i know i only have one shot, and it ain't an easy one.
maura's been in a good mood all day — well, a maura version of a good mood, which means the forecast calls for
drizzle instead of thunderstorms. she hasn't brought up the
gay thing, and lord knows i haven't either.

i wait until last period, knowing that if the pressure's
on, she's more likely to say yes. even though we're sitting
next to each other, i take my phone out under the desk and
text her.

me: whatre u doing tmrw night?
maura: nothing. wanna do something?

me: i wish. i have to go to chicago with my mom.
maura: fun?
me: i need you to sub for me in mathletes. otherwise
    s&d are screwed.
maura: ure kidding, right?
me: no, theyll really be screwed.
maura: and y would i?
me: because ill o u 1. and ill give you 20 bucks.
maura: o me 3 and make it 50.
me: deal.
maura: im saving these texts.

truth? i probably just rescued maura from an afternoon of shopping with her mom or doing homework or poking a pen into her veins to get some material for her poetry. after class, i tell her that she'll no doubt meet some other deadbeat fourth-string mathlete from some town we've never heard of, and the two of them will sneak out for clove cigarettes and talk about how lame everyone else is while derek and simon and that stupid freshman get smashed on theorems and rhombazoids. really, i'm doing wonders for her social life.

maura: don't push it.
me: i swear, it'll be hot.
maura: i want twenty bucks up front.

i'm just glad i didn't have to lie and say that i had to go visit my sick grandma or something. those kind of lies are dangerous, because you know the minute you say your grandma's sick the phone's going to ring and your mom's going to come into the room with really bad news about grandma's pancreas, and even though you'll know that little white lies do not cause cancer, you'll still feel guilty for the rest of your life. maura asks me more about my trip to chicago with my mom, so i make it sound like it's necessary bonding time, and since maura has two happy parents and i have one bummed-out one, i win the sympathy vote. i'm thinking about isaac so much that i'm completely scared i'm just going to blurt him out, but luckily maura's interest keeps me on my guard.

when it's time for her to go her way and me to go mine, she makes one more stab for the truth.

maura: is there anything you want to tell me?
me: yeah. i want to tell you that my third nipple is
    lactating and my butt cheeks are threatening to
      unionize. what do you think i should do about it?
maura: i feel you're not telling me something.

here's the thing about maura: it's always about her. always. now, normally i don't mind this, because if everything's about her, then nothing has to be about me. but sometimes her spotlight clinging drags me in, and that's what i hate.

she's pouting at me now, and, to give her credit, it's a genuine pout. it's not like she's trying to manipulate me by pretending to be annoyed. maura doesn't do that kind of crap, and that's why i put up with her. i can take everything on her face at face value, and that's valuable in a friend.

me: i'll tell you when i have something to tell you,
okay? now go home and practice your math. here . . .
i made you flash cards.

i reach into my bag and take out these cards i made
seventh period, kinda knowing maura was going to say yes.
they're not actually cards, since it's not like i carry a set of
index cards around in my bag for indexing emergencies. but
i made all these dotted lines on the piece of paper so she'll
know where to cut. each card has its own equation.

$2 + 2 = 4$
$50 \times 40 = 2000$
$834620 \times 375002 = who\ really\ gives\ a\ fuck?$
$x + y = z$
$cock + pussy = a\ happy\ rooster\text{-}kitten\ couple$
$red + blue = purple$
$me - mathletes = me + gratitude\ to\ you$

maura looks at them for a second, then folds the piece of
paper along the dotted lines, squaring it together like a map. she
doesn't smile or anything, but she looks unpissed for a second.

me: don't let derek and simon get too frisky, okay?
always wear pocket protection.
maura: i think i'll be able to keep my maidenhead at a
mathletes competition.
me: you say that now, but we'll see in nine months. if
it's a girl, you should name her *logorrhea*. if it's a
boy, go for *trig*.

it does occur to me that because of the way life works, maura probably *will* get some hot math-reject guy to put his plus in her minus, while i bomb out with isaac and come home to the comfort of my own hand.

i decide not to tell maura this, 'cause why jinx us both?

maura gives me an actual 'good-bye' before she goes, and she looks like she has something else to say, but has decided not to say it. another reason for me to be grateful.

i thank her again. and again. and again.

when that's done, i head home and email with isaac once he gets home from school — no work for him today. we go over our plan about two thousand times. he says a friend of his suggested we meet at a place called frenchy's, and since i don't really know chicago that much outside of places where you'd go on a class trip, i tell him that's fine by me, and print out the directions he sends me.

when we're through, i go on facebook and look at his profile for the millionth thousandth time. he doesn't really change it that often, but it's a good enough reminder to me that he's real. i mean, we've exchanged photos and have talked enough for me to know that he's real — it's not like he's some forty-six-year-old who's already prepared a nice spot in the back of his unmarked van for me. i'm not that stupid. we're meeting in a public place, and i have my phone. even if isaac has a psychotic break, i'll be prepared.

before i go to sleep, i look at all the pictures i have of him, as if i haven't already memorized them. i'm sure i'll recognize him the moment i see him. and i'm sure it'll be one of the best moments of my life.

friday after school is brutal. i want to commit murder about a thousand different ways, and it's my closet i want to kill. i have no fucking idea what to wear — and i am *not* a what-do-i-wear kind of guy at all, so it's like i can't even begin to comprehend the task at hand. every single god-damn piece of clothing i own seems to have chosen now to reveal its faults. i put on this one shirt which i've always thought made me look good, and sure enough it makes my chest look like it actually has some definition. but then i realize it's so small that if i raise my arms even an inch, my belly pubes are on full display. so then i try this black shirt which makes me look like i'm trying too hard, and then this white shirt which is cool until i find this stain near the bottom which i'm hoping is orange juice, but is probably from when i tucked before i tapped. band t-shirts are too obvious — if i wear a shirt from one of his favorites, it's like i'm being a kiss-ass, and if i wear one for a band he might not like, he might think my taste is lame. my gray hoodie is too blech and this blue shirt i have is practically the same color as my jeans, and looking all-blue is something only cookie monster can pull off.

for the first time in my life i realize why hangers are called hangers, because after fifteen minutes of trying things on and throwing them aside, all i want to do is hook one to the top of my closet door, lean my neck into the loop, and let my weight fall. my mother will come in and think it's some autoerotic asphyxiation where i didn't even have the time to get my dick out, and i won't be alive enough to tell her that i think autoerotic asphyxiation is one of the dumbest things in the whole universe, right up there with gay republicans.

but, yeah, i'll be dead. and it'll be like an episode of *CSI: FU*, where the investigators will come in and spend forty-three minutes plus commercials scouring over my life, and at the end they'll bring my mother to the station house and they'll sit her down and give her the truth.

cop: ma'am, your son wasn't murdered. he was just
getting ready for a first date.

i'm kind-of smiling, picturing how the scene would be shot, then i remember that i'm standing shirtless in the middle of my room, and i have a train to catch. finally i just pick this shirt that has a little picture of this robot made out of duct tape or something, with the word *robotboy* in small lowercase underneath it. i don't know why i like it, but i do. and i don't know why i think isaac will like it, but i do.

i know i must be nervous, because i'm actually thinking about *how my hair looks*, but when i get to the bathroom mirror, i decide my hair's going to do what it wants to do, and since it usually looks better when it's windy, i'll just stick my head out of the train window or something on my way there. i could use my mother's hair stuff, but i have no desire to smell like butterflies in a field. so i'm done.

i've told mom that the mathletes competition is in chicago — i figured if i was going to lie, she might as well think we made the state finals. i claimed the school had chartered a bus, but instead i head to the train station, no problem. my nerves are completely jangling by now. i try to read *to kill a mockingbird* for english class, but it's like the letters are this nice design on the page and don't mean anything more to me than the patterns on the train seats. it could be an action movie called *die, mockingbird, die!* and i still wouldn't be into it. so i close my eyes and listen to my ipod, but it's like it's been preprogrammed by a mean-ass cupid, because every single song makes me think of isaac. he's become the one the songs are about. and while part of me knows he's probably worth that, another part is yelling at me to *slow the fuck down*. while it's going to be exciting to see isaac, it's also going to be awkward. the key will be to not let that awkwardness get to us.

i take about five minutes to think about my dating history — five minutes is really all i can fill — and i'm sent back to the traumatic experience of drunkenly groping carissa nye at sloan mitchell's party a couple months ago. the kissing part was actually hot, but then when it got more serious, carissa got this stupidly earnest look on her face and i almost cracked up. we had some serious problems with her bra cutting off the circulation to her brain, and when i finally had her boobs in my hands (not that i'd asked for them), i didn't know what to do with them except pet them, like they were puppies. the puppies liked that, and carissa decided to give me a rub or two also, and i liked that, because when it all comes down to it, hands are hands, and touch is touch, and your body's going to react the way your body's going to react. it doesn't give a damn about all the conversations you're going to have afterward — not just with carissa, who wanted to be my girlfriend and who i tried to let down easy, but ended up hurting anyway. no, there was also maura to deal with, because the moment she heard (not from me) she was pissed (all at me). she said she thought carissa was using me, and she acted like she thought i was using carissa, when really the whole thing was useless, and no matter how many times i told maura this, she refused to let me off the hook. for weeks i had her shouting 'well, why don't you give carissa a call, then?' whenever we disagreed. for that alone, the groping wasn't worth it.

isaac, of course, is completely different. not just in the groping sense. although there is certainly that. i'm not heading into the city just to mess around with him. it might not be the last thing on my mind, but it isn't near the first, either.

i thought i was going to be early, but of course by the time i get near where we're supposed to meet, i'm later than a pregnant girl's period. i walk along michigan avenue with the right-before-curfew tourist girls and tourist boys, who all look like they've just come from basketball practice or watching basketball on tv. i definitely eye a few specimens, but it's purely scientific research. for the next, oh, ten minutes, i can save myself for isaac.

i wonder if he's already there. i wonder if he's as nervous as i am. i wonder if he has spent as much time this morning as i did picking a shirt out. i wonder if by some freak of nature we'll be wearing the same thing. like this is so meant to be that god's decided to make it *really* obvious.

sweaty palms. *check.* shaky bones. *check.* the feeling that all oxygen in the air has been replaced by helium. *yup.* i look at the map fifteen times a second. five blocks to go. four blocks to go. three blocks to go. two blocks to go. state street. the corner. looking for frenchy's. thinking it's going to be a hip diner. or a coffee shop. or an indie record store. or even just a rundown restaurant.

then: getting there and finding out . . . it's a porn shop.

thinking maybe the porn shop was named after something else nearby. maybe this is the frenchy's district, and everything is named frenchy's, like the way you can go downtown and find downtown bagels and the downtown cleaners and the downtown yoga studio. but no. i loop the block. i try the other side. i check the address over and over and over.

and there i am. back at the door.

i remember that isaac's friend suggested the place. or at least that's what he said. if that's true, maybe it's a joke, and poor isaac got here first and was mortified and is waiting for me inside. or maybe this is some kind of cosmic test. i have to cross the river of extreme awkwardness in order to get to the paradise on the other side.

what the fuck, i figure.

cold wind blowing all around me, i head inside.

chapter seven

I hear the electronic *bing* and turn around to see a kid walking in. Naturally, he doesn't get carded, and while he is on the hairy side of puberty, there's no way he's eighteen. Small and big-eyed and towheaded and absolutely terrified—as scared as I would probably be had I not already been driven to the brink by the anti-Will Grayson conspiracy encompassing A. Jane, and B. Tiny, and C. The well-pierced specimen behind the counter, and D. Stonedy McKopyShoppy.

But, anyway, the kid is staring at me with a level of intensity that I find very troubling, particularly given that I am holding a copy of *Mano a Mano*. I'm sure there are a number of fantastic ways to indicate to the underage stranger standing next to a Great Wall of Dildos that you are not, in fact, a fan of *Mano a Mano*, but the particular strategy I choose is to mumble, "It's, uh, for a friend." Which is true, but A. It's not a terribly convincing excuse, and B. It implies that I'm the kind of guy who is friends with the kind of guy who likes *Mano a Mano*, and further implies that C. I'm the kind of guy who buys porn magazines for his friends. Immediately after saying "It's for a friend," I realize that I should have said, "I'm trying to learn Spanish."

The kid just continues to stare at me, and then after a while he narrows his eyes, squinting. I hold his stare for a few seconds but then glance away. Finally, he walks past me and into the video aisles. It seems to me that he is looking for something specific, and that the something specific is not related to sex, in which case I rather suspect he will not find it here. He meanders toward the back of the store, which contains an open door that I believe may in some way be related to "Tokens." All I want to do is get the hell out of here with my copy of *Mano a Mano*, so I walk up to the pierced guy and say, "Just this, please."

He rings it up on the cash register. "Nine eighty-three," he says.

"Nine DOLLARS?" I ask, incredulous.

"And eighty-three cents," he adds.

I shake my head. This is turning into an extraordinarily expensive joke, but I'm not very well going to return to the creepy magazine rack and look for a bargain. I reach into my pockets and come out with somewhere in the neighborhood of four dollars. I sigh, and then reach for my back pocket, handing the guy my debit card. My parents look at the statement, but they won't know *Frenchy's* from *Denny's*.

The guy looks at the card. He looks at me. He looks at the card. He looks at me. And just before he talks, I realize: my card says William Grayson. My ID says Ishmael J. Biafra.

Quite loud, the guy says, "William. Grayson. William. Grayson. Where *have* I seen that name before? Oh, right. NOT on your driver's license."

I consider my options for a moment and then say, real quietly, "It's my card. I know my pin. Just—ring it up."

He swipes it through the card machine and says, "I don't give a shit, kid. It all spends the same." And just then I can feel the guy right behind me, looking at me again, and so I wheel around, and he says, "What did you say?" Only he's not talking to me, he's talking to Piercings.

"I said I don't give a shit about his ID."

"You didn't call me?"

"What the fuck are you talking about, kid?"

"William Grayson. Did you say William Grayson? Did someone call here for me?"

"Huh? No, kid. William Grayson is this guy," he says, nodding toward me. "Well, two schools of thought on that, I guess, but that's what *this* card says."

And the kid looks at me confused for a minute and finally says, "What's your name?"

This is freaking me out. Frenchy's isn't a place for *conversation*. So I just say to Piercings, "Can I have the magazine?" and Piercings hands it to me in an unmarked and thoroughly opaque black plastic bag for which I am very grateful, and he gives me my card and my receipt. I walk out the door, jog a half block down Clark, and then sit down on the curb and wait for my pulse to slow down.

Which it is just starting to do when my fellow underage Frenchy's pilgrim runs up to me and says, "Who *are* you?"

I stand up then and say, "Um, I'm Will Grayson."

"W-I-L-L G-R-A-Y-S-O-N?" he says, spelling impossibly fast.

"Uh, yeah," I say. "Why do you ask?"

The kid looks at me for a second, his head turned like he thinks I might be putting him on, and then finally he says, "Because I am also Will Grayson."

"No shit?" I ask.

"Shit," the guy says. I can't decide if he's paranoid or schizophrenic or both, but then he pulls a duct-taped wallet out of his back pocket and shows me an Illinois driver's license. Our middle names are different, at least, but—yeah.

"Well," I say, "good to meet you." And then I start to turn away, because nothing against the guy but I don't care to strike up a conversation with a guy who hangs out at porn stores, even if, technically speaking, I am myself a guy who hangs out at porn stores. But he touches my arm, and he seems too small to be *dangerous*, so I turn back around, and he says, "Do you know Isaac?"

"Who?"

"Isaac?"

"I don't know anyone named Isaac, man," I say.

"I was supposed to meet him at that place, but he's not there. You don't really look like him but I thought—I don't know what I thought. How the—what the hell is going on?" The kid spins a quick circle, like he's looking for a cameraman or something. "Did Isaac put you up to this?"

"I just told you, man, I don't know any Isaac."

He turns around again, but there's no one behind him. He throws his arms in the air, and says, "I don't even know *what* to freak out *about* right now."

"It's been a bit of a crazy day for Will Graysons everywhere," I say.

He shakes his head and sits down on the curb then and I follow him, because there is nothing else to do. He looks over at me, then away, then at me again. And then he actually, physically pinches himself on the forearm. "Of course not. My dreams can't make up shit this weird."

"Yeah," I say. I can't figure out if he wants me to talk to him, and I also can't figure out if I want to talk to him, but after a minute, I say, "So, uh, how do you know meet-me-at-the-porn-store Isaac?"

"He's just—a friend of mine. We've known each other online for a long time."

"Online?"

If possible, Will Grayson manages to shrink into himself even more. His shoulders hunched, he stares intently into the gutter of the street. I know, of course, that there are other Will Graysons. I've Googled myself enough to know that. But I never thought I would see one. Finally he says, "Yeah."

"You've never physically seen this guy," I say.

"No," he says, "but I've seen him in like a thousand pictures."

"He's a fifty-year-old man," I say, matter-of-factly. "He's a pervert. One Will to another: No way that Isaac is who you think he is."

"He's probably just—I don't know, maybe he met another freaking Isaac on the bus and he's stuck in Bizarro World."

"Why the hell would he ask you to go to Frenchy's?"

"Good question. Why *would* someone go to a porn store?" He kind of smirks at me.

"Fair point," I say. "Yeah, that's true. There's a story to it, though."

I wait for a second for Will Grayson to ask me about my story, but he doesn't. Then I start telling him anyway. I tell him about Jane and Tiny Cooper and the Maybe Dead

Cats and "Annus Miribalis" and Jane's locker combination and the copy shop clerk who couldn't count, and I weasel a couple of laughs out of him along the way, but mostly he just keeps glancing back toward Frenchy's, waiting for Isaac. His face seems to alternate between hope and anger. He pays very little attention to me actually, which is fine, really, because I'm just telling my story to tell it, talking to a stranger because it's the only safe kind of talking you can do, and the whole time my hand is in my pocket holding my phone, because I want to make sure I feel it vibrate if someone calls.

And then he tells me about Isaac, about how they've been friends for a year and that he always wanted to meet him because there's just no one like Isaac out in the suburb where he lives, and it dawns on me pretty quickly that Will Grayson likes Isaac in a not-altogether-platonic way. "So, I mean what perverted fifty-year-old would do that?" Will says. "What pervert spends a year of his life talking to me, telling me everything about his fake self, while I tell him everything about my real self? And if a perverted fifty-year-old *did* do that, why wouldn't he show up at Frenchy's to rape and murder me? Even on a totally impossible night, that is *totally impossible*."

I mull it over for a second. "I don't know," I say finally. "People are pretty fucking weird, if you haven't noticed."

"Yeah." He's not looking back to Frenchy's anymore, just forward. I can see him out of the corner of my eye, and I'm sure he can see me out of the corner of his, but mostly we are looking not at each other, but at the same spot on the street as cars rumble past, my brain trying to make sense of all the impossibilities, all the coincidences that brought me here, all the true-and-false things. And we're quiet for a while, so long that I take my phone out of my pocket and look at it and confirm that no one has called and then put it back, and then finally I feel Will turning his head away from the spot on the street and toward me and he says, "What do you think it means?"

"What?" I ask.

"There aren't that many Will Graysons," he says. "It's gotta mean something, one Will Grayson meeting another Will Grayson in a random porn store where neither Will Grayson belongs."

"Are you suggesting that God brought two of Chicago-land's underage Will Graysons into Frenchy's at the same time?"

"No, asshole," he says, "but I mean, it must mean *something*."

"Yeah," I say. "It's hard to believe in coincidence, but it's even harder to believe in anything else." And just then, the phone jumps to life in my hand, and as I am pulling it out of my pocket, Will Grayson's phone starts ringing.

And even for me, that's a lot of coincidences. He mutters, "God, it's Maura," as if I'm going to know who Maura is, and he just stares at the phone, seeming unsure of whether to answer. My call is from Tiny. Before I flip open the phone, I say to Will, "It's my friend Tiny," and I'm looking at Will—at cute, confuzzled Will.

I flip open the phone.

"Grayson!" Tiny shouts over the din of the music. "I'm in love with this band! We're gonna stay for like two more songs and then I'm gonna come get you. Where are you, baby! Where's my pretty little baby Grayson!"

"I'm across the street," I shout back. "And you better get down on your knees and thank the sweet Lord, because man, Tiny, have I got a guy for you."

chapter eight

i am so freaked out, you could pull a clown out of my ass and i wouldn't be at all surprised.

it would make maybe a little sense if this OTHER WILL GRAYSON standing right next to me wasn't a will grayson at all but was instead the gold medal champion of the mind-fuck olympics. it's not like when i first saw him i thought to myself, *hey, that kid must be named will grayson, too*. no, the only thing i thought was, *hey, that's not isaac*. i mean, right age, but entirely wrong face pic. so i ignored him. i turned back to the dvd case i was pretending to study, which was for this porno called *the sound and the furry*. it was all about 'moo sex,' with these people pictured on the cover wear-ing cow suits (one udder). i was glad that no real cows were harmed (or pleasured) in the making of the film. but still, not my thing. next to it was a dvd called *as i get laid dying*, which had a hospital scene on the front. it was like *grey's anatomy*, only with less grey and more anatomy. i totally thought for a moment, *i can't wait to tell isaac about this*, forgetting, of course, that he was supposed to be with me.

it's not like i wouldn't have noticed him come in; the place was empty except for me, o.w.g., and the clerk, who looked like the pillsbury doughboy if the dough had been left out for a week. i guess everyone else was using the internet to get their porn. and frenchy's wasn't exactly inviting — it was lit like a 7-eleven, which made all the plastic seem much more plastic, and the metal seem much more metal, and the naked people on the covers of the dvd cases look even less hot and more like cheap porn. passing up *go down on moses* and *afternoon delight in august*, i found myself in this bizarre penis produce section. because my mind is, at heart, full of fucked up shit, i immediately started to picture this sequel to *toy story* called *sex toy story*, where all these dildos and vibrators and rabbit ears suddenly came to life and have to do things like cross the street in order to get back home.

again, as i was having all these thoughts, i was also thinking about sharing them with isaac. that was my default.

i was only distracted when i heard my name being said by the guy behind the counter. which is how i found o.w.g.

so, yeah, i go into a porn shop looking for isaac and i get another will grayson instead.

god, you're one nasty fucker.

of course, right now isaac is ranking up there in nasty fuckerdom, too. i'm hoping that he's actually a nervous fucker instead — like, maybe he showed up and discovered that the place his friend recommended was a porn shop and was so mortified that he ran away crying. i mean, it's possible. or maybe he's just late. i have to give him at least an hour. his train could've gotten stuck in a tunnel or something. it's not unheard of. he's coming from ohio, after all. people in ohio are late all the time.

my phone rings at practically the same time as o.w.g.'s. even though it's pathetically unlikely that it's going to be isaac, my hopes still do the up thing.

then i see it's maura.

me: god, it's maura.

at first i'm not going to answer, but then o.w.g. answers his.

o.w.g.: it's my friend tiny.

if o.w.g. is going to answer his, i figure i'd better answer mine, too. i also remember maura's doing me a favor today. if later on i learn that the mathletic competition was attacked by an uzi-wielding squad of frustrated humanties nerds, i'll feel guilty that i didn't answer the phone and let maura say good-bye.

me: quick — what's the square root of my underwear?
maura: hey will.
me: that answer earns you zero points.
maura: how's chicago?
me: there's no wind at all!
maura: what are you doing?
me: oh, hanging out with will grayson.
maura: that's what i thought.
me: what do you mean?
maura: where's your mom?

uh-oh. smells like a trap. has maura called my house? has she talked to my mom? pedal motion, backward!

me: am i my mother's keeper? (ha ha ha)
maura: stop lying, will.
me: okay, okay. i kinda needed to sneak in on my own.
    to go to a concert later.
maura: what concert?

fuck! i can't remember which concert o.w.g. said he was going to. and he's still on the phone, so i can't ask.

me: some band you've never heard of.
maura: try me.
me: um, that's their name. 'some band you've never
    heard of.'
maura: oh, i've heard of them.
me: yeah.
maura: i was just reading a review of their album in
    spin.
me: cool.
maura: yeah, the album's called 'isaac's not coming,
    you fucking liar.'

this is not good.

me: that's a pretty stupid name for an album.

what? what what what?

maura: give up, will.

me: my password.

maura: what?

me: you totally hacked my password. you've been reading my emails, haven't you?

maura: what are you talking about?

me: isaac. how do you know about me meeting up with isaac?

she must have looked over my shoulder when i checked my email at school. she must have seen the keys i typed. she stole my dumbass password.

maura: i *am* isaac, will.

me: don't be stupid. he's a guy.

maura: no he's not. he's a profile. i made him up.

me: yeah, right.

maura: i did.

no. no no no no no no no no no no no no no.

me: what?

no please no what no no please no fuck no NO.

maura: isaac doesn't exist. he's never existed.

me: you can't —

maura: you're so caught.

I'M so caught*?!?*

what the FUCK.

me: tell me you're joking.
maura: . . .
me: this can't be happening.

other will grayson's finished his conversation and is looking at me now.

o.w.g.: are you okay?

it's hitting. that moment of 'did an anvil really just fall on my head?' has passed and i am feeling that anvil. oh lord am i feeling that anvil.

me: you. despicable. cunt.

yes, the synapses are conveying the information now. newsflash: isaac never existed. it was only your friend posing. it was all a lie.
    all a lie.

me: you. horrendous. bitch.
maura: why is it that girls are never called assholes?
me: i am not going to insult assholes that way. they at
    least serve a purpose.
maura: look, i knew you'd be mad . . .
me: you *KNEW* i would be *MAD*!?!
maura: i was going to tell you.
me: gee, thanks.

maura: but you never told me.

o.w.g.'s looking very concerned now. so i put my hand over the phone for a second and speak to him.

me: i'm actually not okay. in fact, i am probably having the worst minute of my life. don't go anywhere.

o.w.g. nods.

maura: will? look, i'm sorry.
me: . . .
maura: you didn't actually think he was meeting you at a porn store, did you?
me: . . .
maura: it was a joke.
me: . . .
maura: will?
me: it is only my respect for your parents that will prevent me from murdering you outright. but please understand this: i am never, ever speaking to you or passing notes to you or texting you or doing fucking sign language with you ever again. i would rather eat dog shit full of razor blades than have anything to do with you.

i hang up before she can say anything else. i switch off the phone. i sit down on the curb. i close my eyes. and i scream. if my whole world is going to crash down around me, then i am going to make the sound of the crashing. i want to scream until all my bones break.

once. twice. again.

then i stop. i feel the tears, and hope that if i keep my eyes closed i can keep them inside. i am so beyond pathetic because i want to open my eyes and see isaac there, have him tell me that maura's out of her mind. or have the other will grayson tell me that this, too, can be dismissed as coincidence. *he's* really the will grayson that maura's been emailing with. she's gotten her will graysons mixed up.

but reality. well, reality is the anvil.

i take a deep breath and it sounds clogged.

the whole time.

the whole time it was maura.

not isaac.

no isaac.

never.

there's hurt. there's pain. and there's hurt-and-pain-at-once.

i am experiencing hurt-and-pain-at-once.

o.w.g.: um . . . will?

he looks like he can see the hurt-and-pain-at-once very clearly on my face.

me: you know that guy i was supposed to meet?
o.w.g.: isaac.
me: yeah, isaac. well, it ends up he wasn't a fifty-year-old after all. he was my friend maura, playing a joke.
o.w.g.: that's one helluva mean joke.
me: yeah. i'm feeling that.

i have no idea whether i'm talking to him because he's also named will grayson or because he told me a little about what's going on with him or because he's the only person in the world who's willing to listen to me right now. all of my instincts are telling me to curl into a tiny ball and roll into the nearest sewer — but i don't want to do that to o.w.g. i feel he deserves more than being an eyewitness to my self-destruction.

me: anything like this ever happen to you before?

o.w.g. shakes his head.

o.w.g.: i'm afraid we're in new territory here. my best friend tiny was once going to enter me into *seventeen* magazine's boy of the month contest without telling me, but i don't think that's really the same thing.
me: how did you find out?
o.w.g.: he decided he needed someone to proofread his entry, so he asked me to do it.
me: did you win?
o.w.g.: i told him i'd mail it for him and then filed it away. he was really upset that i didn't win . . . but i think it would've been worse if i had.
me: you might have gotten to meet miley cyrus. jane would've died of jealousy.
o.w.g.: i think jane would've died of laughter first.

i can't help it — i imagine isaac laughing, too.
and then i have to kill that image.

because isaac doesn't exist.
i feel like i'm going to lose it again.

me: why?
o.w.g.: why would jane die laughing?
me: no, why would maura do this?
o.w.g: i can't honestly say.

maura. isaac.
isaac. maura.
anvil.
anvil.
anvil.

me: you know what sucks about love?
o.w.g.: what?
me: that it's so tied to truth.

the tears are starting to come back. because that pain
— i know i'm giving it all up. isaac. hope. the future. those
feelings. that word. i'm giving it all up, and that hurts.

o.w.g.: will?
me: i think i need to close my eyes for a minute and
      feel what i need to feel.

i shut my eyes, shut my body, try to shut out everything
else. i feel o.w.g. stand up. i wish he were isaac, even though
i know he's not. i wish maura weren't isaac, even though i
know she is. i wish i were someone else, even though i know

i'll never, ever be able to get away from what i've done and what's been done to me.

lord, send me amnesia. make me forget every moment i ever didn't really have with isaac. make me forget that maura exists. this must be what my mother felt when my dad said it was over. i get it now. i get it. the things you hope for the most are the things that destroy you in the end.

i hear o.w.g. talking to someone. a murmured recap of everything that's just happened.

i hear footsteps coming closer. i try to calm myself a little, then open my eyes . . . and see this *ginormous* guy standing in front of me. when he notices me noticing him, he gives me this broad smile. i swear, he has dimples the size of a baby's head.

ginormous guy: hello there. i'm tiny.

he offers his hand. i'm not entirely in a shaking mood, but it's awkward if i just leave him there, so i hold out my hand, too. instead of shaking it, though, he yanks me up to my feet.

tiny: did someone die?
me: yeah, i did.

he smiles again at that.

tiny: well, then . . . welcome to the afterlife.

chapter nine

You can say a lot of bad things about Tiny Cooper. I know, because I have said them. But for a guy who knows absolutely nothing about how to conduct his own relationships, Tiny Cooper is kind of brilliant when it comes to dealing with other people's heartbreak. Tiny is like some gigantic sponge soaking up the pain of lost love everywhere he goes. And so it is with Will Grayson. The other Will Grayson, I mean.

Jane's a storefront down standing in a doorway, talking on the phone. I look over at her, but she's not looking at me, and I'm wondering if they played the song. Something Will—the other Will—said right before Tiny and Jane walked up keeps looping around my head: love is tied to truth. I think of them as unhappily conjoined twins.

"Obviously," Tiny is saying, "she's just a hot smoldering pile of suck, but even so, I give her full credit for the name. *Isaac. Isaac.* I mean, I could almost fall in love with a girl, if she were named *Isaac.*"

The other Will Grayson doesn't laugh, but Tiny is undeterred. "You must have been so totally freaked out when you realized it was a porn store, right? Like, who wants to meet *there.*"

"And then also when his namesake was buying a maga-zine," I say, holding up the black bag, thinking that Tiny will snatch it and check out my purchase. But he doesn't. He just says, "This is even worse than what happened to me and Tommy."

"What happened with you and Tommy?" Will asks.

"He said he was a natural blonde, but his dye job was so bad it looked like a weave from Mattel—like Barbie. Also, Tommy wasn't short for *Tomas*, like he told me. It was short for regular old Thomas."

Will says, "Yes, this is worse. Much worse."

I clearly don't have much to contribute to the conver-sation, and anyway, Tiny is acting like I don't exist, so I smile and say, "I'm gonna leave you two boys alone now." And then I look at the other Will Grayson, and he's sort of swaying like he might fall over if the wind kicks up. I want to say something, because I feel really bad for him, but I never know what to say. So I just say what I'm thinking. "I know it sucks, but in a way, it's good." He looks at me like I've just said something absolutely idiotic, which of course I have. "Love and truth being tied together, I mean. They make each other possible, you know?"

The kid gives me about an eighth of a smile and then turns back to Tiny, who—to be fair—is clearly the better therapist. The black bag with *Mano a Mano* doesn't seem funny anymore, so I just drop it on the ground next to Tiny and Will. They don't even notice.

Jane's standing on the curb on her tiptoes now, almost leaning out into a street choked thick with cabs. A group of college guys walk past and look at her, one raising his eyebrows to another. I'm still thinking about the tying of love and truth—and it makes me want to tell her the truth—the whole, contradictory truth—because otherwise, on some level, am I not that girl? Am I not that girl pretending to be Isaac?

I walk over to her and try to touch the back of her elbow, but my touch is too soft and I only get her coat. She turns to me and I see that she's still on her cell. I make a gesture that is intended to convey, "Hey, no hurry, talk as long as you'd like," and probably actually conveys, "Hey, look at me! I have spastic hands." Jane holds up a finger. I nod. She speaks softly, cutely into the phone, saying, "Yeah, I know. Me too."

I step backward across the sidewalk and lean against the brick wall between Frenchy's and a closed sushi restaurant. To my right, Will and Tiny talk. To my left, Jane talks. I pull out my cell as though I'm going to send a text, but I just scroll through my contact list. Clint. Dad. Jane. Mom. People I used to be friends with. People I sorta know. Tiny. Nothing after the *T*'s. Not much for a phone I've had three years.

"Hey," Jane says. I look up, flip the phone shut, and smile at her. "Sorry about the concert," she says.

"Yeah, it's okay," I answer, because it is.

"Who's the guy?" she asks, gesturing toward him.

"Will Grayson," I say. She squints at me, confused. "I met a guy named Will Grayson in that porn store," I say. "I was there to use my fake ID, and he was there to meet his fake boyfriend."

"Jesus, if I'd known that was gonna happen, I would've skipped the concert."

"Yeah," I say, trying not to sound annoyed. "Let's take a walk."

She nods. We walk over toward Michigan Avenue, the Magnificent Mile, home to all of Chicago's biggest, chainiest stores. Everything's closed now, and the tourists who flood the wide sidewalks during the day have gone back to their hotels, towering fifty stories above us. The homeless people who beg off the tourists are gone, too, and it is mostly just Jane and me. You can't tell the truth without talking, so I'm telling her the whole story, trying to make it funny, trying to make it grander than any MDC concert could ever be. And when I finish there's a lull and she says, "Can I ask you something random?"

"Yeah, of course." We're walking past Tiffany, and I stop for a second. The pale yellow streetlights illuminate the storefront just enough that through triple-paned glass and a security grate, I can see an empty display—a gray velvet outline of a neck wearing no jewelry.

"Do you believe in epiphanies?" she asks. We start walking again.

"Um, can you unpack the question?"

"Like, do you believe that people's attitudes can change? One day you wake up and you realize something, you see something in a way that you never saw it before, and boom, epiphany. Something is different forever. Do you believe in that?"

"No," I say. "I don't think anything happens all at once. Like, Tiny? You think Tiny falls in love every day? No way. He *thinks* he does, but he doesn't really. I mean, anything that happens all at once is just as likely to *un*happen all at once, you know?"

She doesn't say anything for a while. She just walks. My hand is down next to her hand, and they brush but nothing happens between us. "Yeah. Maybe you're right," she says finally.

"Why do you ask?" I say.

"I don't know. No reason, really." The English language has a long and storied history. And in all that time, no one has ever asked a "random question" about "epiphanies" for "no reason." "Random questions" are the least random of all questions.

"Who had the epiphany?" I ask.

"Um, I think you're actually, like, the worst possible person to talk to about this," she says.

"How's that?"

"I know it was pretty lame of me to go to the concert," she says randomly. We come to a plastic bench and she sits down.

"It's okay," I say, sitting down next to her.

"It's actually not okay on, like, the grandest possible scale. I guess the thing is that I'm a little confused." Confused. The phone. The sweet, girly voice. Epiphanies. I finally realize the truth.

"The ex-boyfriend," I say. I feel my gut sinking down like it's swimming in the ocean deep, and I learn the truth: I like her. She's cute and she's really smart in precisely the right slightly pretentious way, and there's a softness to her face that sharpens everything she says, and I like her, and it's not just that I *should* be honest with her; I want to. Such is the way these things are tied together, I guess. "I have an idea," I say.

I can feel her looking at me, and I cinch the hood of my coat. My ears feel cold like burning.

And she says, "What's the idea?"

"The idea is that for ten minutes, we forget that we have feelings. And we forget about protecting ourselves or other people and we just say the truth. For ten minutes. And then we can go back to being lame."

"I like the idea," she says. "But you have to start."

I push my coat sleeve back and look at my watch. 10:42. "Ready?" I ask. She nods. I look at my watch again. "Okay, and . . . go. I like you. And I didn't know whether I liked you until I thought of you at that concert with some other guy, but now I do know, and I realize that makes me a bitchsquealer, but yeah, I like you. I think you're great, and very cute—and by cute I mean beautiful but don't want to say beautiful because it's cliché but you are—and I don't even mind that you're a music snob."

"It's not snobbery; it's good taste. So I used to date this boy and I knew he was going to be at the concert and I wanted to go with you partly because I knew Randall would be there but then I wanted to go even without you because I knew he would be there and then he saw me while MDC was playing 'A Brief Overview of Time Travel Paradoxes,' and he was screaming in my ear about how he had an epiphany and he now knows that we're supposed to be together and I was, like, I don't think so and he quoted this e. e. cummings poem about how kisses are a better fate than wisdom and then it turns out that he had MDC dedicate a song to me which was the kind of thing that he would never have done before and I feel like I deserve someone who consistently likes me which you kind of don't and I don't know."

"What song?"

"'Annus Miribalis.' Uh, he's the only person who knows my locker combination, and he had them dedicate it to my locker combination, which is just, I mean, I don't know. That's just. Yeah."

Even though these are the minutes of truth, I don't tell her about the song. I can't. It's too embarrassing. The thing is, coming from your ex-boyfriend, it's sweet. And coming from the guy who wouldn't kiss you in your orange Volvo, it's just weird and maybe even mean. She's right that she deserves someone consistent, and maybe I can't be that. Nonetheless, I shred the guy. "I fucking hate guys who quote poetry to girls. Since we are being honest. Also, wisdom is a better fate than the vast majority of kisses. Wisdom is certainly a better fate than kissing douches who only read poetry so they can use it to get in girls' pants."

"Oh, my," she says. "Honest Will and Regular Will are so fascinatingly different!"

"To tell you the truth, I prefer just your average, run-of-the-mill, everyday jackass with his glass-eyed, slack-jawed obliviousness to the guys who try to hijack my cool by reading poetry and listening to halfway-good music. I worked hard for my cool. I got my ass kicked in middle school for my cool. I came by this shit honestly."

"Well, you don't even know him," she says.

"And I don't need to," I answer. "Look, you're right. Maybe I don't like you the way someone should like you. I don't like you in the call-you-and-read-you-a-poem-every-night-before-you-go-to-bed way. I'm crazy, okay? Sometimes I think, like, God, she's superhot and smart and kind of pretentious but the pretentiousness just makes me kind of *want* her, and then other times I think it's an amazingly bad idea, that dating you would be like a series of unnecessary root canals interspersed with occasional makeout sessions."

"Jesus, that's a burn."

"But not really, because I think both! And it doesn't matter, because I'm your Plan B. Maybe I'm your Plan B because I feel that way, and maybe I feel that way because I'm your Plan B, but regardless, it means you're supposed to be with Randall and I'm supposed to be in my natural state of self-imposed hookup exile."

"So different!" she says again. "Can you be like this permanently?"

"Probably not," I say.

"How many minutes do we have?"

"Four," I say.

And then we're kissing.

I lean in this time, and she doesn't turn away. It's cold, and our lips are dry, noses a little wet, foreheads sweaty beneath wool hats. I can't touch her face, even though I want to, because I'm wearing gloves. But God, when her lips come apart, everything turns warm and her sugar sweet breath is in my mouth, and I probably taste like hot dogs but I don't care. She kisses like a sweet devouring, and I don't know where to touch her because I want all of her. I want to touch her knees and her hips and her stomach and her back and her everything, but we're encased in all these clothes, so we're just two marshmallows bumping against each other, and she smiles at me while still kissing because she knows how ridiculous it is, too.

"Better than wisdom?" she asks, her nose touching my cheek.

"Tight race," I say, and I smile back as I pull her tighter to me.

I've never known before what it feels like to *want* someone—not to want to hook up with them or whatever, but to *want* them, to want *them*. And now I do. So maybe I do believe in epiphanies.

She pulls away from me just enough to say, "What's my last name?"

"I have no idea," I answer immediately.

"Turner. It's Turner." I slip in one last peck, and then she sits up properly, although her gloved hand still rests against my jacketed waist. "See, we don't even *know* each other. I have to find out if I believe in epiphanies, Will."

"I can't believe his name is Randall. He doesn't go to Evanston, does he?"

"No, he goes to Latin. We met at a poetry slam."

"Of course you did. My God, I can picture the slimy bastard: He's tall and shaggy-haired, and he plays a sport— soccer, probably—but he pretends like he doesn't even like it because all he likes is poetry and music and you, and he thinks you're a poem and tells you so, and he's slathered in confidence and probably body spray." She laughs, shaking her head. "What?" I ask.

"Water polo," she says. "Not soccer."

"Oh, Jesus. *Of course.* Water polo. Yeah, nothing says punk rock like water polo."

She grabs my arm and looks at my watch. "One minute," she says.

"You look better when your hair is pulled back," I tell her in a rush.

"Really?"

"Yeah, otherwise you look kinda like a puppy."

"You look better when you stand up straight," she says.

"Time!" I say.

"Okay," she says. "It's a shame we can't do that more often."

"Which part?" I ask smiling. She stands up.

"I should get home. Stupid midnight weekend curfew."

"Yeah," I say. I pull out my phone. "I'll call Tiny and tell him we're headed out."

"I'll just take a cab."

"I'll just call—"

But she's already standing on the edge of the sidewalk, the toes of her Chucks off the curb, her hand raised. A cab pulls over. She hugs me quickly—the hug all fingertips and shoulder blades—and is gone without another word.

I've never been alone in the city this late, and it's deserted. I call Tiny. He doesn't answer. I get the voice mail. "You've reached the voice mail of Tiny Cooper, writer, producer, and star of the new musical *Tiny Dancer: The Tiny Cooper Story*. I'm sorry, but it appears something more fabulous than your phone call is happening right now. When fabulous levels fall a bit, I'll get back to you. BEEP."

"Tiny, the next time that you try to set me up with a girl with a secret boyfriend can you at least *inform* me that she has a secret boyfriend? Also, if you don't call me back within five minutes, I'm going to assume you found a way back to Evanston. Furthermore, you are an asshat. That is all."

There are cabs on Michigan Avenue and a steady flow of

traffic, but once I get onto a side street, Huron, it's quiet. I walk past a church and then up State Street toward Frenchy's. I can tell from three blocks away that Tiny and Will aren't there anymore, but I still walk all the way to the storefront. I look up and down the street but see no one, and anyway, Tiny never shuts up, so I would hear him if he were nearby.

I fish through my coat pocket's detritus for my keys, then pull them out. The keys are wrapped in the note that Jane wrote me, the note from the Locker Houdini.

I'm walking down the street toward the car when I see a black plastic bag on the sidewalk, fluttering in the wind. *Mano a Mano*. I leave it, thinking I've probably just made someone's tomorrow.

For the first time in a long time, I drive with no music. I'm not happy—not happy about Jane and Mr. Randall Water Polo Doucheface IV, not happy about Tiny abandoning me without so much as a phone call, not happy about my insufficiently fake fake ID—but in the dark on Lake Shore with the car eating up all the sound, there's something about the numbness in my lips after having kissed her that I want to keep and hold onto, something in it that seems *pure*, that seems like the singular truth.

I get home four minutes before curfew, and my parents are on the couch, Mom's feet in Dad's lap. Dad mutes the TV and says, "How was it?"

"Pretty good," I say.

"Did they play 'Annus Miribalis?'" Mom asks, because I liked it so much I played it for her. I figure she's asking partly to seem hip and partly to make sure I went to the concert. She'll probably check the set list later. I *didn't* go to the concert, of course, but I know they played the song.

"Yeah," I say. "Yeah. It was good." I stare at them for a second, and then say, "Okay, I'm gonna go to bed."

"Why don't you watch some TV with us?" Dad asks.

"I'm tired," I say flatly, and turn to go.

But I don't go to bed. I go to my room and get online and start reading about e. e. cummings.

The next morning I get a ride to school early with Mom. In the hallways, I pass poster after poster for *Tiny Dancer*.

AUDITIONS TODAY NINTH PERIOD IN THE THEATER. PREPARE TO SING. PREPARE TO DANCE. PREPARE TO BE FABULOUS.

IN CASE YOU FAILED TO SEE THE PREVIOUS POSTER, AUDITIONS ARE TODAY.

SING & DANCE & CELEBRATE TOLERANCE IN THE MOST IMPORTANT MUSICAL OF OUR TIME.

I jog through the halls and then go upstairs to Jane's locker and carefully slip the note I wrote last night through the vent:

To: The Locker Houdini
From: Will Grayson
Re: An Expert in the Field of Good Boyfriends?

Dear Jane,

Just so you know: e. e. cummings cheated on both
of his wives. With prostitutes.

Yours,
Will Grayson

chapter ten

tiny cooper.

tiny cooper.

tiny cooper.

i am saying his name over and over in my head.

tiny cooper.

tiny cooper.

it's a ridiculous name, and the whole thing is ridiculous, and i couldn't stop it if i tried.

tiny cooper.

if i say it enough times, maybe it will be okay that isaac doesn't exist.

it starts that night. in front of frenchy's. i am still in shock. i can't tell whether it's post-traumatic stress or post-stress trauma. whatever it is, a good part of my life has just been erased, and i have no desire to fill in the new blank. leave it empty, i say. just let me die.

tiny, though, won't let me. he's playing the i've-had-it-worse game, which never works, because either the person says something that's not worse at all ('he wasn't a natural blond') or they say something that's so much worse that you feel like all your feelings are being completely negated. ('well, i once had a guy stand me up for a date . . . and it ended up that he'd been eaten by a lion! his last word was my name!')

still, he's trying to help. and i guess i should take some when i need some.

for his part, o.w.g. is also trying to help. there's a girl hovering in the background, and i have no doubt it's the (in)famous jane. at first, o.w.g.'s attempt at help is even lamer than tiny's.

o.w.g.: i know it sucks, but in a way, it's good.

this is about as inspirational as a movie of hitler making out with his girlfriend and having a good time. it runs afoul of what i call the birdshit rule. you know, how people say it's good luck if a bird shits on you? and people believe it! i just want to grab them and say, 'dude, don't you realize this whole superstition was made up because no one could think of anything else good to say to a person who'd just been shit upon?' and people do that all the time — and not with something as temporary as birdshit, either. you lost your job? great opportunity! failed at life? there's only one way to go — up! dumped by a boyfriend who never existed? i know it sucks, but in a way, it's good!

i'm about to strip o.w.g. of his right to be a will grayson, but then he goes on.

o.w.g.: love and truth being tied together, i mean. they make each other possible, you know?

i don't know what hits me more — the fact that some stranger would listen to me, or the fact that he is, technically, absolutely correct.

the other will grayson heads off, leaving me with my new refrigerator-size companion, who's looking at me with such sincerity that i want to slap him.

me: you don't have to stay. really.
tiny: what, and leave you here to mope?
me: this is so far beyond moping. this is out-and-out
    despair.
tiny: *awwww.*

and then he hugs me. imagine being hugged by a sofa. that's what it feels like.

me (choking): i'm choking.
tiny (patting my hair): there, there.
me: dude, you're not helping.

i push him away. he looks hurt.

tiny: you just duded me!
me: i'm sorry. it's just, i —
tiny: i'm only trying to help!

this is why i should carry around extra pills. i think we could both use a double dose right now.

me (again): i'm sorry.

he looks at me then. and it's weird, because i mean, he's *really* looking at me. it makes me completely uncomfortable.

me: what?
tiny: do you want to hear a song from *tiny dancer: the tiny cooper story*?
me: excuse me?
tiny: it's a musical i'm working on. it's based on my life. i think one of the songs might help right now.

we are on a street corner in front of a porn shop. there are people passing by. *chicagoans* — you can't be less musical than chicagoans. i am in a completely demolished state. my mind is having a heart attack. the last thing i need is for the fat lady to sing. but do i protest? do i decide to live the rest of my life within the subway system, feeding off the rats? no. i just nod dumbly, because he wants to sing this song so badly that i'd feel like a jerk to say no.

with a dip of his head, tiny starts to hum a little to himself. once he's gotten the tune, he closes his eyes, opens his arms, and sings:

i thought you'd make my dreams come true
but it wasn't you, it wasn't you

i thought this time it would all be new
but it wasn't you, it wasn't you

i pictured all the things we'd do
but it wasn't you, it wasn't you

and now i feel my heart is through
but it isn't true, it isn't true

i may be big-boned and afraid
but my faith in love won't be mislaid!

though i've been completely knocked off course
i'm not getting off my faithful horse!

it wasn't you, it's true
but there's more to life than you

i thought you were a boy with a view,
you stuck-up, selfish, addled shrew

you may have kicked me till i was blue
but from that experience i grew

it's true, fuck you
there are better guys to woo

it won't be you, comprende vous?
it will never be you.

tiny doesn't just sing these words — he belts them. it's like a parade coming out of his mouth. i have no doubt the words travel over lake michigan to most of canada and on to the north pole. the farmers of saskatchewan are crying. santa is turning to mrs. claus and saying 'what the fuck is *that*?' i am completely mortified, but then tiny opens his eyes and looks at me with such obvious caring that i have no idea what to do. no one's tried to give me something like this in ages. except for isaac, and he doesn't exist. whatever you might say about tiny, he definitely exists.

he asks me if i want to walk. once again, i nod dumbly. it's not like i have anything better to do.

me: who *are* you?
tiny: tiny cooper!
me: you can't really be named tiny.
tiny: no. that's irony.
me: oh.
tiny (tsking): no need to 'oh' me. i'm fine with it. i'm big-boned.
me: dude, it isn't just your bones.
tiny: just means there's more of me to love!
me: but that requires so much more effort.
tiny: darling, i'm worth it.

the sick thing is, i have to admit there's something a little bit attractive about him. i don't get it. it's like, you know how sometimes you see a really sexy baby? wait, that sounds fucked up. that's not what i mean. but it's like, even though he's as big as a house (and i'm not talking about a poor person's house, either), he's got super-smooth skin and really green eyes and everything is in, like, proportion. so i'm not feeling the repulsion i would expect to feel toward someone three times my size. i want to tell him i should be out killing some people now, not taking a stroll with him. but he takes a little of the murder off my mind. it's not like it won't be there later.

as we walk over to millennium park, tiny tells me all

about *tiny dancer* and how hard he's struggled to write, act, direct, produce, choreograph, costume-design, lighting-design, set-design, and attain funding for it. basically, he's out of his mind, and since i'm trying really hard to get out of my mind, too, i attempt to follow. like with maura (fucking witch ass bitch mussolini al-qaeda darth vader non-entity), i don't have to say a word myself, which is fine.

when we get to the park, tiny makes a great-big beeline to the bean. somehow i'm not surprised.

the bean is this really stupid sculpture that they did for millennium park — i guess at the millennium — which originally had another name, but everyone started calling it the bean and the name stuck. it's basically this big reflective metal bean that you can walk under and see yourself all distorted. i mean, i've been here before on school trips, but i've never been here with someone as huge as tiny before. usually it's hard at first to locate yourself in the reflection, but this time i know i'm the wavy twig standing next to the big blob of humanity. tiny giggles when he sees himself like that. a genuine, tee-hee-hee giggle. i hate it when girls do that shit, because it's always so fake. but with tiny it isn't fake at all. it's like he's being tickled by life.

after tiny has tried ballerina pose, swing-batter-batter pose, pump-up-the-jam pose, and top-of-the-mountain-*sound-of-music* pose in the reflection of the bean, he walks us to a bench overlooking lake shore drive. i think he'll be all sweaty because, let's face it, most fat people get sweaty just from lifting the twinkie to their mouth. but tiny is just too fabulous to sweat.

tiny: so tell tiny your problems.

i can't answer, because the way he says it, it's like you could substitute the word 'mama' for the word 'tiny' and the sentence would still sound the same.

me: can tiny talk normal?
tiny (in his best anderson cooper voice): yes, he can.
    but it's not nearly as fun when he does it.
me: you just sound so gay.
tiny: um . . . there's a reason for that?
me: yeah, but. i dunno. i don't like gay people.
tiny: but surely you must like yourself?

holy shit, i want to be from this boy's planet. is he serious? i look at him and see that, yes, he is.

me: why should i like myself? nobody else does.
tiny: i do.
me: you don't know me at all.
tiny: but i want to.

it's so stupid, because all of a sudden i'm screaming

me: shut up! just shut up!

and he looks so hurt, so i have to say

me: no, ha, it's not you. okay? you're nice. i'm not. i'm
    not nice, okay? stop it!

because now he doesn't look hurt; he looks sad. sad for me. he sees me. christ.

me: this is so stupid.

it's like he knows that if he touches me, i will probably lose it on him and start hitting him and start crying and never want to see him again. so instead he just sits there as i put my head in my hands, as if i'm literally trying to hold my head together. and the thing is, he doesn't need to touch me, because with someone like tiny cooper, if he's next to you, you know it. all he has to do is stay, and you know he's there.

me: shit shit shit shit shit shit shit

here's the sick, twisted thing: part of me thinks i *deserve* this. that maybe if i wasn't such an asshole, isaac would have been real. if i wasn't such a lame excuse for a person, something right might happen to me. it's not fair, because i didn't ask for dad to leave, and i didn't ask to be depressed, and i didn't ask for us to have no money, and i didn't ask to want to fuck boys, and i didn't ask to be so stupid, and i didn't ask to have no real friends, and i didn't ask to have half the shit that comes out of my mouth come out of my mouth. all i wanted was one fucking break, one idiotic good thing, and that was clearly too much to ask for, too much to want.

i don't understand why this boy who writes musicals about himself is sitting with me. am i that pathetic? does he get a merit badge for picking up the pieces of a wrecked human being?

i let go of my head. it's not helping. when i surface, i look at tiny, and it's strange all over again. he's not just watching me — he's still *seeing* me. his eyes are practically gleaming.

tiny: i never kiss on the first date.

i look at him with total incomprehension, and then he adds

tiny: . . . but sometimes i make exceptions.

so now my shock from before is turning into a different kind of shock, and it's a charged shock, because at that moment, even though he's enormous, and even though he doesn't know me at all, and even though he's taking up roughly three times more of the bench than i am, tiny cooper is surprisingly, undeniably attractive. yeah, his skin is smooth, his smile is gentle, and most of all his eyes — his eyes have this crazy hope and crazy longing and ridiculous giddiness in them, and even though i think it's completely stupid and even though i am never going to feel the things that he feels, at the very least i don't mind the idea of kissing him and seeing what happens. he is starting to blush from what he's said, and he's actually too shy to lean down to me, so i find myself lifting to kiss him, keeping my eyes open because i want to see his surprise and see his happiness because there's no way for me to see or even feel my own.

it's not like kissing a sofa. it's like kissing a boy. finally, a boy.

he closes his eyes. he smiles when we stop.

tiny: this is not where i thought the night was going.
me: tell me about it.

i want to run away. not with him. i just don't want to go back to school or to life. if my mom wasn't waiting on the other end for me, i would probably do it. i want to run away because i've lost everything. i'm sure if i said this to tiny cooper, he'd point out that i've lost the bad things as well as the good things. he'd tell me the sun will come out tomorrow, or some shit like that. but then i wouldn't believe him. i don't believe any of it.

tiny: hey — i don't even know your name.
me: will grayson.

with that, tiny jumps off the bench, nearly knocking me to the grass.

tiny: no!
me: um . . . yes?
tiny: well, doesn't that just take the cake?

with that, he starts laughing, and calling out

tiny: i kissed will grayson! i kissed will grayson!

when he sees that this freaks me out more than sharks do, he sits back down and says

tiny: i'm glad it was you.

i think about the other will grayson. i wonder how he's doing with jane.

me: it's not like i'm *seventeen* magazine material, right?

tiny's eyes light up.

tiny: he told you about that?
me: yeah.
tiny: he was totally robbed. i was so mad, i wrote a
    letter to the editor. but they never printed it.

i have this deep pang of jealousy, that o.w.g. has a friend like tiny. i can't imagine anyone ever writing a letter to the editor for me. i can't even imagine them giving a quote for my obituary.

i think of everything that's happened, and how when i go home i won't really have anyone to tell it to. then i look at tiny and, surprising myself, kiss him again. because what the fuck. completely, what the fuck.

this goes on for some time. i am getting totally big-boned from kissing someone big-boned. and in between the making out, he's asking me where i live, what happened tonight, what i want to do with my life, what my favorite ice-cream flavor is. i answer the questions i can (basically, where i live and the ice-cream flavor) and tell him i have no idea about the rest of it.

nobody's really watching us, but i'm beginning to feel that they are. so we stop and i can't help but think about isaac, and how even though this whole tiny thing is an interesting development, all-in-all things still suck in a tornado-destroyed-my-home kind of way. tiny's like the one room left standing. i feel i owe him something for that, so i say

me: i'm glad that you exist.
tiny: i'm glad to be existing right now.
me: you have no idea how wrong you are about me.
tiny: you have no idea how wrong you are about
    yourself.
me: stop that.
tiny: only if you stop it.
me: i'm warning you.

i have no idea what truth has to do with love, and vice versa. i'm not even thinking in terms of love here. it's way, way, way early for that. but i guess i am thinking in terms of truth. i want this to be truthful. and even as i protest to tiny and i protest to myself, the truth is becoming increasingly clear.

it's time for us to figure out how the hell this is ever going to work.

chapter eleven

I'm sitting against my locker ten minutes before the first period bell when Tiny comes running down the hallway, his arms a jumble of *Tiny Dancer* audition posters.

"Grayson!" he shouts.

"Hey," I answer. I get up, grab a poster from him, and hold it against the wall. He lets the others fall to the ground and then starts taping, ripping off the masking tape with his teeth. He tapes the poster up, then we gather up the ones he dropped, walk a few paces, and repeat. And all the while, he talks. His heart beats and his eyelids blink and he breathes and his kidneys process toxins and he talks, and all of it utterly involuntary.

"So I'm sorry I didn't go back to Frenchy's to meet you, but I figured you'd guess I just took a cab, which I did, and anyway, Will and I had walked all the way down to the Bean and, like, Grayson, I know I've said this before but I *really like him*. I mean, you have to *really* like someone to go all the way to the Bean with them and listen to them talk about their boyfriend who was neither boy nor friend and also I sang for him. And Grayson, I mean really: can you believe I kissed Will Grayson? I. Freaking. Kissed. Will.

Grayson. And like nothing personal because like I've told you a gajillion times, I think you're a top-shelf person, but I would have bet my left nut that I would never make out with Will Grayson, you know?"

"Uh-hu—" I say, but he doesn't even wait for me to get through the *huh* before he starts up again.

"And I get texts from him like every forty-two seconds and he's a brilliant texter, which is nice because it's just a little pleasant leg vibration, just a reminder-in-the-thigh that he's—see, there's one." I keep holding up the poster while he pulls his phone out of his jeans. "Aww."

"What's it say?" I ask.

"Confidential. I think he kinda trusts me not to blab his texts, you know?"

I might point out the ridiculousness of anyone trusting Tiny not to blab anything, but I don't. He tapes up the poster and starts walking down the hallway. I follow.

"Well, I'm glad your night was so awesome. Meanwhile I was being blindsided about Jane's water polo–playing ex-boyf—"

"Well, first off," he says, cutting me off, "what do you care? You're *not into* Jane. And second off, I wouldn't call him a boy. He is a *man*. He is a sculpted, immaculately conceived, rippling hunk of ex-*man*friend."

"You're not helping."

"I'm just saying—not my type, but he is truly a wonder to behold. And his eyes! Like sapphires burning into the darkened corners of your heart. But anyway, I didn't know they ever dated. I'd never even heard of the guy. I just thought he was a hot guy hitting on her. Jane never talks to me about guys. I don't know why; I'm totally trustworthy about that sort of thing." There's enough sarcasm in his voice—just enough—that I laugh. Tiny talks over the laugh. "It's amazing what you don't know about people, you know? Like, I was thinking about that all weekend talking to Will. He fell for Isaac, who turned out to be made up. That *seems* like something that only happens on the Internet, but really it happens all the time i-r-l, too."

"Well, Isaac wasn't made up. He was just a girl. I mean, that girl Maura is Isaac."

"No, she's not," he says simply. I'm holding up the last of the posters as he tapes it to a boys' bathroom door. It says ARE YOU FABULOUS? IF SO, SEE YOU NINTH PERIOD TODAY AT THE AUDITORIUM. He finishes it up and then we walk toward precalc, the halls beginning to fill up.

The Isaac/Maura namescrewing reminds me of something. "Tiny," I say.

"Grayson," he answers.

"Will you please rename that character in your play, the sidekick guy?"

"Gil Wrayson?" I nod. Tiny throws his hands up in the air and announces, "I can't change Gil Wrayson's name! It's thematically *vital* to the whole production."

"I'm really not in the mood for your bullshit," I say.

"I'm not bullshitting you. His name has to be Wrayson. Say it slow. Ray-sin. Rays-in. It's a double meaning—Gil Wrayson is undergoing a transformation. And he has to let the *rays* of sunlight *in*—those rays of sunlight coming in the form of Tiny's songs—in order to become his true self—no longer a plum, but a sun-soaked raisin. Don't you see?"

"Oh, come on, Tiny. If that's true, why the hell is his name *Gil*?"

That stops him for a moment. "Hmm," he says, squinting down the still-quiet hallway. "It just always sounded right to me. But I suppose I *could* change it. I'll think about it, okay?"

"Thank you," I say.

"You're welcome. Now please stop being a pussy."

"What?"

We get to our lockers, and even though other people can hear him, he talks as loud as ever. "Wah-wah, Jane doesn't like me even though I don't like her. Wah-wah, Tiny named a character after me in his play. Like, there are people in the world with real problems, you know? You gotta keep it in perspective."

"Dude, YOU'RE telling ME to keep it in perspective? Jesus Christ, Tiny. I just wanted to know she had a boyfriend."

Tiny closes his eyes and takes a deep breath like I'm the annoying one. "As I said, I didn't even know he *existed*, okay? But then I saw him talking to her, and I could tell he was into her just from his posture. And when he left, I just had to go up and ask who he was, and she was, like, 'My ex-boyfriend,' and I was, like, '*Ex*?! You need to scoop that beautiful man back up immediately!'"

I'm staring into the broad side of Tiny Cooper's face. He's looking away from me, into his locker. He looks sort of bored, but then his eyebrows dart up, and I think for a second he realizes how pissed I am about what he just said, but then he reaches into his jeans and pulls out the phone. "You didn't," I say.

"Sorry, I know I shouldn't read texts while we're talk-ing, but I'm a little twitterpated at the moment."

"I'm not talking about *texts*, Tiny. You didn't tell Jane to get back together with that guy."

"Well, of course I did, Grayson," he answers, still look-ing at the phone. Now he's writing Will back while talking. "He was *gorgeous*, and you told me you didn't like her. So you like her now? Typical *boy*—you're interested as long as she isn't."

I want to slug him in the kidney, for being wrong and for being right. But it would only hurt me. I'm nothing but a bit character in the Tiny Cooper story, and there isn't a damn thing I can do about it except get jerked around until high school is over and I can finally escape his orbit, can finally stop being a moon of his fat planet.

And then I realize what I can do. The weapon I have. Rule 2: Shut up. I step past him and walk toward class.

"Grayson," he says.

I don't answer.

I say nothing in precalculus, when he miraculously inserts himself into his desk. And then I say nothing when he tells me that right now I am not even his favorite Will Gray-son. I say nothing when he tells me how he has texted the other Will Grayson forty-five times in the last twenty-four hours, and do I think that's too much. I say nothing when he holds his phone under my nose, showing me some text from Will Grayson that I am supposed to find adorable. I say nothing when he asks me why the hell I'm not saying anything. I say nothing when he says, "Grayson, you were just getting on my nerves, and I only said all that stuff to

155

shut you up. But I didn't mean to shut you up *this much*." I say nothing when he says, "No seriously, talk to me," and nothing when he says under his breath but still plenty loud enough for people to hear, "Honestly, Grayson, I'm sorry, okay? I'm sorry."

And then, blessedly, class starts.

Fifty minutes later, the bell rings, and Tiny follows me out into the hallway like a swollen shadow, saying, "Seriously, come on, this is ridiculous." It's not even that I want to torture him anymore. I'm just reveling in the glory of not having to hear the neediness and impotence of my own voice.

At lunch, I sit down by myself at the end of a long table featuring several members of my former Group of Friends. This guy Alton says, "How's it going, faggot?" and I say, "Pretty good," and then this other guy Cole says, "You coming to the party at Clint's? It's gonna be sick," which makes me think these guys don't in fact dislike me even though one of them just called me a faggot. Apparently, having Tiny Cooper as your best-and-only friend does not leave you well-prepared for the intricacies of male socialization.

I say, "Yeah, I'll try to stop by," even though I don't know when the party will be occurring. Then this shave-headed guy Ethan says, "Hey, are you trying out for Tiny's gay-ass play?"

"Hell, no," I say.

"I think I am," he says, and it takes me a second to tell if he's kidding. Everyone starts laughing and talking all at once, trying to get in the first insult, but he just laughs them off and says, "Girls love a sensitive man." He turns around in his chair and shouts at the table behind him, where his girlfriend, Anita, is sitting. "Baby, ain't my singing sexy?"

"Hell, yeah," she says. Then he just looks, satisfied, at all of us. Still, the guys rag on him. I mostly stay quiet, but by the end of my ham and cheese, I'm laughing at their jokes at the appropriate times, which I guess means I'm having lunch with them.

Tiny finds me when I'm putting my tray onto the conveyor belt, and he's got Jane with him, and they walk with me. Nobody talks at first. Jane is wearing an army green hoodie, the hood pulled up. She looks almost unfairly adorable, like she picked it out for the express purpose of taunting. Jane says, "Hilarious note, Grayson. So Tiny tells me you've taken a vow of silence."

I nod.

"Why?" she asks.

"I'm only talking to cute girls today," I answer, and smile. Tiny's right—the existence of the water-polo guy makes it easy to flirt.

Jane smiles. "I think Tiny's a fairly cute girl."

"But *why?*" Tiny begs as I turn down a hallway. The maze of identical hallways differentiated only by different Wildkit murals that used to scare the hell out of me. God, to go back to when my biggest fear was a hallway. "Grayson, please. You're KILLING me."

I am aware that for the first time in my memory, Tiny and Jane are following me.

Tiny decides to ignore me, and he tells Jane that he hopes one day to have enough texts from Will Grayson to turn them into a book, because his texts are like poetry.

Before I can stop myself, I say, "'Shall I compare thee to a summer's day' becomes 'u r hawt like august.'"

"He speaks!" Tiny shouts, and puts his arm around me. "I knew you'd come around! I'm so happy I'm renaming Gil Wrayson! He shall now be known as Phil Wrayson! Phil Wrayson, who must *fill* up on the rays of Tiny's sun in order to become his true self. It's perfect." I nod. People will still assume it's me, but he's—well, he's pretending to try. "Oh, text!" Tiny pulls out his phone, reads the text, sighs loudly, and begins trying to type a response with his meaty hands. While he's thumbing, I say, "I get to pick who plays him."

Tiny nods distractedly.

"Tiny," I repeat, "I get to pick who plays him."

He looks up. "What? No no no. I'm the director. I'm the writer, producer, director, assistant-costume designer, and casting director."

And Jane says, "I saw you nod, Tiny. You already agreed to it." He just scoffs, and then we're at my locker, and Jane kind of pulls me by the elbow away from Tiny and says quietly, "You know, you can't say that stuff."

"Damned if I talk, damned if I don't," I say, smiling.

"I just. Grayson, I just—you can't say those things."

"What things?"

"Cute girl things."

"Why not?" I ask.

"Because I am still doing research on the relationship between water polo and epiphanies." She tries a small, tight-lipped smile.

"You wanna go to the *Tiny Dancer* tryouts with me?" I ask. Tiny is still thumbing away.

"Grayson, I can't—I mean, I am kind of taken, you know?"

"I'm not asking you on a *date*. I'm asking you to an extracurricular activity. We will sit in the back of an auditorium and laugh at the kids auditioning to play me."

I haven't read Tiny's play since last summer, but as I recall, there are about nine meaty parts: Tiny, his mom (who has a duet with Tiny), Phil Wrayson, Tiny's love interests Kaleb and Barry, and then this fictional straight couple who make the character Tiny believe in himself or whatever. And there's a chorus. Altogether, Tiny needs thirty cast members. I figure there will be maybe twelve people at the auditions.

But when I arrive in the auditorium after chem, there are already at least fifty people lounging around the stage and the first few rows of seats waiting for the auditions to start. Gary is running around handing everyone safety pins and pieces of paper with handwritten numbers on them, which the auditioners are pinning to themselves. And, since they are theater people, they are all talking. All of them. Simultaneously. They do not need to be heard; they only need to be speaking.

I take a seat in the back row, one in from the aisle so that Jane can have the aisle. She shows up just after I do and sits down next to me, appraises the situation for a second, and then says, "Somewhere down there, Grayson, there's someone who will have to look into your soul in order to properly embody you."

I'm about to respond when Tiny's shadow passes over us. He kneels next to us, handing us each a clipboard. "Please write a brief note about each person who you'd consider for the role of Phil. Also I'm thinking of writing in a small role for a character named Janey."

Then he marches confidently down the aisle. "People!"

he shouts. "People, please take a seat." People scurry into the first few rows as Tiny hurtles onto the stage. "We haven't much time," he says, his voice weirdly affected. He's talking like he thinks theater people talk, I guess. "First, I need to know if you can sing. One minute of a song from each of you; if you're called back, you'll read for a part then. You may choose your song, but know this: Tiny. Cooper. Hates. Over. The. Rainbow."

He jumps off the stage dramatically, and then shouts, "Number One, make me love you."

Number 1, a mousy blonde who identifies herself as Marie F, climbs the stairs beside the stage and slouches to a microphone. She looks up through her bangs toward the back of the auditorium, where it says in large purple block letters WILDKITS ROCK. She proceeds to prove otherwise with a stunningly bad rendition of a Kelly Clarkson ballad.

"Oh, my God," Jane says under her breath. "Oh, God. Make it end."

"I don't know what you're talking about," I mumble. "This chick's a lock for the role of Janey. She sings off-key, loves corporate pop, and dates bitchsquealers." She elbows me.

Number 2 is a boy, a husky lad with hair too long to be considered normal but too short to be considered long. He sings a song by a band apparently called Damn Yankees—Jane knows them, natch. I don't know how the original sounds, but this guy's howler-monkey a cappella rendition of it leaves a lot to be desired. "He sounds like someone just kicked him in the nuts," Jane says; to which I respond, "If he doesn't stop soon, someone will." By Number 5, I'm *wishing* for a mediocre rendition of something inoffensive like "Over the Rainbow," and I suspect Tiny is, too, from the way his peppy, "That was great! We'll get back to you." has devolved into a, "Thanks. Next?"

The songs vary from jazz standards to boy band covers, but all the performers have one thing in common: they sort of suck. I mean, certainly, not everyone sucks in the same way, and not everyone sucks equally, but everyone sucks at least a little. I'm stunned when my lunch companion Ethan, Number 19, proves to be the best singer so far, singing a song from some musical called *Spring Awakening*. The dude can belt.

"He could play you," Jane says. "If he grew his hair out and developed a bad attitude."

"I don't have a bad attitude—"

"—is the kind of thing that people with bad attitudes say." Jane smiles.

I see a couple potential Janes over the next hour. Number 24 sings a weirdly good sticky-sweet version of a song from *Guys and Dolls*. The other girl, Number 43, has straight bleached hair streaked with blue and sings "Mary Had a Little Lamb." Something about the distance between children's songs and blue hair seems pretty Janeish to me.

"I vote for her," Jane says as soon as the girl gets to the second *Mary*.

The last auditionee is a diminutive, large-eyed creature named Hazel who sings a song from *Rent*. After she's finished, Tiny runs up onto the stage to thank everyone, and to say how brilliant they all were, and how impossibly hard this will be, and how callbacks will be posted the day after tomorrow. Everyone files out past us, and then finally Tiny slouches up the aisle.

"You've got your work cut out for you," I tell him.

He makes a dramatic gesture of futility. "We did not see a lot of future Broadway stars," he acknowledges.

Gary comes up and says, "I liked numbers six, nineteen, thirty-one, and forty-two. The others, well," and then Gary puts his hand to his chest and begins to sing, "Somewhere over the rainbow, way up high / The sound of singing Wildkits, makes me want to die."

"Jesus," I say. "You're like a *real singer*. You sound like Pavarotti."

"Well, except he's a baritone," Jane says, her music pretension apparently extending even to the world of opera.

Tiny snaps the fingers of one hand excitedly while pointing at Gary. "You! You! You! For the part of Kaleb. Congratulations."

"You want me to play a fictionalized version of my own ex-boyfriend?" Gary asks. "I think not."

"Then Phil Wrayson! I don't care. Pick your part. My God, you sing better than all of them."

"Yes!" I say. "I cast you."

"But I'd have to kiss a girl," he says. "Ew." I don't remember my character kissing any girls, and I start to ask Tiny about it, but he cuts me off, saying, "I've been in rewrites." Tiny flatters Gary some more and then he agrees to play the part of me, and honestly, I'll take it. As we walk up the aisle on the way out of the cafeteria, Gary turns to me, cocking his head and squinting. "What's it like to *be* Will Grayson? I need to know what it's like from the inside."

He's laughing, but then he also seems to be waiting for an answer. I always thought that being Will Grayson meant being me, but apparently not. The other Will Grayson is also Will Grayson, and now Gary will be, too.

"I just try to shut up and not care," I say.

"Such stirring words." Gary smiles. "I will base your character upon the attributes of the boulders on the lakeshore: silent, apathetic, and—considering how little they exercise—surprisingly chiseled." Everybody laughs, except Tiny, who's texting. As we exit the hallway, I see Ethan standing against the Wildkit trophy stand, his backpack on. I walk up to him and say, "Not bad today," and he smiles and says, "I just hope I'm not too hot to play you." He smiles. I smile back, even though he seems a little serious. "See you on Friday at Clint's?" he asks.

"Yeah, maybe," I say. He adjusts the backpack over one shoulder and takes off with a nod. Behind me, I hear Tiny dramatically plead, "Someone tell me it will be okay!"

"It'll be okay," Jane says. "Mediocre actors rise to great material."

Tiny takes a deep breath, shakes some thought out of his mind, and says, "You're right. Together they will be greater than the sum of their parts. Fifty-five people tried out for my play! My hair looks amazing today! I got a B on an English paper!" His phone chirps. "And I just got a text from my new favorite Will Grayson. You're totally right, Jane: everything's coming up Tiny."

chapter twelve

it starts when i get home from chicago. i already have twenty-seven texts from tiny on my phone. and he has twenty-seven texts from me. that took up most of the train ride. the rest of the time, i figured out what i needed to do the moment i walked through the door. because if isaac's nonexistence is going to weigh me down, i have to let go of some other things in order not to crash right into the ground. i no longer give a fuck. i mean, i didn't think i gave a fuck before. but that was amateur not-giving-a-fuck. this is stop-at-nothing, don't-give-a-fuck freedom.

mom's waiting for me in the kitchen, sipping some tea, flipping through one of those stupid rich-celebrities-show-off-their-houses magazines. she looks up when i come in.

mom: how was chicago?
me: look, mom, i'm totally gay, and i'd appreciate it if you could get the whole freakout over with now, because, yeah, we have the rest of our lives to deal with it, but the sooner we get through the agony part, the better.
mom: the agony part?

me: you know, you praying for my soul and cursing me
for not giving you grandbabies with a wifey and
saying how incredibly disappointed you are.
mom: you really think i'd do that?
me: it's your right, i guess. but if you want to skip that
step, it's fine with me.
mom: i think i want to skip that step.
me: really?
mom: really.
me: wow. i mean, that's cool.
mom: can i at least have a moment or two for surprise?
me: sure. i mean, it can't be the answer you were
expecting when you asked me how chicago was.
mom: i think it's safe to say that wasn't the answer i
was expecting.

i'm looking at her face to see if she's holding things back,
but it seems like it is what it is. which is pretty spectacular,
all things considered.

me: are you going to tell me you knew all along?
mom: no. but i was wondering who isaac was.

oh, shit.

me: isaac? were you spying on me, too?
mom: no. it's just —
me: what?
mom: you would say his name in your sleep. i wasn't
spying. but i could hear it.

me: wow.

mom: don't be mad.

me: how could i be mad?

i know that's a silly question. i've proven that i can be mad about pretty much anything. there was this one time i woke up in the middle of the night and swore that my mother had installed a smoke alarm on the ceiling while i was asleep. so i burst into her room and started yelling about how could she just go and put something in my room without telling me, and she woke up and calmly told me the smoke alarm was in the hallway, and i actually dragged her out of bed to show her, and of course there wasn't anything on the ceiling — i'd just dreamed it. and she didn't yell at me or anything like that. she just told me to go back to sleep. and the next day was total crap for her, but not once did she say it was tied to me waking her up in the middle of the night.

mom: did you see isaac when you were in chicago?

how can i explain this to her? i mean, if i tell her i just traveled into the city to go to a porn store to meet some guy who didn't end up existing, the next few weeks' poker night earnings are going to be spent on a visit to dr. keebler. but she can tell when i'm lying if she's looking for it. i don't want to lie right now. so i bend the truth.

me: yeah, i saw him. his nickname's tiny. that's what i call him, even if he's huge. he's actually, you know, really nice.

we are in completely uncharted mother-son territory here. not just in this house — maybe in all of america.

me: don't get all worried. we just went to millennium
     park and talked a while. some of his friends were
     there, too. i'm not going to get pregnant.

mom actually laughs.

mom: well, *that's* a relief.

she gets up from the kitchen table and, before i know it, she's giving me a hug. and it's like for a moment i don't know what to do with my hands, and then i'm like, *you dumbfuck, hug her back*. so i do, and i expect her to start crying, because one of us should be crying. but she's dry-eyed when she pulls away — a little misty, maybe, but i've seen her when things aren't all right, when things have totally gone to shit, and so i know enough to recognize that this isn't one of those times. we're okay.

mom: maura called a few times. she sounded upset.
me: well, she can go to hell.
mom: will!
me: sorry. i didn't mean to say that out loud.
mom: what happened?
me: i don't want to get into it. i'm just going to tell you
     that she really, really hurt me, and i need for that
     to be enough. if she calls here, i want you to tell
     her that i never want to speak to her again. don't

tell her i'm not here. don't lie when i'm in the other room. tell her the truth — that it's over and it's never going to be un-over. please.

whether it's because she agrees or whether it's because she knows there's no point in disagreeing when i'm like this, mom nods. i have a very smart mom, all things considered.

it's time for her to leave the room — i thought that's what was going to happen after the hug — but since she's still hovering, i make the move.

me: i'm going to head off to bed. i'll see you in the morning.
mom: will . . .
me: really, it's been a long day. thank you for being so, you know, understanding. i owe you one. a big one.
mom: it's not about owing —
me: i know. but you know what i mean.

i don't want to leave until it's clear it's okay for me to leave. i mean, that's the least i can do.

she leans in and kisses me on the forehead.

mom: good night.
me: good night.

then i go back to my room, turn on my computer, and create a new screenname.

willupleasebequiet: tiny?
bluejeanbaby: here!

168

willupleasebequiet: are you ready?
bluejeanbaby: for what?
willupleasebequiet: the future
willupleasebequiet: because i think it just started

*

tiny sends me a file of one of the songs from *tiny dancer*.
he says he hopes it will give me inspiration. i put it on my ipod
and listen to it as i'm heading to school the next morning.

There was a time
When I thought I liked vagina
But then came a summer
When i realized something finer

I knew from the moment he took top bunk
How desperately i wanted into his trunk
Joseph Templeton Oglethorpe the Third
Left my heart singing like a little bird

Summer of gay!
So lovely! So queer!
Summer of gay!
Set the tone for my year!

Mama and Papa didn't know they were lighting the lamp
The moment they sent me to Starstruck Drama Camp

So many Hamlets to choose from
Some tortured, some cute

I was all ready to swordfight
Or take the Ophelia route

There were boys who called me sister
And sistahs who taught me about boys
Joseph whispered me sweet nothings
And i fed him Almond Joys

Summer of gay!
So fruity! So whole!
Summer of gay!
I realized Angel would be my role!

Mama and Papa didn't know how well their money was spent
When I learned about love from our production of Rent

Such kissing on the catwalks
Such competition for the leads
We fell in love so often and fully
Across all races and sexualities and creeds . . .

Summer of gay!
Ended soon! Lasted long!
Summer of gay!
My heart still carries its song!

Joseph and I didn't make it to September
But you can't unlight a gay-colored ember
I will never go back
To the heterosexual way

'Cause now every day
(Yes, every day)
Is the sum-mer
of gay!

since i've never really listened to musicals, i don't know if they all sound this gay, or if it's just tiny's. i suspect that i would find all of them this gay. i'm not entirely sure how this is supposed to inspire me to do anything except join drama club, which right now is about as likely as me asking maura on a date. still, tiny told me i was the first person to hear the song besides his mom, so that counts for something. even if it's lame, it's a sweet kind of lame.

it even manages to take my mind off of school and maura for a few minutes. but once i get there, she's right in front of me, and the mountain reminds me it's a volcano, and i can't help but want to spray lava everywhere. i walk right past the place we usually meet up, but that doesn't stop her. she launches right behind me, saying all the things that would be in a hallmark card if hallmark made cards for people who invented internet boyfriends for other people and then were suddenly caught in the lie.

maura: i'm sorry, will. i didn't mean to hurt you or
anything. i was just playing around. i didn't realize
how serious you were taking it. and i'm a total
bitch for that, i know. but i was only doing it
because it was the only way to get through to you.
don't ignore me, will. talk to me!

i am just going to pretend that she doesn't exist. because all the other options would get me expelled and/or arrested.

maura: please, will. i'm really, really sorry.

she's crying now, and i don't care. the tears are for her own benefit, not mine. let her feel the pain her poetry desires. it has nothing to do with me. not anymore.

she tries to pass me notes during class. i knock them off my desk and leave them on the ground. she sends me texts, and i delete them unread. she tries to come up to me at the beginning of lunch, and i build a wall of silence that no goth sorrow can climb.

maura: fine. i understand that you're mad. but i'm still going to be here when you aren't so angry.

when things break, it's not the actual breaking that prevents them from getting back together again. it's because a little piece gets lost – the two remaining ends couldn't fit together even if they wanted to. the whole shape has changed.

i am never, ever going to be friends with maura again. and the sooner she realizes it, the less annoying it's going to be.

when i talk to simon and derek, i find out that they vanquished the trigonometric challengers yesterday, so at least i know they're not still mad at me for ditching. my seat at the lunch table remains secure. we sit there and eat in silence for at least five minutes until simon speaks.

simon: so how was your big date in chicago?

me: do you really want to know?

simon: yeah — if it was big enough for you to bow out
of our competition, i want to know how it went.

me: well, at first he didn't exist, but then he existed
and it went pretty well. before, when i told you
about it, i was really careful not to use any
pronouns, but i don't give a fuck anymore.

simon: wait a sec — you're gay?

me: yup. i suppose that's the correct conclusion for you
to draw.

simon: that's disgusting!

this is not exactly the reaction i was expecting from simon.
i was betting on something a little closer to indifference.

me: what's disgusting?

simon: you know. that you put your thing in the place
where he, um, defecates.

me: first of all, i haven't put my thing anywhere. and
you do realize, don't you, that when a guy and
a girl get together, he puts his thing where she
urinates and gets her period?

simon: oh. i hadn't thought about that.

me: exactly.

simon: still, it's weird.

me: it's no weirder than jerking off to video game
characters.

simon: who told you that?

he whacks derek on the head with his plastic fork.

simon: did you tell him that?
derek: i didn't tell him anything!
me: i figured it out myself. honestly.
simon: it's only the girl characters.
derek: and some warlocks!
simon: SHUT UP!

this is not, i have to admit, how i thought being gay was going to be.

luckily, tiny texts me every five minutes or so. i don't know how he does it without getting caught in class. maybe he hides the phone in the folds of his stomach or something. whatever the case, i'm grateful. because it's hard to hate life too much when you have someone interrupting your day with things like

I'M THINKING HAPPY GAY THOUGHTS ABOUT U
and
I WANT TO KNIT U A SWEATER. WHAT COLOR?
and
I THINK I JUST FAILED A MATH TEST BECAUSE I WAS THINKING OF U 2 MUCH
and
WHAT RHYMES WITH SODOMY TRIAL?
then
LOBOTOMY VILE?
then
BOTTOM ME, KYLE?

then
BOTTOMY NILE
then
BOTTOMY GUILE!
then
BTW—ITS 4 THE SCENE WHEN OSCAR WILD'S GHOST COMES TO ME IN A DREAM

i only know about half of what he's talking about, and usually that annoys the shit out of me. but with tiny, it doesn't matter as much. maybe someday i'll figure it out. and if not, being oblivious could be fun, too. the fatty's turning me into a softie. it's sick, really.

he also texts me all the questions about how it's going, what i'm doing, how i'm feeling, and when is he going to see me again. i can't help it – i think it's kind of like it was with isaac. only without the distance. this time, i feel i know who i'm talking to. because i get a sense that with tiny, what you see is how he is. he doesn't hold anything back. i want to be like that. only without having to gain, like, three hundred pounds to do it.

after school, maura catches me at my locker.

maura: simon told me you're officially gay now. that
    you 'met somebody' in chicago.

i don't owe you anything, maura. especially not an explanation.

maura: what are you doing, will? why did you tell him
   that?

because i did meet someone, maura.

maura: talk to me.

never. i am going to let the close of my locker speak for
me. i am going to let the sound of my footsteps speak for me.
i am going to let the way i don't look back speak for me.
   you see, maura, i don't give a fuck.

that night, tiny and i exchange IMs for four hours. mom
leaves me alone and even lets me stay up late.
   someone with a fake profile leaves a comment on my
myspace page calling me a fag. i don't think it's maura;
someone else from school must've heard.
   when i look in my mailbox at all the messages i've gathered there, i see isaac's face has been replaced with a gray
box with a red X through it.
   'profile no longer exists,' it says.
   so the mail from him remains, but he's gone.

i see a few people looking at me weird in school the
next day, and i wonder if it would be possible to reconstruct
the path the gossip took from derek or simon to the towering snot-nosed jock glaring at me. of course, it's possible
that the towering snot-nosed jock always glared at me, and
i'm just noticing it now. i try not to give a fuck.

maura's laying low, but i assume it's because she's planning her next assault. i want to tell her it's not worth it. maybe our friendship wasn't meant to last longer than a year. maybe the things that drew us together — doom, gloom, sarcasm — weren't meant to hold us together. the fucked-up thing is, i miss isaac and i don't miss her. even though i know she was isaac. none of those conversations count anymore. i am genuinely sorry that she went to such insane lengths to get me to tell her the truth — we would have been better off if we'd never been friends in the first place. i'm not going to try to punish her — i'm not going to tell everyone what she did, or bomb her locker, or yell at her in front of everyone else. i just want her to go away. that's all. the end.

right before lunch, this kid gideon catches me by my locker. we haven't really talked since seventh grade, when we were lab partners in earth science. then he went on the honors track and i didn't. i've always liked him and we've always been on hi-in-the-halls terms. he dj's a lot, mostly at parties i don't go to.

gideon: hey, will.
me: hey.

i'm pretty sure he's not here to bash me. the lcd sound-system shirt kinda gives that away.

gideon: so, yeah. i heard that you might be, you know . . .
me: ambidextrous? a philatelist? homosexual?

he smiles.

gideon: yeah. and, i don't know, when i realized i was
    gay, it really sucked that nobody was, like, 'way to
    go.' so i just wanted to come over and say . . .
me: way to go?

he blushes.

gideon: well, it sounds stupid like that. but that's the
    gist of it. welcome to the club. it's a very small club
    at this school.
me: i hope there aren't dues?

he stares at his shoes.

gideon: um, no. it's not *really* a club.

if tiny was at our school, i imagine it would be a club.
and he would be the president.
    i smile. gideon looks up and sees it.

gideon: maybe if you'd want to, i don't know, get some
    coffee or something after school . . . ?

it takes me a second.

me: are you asking me out?
gideon: um, maybe?

right here in the halls. there are all these people around us.
amazing.

me: here's the thing. i'd love to hang out. but . . . i have
   a boyfriend.

these words are actually leaving my lips.
uh-mazing.

gideon: oh.

i take out my phone and show him the inbox full of
texts from tiny.

me: i swear, i'm not making it up just to get out of
   going on a date with you. his name's tiny. he goes to
   school in evanston.
gideon: you're so lucky.

this is not a word that's usually thrown my way.

me: why don't you sit with me and simon and derek at
   lunch?
gideon: are they gay, too?
me: only if you're a warlock.

i text tiny a minute later.

MADE NEW GAY FRIEND.

and he texts back

PROGRESS!!!

then

YOU SHOULD FORM A GSA!

to which i reply

ONE STEP AT A TIME, BIG BOY

and he replies

BIG BOY – I LUV THAT!

the texting goes on for the rest of the day and into the night. it's pretty incredible, really, how frequently you can write someone when you're keeping the character count low. it's so stupid, because it feels like tiny's sharing the day with me. like he's there when i'm ignoring maura or talking to gideon or finding out that nobody's going to axe-murder me in gym class because i'm sending out a homosexual vibe.

still, it's not enough. because i felt that way sometimes with isaac. and i won't let this relationship be all in my head.

so that night i call tiny on the phone and talk to him. i tell him i want him to come visit. and he doesn't make excuses. he doesn't say it's not possible. instead, he says

tiny: how soon?

i will admit there's a certain degree of giving a fuck that goes into not giving a fuck. by saying you don't care if the

world falls apart, in some small way you're saying you want
it to stay together, on your terms.

when i hang up with tiny, mom comes into my room.

mom: how's it going?
me: fine.

and it's true, for once.

chapter thirteen

I awake to the sound of my alarm clock, blaring rhythmically, and it seems as loud as an air siren, shouting at me with such ferocity that it sort of hurts my feelings. I roll over in bed, and squint through the darkness: It's 5:43 in the morning. My alarm doesn't go off until 6:37.

And only then do I realize: That sound is not my alarm clock. It is a car horn, honking, sounding some kind of terrible siren song through the streets of Evanston, a howling warning of doom. Horns don't honk this early, not with such insistence. It must be an emergency.

I race out of bed, pull on a pair of jeans, and bolt toward the front door. I'm relieved to see both Mom and Dad alive, racing to the entryway. I say, "Jesus, what's going on?" and my mom just shrugs and my dad says, "Is it a car horn?" I make it to the door first and peer out the glass sidelight.

Tiny Cooper is parked outside my house, honking methodically.

I run outside and only when he sees me does he stop honking. The passenger window rolls down. "Christ, Tiny. You're going to wake the whole neighborhood."

I see a can of Red Bull dancing in his huge, shaky hand.

The other hand remains perched on the horn, ready to honk at any moment.

"We gotta go," he says, his voice rushed. "Gotta go go go go go go go go."

"What's wrong with you?"

"Gotta go to school. I'll explain later. Get in the car." He sounds so frantically serious, and I am so tired, that I don't think to question him. I just race back into the house, pull on some socks and shoes, brush my teeth, tell my parents I'm going to school early, and hurry into Tiny's car.

"Five things, Grayson," he says as he puts the car into drive and speeds off, without ever relinquishing his shaky hold on the can of Red Bull.

"What? Tiny, what's wrong?"

"Nothing's wrong. Everything's right. Things couldn't be righter. Things could be less tired. They could be less busy. They could be less caffeinated. But they couldn't be righter."

"Dude, are you on meth?"

"No, I'm on Red Bull." He hands me the Red Bull, and I sniff at it, trying to figure out whether it's laced with something. "Also coffee," he adds. "So but listen, Grayson. Five things."

"I can't believe you woke up my entire neighborhood at five forty-three for no reason."

"Actually," he says, his voice louder than seems entirely necessary at such a tender hour, "I woke you up for *five* reasons, which is what I've been trying to tell you, except that you keep interrupting me, which is just a very, like, Tiny Cooper thing of you to do."

I've known Tiny Cooper since he was a very large and very gay fifth grader. I've seen him drunk and sober, hungry and sated, loud and louder, in love and in longing. I have seen him in good times and bad, in sickness and in health. And in lo those many years, he has never before made a self-deprecating joke. And I can't help but think: maybe Tiny Cooper should fry his brain with caffeine more often.

"Okay, what are the five things?" I ask.

"One, I finished casting the show last night around eleven while I was skyping with Will Grayson. He helped me. I imitated all the potential auditioners, and then he helped me decide who was least horrible."

"The other Will Grayson," I correct him.

"Two," he says, as if he hasn't heard me. "Shortly thereafter, Will went to bed. And I was thinking to myself, you know, it's been eight days since I met him, and I haven't technically liked someone who liked me back for eight days in my entire life, unless you count my relationship with Bethany Keene in third grade, which obviously you can't, since she's a girl.

"Three, and then I was thinking about that and lying in the bed staring up at the ceiling, and I could see the stars that we stuck up there in like sixth grade or whatever. Do you remember that? The glow-in-the-dark stars and the comet and everything?"

I nod, but he doesn't look over, even though we're stopped at a light. "Well," he goes on, "I was looking at those stars and they were fading away because it had been a few minutes since I'd turned out the light, and then I had a blinding light spiritual awakening. What is *Tiny Dancer* about? I mean, what is its subject, Grayson? You've read it."

I assume that, as usual, he is asking this question rhetorically, so I say nothing so he'll go on ranting, because as painful as it is for me to admit, there is something kind of wonderful about Tiny's ranting, particularly on a quiet street when I am still half asleep. There is something about the mere act of him speaking that is vaguely pleasurable even though I wish it weren't. It is something about his voice, not his pitch or his rapid-fire, caffeinated diction, but the voice itself—the familiarity of it, I guess, but also its inexhaustibility.

But he doesn't say anything for a while and then I realize he actually *does* want me to answer. I don't know what he wants to hear, so in the end I just tell him the truth. "*Tiny Dancer* is about Tiny Cooper," I say.

"*Exactly!*" he shouts, pounding the steering wheel. "And no great musical is ever about a person, not really. And that's the problem. That's the whole problem with the play. It's not about tolerance or understanding or love or anything. It's about *me*. And, like, nothing against me. I mean, I am pretty fabulous. Am I not?"

"You're a pillar of fabulosity in the community," I tell him.

"Yes, exactly," he says. He's smiling, but it's tough to tell how much he's kidding. We're pulling into school now, the place entirely dead, not even a car in the faculty lot. He turns into his usual spot, reaches into the back for his backpack, gets out, and starts walking across the desolate lot. I follow.

"Four," he says. "So I realized, in spite of my great and

terrible fabulousness, the play can't be about me. It must be about something even more fabulous: love. The polychromic many-splendored dreamcoat of love in all its myriad glories. And so it had to be revised. Also retitled. And so I had to stay up all night. And I've been writing like crazy, writing a musical called *Hold Me Closer*. We'll need more sets than I thought. Also! Also! More voices in the chorus. The chorus must be like a fucking *wall* of song, you know?"

"Sure, okay. What's the fifth thing?"

"Oh, right." He wiggles a shoulder out of his backpack and slings it around to his chest. He unzips the front pocket, digs around for a moment, and then pulls out a rose made entirely of green duct tape. He hands it to me. "When I get stressed," Tiny explains, "I get crafty. Okay. Okay. I'm gonna go to the auditorium and start blocking out some scenes, see how the new stuff looks onstage."

I stop walking. "Um, do you need me to help or something?"

He shakes his head no. "No offense, Grayson, but what exactly are your theater credentials?"

He's walking away from me, and I try to stand my ground, but then finally chase after him up the steps to school, because I've got a burning question. "Then why the hell did you wake me up at five forty-three in the morning?"

He turns to me now. It becomes impossible not to feel Tiny's immensity as he stands over me, shoulders back, his width almost entirely blocking the school behind him, his body a bundle of tiny tremors. His eyes are open unnaturally wide, like a zombie's. "Well, I needed to tell *someone*," he says.

I think about that a minute, and then follow him into the auditorium. For the next hour, I watch Tiny as he runs around the theater like a rampaging lunatic, mumbling to himself. He puts masking tape down on the floor to mark the spots of his imaginary sets; he pirouettes across the stage as he hums song lyrics in fast motion; and every so often he shouts, "It's not about Tiny! It's about love!" Then people start to file in for their first period drama class, so Tiny and I go to precalc, and Tiny performs the Big-Man-in-Small-Desk miracle, and I experience the traditional amazement, and school is boring, and then at lunch I'm sitting with Gary and Nick and Tiny, and Tiny is talking about his blinding light spiritual awakening in a manner that—nothing against Tiny—kind of implies that maybe Tiny has not fully internalized the idea that the earth does not spin around the axis of Tiny Cooper, and then I say to Gary, "Hey, where is Jane?"

And Gary says, "Sick."

To which Nick adds, "Sick in the I'm-spending-the-day-with-my-boyfriend-at-the-botanical-gardens kind of way." Gary shoots Nick a disapproving look.

Tiny quickly changes the subject, and I try to laugh at all the appropriate moments for the rest of lunch, but I'm not listening.

I know that she is dating Douchepants McWater Polo, and I know that sometimes when you date people you engage in idiotic activities like going to the botanical gardens, but in spite of all the knowledge that ought to protect me, I still feel like shit for the rest of the day. *One of these days*, I keep telling myself, *you'll learn to truly shut up and not care.*

And until then . . . well, until then I'll keep taking deep breaths because it feels like the wind got knocked out of me. For all my not crying, I sure feel a hell of a lot worse than I did at the end of *All Dogs Go to Heaven*.

I call Tiny after school, but I get his voice mail, so I send him a text: "The Original Will Grayson requests the pleasure of a phone call whenever possible." He doesn't call until 9:30. I'm sitting on the couch watching a dumb romantic comedy with my parents. The plates from our take-out-Chinese-put-on-real-plates-so-you-feel-like-it's-a-homemade dinner fill the coffee table. Dad is falling asleep, as he always does when he's not working. Mom sits closer to me than seems necessary.

Watching the movie, I can't stop thinking about wanting to be at the ridiculous botanical gardens with Jane. Just walking around, her in that hoodie, and me making jokes about the Latin names of the plants, and her saying that *ficaria verna* would be a good name for a nerdcore hip-hop crew that only raps in Latin, and so on. I can picture the whole damned thing, actually, and it almost makes me desperate enough to complain to Mom about the situation, but that will only mean questions about Jane for the next seven to ten years. My parents get so few details about my private life that whenever they do stumble upon some morsel, they cling to it for eons. I wish they'd do a better job of hiding their desire for me to have tons of friends and girlfriends.

Sobutand Tiny calls, and I say, "Hey," and then I get up and go to my room and close the door behind me, and in all that time, Tiny doesn't say anything, so I say, "Hello?"

And he says, "Yeah, hi," distractedly. I hear typing.

"Tiny, are you typing?"

After a moment he says, "Hold on. Let me finish this sentence."

"Tiny, *you* called *me*."

Silence. Typing. And then, "Yeah, I know. But I'm, uh, I gotta change the last song. Can't be about me. Has to be about love."

"I wish I hadn't kissed her. The whole boyfriend thing kind of like gnaws at my brain."

And then I'm quiet for a while, and finally he says, "Sorry, I just got an IM from Will. He's telling me about lunch with this new gay friend he's got. I know it's not a date if it's in the cafeteria, but still. Gideon. He *sounds* hot. It is pretty awesome that Will's so out, though. He like came out to everyone in the entire world. I swear to God I think he wrote the president of the United States and was like, 'Dear Mr. President, I am gay. Yours truly, Will Grayson.' It's fucking beautiful, Grayson."

"Did you even hear what I said?"

"Jane and her boyfriend ate your brain," he answers disinterestedly.

"I swear, Tiny, sometimes . . ." I stop myself from saying something pathetic and start over. "Do you want to do something after school tomorrow? Darts or something at your house?"

"Rehearsal then rewrites then Will on the phone then bed. You can sit in on rehearsal if you want."

"Nah," I say. "It's cool."

After I hang up, I try to read *Hamlet* for a while, but I

don't understand it that well, and I have to keep looking over to the right margin where they define the words, and it just makes me feel like an idiot.

Not that smart. Not that hot. Not that nice. Not that funny. That's me: I'm not that.

I'm lying on top of the covers with my clothes still on, the play still on my chest, eyes closed, mind racing. I'm thinking about Tiny. The pathetic thing I wanted to say to him on the phone—but didn't—was this: When you're a little kid, you have something. Maybe it's a blanket or a stuffed animal or whatever. For me, it was this stuffed prairie dog that I got one Christmas when I was like three. I don't even know where they found a stuffed prairie dog, but whatever, it sat up on its hind legs and I called him Marvin, and I dragged Marvin around by his prairie dog ears until I was about ten.

And then at some point, it was nothing personal against Marvin, but he started spending more time in the closet with my other toys, and then more time, until finally Marvin became a full-time resident of the closet.

But for many years afterward, sometimes I would get Marvin out of the closet and just hang out with him for a while—not for me, but for Marvin. I realized it was crazy, but I still did it.

And the thing I wanted to say to Tiny is that sometimes, I feel like his Marvin.

I remember us together: Tiny and me in gym in middle school, how the athletic wear company didn't make gym shorts big enough to fit him, so he looked like he was wearing a skintight bathing suit. Tiny dominating at dodgeball despite his width, and always letting me finish second just by virtue of putting me in his shadow and not spiking me until the end. Tiny and me at the gay pride parade in Boys Town, ninth grade, him saying, "Grayson, I'm gay," and me being like, "Oh, really? Is the sky blue? Does the sun rise in the east? Is the Pope Catholic?" and him being like, "Is Tiny Cooper fabulous? Do birds weep from the beauty when they hear Tiny Cooper sing?"

I think about how much depends upon a best friend. When you wake up in the morning you swing your legs out of bed and you put your feet on the ground and you stand up. You don't scoot to the edge of the bed and look down to make sure the floor is there. The floor is always there. Until it's not.

It's stupid to blame the other Will Grayson for something that was happening before the other Will Grayson existed. And yet.

And yet I keep thinking about him, and thinking about his eyes unblinking in Frenchy's, waiting for someone who didn't exist. In my memory, his eyes get bigger and bigger, almost like he's a manga character. And then I'm thinking about that guy, Isaac, who was a girl. But the things that were said that made Will go to Frenchy's to meet that guy—those things *were* said. They were real.

All at once I grab my phone from off my bedside table and call Jane. Voice mail. I look at the clock on the phone: it's 9:42. I call Gary. He picks up on the fifth ring.

"Will?"

"Hey, Gary. Do you know Jane's address?"

"Um, yes?"

"Can you give it to me?"

He pauses. "Are you going all stalker on me, Will?"

"No, I swear, I have a question about science," I say.

"You have a Tuesday night at nine forty-two question about science?"

"Correct."

"Seventeen twelve Wesley."

"And where is her bedroom?"

"I have to tell you, man, that my stalker meter is kind of registering in the red zone right now." I say nothing, waiting. And then finally he says, "If you're facing the house, it's front and left."

"Awesome, thanks."

I grab the keys off the kitchen counter on my way out, and Dad asks where I'm going, and I try just getting by with, "Out," but that just results in the pausing of the TV. He comes up close as if to remind me he is just a little bit taller than I am, and sternly asks, "Out with *whom* and to *where*?"

"Tiny wants my help with his stupid play."

"Back by eleven," Mom says from the couch.

"Okay," I say.

I walk down the street to the car. I can see my breath, but I don't feel cold except on my gloveless hands, and I stand outside the car for a second, looking at the sky, the orange light coming from the city to the south, the leafless streetside trees quiet in the breeze. I open the door, which cracks the silence, and drive the mile to Jane's house. I find a spot half a block down and walk back up the street to an old, two-story house with a big porch. Those houses don't come cheap. There's a light on in the front-left room, but as soon as I get there, I don't want to walk up. What if she's changing? What if she's lying in bed and she sees a creepy guy face pressed against the glass? What if she's making out with Randall McBitchsquealer? So I send her a text: "Take this in the least stalkery way possible: Im outside ur house." It's 9:47. I figure I'll wait until the clock turns over to 9:50 and then leave. I shove one hand into my jeans and hold the phone with the other, pressing the volume up button each time the screen goes blank. It's been 9:49 for at least ten seconds when the front door opens and Jane peers outside.

I wave very slightly, my hand not even rising above my head. Jane puts a finger to her lips, and then dramatically tiptoes out of the house and very slowly closes the door behind her. She walks down the steps of the porch, and in the porch light I can see that she's wearing the same green hoodie but now with red flannel pajama pants and socks. No shoes.

She walks up to me and whisper-says, "It's a slightly creepy delight to see you."

And I say, "I have a science question."

She smiles and nods. "Of course you do. You're wondering how it's scientifically possible that you're paying oh-so-much attention to me now that I have a boyfriend when you were totally uninterested in me before. Sadly, science is baffled by the mysteries of boy psychology."

But I do have a science question—about Tiny and me, and about her, and about cats. "Can you explain to me about Schrödinger's cat?"

"Come on," she says, and reaches out for my coat and pulls me down the sidewalk. I'm walking beside her, not saying anything, and she's mumbling, "God God God God God God God," and I say, "What's wrong?" and she says, "You. You, Grayson. You're what's wrong," and I say, "What?" and she says, "You know," and I say, "No I don't," and she—still walking and not looking at me—says, "There are probably some girls who don't want guys to show up at their house randomly on a Tuesday night with questions about Edwin Schrödinger. I am sure such girls exist. But they don't live at my house."

We get five or six houses past Jane's, near to where my car is parked, and then she turns toward a house with a FOR SALE sign and walks up the stairs to a porch swing. She sits down and pats a place next to her.

"Nobody lives here?" I ask.

"No. It's been for sale for, like, a year."

"You've probably made out with the Douche on this swing."

"I probably have," she answers. "Schrödinger was doing a thought experiment. Okay, so, this paper had just come out arguing that if, like, an electron might be in any one of four different places, it is sort of in all four places at the same time until the moment someone determines which of the four places it's in. Does that make sense?"

"No," I say. She's wearing little white socks, and I can see her ankle when she kicks up her feet to keep the swing swinging.

"Right, it totally doesn't make sense. It's mind-bendingly weird. So Schrödinger tries to point this out. He says: put a cat inside a sealed box with a little bit of radioactive stuff that might or might not—depending on the location of its sub-atomic particles—cause a radiation detector to trip a hammer that releases poison into the box and kills the cat. Got it?"

"I think so," I say.

"So, according to the theory that electrons are in all-possible-positions until they are measured, the cat is both alive and dead until we open the box and find out if it is alive or dead. He was not endorsing cat-killing or anything. He was just saying that it seemed a little improbable that a cat could be simultaneously alive and dead."

But it doesn't seem that improbable to me. It seems to me that all the things we keep in sealed boxes *are* both alive and dead until we open the box, that the unobserved is both there and not. Maybe that's why I can't stop think-ing about the other Will Grayson's huge eyes in Frenchy's: because he had just rendered the dead-and-alive cat dead. I realize that's why I never put myself in a situation where I really *need* Tiny, and why I followed the rules instead of kissing her when she was available: I chose the closed box. "Okay," I say. I don't look at her. "I think I get it."

"Well, that's not all, actually. It turns out to be some-what more complicated."

"I don't think I'm smart enough to handle more compli-cated," I say.

"Don't underestimate yourself," she says.

The porch swing creaks as I try to think everything through. I look over at her.

"Eventually, they figured out that keeping the box closed doesn't actually keep the cat alive-and-dead. Even if *you* don't observe the cat in whatever state it's in, the air in the box does. So keeping the box closed just keeps *you* in the dark, not the universe."

"Got it," I say. "But failing to open the box doesn't *kill* the cat." We aren't talking about physics anymore.

"No," she says. "The cat was already dead—or alive, as the case may be."

"Well, the cat has a boyfriend," I say.

"Maybe the physicist likes that the cat has a boyfriend."

"Possible," I say.

"Friends," she says.

"Friends," I say. We shake on it.

chapter fourteen

mom insists that before i go anywhere with tiny, he has to come over for dinner. i'm sure she checks all the sex predator websites beforehand. she doesn't trust that i met him over the internet. and, given the circumstances, i can't really blame her. she's a little surprised when i go along with the plan, even if i do tell her

> me: just don't ask about his forty-three ex-boyfriends,
>   okay? or ask him about why he's carrying around an
>   axe.
> mom: . . .
> me: i'm kidding about the axe part.

but really, nothing i can say can calm the woman down. it's insane. she puts on those yellow rubber gloves and starts scrubbing with the intensity you usually reserve for when someone's thrown up all over the furniture. i tell her she really doesn't have to do that, because it's not like tiny's going to be eating off the floor. but she just waves me away and tells me to clean up my room.

i mean to clean up my room. really, i do. but all i manage to do is wipe the history from my web browser, and then i'm totally exhausted. it's not like i don't wipe the snot flakes from my bed in the morning. i'm a pretty clean guy. all the dirty clothes are shoved in the bottom of my closet. he's not going to see them.

finally, it's time for him to get here. at school, gideon asks me if i'm nervous about tiny coming over, and i tell him i'm totally not. but, yeah, that's a lie. mostly i'm nervous about my mom and how she's going to act.

i'm waiting for him in the kitchen, and mom's running around like a madwoman.

mom: i should fix the salad.
me: why should you fix the salad?
mom: doesn't tiny like salad?
me: i told you, i think tiny would eat baby seals if we
    gave them to him. but i mean, why do you have
    to fix the salad? who broke it? i didn't touch it.
    did you break the salad, mom? if you did, YOU'D
    BETTER FIX IT!

i'm joking, but she's not really finding it funny. and i'm thinking, *aren't i supposed to be the one who's freaking out here?* tiny is going to be the first b-b-b- (i can't do it) boy-f-f-f (c'mon, will) boyf-boyf (here we go) boyfriend of mine that she's ever met. although if she keeps talking about salad, i might have to lock her in her bedroom before he comes over.

mom: you're sure he doesn't have any allergies?
me: calm. down.

like i suddenly have supercanine sound skills, i hear a car pulling into the driveway. before mom can tell me to comb my hair and put on some shoes, i'm out the front door and watching tiny turn off the ignition.

me: run! run!

but the radio's so loud that tiny can't hear me. he just grins. as he opens the door, i get a look at his car.

me: what the——?!?

it's this silver mercedes, the kind of car you'd expect to be driven by a plastic surgeon — and not the kind of plastic surgeon who fixes the fucked-up faces of starving african babies, but the kind of plastic surgeon who convinces women that their lives will be over if they look older than twelve.

tiny: greetings, earthling! i come in peace. take me to
       your leader!

it should be weird to have him right in front of me for only the second time in our boyfriendship, and it should be really exciting that i'm about to be caught up in those big arms of his, but really i'm still stuck on the car.

me: please tell me you stole that.

he looks a little confused, and holds up the shopping bag he's carrying.

tiny: this?

me: no. the car.

tiny: oh. well, i *did* steal it.

me: you did?

tiny: yeah, from my mother. my car was almost out of
      gas.

it's so bizarre. all the times we've been talking or texting
or IMing or whatever, i've always imagined that tiny was in
a house like mine, or a school like mine, or a car like the
one i might get someday — a car almost as old as me, probably bought off an old woman who isn't allowed to drive
anymore. now i'm realizing it's not like that at all.

me: you live in a big house, don't you?

tiny: big enough to fit me!

me: that's not what i mean.

i have no idea what i'm doing. because i've totally slowed
us down, and even though he's right in front of me now, it's
not like it should be.

tiny: come here, you.

and with that, he puts his bag down and opens his arms
to me, and his smile is so wide that i'd be an asshole to do
anything but walk right inside his welcome. once i'm there,
he leans down to kiss me lightly.

tiny: hello.

i kiss him back.

me: hello.

okay, so this is the reality: he is here. he is real. we are real. i shouldn't care about his car.

mom's got her apron off by the time we get inside the house. even though i warned her that he's the shape of utah, there's still a slight moment of astonishment when she first sees tiny in the flesh. he must be used to this, or maybe he just doesn't care, because he glides right over to her and starts saying all the right things, about how excited he is to meet her, and how amazing it is that she cooked dinner, and how wonderful the house looks.

mom gestures him over to the couch and asks him if he wants anything to drink.

mom: we have coke, diet coke, lemonade, orange juice —
tiny: ooh, i love lemonade.
me: it's not real lemonade. it's just lemon-flavored
   crystal light.

both mom and tiny look at me like i'm the fucking grinch.

me: i didn't want you to get all excited for real
   lemonade!

i can't help it — i'm seeing our apartment through his eyes — our whole lives through his eyes — and it all looks so . . .

shabby. the water stains on the ceiling and the dull-colored rug and the decades-old tv. the whole house smells like debt.

mom: why don't you go sit next to tiny, and i'll get you a coke?

i took my pills this morning, i swear. but it's like they ended up in my leg instead of my brain, because i just can't get happy. i sit down on the couch, and as soon as mom is out of the room, tiny's hand is on my hand, fingers rubbing over my fingers.

tiny: it's okay, will. i love being here.

i know he's been having a bad week. i know things haven't been going his way, and that he's worried his show is going to bomb. he's rewriting it daily. ('who knew it would be so complicated to fit love into fourteen songs?') i know he's been looking forward to this — and i know that *i've* been looking forward to this. but now i have to stop looking forward and start looking at where i am. it's hard.

i lean into tiny's meaty shoulder.

i can't believe i'm turned on by anything i'd call 'meaty.'

me: this is the rough part, okay? so just stay tuned for the good part. i promise it'll come soon.

when mom comes back in, i'm still leaning there. she doesn't flinch, doesn't stop, doesn't seem to mind. she puts our drinks down, then runs to the kitchen again. i hear the oven open and close, then the scrape of a spatula against a cookie sheet. a minute later, she's back with a plate of mini hot dogs and mini egg rolls. there are even two little bowls, one with ketchup and one with mustard.

tiny: yum!

we dig in, and tiny starts telling mom about the week he's had, and so many details about *hold me closer* that i can see she's thoroughly confused. as he's talking, she remains hovering above us, until finally i tell her she should join us, sit down. so she pulls over a chair and listens, even having an egg roll or two herself.

it starts to feel more normal. tiny being here. mom seeing the two of us. me sitting so that at least one part of my body is always touching his. it's almost like i'm back in millennium park with him, that we're continuing that first time-bending conversation, and this is where the story is supposed to go. as always, the only question is whether i'll fuck it all up.

when there are no finger foods left to finger, mom clears the dishes and says dinner will be ready in a few minutes. as soon as she's out of the room, tiny turns to me.

tiny: i love her.

yes, i think, he's the type of person who can love someone that easily.

me: she's not bad.

when she comes in to tell us dinner's ready, tiny flies up from the couch.

tiny: ooh! i almost forgot.

he reaches for the shopping bag he brought and hands it to my mother.

tiny: a host gift!

mom looks really surprised. she takes a box out of the bag — it has a ribbon on it and everything. tiny sits back down so she won't feel awkward sitting down to open it. very carefully, she undoes the ribbon. then she gently lifts open the top of the box. there's a black foam cushion, then something surrounded by bubble wrap. With even more care, she undoes the wrapping, and takes out this plain glass bowl.

at first, i don't get it. i mean, it's a glass bowl. but my mother's breath catches. she's blinking back tears. because it's not just a plain glass bowl. it's perfect. i mean, it's so smooth and perfect, we all sit there and stare at it for a moment, as my mother turns it slowly in her hand. even in our shabby living room, it catches the light.

nobody's given her anything like this in ages. maybe ever. nobody ever gives her anything this beautiful.

tiny: i picked it out myself!

he has no idea. he has no clue what he's just done.

mom: oh, tiny . . .

she's lost the words. but i can tell. it's the way she holds that bowl in her hand. it's the way she's looking at it.

i know what her mind is telling her to do — to say it's too much, that she couldn't possibly have such a thing. even if she wants it so badly. even if she loves it that much.

so it's me who says

me: it's beautiful. thank you so much, tiny.

i hug him, really send him my thank you that way, too. then mom is putting the bowl on the coffee table she cleaned to a shine. she's standing up, and she's opening her arms, and then he's hugging her, too.

this is what i never allow myself to need.

and of course i've been needing it all along.

to tell the truth, tiny eats most of the chicken parm at dinner, and takes up most of the conversation as well. mostly, we talk about stupid things — why mini hot dogs taste better than regular-size hot dogs, why dogs are better than cats, why *cats* was so successful in the eighties when sondheim was writing rings around lloyd webber (neither mom or i really contribute much to that one). at one point, tiny sees the da vinci postcard mom has on the refrigerator, and he asks her if she's ever been to italy. so she tells him about the trip she took with three college friends their junior year, and it's an interesting story for once. he tells her he likes naples even more than rome, because the people in naples are so intensely from the place they're from. he says he wrote a song about traveling for his musical, but ultimately it didn't make the cut. he sings us a few lines:

Once you've been to Naples
it's hard to shop at Staples,
And once you've been to Milan
it's hard to eat at Au Bon Pain.

Once you've been to Venice
you turn from iceberg lettuce.
And you learn that baloney's baloney
When Bologna feeds you rigatoni.

Being a transatlantic gay
is a dangerous game to play.
Because once you've been to Rome
it's hard to call a suburb home

for the first time i can recall, mom looks completely tickled. she even hums along a little. when tiny is done, her applause is genuine. i figure it's time to end the lovefest, before tiny and mom run off together and start a band.

i offer to do the dishes, and mom acts like she's completely shocked by this.

me: i do the dishes all the time.

mom looks seriously at tiny.

mom: really, he does.

then she bursts out laughing.

i am not really appreciating this, even though i'm aware there are many worse ways this could've played out.

tiny: i want to see your room!

this is not a hey!-my-zipper's-getting-itchy! request. when tiny says he wants to see your room, it means he wants to see . . . your room.

mom: go ahead. i've got the dishes.
tiny: thanks, mrs. grayson.
mom: anne. call me anne.
tiny: thanks, anne!
me: yeah, thanks, anne.

tiny hits me on the shoulder. i think he means to do it lightly, but i feel like someone's just driven a volkswagen into my arm.

i lead him to my room, and even manage a ta-da! when i open the door. he walks to the center of the room and takes it all in, smiling the whole time.

tiny: goldfish!

he goes right over to the bowl. i explain to him that if goldfish ever take over the world and decide to have a war crimes trial, i am going to be noosebait, because the mortality rate of my little goldfish bowl is much much higher than if they'd lived in the moat at some chinese restaurant.

tiny: what are their names?

oh, lord.

me: samson and delilah.
tiny: really?
me: she's a total slut.

he leans over for a closer look at the fish food.

tiny: you feed them prescription drugs?
me: oh, no. those are mine.

it's the only way i'll remember to feed the fish and take my meds, if i keep them together. still, i'm thinking maybe i should've cleaned a little more. because of course tiny's now blushing and not going to ask anything else, and while i don't want to go into it, i also don't want him to think i'm being treated for scabies or something.

me: it's a depression thing.
tiny: oh, i feel depressed, too. sometimes.

we're coming dangerously close to the conversations i'd have with maura, when she'd say she knew exactly what i was going through, and i'd have to explain that, no, she didn't, because her sadness never went as deep as mine. i had no doubt that tiny *thought* he got depressed, but that was probably because he had nothing to compare it to. still, what could i say? that i didn't just *feel* depressed — instead, it was like the depression was the core of me, of every part of me, from my mind to my bones? that if he got blue, i got black? that i hated those pills so much, because i knew how much i relied on them to live?

no, i couldn't say any of this. because, when it all comes down to it, nobody wants to hear it. no matter how much they like you or love you, they don't want to hear it.

tiny: which one's samson and which one's delilah?
me: honestly? i forget.

tiny scans my bookshelf, runs his hand over my keyboard, spins the globe i got when i graduated fifth grade.

tiny: look! a bed!

for a second, i think he's going to leap onto it, which would kill my bed frame for sure. but with an almost-shy grin, he sits gingerly on its edge.

tiny: comfy!

how have i ended up dating this sprinkled donut of a person? with a not-unfriendly sigh, i sit down next to him. the mattress is definitely canyoning his way.

but before the inevitable next step, my phone vibrates on my desk. i'm going to ignore it, but then it buzzes again and tiny tells me to get it.

i flip open the phone and read what's there.

tiny: who's it from?

me: just gideon. he wants to see how things are
    going.

tiny: gideon, huh?

there's an unmistakable suspicion in tiny's voice. i close
the phone and head back to the bed.

me: you're not jealous of gideon, are you?

tiny: what, that he's cute and young and gay and
    gets to see you every day? what's there to be
    jealous of?

i kiss him.

me: you have nothing to be jealous of. we're just
    friends.

something hits me then, and i start to laugh.

tiny: what?

me: there's a boy in my bed!

it's such a stupid, gay thought. i feel like i have to carve
'I HATE THE WORLD' into my arm about a hundred
times to make up for it.

the bed really isn't big enough for the two of us. twice i
end up on the floor. all our clothes stay on — but it's almost
like that doesn't matter. because we're all over each other.
he's big and strong, but i match him in the push and pull.
soon we're a complete hot mess.

when we've tired ourselves out, we just lie there. his heartbeat is huge.

we hear my mother turn on the tv. the detectives start talking. tiny runs his hand under my shirt.

tiny: where's your dad?

i'm totally not ready for the question. i feel myself tense.

me: i don't know.

tiny's touch tries to soothe me. his voice tries to calm me.

tiny: it's okay.

but i can't take that. i sit up, knocking us right out of our dreamy breathing, making him shift away a little so he can see me clearly. the impulse in me is loud and clear: immediately, i can't do this. not because of my father — i don't really care that much about my father — but because of this whole process of knowing everything.

i argue with myself.

stop.

stay here.

talk.

tiny is waiting. tiny is looking at me. tiny is being kind, because he hasn't realized yet who i am, what i am. i will never be kind back. the best i can do is give him reasons to give up.

tiny: tell me. what do you want to say?

don't ask me, i want to warn him. but then i'm talking.

> me: look, tiny – i'm trying to be on my best behavior,
> but you have to understand – i'm always standing
> on the edge of something bad. and sometimes
> someone like you can make me look the other
> way, so that i don't know how close i am to falling
> over. but i always end up turning my head. always.
> i always walk off that edge. and it's shit i deal with
> every day, and it's shit that's not going away any
> time soon. it's really nice to have you here, but do
> want to know something? do you really want me to
> be honest?

he should take this as the warning it is. but no. he
nods.

> me: it feels like a vacation. i don't think you know what
> that's like. which is good – you don't want to.
> you have no idea how much i hate this. i hate the
> fact that i'm ruining the night right now, ruining
> everything –
> tiny: you're not.
> me: i am.
> tiny: says who?
> me: says me?
> tiny: don't i get any say?
> me: no. i just ruin it. you don't get any say.

tiny touches my ear lightly.

tiny: you know, you get all sexy when you turn
  destructive.

his fingers run down my neck, under my collar.

tiny: i know i can't change your dad or your mom or
  your past. but you know what i can do?

his other hand works its way up my leg.

me: what?
tiny: something else. that's what i can give you.
  something else.

i am so used to bringing out the pain in people. but tiny
refuses to play that game. while we're texting all day, and
even here in person, he's always trying to get to the heart of
it. and that means he always assumes there's a heart to get
to. i think that's ridiculous and admire it at the same time.
i want the something else he has to give me, even though
i know it's never going to be something i can actually take
and have as my own.

i know it's not as easy as tiny says it is. but he's trying so
hard. so i surrender to it. i surrender to something else.

even if my heart isn't totally believing it.

chapter fifteen

The next day, Tiny isn't in precalc. I assume he's hunched over somewhere writing songs into a comically undersized notebook. It doesn't bother me much. I see him between second and third period when I walk past his locker; his hair looks unwashed and his eyes are wide.

"Too much Red Bull?" I ask, walking up to him.

He answers all in a furious rush. "Play opens in nine days, Will Grayson's adorable, everything's cool. Listen, Grayson, I gotta go to the auditorium, I'll see you at lunch."

"The *other* Will Grayson," I say.

"What, huh?" Tiny asks, slamming his locker shut.

"The other Will Grayson's adorable."

"Right, quite right," he answers.

He's not at our table at lunch, and neither is Gary or Nick or Jane or anyone, and I don't want the entire table to myself, so I take my tray to the auditorium, figuring I'll find everyone there. Tiny's standing in the middle of the stage, a notebook in one hand and his cell in the other, gesticulating wildly. Nick's sitting in the first row of seats. Tiny's talking to Gary onstage, and because the acoustics are fantastic in our auditorium, I can hear exactly what he's saying even from the back.

"The thing you've gotta remember about Phil Wrayson is that he is totally freaking terrified. Of everything. He acts like he doesn't care, but he's closer to falling apart than anyone else in the whole freaking play. I want to hear the quiver in his voice when he's singing, the *need* he hopes no one can hear. Because that's gotta be what makes him so annoying, you know? The things he says aren't annoying; it's the *way* he says them. So when Tiny is taping up those Pride posters, and Phil won't shut up about the stupid girl problems he brought on himself, we've gotta *hear* what's annoying. But you can't overdo it, either. It's the slightest little thing, man. It's the pebble in your shoe."

I just stand there for a minute, waiting for him to see me, and then finally he does. "He's a CHARACTER, Grayson," Tiny shouts. "He's a FICTIONAL CHARACTER."

Still holding my tray, I spin around and leave. I sit down outside the auditorium on the tile floor of the hallway, leaning up against a trophy case, and I eat a little.

I'm waiting for him. To come out and apologize. Or else to come out and yell at me for being a pussy. I'm waiting for those dark wood double doors to open and for Tiny to blow through them and start talking.

I know it's immature, but I don't care. Sometimes you need your best friend to walk through the doors. And then, he doesn't. Finally, feeling small and stupid, it's me who gets up and cracks open the door. Tiny is happily singing about Oscar Wilde. I stand there for a moment, still hoping he'll see me, and I don't even know that I'm crying until this crooked sound comes up out of me as I inhale. I close the door. If Tiny ever sees me, he doesn't pause to acknowledge it.

I walk down the hallway, my head down so far that the salt water drips from the tip of my nose. I walk out the main door—the air cold, the sun warm—and down the steps. I follow the sidewalk until I get to the security gate, then I dart into the bushes. Something in my throat feels like it might choke me. I walk through the shrubs just like Tiny and I did freshman year when we skipped to go down to Boys Town for the Pride Parade where he came out to me.

I walk all the way to this Little League field that's half-way between my house and school. It's right by the middle school, and when I was a kid, I used to go there a lot by myself, like after school or whatever, just to think. Sometimes I would bring a sketchbook or something and try to draw, but mostly I just liked to go there. I walk around the backstop fence and sit down on the bench in the dugout, my back against the aluminum wall, warmed by the sunlight, and I cry.

Here's what I like about the dugout: I'm on the third base side, and I can see the diamond of dirt in front of me and the four rows of wooden bleachers on one side; and then on the other side, the outfield and the next diamond over; and then a large park, and then the street. I can see people walking their dogs, and a couple walking into the wind. But with my back to the wall, with this aluminum roof over my head, no one can see me unless I can see them.

The rarity of the situation is the kind of thing that makes you cry.

Tiny and I actually played Little League together—not

in this park, but in one closer to our houses, starting in third grade. That's how we became friends, I guess. Tiny was strong as hell, of course, but not much good with the bat. He did lead the League in getting hit by pitches, though. There was so much to hit.

I played a respectable first base and didn't lead the League in anything.

I put my elbows on my knees like I did back when I was watching games from a dugout like this one. Tiny always sat next to me, and even though he only played because the coach had to play everyone, he was super-enthusiastic. He'd be all, "Hey, batter batter. Hey, batter batter, SWING, batter," and then eventually he'd switch to, "We want a pitcher, not a bellyitcher!"

Then, sixth grade: Tiny was playing third base, and I was at first. It was early in the game, and we were either just barely winning or just barely losing—I don't remember. Honestly, I never even looked at the score when I was playing. Baseball for me was just one of those weird and terrible things parents do for reasons you cannot fathom, like flu shots and church. So the batter hit the ball, and it rolled to Tiny. Tiny gloved it and threw the ball to first with his cannon arm, and I stretched out to make the catch, careful to keep a foot on the bag, and the ball hit me in the glove and then immediately fell out, because I forgot to squeeze the glove shut. The runner was safe, and the mistake cost us a run or something. After the inning ended, I went back to the dugout. The coach—I think his name was Mr. Frye— leaned down toward me. I became aware of the bigness of his head, his cap riding high over his fat face, and he said,

"FOCUS on CATCHING the BALL. CATCH the BALL, okay? Jesus!" My face felt flush, and with that quiver in my voice that Tiny pointed out to Gary, I said, "Suhrry, Coach," and Mr. Frye said, "Me too, Will. Me too."

And then Tiny hauled off and punched Mr. Frye in the nose. Just like that. Thus ended our Little League careers.

It wouldn't hurt if he weren't right—if I hadn't known somewhere that my weakness aggravates him. And maybe he thinks like I do, that you don't pick your friends, and he's stuck with this annoying bitchsquealer who can't handle himself, who can't close his glove around the ball, who can't take a dressing-down from the coach, who regrets writing letters to the editor in defense of his best friend. This is the real story of our friendship: I haven't been stuck with Tiny. He's been stuck with me.

If nothing else, I can relieve him of that burden.

It takes a long time to stop crying. I use my glove as a handkerchief as I watch the shadow of the dugout roof creep down my outstretched legs as the sun rises to the top of the sky. Finally, my ears feel frozen in the shade of the dugout, so I get up and walk across the park and then home. On the way, I scroll through my list of contacts on my phone for a while and then call Jane. I don't know why. I feel like I need to call someone. I feel, weirdly, like I still want *someone* to open the double doors to the auditorium. I get her voice mail.

"Sorry, Tarzan, Jane's unavailable. Leave a message."

"Hey, Jane, it's Will. I just wanted to talk to you. I . . . radical honesty? I just spent like five minutes going through a list of everyone I could call, and you were the only person I wanted to call, because I like you. I just like you a lot. I think you're awesome. You're just . . . er. Smart*er* and fun*nier* and prett*ier* and just . . . *er*. Yeah, okay. That's all. Bye."

When I get home, I call my dad. He picks up on the last ring.

"Can you call the school and tell them I'm sick? I had to go home," I say.

"You okay, bud?"

"Yeah. I'm okay," I say, but the quiver is in my voice, and I feel like I might start up with the sobbing again for some reason, and he says, "Okay. Okay. I'll call."

Fifteen minutes later, I'm slumped on the couch in the living room, my feet up on the coffee table. I'm staring at the TV, only the TV isn't on. I've got the remote in my left hand, but I don't even have the energy to push the goddamned power button.

I hear the garage door open. Dad comes in through the kitchen and sits down next to me, pretty close. "Five hundred channels," he says after a moment, "and nothing's on."

"You get the day off?"

"I can always get someone to cover," he says. "Always."

"I'm okay," I say.

"I know you are. I just wanted to be home with you, that's all."

I blink out some tears, but Dad has the decency not to say anything about it. I turn on the TV then, and we find a show called *The World's Most Amazing Yachts*, which is about yachts that have, like, golf courses on them or whatever, and every time they show some fancy feature, Dad says, "It's UH-MAAZING!" all sarcastically, even though it sort of *is* amazing. It is and isn't, I guess.

And then Dad mutes the TV and says, "You know Dr. Porter?"

And I nod. He's this guy who works with Mom.

"They don't have any kids, so they're rich." I laugh. "But they've got this boat they keep at Belmont Harbor, one of these behemoths with cherry-wood cabinets imported from Indonesia and a rotating king-size bed stuffed with the feathers of endangered eagles and everything else. Your mom and I had dinner with the Porters on the boat years ago, and in the span of a single meal—in that two hours— the boat went from feeling like the most extraordinarily luxurious experience to just being a boat."

"I assume there's a moral to this story."

He laughs. "You're our yacht, bud. All that money that would have gone into a yacht, all that time we would have spent traveling the world? Instead, we got you. It turns out that the yacht is a boat. But you—you can't be bought on credit, and you aren't reducible." He turns his face back toward the TV and after a moment says, "I'm so proud of you that it makes me proud of me. I hope you know that." I nod, tight-throated, staring now at a muted commercial for laundry detergent. After a second, he mumbles to himself, "Credit, people, consumerism. . . . There's a pun in there somewhere."

I say, "What if I didn't want to go to that program at Northwestern? Or what if I don't get in?"

"Well, then I would stop loving you," he says. He keeps a straight face for a second, then laughs and unmutes the TV.

• • •

Later in the day, we decide we're going to surprise Mom with turkey chili for dinner. I'm chopping onions when the doorbell rings. Immediately, I know it's Tiny, and I feel this weird relief radiate out from my solar plexus. "I got it," I say. I squeeze past Dad in the kitchen and then run to the door.

It's not Tiny but Jane. She looks up at me, lips pursed.

"What's my locker combination?"

"Twenty-five-two-eleven," I say.

She hits me playfully on the chest. "*I knew it!* Why didn't you tell me?"

"I couldn't figure out which of several true things was the most true," I answer.

"We gotta open the box," she tells me.

"Um," I say. I step forward so I can close the door behind me, but she doesn't step backward, so now we're almost touching. "The cat has a boyfriend," I point out.

"I'm not the cat, actually. The cat is us. I am a physicist. You are a physicist. The cat is us."

"Um, okay," I say. "The physicist has a boyfriend."

"The physicist does not in fact have a boyfriend. The physicist dumped her boyfriend at the botanical gardens because he wouldn't shut up about how he was going to the Olympics in twenty sixteen, and there was this little voice in the physicist's head named Will Grayson, saying, 'And at the Olympics will you be representing the United States or the Kingdom of Douchelandia?' So the physicist broke up with her boyfriend and insists that the box be opened, because she kind of cannot stop thinking about the cat. The physicist won't mind if the cat is dead; she just needs to know."

We kiss. Her hands are freezing on my face, and she tastes like coffee and the smell of the onion is still stuck in my nose, and my lips are all dry from the endless winter. And it's awesome.

"Your professional physicist opinion?" I ask.

She smiles. "I believe the cat to be alive. And what says my esteemed colleague?"

"Alive," I say. And it truly is. Which makes it all the weirder that as I'm talking to her, some small cut inside me feels unstitched. I thought it would be Tiny at the door, brimming with apologies I would slowly accept. But such is life. We grow up. Planets like Tiny get new moons. Moons like me get new planets. Jane pulls away from me for a second and says, "Something smells good. I mean, in addition to you."

I smile. "We're making chili," I say. "Do you want to—. Do you want to come in and meet my dad?"

"I don't want to imp—"

"No," I say. "He's nice. A little weird. Nice, though. You can stay for dinner."

"Um, okay let me call my house." I stand out there shivering for a second while she talks to her mom, saying, "I'm gonna have dinner at Will Grayson's house. . . . Yes, his dad is here. . . .They're doctors. . . . Yeah. . . . Okay, love you."

I come back inside. "Dad," I say, "this is my friend Jane." He emerges from the kitchen wearing his *Surgeons Do It with a Steady Hand* apron over his shirt and tie. "I give people credit for buying into consumerism!" he says excitedly, having found his pun. I laugh.

Jane extends her hand, the picture of class, saying, "Hello, Dr. Grayson, I'm Jane Turner."

"Ms. Turner, it's a pleasure."

"Is it okay if Jane stays for dinner?"

"Of course, of course. Jane, if you'll excuse us for a moment."

Dad takes me into the kitchen, then leans in and says softly, "This was the cause of your problems?"

"Strangely, no," I say. "But we are sorta yeah."

"You are sorta yeah," he mumbles to himself. "You are sorta yeah." And then quite loudly he says, "Jane?"

"Yes, sir?"

"What is your grade-point average?"

"Um, three point seven, sir?"

He looks at me, his lips scrunched up, and nods slowly. "Acceptable," he says, and then smiles.

"Dad, I don't need your *approval*," I say softly.

"I know," he answers. "But I thought you might like it anyway."

chapter sixteen

four days before his show is supposed to go on, tiny calls me and tells me he needs to take a mental health day. it's not just because the show is in chaos. the other will grayson isn't talking to him. i mean, he's talking to him, but he's not saying anything. and part of tiny is pissed that o.w.g. is 'pulling this shit so close to curtain time' and part of him seems really, really afraid that something is really, really wrong.

> me: what can i do? i'm the wrong will grayson.
> tiny: i just need a will grayson fix. i'll be at your school
>   in an hour. i'm already on the road.
> me: you're what?
> tiny: you just have to tell me where your school is. i
>   google-mapped it, but those directions always suck.
>   and the last thing my mental health day needs is to
>   be google-mapped into iowa at ten in the morning.

i think the idea of a 'mental health day' is something completely invented by people who have no clue what it's like to have bad mental health. the idea that your mind can be aired out in twenty-four hours is kind of like saying heart disease can be cured if you eat the right breakfast cereal. mental health days only exist for people who have the luxury of saying 'i don't want to deal with things today' and then can take the whole day off, while the rest of us are stuck fighting the fights we always fight, with no one really caring one way or another, unless we choose to bring a gun to school or ruin the morning announcements with a suicide.

i don't say any of this to tiny. i pretend that i want him here. i don't let him know how freaked out i am about him seeing more of my life. it seems to me that he's cross-wired on his will graysons. i'm not sure i'm the one who can help him.

it's gotten so intense — more intense than it was with isaac. and not just because tiny is real. i don't know what freaks me out more — that i matter to him, or that he matters to me.

i tell gideon right away about tiny's visit, mostly because he's the only person in the school who i've really talked to about tiny.

gideon: wow, it's sweet that he wants to see you.
me: i hadn't even thought of that.
gideon: most guys will drive over an hour for sex. but
    only a few will drive over an hour just to see you.
me: how do you know this?

it's sort of strange that gideon's become my go-to gay guy, since he's told me the most play he's ever gotten was at boy scout camp the summer before ninth grade. but i guess he's been to enough blogs and chat rooms and things. oh, and he watches hbo-on-demand all the time. i am constantly telling him that i'm not sure the laws of *sex and the city* apply when there's no sex and there's no city, but then he looks at me like i'm throwing spiked darts at the heart-shaped helium balloons that populate his mind, so i let it go.

the funny thing is that most of the school — well, the part that cares, which is not that huge — thinks gideon and i are a couple. because, you know, they see gay me walking in the halls with gay him, and they immediately assume.

i will say this, though — i kind-of don't mind it. because gideon is really cute, and really friendly, and the people who don't beat him up seem to like him a lot. so if i'm going to have a hypothetical boyfriend in this school, i could do much worse.

still, it's weird to think of gideon and tiny finally meeting. it's weird to think of tiny walking the halls with me. it's like inviting godzilla to the prom.

i can't picture it . . . but then i get a text that he's two minutes away, and i have to face facts.

i basically just leave mr. jones's physics class in the middle of a lab — he never really notices me, anyway, so as long as my lab partner, lizzie, covers for me, i'm set. i tell lizzie the truth — that my boyfriend is sneaking into the school to meet me — and she becomes my accomplice, because even if she wouldn't ordinarily do it for me, she'll definitely do it for LOVE. (well, LOVE and gay rights — three cheers for straight girls who max out on helping gay guys.)

the only person who gives me grief is maura, who snorts out a black cloud when i explain my story to lizzie. she's been trying to fuck up my silent treatment by eavesdropping on me whenever she can. i don't know whether the snort is because she thinks i'm making it up or because she's disgusted that i'm mistreating my physics lab. or maybe she's just jealous of lizzie, which is funny because lizzie has acne so bad that it looks like bee stings. but whatever. maura can snort until all the brain-mucus has left her head and pooled at her feet. i will not respond.

i find tiny easily enough in front of the school, shifting from foot to foot. i am not about to start making out with him on school grounds, so i give him a guy-hug (two points of contact! only two!) and tell him that if anyone asks, he should say he's moving to town in the fall and is checking out the school ahead of time.

he's a little different than when i last saw him — tired, i guess. otherwise, though, his mental health seems perfectly fine.

tiny: so this is where the magic happens?
me: only if you consider blind enslavement to
    standardized tests and college applications to
    be a form of magic.
tiny: it remains to be seen.
me: how's the play going?
tiny: what the chorus lacks in voice, it makes up
    for in energy.
me: i can't wait to see it.
tiny: i can't wait for you to see it.

the bell for lunch rings when we're halfway to the

cafeteria. suddenly, there are people all around us, and they're noticing tiny the same way they'd notice someone who decided to go from class to class on horseback. the other day i was joking with gideon that the reason the school made all of our lockers gray was so kids like me could blend in and make it through the hallways safely. but with tiny, that's not an option. heads turn.

me: do you always get this much attention?
tiny: not so much. i guess people notice my
    extraordinary hugeness more here. do you mind
    if i hold your hand?

the truth is, i do mind. but i know that since he's my boyfriend, the answer should be that i don't mind at all. he'd probably carry me to class in his arms, if i asked him nicely.

i take his hand, which is big and slippery. but i guess i can't hide the worry on my face, because he takes one look and lets go.

tiny: never mind.
me: it's not you. i'm just not a hand-holding-in-
    hallways kind of guy. not even if you were a girl.
    not even if you were a cheerleader with big tits.
tiny: but i *was* a cheerleader with big tits.

i stop and look at him.

me: you're kidding.
tiny: only for a few days. i totally ruined the pyramid.

we walk a little farther.

tiny: i suppose putting my hand in your back pocket is
    out of the question?
me: *cough*
tiny: that was a joke.
me: can i at least buy you lunch? maybe there's even a
    casserole!

i have to keep reminding myself that this is what i wanted
— this is what everybody is supposed to want. here's a boy
who wants to be affectionate with me. a boy who will get in
his car and drive to see me. a boy who isn't afraid of what
everyone else is going to think when they see us together. a
boy who thinks i can improve his mental health.

one of the lunch ladies actually laughs when tiny gets
all gleeful about the empanadas that they're serving in celebration of latino heritage week (or maybe it's latino heritage
month). she calls him sweetie when she hands it to him,
which is pretty funny, since i've spent the last three years
trying to win her over enough to stop getting the smallest
piece of pizza from the tray.

when we get to the table, derek and simon are already
there — gideon's the only one missing. since i haven't warned
them about our special guest star, they look surprised and
petrified when we walk over.

me: derek and simon, this is tiny. tiny, this is derek and
    simon.
tiny: lovely to meet you!

simon: ermm . . .

derek: nice to meet you, too. who are you?

tiny: i'm will's boyfriend. from evanston.

okay, now they're looking at him like he's a magical beast from world of warcraft. derek's amused, in a friendly way. simon is looking at tiny, then looking at me, then looking at tiny, in a way that can only mean that he's wondering how someone so big and someone so wiry can have sex.

i feel a hand on my shoulder.

gideon: there you are!

gideon seems to be the only person in the school who doesn't seem shocked by tiny's appearance. without missing a beat, he leans his other hand out to shake.

gideon: you must be tiny.

tiny looks at the hand gideon has on my shoulder before shaking the hand that gideon's offered. he doesn't sound too happy when he says

tiny: . . . and you must be gideon.

his handshake has to be a little firmer than usual, since gideon actually winces before it's through. then he leaves to pull up an extra chair to the table, offering tiny the place where he usually sits.

tiny: now, isn't this cozy?

well, no. the smell of his beef empanada makes me feel like i'm locked in a small, warm room full of dog food. simon, i fear, is on the verge of saying something wrong, and derek looks like he's going to blog about the whole thing. gideon starts asking tiny friendly questions, and tiny keeps giving one-word answers.

gideon: how was the traffic getting here?
tiny: fine.
gideon: is this a lot like your school?
tiny: meh.
gideon: i hear you're putting on a musical.
tiny: yup.

finally, gideon gets up to buy a cookie, allowing me to lean over to tiny and ask

me: why are you treating him like someone who
    dumped you?
tiny: i'm not!
me: you don't even know him.
tiny: i know his type.
me: what type?
tiny: the wispy cute type. they're *poison*.

i think he knows he's gone a little too far there, because he immediately adds

tiny: but he seems really nice.

he looks around the cafeteria.

tiny: which one's maura?

me: two tables to the left of the door. sitting by herself,
   poor slaughtered lamb. scribbling in her notebook.

as if sensing our glance, she looks up in our direction,
then puts her head down and scribbles more furiously.

derek: how is the beef empanada? in all my years here,
   you're the first person i've ever seen finish it.

tiny: not bad, if you don't mind salty. it's like someone
   made a pop-tart out of beef jerky.

simon: and how long have the two of you been, like,
   together?

tiny: i dunno? four weeks, two days, and eighteen
   hours, i think.

simon: so you're the guy.

tiny: what guy?

simon: the guy who almost lost us the mathletic
   competition.

tiny: if that's true, then i'm very sorry.

simon: well, you know what they say.

derek: simon?

simon: gay guys always put dicks before math.

me: in the whole history of the world, no one has ever
   said that.

derek: you're just upset that the girl from naperville —

simon: don't go there!

derek: — wouldn't sit on your lap when you asked her to.

simon: it was a crowded bus!

gideon comes back with cookies for all of us.

gideon: it's a special occasion. what did i miss?

me: dicks before math.

gideon: that makes no sense.

me: exactly.

tiny is starting to fidget, and he's not even touching his cookie. it's a soft cookie. with chocolate chips. it should be in his digestive system by now.

if tiny's losing his appetite, there's no way we're going to make it through the rest of the school day. it's not like i have any desire to go to class — why would tiny? if he wants to be with me, i should be with him. and this school will never let me.

me: let's leave.

tiny: but i just got here.

me: you have just met the only people i ever interact
    with. you have sampled our fine cuisine. if you'd
    like, i can show you the trophy case on the way
    out so you can bask in the achievements of the
    alumni who are now old enough to be suffering
    from erectile dysfunction, memory loss, and death. i
    am never, ever, going to be able to display affection
    for you here, but if you get me in private, it will be
    another matter entirely.

tiny: dicks before math.

me: yes. dicks before math. even though i already had
    math class today. i'll skip it retroactively to be with
    you.

derek: go! go!

tiny seems very pleased by this turn of events.

tiny: i'll have you all to myself?

this is borderline embarrassing to admit in front of other people, so i just nod.

we gather our trays and say our good-byes. gideon looks a little bummed, but sounds sincere when he tells tiny he hopes we'll all get a chance to hang out later. tiny says he hopes so, too, but not like he means it.

as we're about to leave the cafeteria, tiny says he needs to make one more stop.

tiny: there's something i have to do.
me: the restroom's down that hallway, to the left.

but that's not his destination.
he's heading straight for maura's table.

me: what are you doing? we don't talk to her.
tiny: you might not — but i have a thing or two i'd
    like to say.

she's looking up at us now.

me: stop.
tiny: step aside, grayson. i know what i'm doing.

she makes a big production of putting down her pen and closing her notebook.

me: don't, tiny.

but he steps forward and hovers over her. the mountain has come to maura, and it has something to say.

there's a flash of nervousness across tiny's face before he begins. he takes a deep breath. she looks at him with a studied blankness.

> tiny: i just wanted to come over and thank you. i'm
> tiny cooper, and i've been dating this will grayson
> for four weeks, two days, and eighteen hours now.
> if you hadn't been such an evil, selfish, deceitful,
> vindictive frenemy to him, we would have never
> met. it just goes to show, if you try to ruin
> someone's life, it only gets better. you just don't
> get to be a part of it.
>
> me: tiny, enough.
>
> tiny: i think she needs to know what she's missing,
> will. i think she needs to know how happy —
>
> me: ENOUGH!

a lot of people hear it. tiny certainly does, because he stops. and maura certainly does, because she stops staring blankly at him and starts staring blankly at me. i am so mad at both of them right now. i take tiny by the hand, but this time it's to pull him away. maura smirks at that, then opens her notebook and starts writing again. i make it to the door, then let go of tiny's hand, head back to maura's table, grab the notebook, and rip out the page that she's writing on. i don't even read it. i just rip it out and crumple it up and then throw the notebook back on the table, knocking over her diet coke. i don't say a word. i just leave.

i am so angry i can't speak. tiny is behind me, saying

tiny: what? what did i do?

i wait until we're out of the building. i wait until we're in the parking lot. i wait until he's led me to his car. i wait until we're inside the car. i wait until i feel i can open my mouth without screaming. and then i say:

me: you really shouldn't have done that.
tiny: why?
me: WHY? because i'm not talking to her. because i've managed to avoid her for a month, and now you just dragged me over to her and made her feel like she matters in my life.
tiny: she needed to be taught a lesson.
me: what lesson? that if she tries to ruin someone's life, *it only gets better*? that's a great lesson, tiny. now she can try to ruin more people's lives, because at least she'll have the satisfaction of knowing she's doing them a favor. maybe she can even start a matchmaking service. clearly, it worked for us.
tiny: stop it.
me: stop what?
tiny: stop talking to me like i'm stupid. i'm not stupid.
me: i know you're not stupid. but you sure as hell did a stupid thing.

he hasn't even started the car yet. we're still sitting in the parking lot.

tiny: this isn't how the day was supposed to go.

me: well, you know what? a lot of the time, you have
     no control over how your day goes.

tiny: stop. please. i want this to be a nice day.

he starts the car. it's my turn to take a deep breath. who
the hell wants to be the one to tell a kid that santa claus isn't
real. it's the truth, right? but you're still a jerk for saying it.

tiny: let's go somewhere you like to go. where should
     we go? take me somewhere that matters to you.

me: like what?

tiny: like . . . i don't know. for me, if i need to feel
     better, i go alone to super target. i don't know why,
     but seeing all of those things makes me happy.
     it's probably the design. i don't even have to buy
     anything. just seeing all the people together, seeing
     all the things i *could* buy — all the colors, aisle
     after aisle — sometimes i need that. for jane, it's
     this indie record store we'll go to so she can look
     at old vinyl while i look at all the boy band cds
     in the two-dollar bin and try to figure out which
     one i think is the cutest. or the other will grayson
     — there's this park in our town, where all the little
     league teams play. and he loves the dugout, because
     when no one else is around, it's really quiet there.
     when there's not a game on, you can sit there and
     all that exists are the things that happened in the
     past. i think everyone has a place like that. you
     must have a place like that.

i think hard about it for a second, but i figure if i had a place like that, i'd know it right away. but no place really matters to me. it didn't even occur to me that i was supposed to have a place that mattered to me.

i shake my head.

me: nothing.
tiny: c'mon. there has to be someplace.
me: there isn't, okay? just my house. my room. that's it.
tiny: fine — then where's the nearest swing set?
me: are you kidding me?
tiny: no. there has to be a swing set around here.
me: at the elementary school, i guess. but school isn't out yet. if they catch us there, they'll think we're kidnappers. i'll be okay, but i bet you'd be tried as an adult.
tiny: okay, besides the elementary school.
me: i think my neighbors have one.
tiny: do the parents work?
me: i think so.
tiny: and the kids are still in school. perfect! lead the way.

this is how we end up parking in front of my house and breaking into my next-door neighbor's yard. the swing set is pretty sad, as swing sets go, but at least it's made for older kids, not toddlers.

me: you're not actually going to sit on that, are you?

but he does. and i swear the metal frame bends a little. he gestures to the swing next to his.

tiny: join me.

it's probably been ten years since i sat on a swing. i only do it to shut tiny up for a second. neither of us actually swings — i don't think the frame could take that. we just sit there, dangling over the ground. tiny twists around so he's facing me. i twist, too, putting my feet on the ground to prevent the chain from unwinding me.

tiny: now, isn't this better?

and i can't help it. i say

me: better than what?

tiny laughs and shakes his head.

me: what? why are you shaking your head.
tiny: it's nothing.
me: tell me.
tiny: it's just funny.
me: WHAT'S funny?
tiny: you. and me.
me: i'm glad you find it funny.
tiny: i wish you'd find it funnier.

i don't even know what we're talking about anymore.

tiny: you know what's a great metaphor for love?
me: i have a feeling you're about to tell me.

he turns away and makes an attempt to swing high. the swing set groans so much that he stops and twists back my way.

tiny: sleeping beauty.
me: sleeping beauty?
tiny: yes, because you have to plow through this incredible thicket of thorns in order to get to beauty, and even then, when you get there, you still have to wake her up.
me: so i'm a thicket?
tiny: and the beauty that isn't fully awake yet.

i don't point out that tiny is hardly what little girls think of when you say the words *prince charming*.

me: it figures you'd think that way.
tiny: why?
me: well, your life is a musical. literally.
tiny: do you hear me singing now?

i almost do. i'd love to live in his musical cartoon world, where witches like maura get vanquished with one heroic word, and all the forest creatures are happy when two gay guys walk hand-in-hand through the meadow, and gideon is the himbo suitor you know the princess can't marry, because her heart belongs to the beast. i'm sure it's a lovely world, where these things happen. a rich, spoiled, colorful world. maybe one day i'll get to visit, but i doubt it. worlds like that don't tend to issue visas to fuckups like me.

me: it puzzles me how someone like you could drive all this way to be with someone like me.

tiny: not that again!

me: excuse me?

tiny: we're always having this conversation. but if you keep focusing on why you have it so bad, you'll never realize how you could have it so good.

me: easy for you to say!

tiny: what do you mean?

me: pretty much exactly that. i'll break it down for you. *easy* — with no difficulty whatsoever. *for you* — the opposite of 'for me.' *to say* — to vocalize, sometimes ad nauseam. you have it so good that you don't realize that when you have it bad, it's not a choice you're making.

tiny: i know that. i wasn't saying . . .

me: yes?

tiny: i do understand.

me: you DON'T understand. because you have it so easy.

now i've riled him up. he steps out of the swing and stands right in front of me. there's a vein in his neck that's actually pulsing. he can't look angry without also looking sad.

tiny: STOP TELLING ME I HAVE IT SO EASY! do you have any idea what you're talking about?

because i'm a person, too. and i have problems, too. and even though they might not be your problems, they're still problems.

me: like what?

tiny: you may not have noticed, but i'm not what you'd call conventionally beautiful. in fact, you might say that i'm the opposite of that. *say*, you know — to vocalize, sometimes ad nauseam? do you think that there's any minute in any day when i'm not aware of how big i am? do you think there's a single minute that goes by when i'm not thinking about how other people see me? even though i have no control whatsoever over that? don't get me wrong — i love my body. but i'm not so much of an idiot to think that everybody else loves it. what really gets to me — what *really* bothers me — is that it's all people see. ever since i was a not-so-little kid. *hey, tiny, want to play football? hey, tiny, how many burgers did you eat today? hey, tiny, you ever lose your dick down there? hey, tiny, you're going to join the basketball team whether you like it or not. just don't try to look at us in the locker room!* does that sound easy to you, will?

i'm about to say something, but he holds up his hand.

tiny: you know what? i'm totally at peace with being big-boned. and i was gay long before i knew what sex was. it's just who i am, and that's great. i don't want to be thin or conventionally beautiful or straight or brilliant. no, what i really want — and what i never get — is to be *appreciated*. do you know what it's like to work so hard to make sure everyone's happy, and to have not a single person recognize it? i can work my ass off bringing together the other will grayson and jane — no appreciation, only grief. i write this whole musical that's basically about love, and the main character in it — besides me, of course — is phil wrayson, who needs to figure some things out, but is all-in-all a pretty wonderful guy. and does will get that? no. he freaks out. i do everything i can to be a good boyfriend with you — no appreciation, only grief. i try to make this musical so it can create something, to show that we all have something to sing — no appreciation, only grief. this musical is a gift, will. my gift to the world. it's not about me. it's about what i have to share. there's a difference — i see it, but i am worried that i am the only frickin' one who sees it. you think i have it easy, will? are you really dying to try on these size fifteens? because every morning when i wake up, i have to convince myself that, yes, by the end of the day, i will be able to do something good. that's all i ask — to be able to do something good. not for myself, you whiny shithead bastard complainer who, incidentally, i really, really like. but for my friends. for other people.

me: but why me? i mean, what do you see in me?
tiny: you have a heart, will. you even let it slip out every

now and then. i see that in you. and i see that you
need me.

i shake my head.

me: don't you get it? i don't need anyone.
tiny: that only means you need me more.

it's so clear to me.

me: you're not in love with me. you're in love with my
need.
tiny: who said i was in love with anything? i said
'really, really like.'

he stops now. pauses.

tiny: this always happens. some variation of this always
happens.
me: i'm sorry.
tiny: they always say 'i'm sorry,' too.
me: i can't do this, tiny.
tiny: you can, but you won't. you just won't.

it's like i don't have to break up with him, because he's
already had the conversation in his head. i should feel relieved that i don't have to say anything. but instead, i only
feel worse.

me: it's not your fault. i just can't feel anything.

tiny: really? are you really feeling nothing right now? nothing at all?

i want to tell him: nobody ever told me how to deal with things like this. shouldn't letting go be painless if you've never learned how to hold on?

tiny: i'm going to go now.

and i'm going to stay. i'm going to stay on this swing as he walks away. i'm going to stay silent as he gets in his car. i'm going to stay still as i hear the car start, then drive away. i'm going to stay in the wrong, because i don't know how to get through the thicket of my own mind in order to reach whatever it is that i'm supposed to do. i'm going to stay the same, and the same, and the same, until i die of it.

minutes have to pass before i can admit that, yes, even though i tell myself i'm feeling nothing, it's a lie. i want to say i'm feeling remorse or regret or even guilt. but none of those words seem like enough. what i'm feeling is shame. raw, loathing shame. i don't want to be the person i am. i don't want to be the person who just did what i did.

it's not even about tiny, really.

i am awful.

i am heartless.

i am scared that these things are actually true.

i run back to my house. i am starting to sob — i'm not even thinking about it, but my body is falling to pieces. my hand is shaking so much that i drop the keys before i finally get them in the door. the house is empty. i am empty. i try to eat. i try to crawl into bed. nothing works. i do feel things. i feel everything. and i need to know i'm not alone. so i'm getting out the phone. i'm not even thinking about it. i'm pressing the number and i'm hearing the ring and as soon as it's answered, i'm shouting into the phone:

me: I LOVE YOU. DO YOU HEAR ME, I LOVE YOU?

i'm screaming it, and it sounds so angry and so frightened and so pathetic and desperate. on the other end of the phone, my mother is asking me what's wrong, where am i, what's happening, and i'm telling her that i'm at home and that everything's a mess, and she's saying she'll be home in ten minutes, will i be okay for ten minutes? and i want to tell her i'll be okay, because that's what she wants to hear, but then i realize that maybe what she wants to hear is the actual truth, so i tell her that i feel things, i really do, and she tells me of course i do, i always have had these feelings, and that's what makes life hard for me sometimes.

just hearing her voice makes me feel a little better, and i realize that, yes, i appreciate what she's saying, and i appreciate what she's doing, and that i need to let her know that. although i don't say it right away, since i think that will only worry her more, but when she gets home i say it to her, and she says she knows.

i tell her a little about tiny, and she says it sounds like we were putting too much pressure on ourselves, and that it doesn't have to be love immediately, or even love eventually. i want to ask her which it was with my father, and when it was that everything turned into hate and sadness. but maybe i don't really want to know. not right now.

> mom: need is never a good basis for any relationship. it
>   has to be much more than that.

it's good to talk to her, but it's also strange, because she's my mom, and i don't want to be one of these kids who thinks his mom's his best friend. by the time i've recovered enough, school is long over, and i figure i can go online and see if gideon's there. then i realize i can text him instead. then i realize that i can actually call him. finally, i realize i can actually call him and see if he wants to do something. because he's my friend, and that's what friends do.

i call, he answers. i need him, he answers. i go over to his house and tell him what's happened, and he answers. it's not like it was with maura, who always wanted to take the dark road. it's not like it was with tiny, because with him i was feeling all these expectations to be a good boyfriend, whatever that is. no, gideon's ready to believe both the best and the worst in me. in other words: the truth.

when we're done talking, he asks me if i'm going to call tiny. i tell him i don't know.

it's not until later that i decide. i'm on IM, and i see he's on, too.

i don't really think i can salvage us being boyfriends, but at the very least i want to tell him that even if he was wrong about me, he wasn't wrong about himself. i mean, someone should be trying to do good in the world.

so i try.

8:15pm
willupleasebequiet: bluejeanbaby?
willupleasebequiet: tiny?

8:18pm
willupleasebequiet: are you there?

9:33pm
willupleasebequiet: are you there?

10:10pm
willupleasebequiet: please?

11:45pm
willupleasebequiet: are you there?

1:03am
willupleasebequiet: are you there?
willupleasebequiet: are you there?
willupleasebequiet: are you there?
willupleasebequiet: are you there?
willupleasebequiet: are you there?

chapter seventeen

Three days before the play, Tiny and I are talking again as we wait for precalc to start, but there's nothing inside our words. He sits down next to me and says, "Hey, Grayson," and I say, "Hey," and he says, "What's new?" and I say, "Not much, you?" and he says, "Not much. The play is kicking my ass, man," and I say, "I bet," and he says, "You're dating Jane, huh?" and I say, "Sorta, yeah," and he says, "That's awesome," and I say, "Yeah. How's the other Will Grayson," and he says, "Fine," and that's it. Honestly, talking to him is worse than not. Talking to him makes me feel like I'm drowning in lukewarm water.

Jane's standing by my locker with her hands behind her back when I get there after first period, and when I get to her, there's this awkward but not unpleasant should-we-kiss moment, or at least I think that's what the moment is, but then she says, "Sucks about Tiny, huh?"

"What does?" I ask.

"He and the other Will Grayson. Kaput."

I tilt my head at her, baffled. "No, he just said they were fine. I asked him in precalc."

"Happened yesterday, at least according to Gary and Nick and the twenty-three other people who told me about it. On a swing set, apparently. Oh, the metaphorical resonance."

"Then why didn't he tell me?" I hear my voice catch as I say it.

Jane grabs my hand and stands up to say into my ear, "Hey," and then I look back at her, trying to act like it doesn't matter. "Hey," she says again.

"Hey," I say.

"Just go back to normal with him, huh? Just *talk* to him, Will. I don't know if you've noticed, but everything goes better for you when you talk to people."

"You wanna come over after school?" I ask.

"Absolutely." She smiles, then spins a half-circle in place and walks off. She takes a few steps before turning back and saying, "Talk. To. Tiny."

For a while, I just stand there at my locker. Even after the bell rings. I know why he didn't tell me: it isn't because he feels weird that for the first time in human history, he's single and I'm taken(ish). He said the other Will Grayson was fine because I don't matter.

Tiny might ignore you when he's in love. But when Tiny Cooper lies to you about his heartbreak, the Geiger counter has tripped the hammer. The radiation has been released. The friendship is dead.

That day after school Jane's at my house, sitting across a Scrabble board from me. I spell *hallow*, which is a great word but also opens up a triple-word-score spot for her.

"Oh my God, I love you," she says, and it must be close enough to true, because if she'd said that a week before I wouldn't have thought anything of it, and now it hangs in the air forever until she finally bursts the awkwardness by saying, "That would be a weird thing to say to someone you just started dating! Boy-howdy, is this awkward!" After a moment of silence, she keeps going, "Hey, to extend the weird, are we dating?"

And the word turns my stomach a little and I say, "Can we be not not-dating?"

She smiles and spells *cowed* for thirty-six points. It's absolutely amazing, the whole thing. Her shoulder blades are amazing. Her passionately ironic love for 1980s television dramas is amazing. The way she laughs at my jokes really loudly is amazing—all of which only makes it more amazing that she doesn't fill the Tiny hole left by his absence.

To be perfectly honest, I felt it last semester when he went off to become the GSA president and I fell into the Group of Friends. Probably that's why I wrote the letter to the editor and signed it. Not because I wanted the school to know I'd written it, but because I wanted Tiny to know.

The next day, Mom drops me off early. I go in and slip a note in Jane's locker, which I've gotten in the habit of doing. It's always just a line or two that I found from some poem in the gigantic poetry anthology my sophomore English teacher taught from. I said I wouldn't be the kind of boyfriend who reads her poetry, and I'm not, but I guess I am the kind of cheesy bastard who slips lines of poetry into her mornings.

Today's: I see thee better in the dark / I do not need a light. —Emily Dickinson

And then I settle into my precalc seat twenty minutes early. I try to study a little for chem but give up within twenty seconds. I get out my phone and check my email. Nothing. I keep looking over at his empty chair, the chair he fills with a completeness unimaginable to the rest of us.

I decide to write him an email, thumbing it out on my tiny keyboard. I'm just passing time, really. I keep using unnecessarily long words because they make the writing soak up the minutes.

> *it's not like i feel some urgent desire to be friends, but i wish we could be one thing or the other. this, even though rationally i know that your departure from my life is a bountiful blessing, that on most days you are nothing but a 300-pound burden shackled to me, and that you clearly never liked me. i always complained about you and your general hugeness, and now i miss it. typical guy, you'd say. they don't know what they've got till it's gone. and maybe you're right, tiny. i'm sorry about will grayson. both of us.*

The first bell finally rings. I save the email as a draft.

Tiny sits down next to me and says, "Hey, Grayson," and I say, "Hey, how's it going?" and he says, "Good, man. Dress rehearsal today," and I say, "Awesome," and he says, "What's going on with you?" and I say, "This paper for English is killing me," and he says, "Yeah, my grades are in the tank," and I say, "Yeah," and the second bell rings and we turn our attention to Mr. Applebaum.

• • •

Four hours later: I'm in the middle of the line of people rushing out of the physics classroom fifth period when I see Tiny walking past the window. He stops, dramatically pivots toward the door, and waits for me.

"We broke up," he says matter-of-factly.

"So I heard. Thanks for letting me know—after telling everyone else."

"Yeah, well," he says. People weave around us like we're a blood clot in the hallway's artery. "Rehearsal's gonna go late—we're gonna do a run-through after dress—but you wanna get some late-night dinner? Hot Dog Palace or something?"

I consider it a minute, thinking about the unsent email in my drafts folder, and the other Will Grayson, and Tiny up onstage telling me the truth behind my back, and then I say, "I don't think so. I'm tired of being your Plan B, Tiny."

It doesn't faze him, of course. "Well, I guess I'll see you at the play then."

"I don't know if I can make it, but yeah, I'll try."

It's hard to read Tiny's face for some reason, but I think I've gotten a shot in. I don't know exactly why I want to make him feel like crap, but I do.

I'm walking to Jane's locker to find her when she comes up behind me and says, "Can I talk to you for a minute?"

"You can talk to me for billions of minutes." I smile.

We duck into an abandoned Spanish classroom. She spins a chair around and sits, the chair's back like a shield. She's wearing a tight T-shirt underneath a peacoat, which she presently takes off, and she looks awfully good, good enough that I wonder aloud if we can't talk at home.

"I get distracted at your house." She raises her eyebrows and smiles, but I see the fake in it. "You said yesterday that we were not not-dating, and like it's not a big deal, and I realize that it has been one week and one week only, but I actually don't want to not not-date you; I want to be your girlfriend or not, and I would think by now you're qualified to make at least a temporary decision on the topic, because I know I am."

She looks down for a second, and I notice her hair parted in the middle has an accidental zigzag at the top of her head, and I inhale to talk, but then she says, "Also, I'm not going to be *devastated* or anything either way. I'm not that kind of person. I just think if you don't *say* the honest thing, sometimes the honest thing never becomes true, you know, and I—" she says, but then I hold up my finger, because I need to hear the thing she just said, and she talks too fast for me to keep up. I keep holding up my hand, thinking *if you don't say the honest thing, it never becomes true.*

I put my hands on her shoulders. "I just realized something. I really really like you. You're amazing, and I so want to be your boyfriend, because of what you just said, and also because that shirt makes me want to take you home now and do unspeakable things while we watch live-action Sailor Moon videos. But but but you're totally right about saying the honest thing. I think if you keep the box closed long enough you do kill the cat, actually. And—God, I hope you won't take this personally—but I love my best friend more than anyone in the world."

She's looking at me now, squinting confusion.

"I do. I fucking love Tiny Cooper."

Jane says, "Um, okay. Are you asking me to be your girlfriend, or are you telling me that you're gay?"

"The first one. The girlfriend one. I gotta go find Tiny."

I stand up and kiss her on the zigzag and then bolt.

I call him while running across the soccer field, holding down 1 to speed dial. He doesn't pick up, but I think I know where he thinks I'm going, so I go there.

Once I see the park to my left, I slow to a fast-walk, heaving breaths, my shoulders burning beneath the backpack straps. Everything depends upon him being in the dugout, and it's so unlikely that he would go there, three days before the opening of the play, and as I walk, I start to feel like an idiot: His phone is off because he's in rehearsal, and I ran *here* instead of running to the auditorium, which means that now I am going to have to run *back* to the auditorium, and my lungs were not designed for such rigorous use.

I slow further when I hit the park, half because I'm out of breath and half because so long as I can't see into the dugout, he's there and he isn't. I watch this couple walking on the lawn, knowing that they can see into the dugout, trying to tell from their eyes whether they see a gigantic someone sitting in the visitors' dugout of this Little League field. But their eyes give me nothing, and I just watch them as they hold hands and walk.

Finally, the dugout comes into view. And damned if he isn't sitting right in the middle of that wooden bench.

I walk over. "Don't you have dress rehearsal?" He doesn't say anything until I sit down next to him on the cold wooden bench.

"They need a run-through without me. Otherwise, they may mutiny. We'll do the dress a little later tonight."

"So, what brings you to the visitors' dugout?"

"You remember after I first came out, you used to say, instead of like saying, 'Tiny plays for the other team,' you'd say, 'Tiny plays for the White Sox.'"

"Yeah. Is that homophobic?" I ask.

"Nah," he says. "Well, probably it is, but it didn't bother me. Anyway, I want to apologize."

"For what?"

Apparently, I've uttered the magic words, because Tiny takes a deep breath before he starts talking, as if—fancy this—he has a lot to say. "For not saying to your face what I said to Gary. I'm not gonna apologize for saying it, because it's true. You and your damn rules. And you do get tag-alongy sometimes, and there's something a little Drama Queeny about your anti-Drama Queenyness, and I know I'm difficult but so are you and your whole put-upon act gets really old, and also you are so self-involved."

"Said the pot to the kettle," I say, trying not to get pissed. Tiny is awfully talented at puncturing the love bubble I felt for him. Perhaps, I think, this is why he gets dumped so much.

"Ha! True. True. I'm not saying I'm innocent. I'm saying you're guilty, too."

The couple walks out of my view. And then finally I feel ready to banish the quiver Tiny apparently thinks is weakness. I stand up so he has to look at me, and so I have to look at him, and for once, I'm taller. "I love you," I say.

He tilts his fat lovable head like a confused puppy.

"You are a terrible best friend," I tell him. "Terrible!

You totally ditch me every time you have a boyfriend, and then you come crawling back when you're heartbroken. You don't listen to me. You don't even seem to *like* me. You get obsessed with the play and totally ignore me except to insult me to our friend behind my back, and you exploit your life and the people you say you care about so that your little play can make people love you and think how awesome you are and how liberated you are and how wondrously gay you are, but you know what? Being gay is not an excuse for being a dick.

"But you're one on my speed dial and I want you to stay there and I'm sorry I'm a terrible best friend, too, and I love you."

He won't stop it with the turned head. "Grayson, are you coming out to me? Because I'm, I mean, don't take this personally, but I would sooner go straight than go gay with you."

"NO. No no no. I don't want to *screw* you. I just *love* you. When did who you want to screw become the whole game? Since when is the person you want to screw the only person you get to love? It's so stupid, Tiny! I mean, Jesus, who even gives a fuck about sex?! People act like it's the most important thing humans do, but come on. How can our sentient fucking lives revolve around something *slugs* can do. I mean, who you want to screw and whether you screw them? Those are important questions, I guess. But they're not *that* important. You know what's important? Who would you *die* for? Who do you wake up at five forty-five in the morning for even though you don't even know why he needs you? Whose drunken nose would you pick?!"

I'm shouting, my arms whirling with gesticulations, and I don't even notice until I run out of important questions that Tiny is crying. And then softly, the softest I've ever heard Tiny say anything, he says, "If you could write a play about anybody . . ." and then his voice trails off.

I sit down next to him, put my arm around him. "Are you okay?"

Somehow, Tiny Cooper manages to contort himself so that his massive head cries on my narrow shoulder. And after a while he says, "Long week. Long month. Long life."

He recovers quickly, wiping his eyes with the popped collar of the polo shirt he's wearing beneath a striped sweater. "When you date someone, you have the markers along the way, right: You kiss, you have The Talk, you say the Three Little Words, you sit on a swing set and break up. You can plot the points on a graph. And you check up with each other along the way: Can I do this? If I say this, will you say it back?

"But with friendship, there's nothing like that. Being in a relationship, that's something you choose. Being friends, that's just something you are."

I just stare out at the ball field for a minute. Tiny sniffles. "I'd pick you," I say. "Fuck it, I *do* pick you. I want you to come over to my house in twenty years with your dude and your adopted kids and I want our fucking kids to hang out and I want to, like, drink wine and talk about the Middle East or whatever the fuck we're gonna want to do when we're old. We've been friends too long to pick, but if we could pick, I'd pick you."

"Yeah, okay. You're getting a little feelingsy, Grayson," he says. "It's kinda freaking me out."

"Got it."

"Like, don't ever say you love me again."

"But I do love you. I'm not embarrassed about it."

"Seriously, Grayson, stop it. You're making me throw up in the back of my mouth a little."

I laugh. "Can I help with the play?"

Tiny reaches into his pocket and produces a neatly folded piece of notebook paper and hands it to me. "I thought you'd never ask," he says, smirking.

Will (and to a lesser extent Jane),

Thank you for your interest in assisting me in the run-up to *Hold Me Closer*. I would greatly appreciate it if you would both be backstage opening night to assist with costume changes and to generally calm cast members (okay, let's just say it: me). Also, you'll have an excellent view of the play.

Also, the Phil Wrayson costume is excellent as is, but it'd be even better if we had some Will Grayson-ish clothes for Gary to wear.

Furthermore, I thought I would have time to make a preshow mix in which the odd-numbered tracks are punk rock and the even-numbered tracks are from musicals. I will not, in fact, have time to do this; if you do, it would be truly fabulous.

You are a cute couple, and it was my distinct pleasure to set you up, and I do not in any way resent either of you for failing to have thanked me for making your love possible.

I remain . . .

Your faithful matchmaker and servant . . .

Toiling alone and newly single in an ocean of pain
so that some light may be brought into your lives . . .
Tiny Cooper

I laugh while I read it, and Tiny laughs, too, nodding his head, appreciating his own awesome.

"I'm sorry about the other Will Grayson," I say.

His smile folds in upon itself. His response seems directed more toward my namesake than me. "There's never been anybody like him."

I don't trust the words as he says them, but then he exhales through pursed lips, his sad eyes squinting at the distance, and I believe him.

"I should probably get started on this, eh? Thanks for the backstage invite."

He gets up and starts nodding like he sometimes does, the repetitive nodding that tells me he's convincing himself of something. "Yeah, I should get back to infuriating the cast and crew with my tyrannical direction."

"I'll see you tomorrow then," I say.

"And all the other days," he says, patting me too hard between the shoulder blades.

chapter eighteen

i start holding my breath. not like you do when you pass a graveyard or something like that. no. i'm trying to see how long i can do it before i pass out or die. it's a really convenient pastime — you can do it pretty much anywhere. class. lunch. at the urinal. in the discomfort of your own room.

the sucky part is that the moment always comes when i take the next breath. i can only push myself so far.

i've given up on hearing from tiny. i hurt him, he hates me — it's as simple as that. and now that he's not texting me, i realize that no one else texts me. or messages me. or cares.

now that he isn't into me, i realize that no one else is all that into me, either.

okay, so there's gideon. he's not much of a texter or a messager, but when we're at school, he's always asking me how things are going. and i always stop not-breathing in order to answer him. sometimes i even tell the truth.

me: seriously, is this what the rest of my life is going to be? i don't think i signed up for this.

i know it sounds like teenage idiocy — the needles! in my heart! and my eyes! — but the pattern seems inescapable. i am never going to get better at being a good person. i am always going to be the blood and shit of things.

gideon: just breathe.

and i wonder how he knows to say that.

the only time that i pretend i have it all together is when maura's around. i don't want her to see me falling apart. worst case scenario: she stomps on all the pieces. worse-than-that case scenario: she tries to put them together again. i realize: i am now where she was with me. on the other side of the silence. you'd think that silence would be peaceful. but really, it's painful.

at home, mom is keeping close watch on me. which makes me feel worse, because now i'm putting her through it, too.

that night — the night i screwed everything up with tiny — she hid the glass bowl he gave her. while i was asleep, she put it away. and the stupid thing was, when i saw it was gone, the first thing i thought was that she was afraid i'd smash it. then i realized she was only trying to protect me from seeing it, from getting upset.

at school, i ask gideon

me: why is it *up*set? shouldn't it be *down*set?
gideon: i will file a lawsuit against the dictionaries first
    thing tomorrow morning. we're going to tear merriam
    a new asshole and throw webster inside of it.

me: you are such a dork.

gideon: only if you catch me on a good day.

i don't tell gideon that i feel guilty being around him. because what if the threat tiny felt turns out to be true? what if i was cheating on him without knowing it?

me: can you cheat on someone without knowing it?

i am not asking gideon this. i am asking my mother.

she has been so careful with me. she has been tiptoeing around my moods, acting like everything's okay. but now she just freezes.

mom: why are you asking me that? did you cheat on tiny?

and i'm thinking, oh shit, i should not have asked that question.

me: no. i didn't. why are you so mad?

mom: nothing.

me: no, why? did dad cheat on you?

she shakes her head.

me: did you cheat on dad?

she sighs.

mom: no. it's not that. it's . . . i don't want you to ever be
     a cheater. not on people. sometimes it's okay to cheat

on things — but don't ever cheat on people. because once you start, it's very hard to stop. you find out how easy it is to do.

me: mom?

mom: that's all. why are you asking?

me: no reason. just wondering.

i've been wondering a lot lately. sometimes, when i'm passing the minute mark on holding my breath, besides imagining being dead, i'm also imagining what tiny is doing. sometimes i picture the other will grayson there. most of the time, they're onstage. but i can never understand what they're singing.

and the weird thing is, i'm thinking about isaac again. and maura. and how weird it is that it was a lie that made me happiest.

tiny doesn't respond to any of my instant messages. then, the night before the musical, i decide to type in the other will grayson's screenname. and there he is. it's not like i think he'll completely understand. yeah, we have the same name, but it's not like we're psychic twins. it's not like he'll wince in pain if i burn myself or anything. but that one night in chicago, i felt he understood a little of it. and, yeah, i also want to see if tiny's okay.

willupleasebequiet: hey

willupleasebequiet: it's will grayson.

willupleasebequiet: the other one.

WGrayson7: wow. hello.

willupleasebequiet: is this okay? me talking to you.

WGrayson7: yeah. what are you doing up at 1:33:48?

willupleasebequiet: waiting to see if 1:33:49 is any
    better. you?

WGrayson7: if i'm not mistaken, i just saw, via webcam,
    a revised musical number that involved oscar wilde's
    ghost, live from the bedroom of the musical's

WGrayson7: director-writer-star-etc-etc

willupleasebequiet: how was it?

willupleasebequiet: no.

willupleasebequiet: i mean, how is he?

WGrayson7: truth?

willupleasebequiet: yes.

WGrayson7: i don't think i've ever seen him more
    nervous. and not because he's the director-writer-
    star-etc-etc. but because it means so much to him,
    you know? he really thinks he can change the
    world.

willupleasebequiet: i can imagine.

WGrayson7: sorry, it's late. and i'm not even sure if i
    should be talking about tiny with you.

willupleasebequiet: i just checked the bylaws of the
    international society of will graysons, and i can't
    find anything in there about it. we're in vastly
    uncharted territory.

WGrayson7: exactly. here be dragons.

willupleasebequiet: will?

WGrayson7: yes, will.

willupleasebequiet: does he know i'm sorry?

WGrayson7: dunno. in my recent experience, i'd say
    hurt tends to drown out sorry.

willupleasebequiet: i just couldn't be that person for him.

WGrayson7: that person?

willupleasebequiet: the one he really wants.

willupleasebequiet: i just wish it wasn't all trial and error.

willupleasebequiet: because that's what it is, isn't it?

willupleasebequiet: trial and error.

willupleasebequiet: i guess there's a reason they don't call it 'trial and success'

willupleasebequiet: it's just try-error

willupleasebequiet: try-error

willupleasebequiet: try-error

willupleasebequiet: i'm sorry. are you still here?

WGrayson7: yes.

WGrayson7: if you'd caught me two weeks ago, i would have had to agree with you fullheartedly.

WGrayson7: now i'm not so sure.

willupleasebequiet: why?

WGrayson7: well, i agree that 'trial and error' is a pretty pessimistic name for it. and maybe that's what it is most of the time.

WGrayson7: but i think the point is that it's not just try-error.

WGrayson7: most of the time it's try-error-try

WGrayson7: try-error-try

WGrayson7: try-error-try

WGrayson7: and that's how you find it.

willupleasebequiet: it?

WGrayson7: you know. *it.*

willupleasebequiet: yeah, *it.*

willupleasebequiet: try-error-try-*it*

WGrayson7: well . . . i haven't become *that* optimistic.

WGrayson7: it's more like try-error-try-error-try-error-
try-error-try-error-try . . . at least fifteen more
rounds . . . then try-error-try-*it*

willupleasebequiet: i miss him. but not in the way he
would want me to miss him.

WGrayson7: are you coming tomorrow?

willupleasebequiet: i don't think that would be a good
idea. do you?

WGrayson7: it's up to you. it could be another error. or
it could be *it*. just do me a favor and give me a call
first so i can warn him.

that seems fair. he gives me his phone number and i give
him mine. i type it into my phone before i forget. when it asks
for the name to go with the number, i just type *will grayson.*

willupleasebequiet: what's the secret to your wisdom,
will grayson?

WGrayson7: i think it's that i hang out with the right
people, will grayson.

willupleasebequiet: well, thank you for your help.

WGrayson7: i like to be on call for all of my best
friend's ex-boyfriends.

willupleasebequiet: it takes a village to date tiny cooper.

WGrayson7: exactly.

willupleasebequiet: good night, will grayson.

WGrayson7: good night, will grayson.

i want to say this calms me. i want to say i fall immediately to sleep. but the whole night my mind goes
try-error-?

try-error-?
try-error-?

by the morning, i am wreckage. i wake up and i think, *today's the day*. and then i think, *it has nothing to do with me*. it's not like i even helped him with it. it's just that now i'm not getting to see it. i know that's fair, but it doesn't feel fair. it feels like i've screwed myself over.

mom notices my unparalleled self-hatred at breakfast. it's probably the way i drown the cocoa puffs until the milk overflows that tips her off.

mom: will, what's wrong?
me: what isn't?
mom: will . . .
me: it's okay.
mom: no, it's not.
me: how can you tell me it's not? isn't that my choice?

she sits down across from me, puts her hand on my hand even though there's now a puddle of cocoa-colored milk under her wrist.

mom: do you know how much i used to scream?

i have no idea what she's talking about.

me: you don't scream. you fall silent.
mom (shaking her head): even when you were little,

but mostly when your father and i were going
through what we went through — there were times
when i had to go outside, get in the car, drive
around the corner, and scream my head off. i
would scream and scream and scream. sometimes
just noise. and sometimes curses — every curse you
can think of.

me: i can think of a lot of them. did you ever scream
'shitmonger!'

mom: no, but . . .

me: 'fuckweasel!'

mom: will —

me: you should try 'fuckweasel.' it's kinda satisfying.

mom: my point is that there are times when you just
have to let it all out. all of the anger, all of the pain.

me: have you thought of talking to someone about
this? i mean, i have some pills that might interest
you, but i think you're supposed to have a
prescription. it's okay — it only takes up an hour
of your time for them to diagnose it.

mom: will.

me: sorry. it's just that it's not really anger or pain i'm
feeling. just anger at myself.

mom: that's still anger.

me: but don't you feel like that shouldn't count? i
mean, not the same as being angry at someone else.

mom: why this morning?

me: what do you mean?

mom: why are you especially angry at yourself this
morning?

it's not like i'd been planning on advertising the fact that i'm angry. she kinda traps me into it. i of all people can respect that. so i tell her that today's the day of tiny's musical.

mom: you should go.

now it's my turn to shake my head.

me: no way.
mom: way. and will?
me: yes?
mom: you should also talk to maura.

i bolt down the cocoa puffs before there's any way for her to persuade me. when i get to school, i sail past maura at her perch and try to use the day as a distraction. i try to pay attention in classes, but they are so boring that it's like the teachers are trying to drive me back to my own thoughts. i am afraid of what gideon will say to me if i confide in him, so i try to pretend like it's just an ordinary day, and that i'm not cataloging all of the things i've done wrong over the past few weeks. did i really give tiny a chance? did i give maura a chance? shouldn't i have let him calm me down? shouldn't i have let her explain why she did what she did?

finally, at the end of the day, i can't deal with it on my own anymore, and gideon's the one i want to turn to. part of me is hoping that he'll tell me i have nothing to be ashamed of, that i've done nothing wrong. i find him at his locker and say

me: can you believe it? my mom said i should crash
    tiny's show *and* talk to maura.
gideon: you should.
me: did your sister use your mouth as a crack pipe last
    night? are you insane?
gideon: i don't have a sister.
me: whatever. you know what i'm saying.
gideon: i'll go with you.
me: what?
gideon: i'll borrow my mom's car. do you know where
    tiny's school is?
me: you're joking.

and that's when it happens. it's almost astonishing, really.
gideon becomes a little — just a little — more like me.

gideon: can we just say 'fuck you' to the 'you're joking'
    part? all right? i'm not saying you and tiny should
    be together forever and have huge, depressed
    babies that have periods of manic thinness, but
    i do think the way the two of you left it is pretty
    unhelpful, and i'd bet twenty dollars if i had
    twenty dollars that he is suffering from the same
    waves of crappiness that you're suffering from. or
    he's found a new boyfriend. maybe also named will
    grayson. whatever the case, you are going to be
    this walking, talking *splinter* unless someone takes
    your ass to wherever he is, and in this particular
    case, and in any other particular case where you
    need me, i am that someone. i am the knight with

271

a shining jetta. i am your fucking steed.

me: gideon, i had no idea . . .

gideon: shut the fuck up.

me: say it again!

gideon (laughing): shut the fuck up!

me: but why?

gideon: why should you shut the fuck up?

me: no — why are you my *fucking steed*?

gideon: because you're my friend, wingnut. because
    underneath all that denial, you're someone who's
    deeply, deeply nice. and because ever since you
    first mentioned it to me, i've been dying to see this
    musical.

me: okay, okay, okay.

gideon: and the second part?

me: what second part?

gideon: talking to maura.

me: you're kidding.

gideon: not one bit. you have fifteen minutes while i
    get the car.

me: i don't want to.

gideon gives me a hard look.

gideon: what are you, three years old?

me: but why should i?

gideon: i bet you can answer that one yourself.

i tell him he's totally out of line. he waves me off and
says i need to do it, and that he'll honk when he gets here
to pick me up.

the sick thing is, i know he's right. this whole time, i've thought the silent treatment was working. because it's not like i miss her. then i realize that missing her or not missing her isn't the point. the point is that i'm still carrying around what happened as much as she is. and i need to get rid of it. because both of us poured the toxins into our toxic friendship. and while i didn't exactly invent an imaginary boyfriend trap, i certainly contributed enough errors to our trials. there's no way we're ever going to find an ideal state of *it*. but i guess i'm seeing that we have to at least make it to an *it* we can bear.

i walk outside and she's right there in the same place at the end of the day that she is at the start of the day. perching on a wall, notebook out. staring at the other kids as they walk by, no doubt looking down at each and every one of them, including me.

i feel like i should've prepared a speech. but that would require me to know what i'm going to say. i have no idea, really. the best i can come up with is

me: hey

to which she says

maura: hey

she gives me that blank stare. i look at my shoes.

maura: to what do i owe this pleasure?

this is the way we talked to each other. always. and i

don't have the energy for it anymore. that's not how i want
to talk with friends. not always.

> me: maura, stop.
> maura: stop? you're kidding, right? you don't talk to me
>   for a month, and when you do, it's to tell me to stop?
> me: that's not why i came over here. . . .
> maura: then why did you come over here?
> me: i don't know, okay?
> maura: what does that mean? of course you know.
> me: look. i just want you to know that while i still
>   think what you did was completely shitty, i realize
>   that i was shitty to you, too. not in the elaborately
>   shitty way that you were to me, but still pretty shitty.
>   i should have just been honest with you and told you
>   i didn't want to talk to you or be your boyfriend or
>   be your best friend or anything like that. i tried – i
>   swear i tried. but you didn't want to hear what i was
>   saying, and i used that as an excuse to let it go on.
> maura: you didn't mind me when i was isaac. when we
>   would chat every night.
> me: but that was a lie! a complete lie!

now maura looked me right in the eye.

> maura: c'mon, will – you know there's no such thing as
>   a complete lie. there's always some truth in there.

i don't know how to react to that. i just say the next
thing that comes to my mind.

me: it wasn't you i liked. it was isaac. i liked isaac.

the blankness has disappeared now. there's sadness instead.

maura: . . . and isaac liked you.

i want to say to her: i just want to be myself. and i want to be with someone who's just himself. that's all. i want to see through all the performance and all the pretending and get right to the truth. and maybe this is the most truth that maura and i will ever find — an acknowledgment of the lie, and of the feelings that fell behind it.

me: i'm sorry, maura.
maura: i'm sorry, too.

this is why we call people exes, i guess — because the paths that cross in the middle end up separating at the end. it's too easy to see an X as a cross-out. it's not, because there's no way to cross out something like that. the X is a diagram of two paths.

i hear a honk and turn to see gideon pulling up in his mom's car.

me: i gotta go.
maura: so go.

i leave her and get in the car with gideon and tell him everything that just happened. he says he's proud of me, and i don't know what to do with that. i ask him me: why?

and he says

gideon: for saying you were sorry. i wasn't sure if you'd
   be able to do that.

i tell him i wasn't sure, either. but it's how i felt. and i
wanted to be honest.

suddenly — it's like the next thing i know — we're on the
road. i'm not even sure if we're going to make it to tiny's
show on time. i'm not even sure i should be there. i'm not
even sure that i want to see tiny. i just want to see how the
play turned out.

gideon is whistling along to the radio beside me. normally that kind of shit annoys me, but this time it doesn't.

me: i wish i could show him the truth.
gideon: tiny?
me: yeah. you don't have to date someone to think
   they're great, right?

we drive some more. gideon starts whistling again. i
picture tiny running around backstage. then gideon stops
whistling. he smiles and hits the steering wheel.

gideon: by jove, i think i've got it!
me: did you really just say that?
gideon: admit it. you love it.
me: strangely, i do.

gideon: i think i have an idea.

so he tells me. and i can't believe i have such a sick and twisted and brilliant individual sitting at my side.

even more than that, though, i can't believe i'm about to do what he's suggesting.

chapter nineteen

Jane and I spend the hours before Opening Night constructing the perfect preshow playlist, which comprises—as requested—odd-numbered pop punk songs and even-numbered tunes from musicals. "Annus Miribalis" makes an appearance; we even include the punkest song from the resolutely unpunk Neutral Milk Hotel. As for the songs from musicals, we choose nine distinct renditions of "Over the Rainbow," including a reggae one.

Once we're finished debating and downloading, Jane heads home to change. I'm anxious to get to the auditorium, but it seems unfair to Tiny merely to wear jeans and a Willy the Wildkit T-shirt to the most important event of his life. So I put one of Dad's sports coats over the Wildkit shirt, fix my hair, and feel ready.

I wait at home until Mom pulls in, take the keys from her before she can even get the door all the way open, and drive to school.

I walk into the mostly empty auditorium—curtain time is still more than an hour away—and I'm met by Gary, whose hair is dyed lighter, and chopped short and messy like mine.

Also, he's wearing my clothes, which I delivered to him yesterday: khakis; a short-sleeve, plaid button-down I love; and my black Chucks. The entire effect would be surreal except the clothes are ridiculously wrinkled.

"What, Tiny couldn't find an iron?" I ask.

"Grayson," Gary says, "look at your pants, man."

I do. Huh. I didn't even know that jeans *could* wrinkle. He puts his arm around me and says, "I always thought it was part of your look."

"It is now," I say. "How's it going? Are you nervous?"

"I'm a little nervous, but I'm not Tiny nervous. Actually, could you go back there and, um, try to help? This," he says, gesturing at the outfit, "was for dress rehearsal. I gotta put on my White Sox garb."

"Done and done," I say. "Where is he?"

"Bathroom backstage," Gary answers. I hand him the preshow CD, jog down the aisle, and snake behind the heavy red curtain. I'm met by a gaggle of cast and crew in various stages of costume, and for once they are quiet, working away on each other's makeup. All the guys in the cast wear White Sox uniforms, complete with cleats and high socks pulled up over their tight pants. I say hi to Ethan, the only one I really know, and then I'm about to look for the bathroom when I notice the set. It's a very realistic baseball field dugout, which surprises me. "This is the set for the whole play?" I ask Ethan.

"God no," he says. "There's a different one for each act."

I hear in the distance a thunderous roar followed by a horrifying series of splashes, and my first thought is, *Tiny has written an elephant into the play, and the elephant has just vomited*, but then I realize that Tiny is the elephant.

Against my better judgment, I follow the sound to a bathroom, whereupon it promptly happens again. I can see his feet peeking out the bottom of the stall. "Tiny," I say.

"BLLLLAAARRRRGGGGH," he answers, and then sucks in a desperate wheezing breath before more pours forth. The smell is overpowering, but I step forward and push the door open a bit. Tiny, wearing the world's largest Sox uniform, hugs the toilet. "Nerves or sickness?" I ask.

"BLLLLLAAAAAAOOOO." One cannot help but be surprised by the sheer volume of what pours forth from Tiny's distended mouth. I notice some lettuce and wish I hadn't, because then I begin to wonder: Tacos? Turkey sandwich? I start to feel like I may join him.

"Okay, bud, just get it all up and you'll be fine."

Nick bursts into the bathroom then, moaning, "The smell, the smell," and then says, "Do not fuck your hair up, Cooper! Keep that head out of the toilet. We spent hours on that hair!"

Tiny sputters and coughs a bit and then croaks, "My throat. So raw." He and I realize simultaneously: the central voice of the show is shot.

I take one armpit and Nick takes another and we pull him up and away. I flush, trying not to look into the unspeakable horror in the toilet. "What did you *eat*?"

"A chicken burrito and a steak burrito from Burrito Palace," he answers. His voice sounds all weird, and he knows it, so he tries to sing. "What's second base for a—shit shit shit shit shit I wrecked my voice. Shit."

With Nick still beneath one Tiny arm and me beneath the other, we walk back toward the crew, and I shout, "I need some warm tea with a lot of honey and some Pepto-Bismol immediately, people!"

Jane runs up wearing a white, men's v-neck T-shirt, Sharpie-scrawled with the words *I'm with Phil Wrayson*.

"I'm on it," she says. "Tiny, you need anything else?" He holds up a hand to quiet us and then groans, "What is that?"

"What is what?" I ask.

"That noise. In the distance. Is that—is that—goddamn it, Grayson, did you put 'Over the Rainbow' on the preshow CD?"

"Oh yes," I say. "Repeatedly."

"TINY COOPER HATES 'OVER THE RAINBOW'!" His voice cracks as he screams. "Shit, my voice is so gone. Shit."

"Stay quiet," I say. "We're gonna fix this, dude. Just don't puke anymore."

"I am bereft of burrito to puke," he answers.

"STAY QUIET," I insist.

He nods. And for a few minutes, while everyone runs around fanning their pancake faces and whispering to one another how great they'll be, I'm alone with a silent Tiny Cooper. "I didn't know you could get nervous. Do you get nervous before football games?" He shakes his head no. "Okay, just nod if I'm right. You're scared the play isn't actually that good." He nods. "Worried about your voice." Nod. "What else? Is that it?" He shakes his head no. "Um, you're worried it won't change homophobic minds." No. "You're worried you'll hurl onstage." No. "I don't know, Tiny, but whatever you're worried about, you're bigger than the worries. You're gonna *kill* out there. The ovation will last for *hours*. Longer than the play itself."

"*Will*," he whispers.

"Dude, save the voice."

"Will," he says again.

"Yeah?"

"No. *Will*."

"You mean the other Will," I say, and he just raises his eyebrows at me and smirks.

"I'll go look," I say. Twenty minutes to curtain, and the auditorium is now damn near full. I stand on the edge of the stage looking out for a second, feeling a little bit famous. Then I jog down the stairs and slowly walk up the stage-right aisle. I want him here, too. I want it possible for people like Will and Tiny to be friends, not just tried errors.

Even though I feel like I know Will, I barely remember what he looks like. I try to exclude each face in each row. A thousand people texting and laughing and squirming in their seats. A thousand people reading the program in which, I later learn, Jane and I are specially thanked for "being awesome." A thousand people waiting to see Gary pretend to be me for a couple hours, with no idea what they're about to see. And I don't know, either, of course—I know the play has changed in the months since I read it, but I don't know how.

All these people, and I try to look at every last one of them. I see Mr. Fortson, the GSA advisor, sitting with his partner. I see two of our assistant principals. And then as I get into the middle, my eyes scanning faces looking for Will Graysony ones, I see two older faces staring back at me on the aisle. My parents.

"What are you doing here?"

My father shrugs. "You will be surprised to learn it was not my idea."

Mom nudges him. "Tiny wrote me a very nice Facebook message inviting us *personally*, and I just thought that was so sweet."

"You're Facebook friends with Tiny?"

"Yes. He request-friended me," Mom says, epically failing to speak Facebook.

"Well, thanks for coming. I'm gonna be backstage but I'll, um, see you after."

"Say hi to Jane for us," Mom says, all smiley and conspiratorial.

"Will do."

I finish making my way up the aisle and then walk back the stage-left aisle. No Will Grayson. When I get backstage, I see Jane holding a supersize bottle of Pepto-Bismol.

She turns it upside down and says, "He drank it all."

Tiny jumps out from behind the set and sings, "And now I feel GrrrrrEAT!" His voice sounds fine for the moment.

"Rock 'n' roll," I tell him. He walks up to me and looks at me askingly. "There's like twelve hundred people in the audience, Tiny," I say.

"You didn't see him," he says, nodding softly. "Okay. Yeah. Okay. That's okay. Thanks for making me shut up."

"And flushing your ten thousand gallons of vomit."

"Sure, also that." He takes a big breath and puffs out his cheeks, rendering his face almost perfectly circular. "I guess it's time."

Tiny gathers the cast and crew around him. He kneels

in the center of a thick mass of people, everyone touching everyone because one of the laws of nature is that theater people love to be touchy. The cast is in the first circle around Tiny, everyone—guy and girl—dressed like White Sox. Then the chorus, dressed all in black for the moment. Jane and I lean in, too. Tiny says, "I just want to say thank you and you're all amazing and it's all about falling. Also I'm sorry I hurled earlier. I was hurling because I actually got awesome-poisoning from being around so many awesome people." That gets a bit of nervous laughter. "I know you're freaked out but just trust me: you're fabulous. And anyway, it's not about you. Let's go make some dreams come true."

Everyone kind of shouts and does this thing where we raise up one hand to the ceiling, and then there are a lot of jazz fingers. The light beneath the curtain is extinguished. Three football players push the set forward into its place. I step off to the side, standing in cave-darkness next to Jane, whose fingers interlace with mine. My heart pounds, and I can only imagine what it's like to be Tiny now, praying that a quart of Pepto-Bismol will coat his vocal cords, that he won't forget a line or fall or pass out or hurl. It's bad enough in the wings, and I realize the courage it actually takes to get onstage and tell the truth. Worse, to *sing* the truth.

A disembodied voice says, "To prevent interruptions of the fabulousness, please turn off your cell phones." I reach into a pocket with my free hand and click mine over to vibrate. I whisper to Jane, "*I* might puke," and she says, "*Shh*," and I whisper, "Hey, are my clothes always superwrinkly?" and she whispers, "Yes. *Shh*," and squeezes my hand. The curtain parts. The applause is polite.

Everyone in the cast sits on the dugout bench except for Tiny, who walks nervously back and forth in front of the players. "Come on, Billy. Be patient, Billy. Wait for your pitch." I realize that Tiny isn't playing Tiny; he's playing the coach.

Some pudgy freshman plays Tiny instead. He can't stop moving his legs around; I can't tell if he's acting or nervous. He says, all exaggeratedly effeminate, "Hey, Batta Batta THWING batta." It sounds like he's flirting with the batter.

"Idiot," someone on the bench says. "*Our guy* is batting."

Gary says, "Tiny's rubber. You're glue. Whatever you say bounces off him and sticks to you." I can tell from his sloping shoulders and meek look that Gary's me.

"Tiny's gay," adds someone else.

The coach wheels around to the bench and shouts. "Hey! HEY! No insulting teammates."

"It's not an insult," Gary says. But he isn't Gary anymore. It isn't Gary talking. It's me. "It's just a thing. Like, some people are gay. Some people have blue eyes."

"Shut up, Wrayson," the coach says.

The kid playing Tiny glances gratefully at the kid playing me, and then one of the bullies stage-whispers, "You're so gay for each other."

And I say, "We're not *gay*. We're *eight*." This happened. I'd forgotten it, but seeing the moment resurrected, I remember.

And the kid says, "You want to go to second base . . . WITH TINY."

The me onstage just rolls his eyes. And then the pudgy kid playing Tiny stands up and takes a step forward, in front of the coach and sings, "What's second base for a gay man?" And then Tiny takes a step forward and joins him, harmonizing, and they launch into the greatest musical song I've ever heard. The chorus goes:

What's second base for a gay man?
Is it tuning in Tokyo?
I can't see how that would feel good
But maybe that's how it should go?

Behind the two Tinys singing arm in arm, the guys in the chorus—including Ethan—pull off a hilariously elaborate old-fashioned, high-stepping, highly choreographed dance, their bats used as canes and their ball caps as top hats. Midway through, half the guys swing their bats toward the heads of half the others, and even though from my side view I can see it's totally faked, when the other boys fall backward dramatically and the music cuts out, I gasp with the audience. Moments later, they all jump up in a single motion and the song starts up again. When it's done, Tiny and the kid dance offstage to thunderous shouts from the crowd, and as the lights cut, Tiny damn near lands in my arms, bathed in sweat.

"Not bad," he says.

I just shake my head, amazed. Jane helps him out of his shoes and says, "Tiny, you're kind of a *genius*." He rips off his baseball uniform to reveal a very Tiny purple polo shirt and chino shorts.

"I know, right?" he says. "Okay, time to come out to the folks," he says, and hustles out onto the stage. Jane grabs my hand and kisses me on the neck.

It's a quiet scene, as Tiny tells his parents he's "probably kinda gay." His dad is sitting silent while his mom sings about unconditional love. The song is only funny because Tiny keeps cutting in with other comings-out each time his mom sings, "We'll always love our Tiny," like, "Also, I cheated in algebra," and, "There's a reason your vodka tastes watered down," and "I feed my peas to the dog."

When the song ends, the lights go down again, but Tiny doesn't leave the stage. When the lights go back up, there's no set, but judging from the elaborately costumed cast, I gather we're at a Gay Pride Parade. Tiny and Phil Wrayson stand center stage as people march past, chanting their chants, waving dramatically. Gary looks so much like me it's weird. He looks more like freshman-year me than Tiny looks like freshman-year Tiny.

They talk for a minute and then Tiny says, "Phil, I'm gay."

Stunned, I say, "No."

And he says, "It's true."

I shake my head. "You mean, like, you're happy?"

"No, I mean, like, that guy," he points at Ethan, who's wearing a skintight yellow wifebeater, "is hot and if I talked to him for a while and he had a good personality and respected me as a person I would let him kiss me on the mouth."

"You're gay?" I say, seemingly uncomprehending.

"Yeah. I know. I know it's a shock. But I wanted you to be the first to know. Other than my parents, I mean."

And then Phil Wrayson breaks out into song, singing more or less exactly what I said when this really happened:

"Next you're gonna tell me the sky is blue, that you use girl shampoo, that critics don't appreciate Blink 182. Oh, next you're gonna tell me the Pope is Catholic, that hookers turn tricks, that Elton John sucks HEY."

And then the song turns into a call and response, with Tiny singing his surprise that I knew he was gay and me singing that it was obvious.

"But I'm a football player."

"Dude, you couldn't be gayer."

"I thought my straight-acting deserved a Tony."

"But, Tiny, you own a thousand My Little Ponies!"

And so on. I can't stop laughing, but more than that, I can't believe how well he remembers it all, how good—for all of our bad—we've always been to each other. And I sing, "You don't want me, do you?" And he answers, "I would prefer a kangaroo," and behind us the chorus high-kicks like the Rockettes.

Jane puts her hands on a shoulder to bend me down and whispers, "See? He loves you, too," and I turn to her and kiss her in the quick dark moment between the end of the song and the beginning of the applause.

As the curtain closes for a set change, I can't *see* the standing ovation, but I can hear it.

Tiny runs offstage, shouting "WOOOOOOOOOT!"

"It could actually go to Broadway," I tell him.

"It got a lot better when I made it about love." He looks at me, smiling with half his mouth, and I know that's as close as he'll ever come. Tiny's the gay one, but I'm the sentimentalist. I nod and whisper *thanks*.

"Sorry if you come across a little annoying in this next

part." Tiny reaches up to touch his hair and Nick appears out of nowhere, diving over an amp to grab Tiny's arm, screaming, "DO NOT TOUCH YOUR PERFECT HAIR." The curtain rises, and the set is a hallway in our school. Tiny's putting up posters. I'm annoying him, that catch in my voice. I don't mind it, or at least I don't mind it much—love is bound up in truth, after all. Just after that scene, there's one with Tiny drunk at a party in which the character Janey gets her only time onstage—a duet with Phil Wrayson sung on opposite sides of a passed-out Tiny, the song culminating in Gary's voice suddenly toughening into confidence and then Janey and me leaning over Tiny's mumbling half-conscious body and kissing. I can only half watch the scene, because I keep wanting to see Jane's smile as she watches.

The songs get better and better from there, until, in the last song before intermission, the whole audience is singing along as Oscar Wilde sings over a sleeping Tiny,

> The pure and simple truth
> Is rarely pure and never simple.
> What's a boy to do
> When lies and truth are both sinful?

As that song ends, the curtain closes and the house lights come up for intermission. Tiny runs up to us and puts a paw on each of our shoulders and lets forth a yawp of joy. "It's hilarious," I tell him. "Really. It's just . . . awesome."

"Woot! The second half's a lot darker, though. It's the romantic part. Okay okay okay okay, see you after!" he says, and then races off to congratulate, and probably chastise, his cast. Jane takes me off into a corner backstage, secluded behind the set, and says, "You really did all that? You looked after him in Little League?"

"Eh, he looked after me, too," I say.

"Compassion is hot," she says as we kiss. After a while, I see the houselights dim and then come back up. Jane and I head back to our stage-side vantage point. The houselights go down again, signaling the end of intermission. And after a moment, a voice from on high says, "Love is the most common miracle."

At first I think God is, like, talking to us, but I quickly realize it's Tiny coming in over the speakers. The second half is beginning.

Tiny sits on the front edge of the stage in the dark, saying, "Love is always a miracle, everywhere, every time. But for us, it's a little different. I don't want to say it's *more* miraculous," he says, and people laugh a little. "It is, though." The lights come up slowly, and only now do I see that behind Tiny is an actual honest-to-God swing set that seems to have been possibly literally dug out of a playground and transported to the stage. "Our miracle is different because people say it's impossible. As it sayeth in Leviticus, 'Dude shall not lie with dude.'" He looks down, and then out into the audience, and I can tell he is looking for the other Will and not finding him. He stands up.

"But it doesn't say that dude shall not fall in love with dude, because that's just impossible, right? The gays are animals, answering their animal desires. It's impossible for animals to fall in love. And yet—"

Suddenly, Tiny's knees buckle and he collapses in a

heap. I jolt up and start to run onstage to pick him up, but Jane grabs a fistful of my shirt as Tiny raises his head toward the audience and says, "I fall and I fall and I fall and I fall and I fall."

And at that very moment, my phone buzzes in my pocket. I dig it out of my pocket. The caller ID reads *Will Grayson*.

chapter twenty

what's in front of me is the trippiest thing i've ever seen. by far.

i honestly didn't think gideon and i would make it on time. chicago traffic is unkind to begin with, but in this case it was moving slower than a stoner's thoughts. gideon and i had to have a swearing contest in order to calm ourselves down.

now that we've made it, i'm guessing there's no way our plan is going to work. it's both insane and genius, which is what tiny deserves. and it required me to do a lot of things i don't usually do, including:

- talking to strangers
- asking strangers for favors
- being willing to make a complete fool of myself
- letting someone else (gideon) help me

it also relies on a number of things beyond my control, including:

- the kindness of strangers

- the ability of strangers to be spontaneous
- the ability of strangers to drive quickly
- tiny's musical lasting more than one act

i'm sure it's going to be a total disaster. but i guess the point is that i'm going to do it anyway.

i know i've cut it real close, because when gideon and i walk into the auditorium, they're carrying a swing set onto the stage. and not just any swing set. i recognize that swing set. that *exact same* swing set. and that's when the trippiness kicks in, big-time.

gideon: holy shit.

at this point, gideon knows everything that went on. not just with me and tiny, but with me and maura, and me and my mom, and basically me and the whole world. and not once has he told me i was stupid, or mean, or awful, or beyond help. in other words, he hasn't said any of the things i've been saying to myself. instead, in the car ride over, he said

gideon: it all makes sense.
me: it does?
gideon: completely. i would've done the same things you did.
me: liar.
gideon: no lie.

then, completely out of nowhere, he held out his pinkie.

gideon: pinkie swear, no lie.

and i hooked my pinkie in his. we drove that way for a little bit, with my little finger curled into his little finger.

me: next thing you know, we'll be blood brothers.
gideon: and we'll be having sleepovers.
me: in the backyard.
gideon: we won't invite the girls.
me: what girls?
gideon: the hypothetical girls that we won't invite.
me: will there be s'mores?
gideon: what do you think?

i knew there would be s'mores.

gideon: you know you're insane, right?
me: this is news?
gideon: for doing what you're about to do.
me: it was your idea.
gideon: but you did it, not me. i mean, you're doing it.
me: we'll see.

and it was strange, because as we drove on, it wasn't gideon or tiny i was thinking about, but maura. as i was in that car with gideon, so completely comfortable with myself, i couldn't help but think that this was what she wanted from me. this is what she always wanted from me. and it was never going to be like this. but i guess for the first time i saw why she would try so hard for it. and why tiny tried so hard for it.

now gideon and i are standing in the back of the theater. i'm looking around to see who else is here, but i can't
really tell in the darkness.

the swing set stays in the back of the stage as a chorus
line of boys dressed as boys and girls dressed as boys lines
up in front of it. i can tell this is meant to be a parade of tiny's ex-boyfriends because as they line up, they are singing,

chorus: we are the parade of ex-boyfriends!

i have no doubt the kid at the end is supposed to be me.
(he's dressed all in black and looks really moody.)

they all start singing their breakup lines:

ex-boyfriend 1: you're too clingy
ex-boyfriend 2: you're too singy
ex-boyfriend 3: you're so massive
ex-boyfriend 4: i'm too passive.
ex-boyfriend 5: i'd rather be friends.
ex-boyfriend 6: i don't date tight ends.
ex-boyfriend 7: i found another guy.
ex-boyfriend 8: i don't have to tell you why.
ex-boyfriend 9: i don't feel the spark.
ex-boyfriend 10: it was only a lark.
ex-boyfriend 11: you mean you won't put out?
ex-boyfriend 12: i can't conquer my doubt.
ex-boyfriend 13: i have other things to do.
ex-boyfriend 14: i have other guys to screw.
ex-boyfriend 15: our love has all been in your head.
ex-boyfriend 16: i'm worried that you'll break my bed.

ex-boyfriend 17: i think I'll just stay home and read.
ex-boyfriend 18: i think you're in love with my need.

that's it — hundreds of texts and conversations, thousands upon thousands of words spoken and sent, all boiled down into a single line. is that what relationships become? a reduced version of the hurt, nothing else let in. it was more than that. i know it was more than that.

and maybe tiny knows, too. because all the other boyfriends leave the stage except for boyfriend #1, and i realize that we're going to go through them all, and maybe each one will have a new lesson for tiny and the audience.

since it's going to be a while before we get to ex-boyfriend #18, i figure it's a good time for me to call the other will grayson. i'm worried he'll have his phone off, but when i go out to the lobby to call (leaving gideon to save me a seat), he picks up and says he'll meet me in a minute.

i recognize him right away, even though there's something different about him, too.

me: hey
o.w.g.: hey
me: one helluva show in there.
o.w.g.: i'll say. i'm glad you came.
me: me too. because, you see, i had this idea. well,
    actually, it was my friend's idea. but here's
    what we're doing. . . .

i explain it to him.

o.w.g.: that's insane.

me: i know.

o.w.g.: do you think they're really here?

me: they said they would be. but even if they're not, at least there's you and me.

the other will grayson looks terrified.

o.w.g.: you're going to have to go first. i'll back you up, but i don't think i could go first.

me: you have a deal.

o.w.g.: this is totally crazy.

me: but tiny's worth it.

o.w.g.: yeah, tiny's worth it.

i know we should go back to the play. but there's something i want to ask him, now that he's in front of me.

me: can i ask you something personal, will grayson to will grayson?

o.w.g.: um . . . sure.

me: do you feel things are different? i mean, since the first time we met?

o.w.g. thinks about it for a second, then nods.

o.w.g.: yeah. i guess i'm not the will grayson i used to be.

me: me neither.

i open the door to the auditorium and peek in again. they're already on ex-boyfriend #5.

> o.w.g.: i better return backstage. jane's going to wonder where i went.
> me: jane, eh?
> o.w.g.: yeah, jane.

it's so cute — there are like two hundred different emotions that flash across his face when he says her name — everything from extreme anxiety to utter bliss.

> me: well, let's take our places.
> o.w.g.: good luck, will grayson.
> me: good luck to us all.

i sneak back in and find gideon, who fills me in on what's going on.

> gideon (whispering): ex-boyfriend six was all about the jockstraps. to the point of fetish, i'd say.

almost all the ex-boyfriends are like this — never really three-dimensional, but it soon becomes apparent that this is deliberate, that tiny's showing how he never got to know all of their dimensions, that he was so caught up in being in love that he didn't really take the time to think about what he was in love with. it's agonizingly truthful, at least for exes like me. (i see a few more boys shifting in their seats, so i'm probably not the only ex in the audience.) we make it through the first seventeen exes, and then there's a blackout and the swing set is moved to the center of the stage. suddenly, tiny's in the spotlight, on the swing, and it's like my life has rewound and is playing back to me, only in musical form. it's exactly as i remember it . . . until it's not, and tiny's inventing this new dialogue for us.

> me-on-stage: i'm really sorry.
> tiny: don't be. i fell for you. i know what happens at the end of falling — landing.
> me-on-stage: i just get so pissed off at myself. i'm the worst thing in the world for you. i'm your pinless hand grenade.
> tiny: i like my pinless hand grenade.

it's funny — i wonder if i'd said that, and if he'd said that, then maybe things would have played out differently. because i would have known that he understood, at least a little. but i guess he needed to be writing it as a musical to see it. or say it.

> me-on-stage: well, i don't like being your pinless hand grenade. or anybody's.

but the weird thing is, for once i feel the pin is in.

tiny's looking out into the audience right now. there's no way for him to know i'm here. but maybe he's looking for me anyway.

tiny: i just want you to be happy. if that's with me or
with someone else or with nobody. i just want you
to be happy. i just want you to be okay with life.
with life as it is. and me, too. it is so hard to accept
that life is falling. falling and landing and falling
and landing. i agree it's not ideal. i agree.

he's talking to me. he's talking to himself. maybe there's
no difference.

i get it. i understand it.

and then he loses me.

tiny: but there is the word, this word phil wrayson
taught me once: *weltschmerz*. it's the depression you
feel when the world as it is does not line up with
the world as you think it should be. i live in a big
goddamned *weltzschermz* ocean, you know? and so
do you. and so does everyone. because everyone
thinks it should be possible just to keep falling
and falling forever, to feel the rush of the air on
your face as you fall, that air pulling your face into
a brilliant goddamned smile. and that *should* be
possible. you *should* be able to fall forever.

and i think: no.

seriously. no.

because i have spent my life falling. not the kind that
tiny's talking about. he's talking about love. i'm talking
about life. in my kind of falling, there's no landing. there's
only hitting the ground. hard. dead, or wanting to be dead.
so the whole time you're falling, it's the worst feeling in the

world. because you feel you have no control over it. because you know how it ends.

i don't want to fall. all i want to do is stand on solid ground.

and the weird thing is, i feel like i'm doing that now. because i am trying to do something good. in the same way that tiny is trying to do something good.

> tiny: you're still a pinless grenade over the world not
> being perfect.

no, i am a pinless grenade over the world being cruel. but every time i'm proven wrong, that pin goes in a little more.

> tiny: and i'm still — every time this happens to me,
> everytime i land, it still hurts like it has never
> happened before.

he's swinging higher now, kicking his legs hard, the swing set groaning. it looks like he's going to bring the whole contraption down, but he just keeps pumping his legs and pulling against the chain with his arms and talking.

> tiny: because we can't stop the *weltschmerz*. we can't
> stop imagining the world as it might be. which is
> awesome! it is my favorite thing about us!

when he gets to the top of his arc now, he's above the reach of the lights, screaming down at the audience from the darkness. then he swings back into view, his back and ass rushing toward us in the audience.

tiny: and if you're gonna have that, you're gonna have
falling. they don't call it *rising* in love. that's why i
love us!

at the top of the arc, above the lights, he kicks out of the
swing. he is so goddamned nimble and quick about it, i can
barely see it, but he lifts himself up by the arms and pulls
his legs up and then just lets go and grabs onto a rafter. the
swing falls before he does, and everyone — the audience,
the chorus — gasps.

tiny: because we know what will happen when we fall!

the answer to this is, of course, that we will crash
right on our ass. which is exactly what tiny does. he lets
go of the rafters, crashes down right in front of the swing
set, and collapses in a heap. i flinch, and gideon grabs my
hand.

i can't tell whether the kid playing me is supposed to be
in character or out of character when he asks tiny if he's all
right. whatever the case, tiny waves the imitation me away,
motions to the conductor, and a moment later, it starts — a
quiet song, all piano keys spaced far apart. tiny recovers his
breath during the intro and starts to sing again.

tiny:
it's all about falling
you land and get up so you can fall again
it's all about falling
i won't be afraid to hit that wall again

it's chaos up there. the chorus is desperately clinging to the chorus. they keep singing how it's about the falling, and then tiny steps forward and says his lines over them.

tiny: maybe tonight you're scared of falling, and maybe there's somebody here or somewhere else you're thinking about, worrying over, fretting over, trying to figure out if you want to fall, or how and when you're gonna land, and i gotta tell you friends that to stop thinking about the landing, because it's all about falling.

it's incredible. it's like he's lifting off the stage, he believes in his words so strongly. and i realize what it is that i have to do. i have to help him realize that it's the belief, not the words, that mean everything. i have to make him realize the point isn't the falling. it's the floating.

tiny calls for them to bring up the houselights. he's looking around, but he doesn't see me.

i gulp.

gideon: ready?

the answer to this question is always going to be no. but i have to do it anyway.

tiny: maybe there is something you're afraid to say, or someone you're afraid to love, or somewhere you're afraid to go. it's gonna hurt. it's gonna hurt because it matters.

no, i think. NO.

it doesn't have to hurt.

i stand up. and then i almost sit down again. it is taking all of my strength to stand up.

i look at gideon.

tiny: but i just fell and landed and i am still standing
here to tell you that you've gotta learn to love the
falling, because it's all about falling.

i reach out my pinkie. gideon takes it in his.

tiny: just fall for once. let yourself fall!

the whole cast is on the stage now. i see that the other will grayson has snuck on, too, and he's wearing these wrinkled jeans and a plaid shirt. right next to him is a girl who must be jane, wearing this shirt that says *I'm with Phil Wrayson*.

tiny makes a gesture, and suddenly everyone onstage is singing.

chorus: hold me closer, hold me closer

and i'm still standing. i'm making eye contact with the other will grayson, who looks nervous but smiles anyway. and i'm seeing a few people nod in my direction. god, i hope they're who i want them to be.

suddenly, with a grand wave of his arms, tiny stops the music. he moves to the front of the stage and the rest of the stage goes dark. it's just him in a spotlight, looking out into the audience. he just stands there for a moment, taking it all in. and then he closes the show by saying:

tiny: my name is tiny cooper. and this is my story.

there's a silence then. people are waiting for the curtain to go down, for the show to definitely be over, for the ovations to start. i have less than a second. i squeeze gideon's pinkie tight, then let go. i raise my hand.
tiny sees me.
other people in the audience see me.
i yell

me: TINY COOPER!

and that's it.
i really hope this is going to work.

me: my name is will grayson. and i appreciate you, tiny cooper!

now everyone's looking at me, and many of them are confused. they have no idea whether this is still part of the show.
what can i say? i'm giving it a new ending.
now this twentysomething-year-old man in a hipster vest stands up. he looks to me for a second, smiles, then turns to tiny and says

man: my name is also will grayson. i live in wilmette.
and i also appreciate you, tiny cooper.

cue the seventy-nine-year-old in the back row.

old guy: my name is william t. grayson, but you can
call me will. and i sure as heck appreciate you, tiny
cooper.

thank you, google. thank you, internet telephone direc-
tories. thank you, keepers of the name.

fortysomething woman: hi! i'm wilma grayson, from
hyde park. and i appreciate you, tiny cooper.

ten-year-old boy: hey. i'm will grayson. the fourth. my
dad couldn't be here, but we both appreciate you,
tiny cooper.

there should be one other. a sophomore at northwestern.
there's a dramatic pause. everyone's looking around.
and then HE stands up. if frenchy's could bottle him up
and sell him as porn, they'd probably own half of chicago
within a year. he's what would happen after nine months if
abercrombie fucked fitch. he's like a movie star, an olympic
swimmer, and america's next top male model all at once.
he's wearing a silver shirt and pink pants. everything about
him sparkles.
not my type at all. but . . .

Gay God: my name is will grayson. and i *love* you, tiny
cooper.

finally, tiny, who's been uncharacteristically speechless the whole time, gets out some words.

tiny: 847-555-3982
Gay God: 847-555-7363
tiny: WILL SOMEONE PLEASE WRITE THAT
    DOWN FOR ME?

half the audience nods.

and then it's quiet again. in fact, it's a little awkward. i don't know whether to sit down or what.

then there's a rustling from the dark part of the stage. the other will grayson walks out of the chorus. he walks right up to tiny and looks him in the eye.

o.w.g.: you know my name. and i love you, tiny cooper.
    although not in the same way that the guy in the
    pink pants might love you.

and then the girl who must be jane chimes in.

girl: my name is not will grayson, and i appreciate you
    a helluva lot, tiny cooper.

it's the strangest thing ever. one by one, everyone on-stage tells tiny cooper they appreciate him. (even the guy named phil wrayson — what are the odds?) then the audience gets into the act. row by row. some say it. some sing it. tiny's crying. i'm crying. everyone's crying.

i lose track of how long it takes. then, when it's all over, the applause starts. the loudest applause you've ever heard.

tiny steps to the front of the stage. people throw flowers.

he's brought us all together. we all feel that.

gideon: you did good.

i link our pinkies again.

me: yeah, we did good.

i nod to the other will grayson, up onstage. he nods to me. we have something between us, him and me.

but the truth?

everybody has it.

that's our curse and our blessing. that's our trial and our error and our *it*.

the applause continues. i look up at tiny cooper.

he may be heavy, but right now he floats.

ACKNOWLEDGMENTS:

We acknowledge that Jodi Reamer is a kickass agent, and furthermore acknowledge that she could beat both of us at once at arm-wrestling.

We acknowledge that picking your friend's nose is a personal choice, and may not be suitable with all personalities.

We acknowledge that this book probably wouldn't exist if Sarah Urist Green hadn't laughed out loud when we read the first two chapters to her a long time ago in an apartment far, far away.

We acknowledge that we were a little disappointed to learn that the Penguin clothing brand is in no way related to the Penguin publishing company, because we were hoping for a discount on smart polo shirts.

We acknowledge the unadulterated fabulousness of Bill Ott, Steffie Zvirin, and John's fairy godmother, Ilene Cooper.

We acknowledge that in the same way that you could never see the moon if it wasn't for the sun, there's no way you'd ever get to see us if it wasn't for the magnificent and continual brightness of our author friends.

We acknowledge that one of us cheated on the SATs, but he didn't mean to.

We acknowledge that nerdfighters are made of awesome.

We acknowledge that being the person God made you cannot separate you from God's love.

We acknowledge that we timed the completion of this book in order to persuade our masterful editor, Julie Strauss-Gabel, to name her child Will Grayson, even if it's a girl. Which is somewhat disingenuous, because we should probably be the ones naming babies after her. Even if they're boys.

A Conversation between
John Green AND David Levithan

John Green: Okay, so admittedly I've heard the story before, but I never tire of it: How'd you come up with the idea for this book?

David Levithan: Funny you should ask. The idea of doing a book about two boys with the same name came from the fact that one of my best friends is named David Leventhal. Not the same name, but close enough. We both went to Brown, and were mistaken for each other a lot. Not only in the normal ways (mixed-up mail and phone calls) but also in some rather awkward, ultimately laughable ways. You see, David Leventhal is an extraordinary dancer. I, David Levithan, am not. So people would come up to me and say, "I saw you onstage last night—you seem to be such an oafish, clumsy guy; but when you dance, you're so graceful!" And I'd have to reply, "Um, that wasn't me onstage last night." It was like my alter ego was walking around campus; and eventually, right before I graduated, I called him up and we met up and became great friends. I wouldn't say our book is about How to Love Your Alter Ego, but it is about how another person can unlock—often inadvertently—the potential of your personality. Oh! And the punch line (which I often forget) is that one of David Leventhal's roommates/best friends in college was named . . . Jon Green. Totally coincidental. But that's a nice lead-in to my question: What has your experience been with other John Greens?

JG: There are, of course, hundreds of us—from real estate brokers in Mississippi to Australian botanists. I've met several John Greens, and they've all been delightful; but I did have one unpleasant run-in a few years ago. There is a John Green in Canada who is a Very Big Deal in the field of Bigfoot research, also known as Sasquatch-ery. (He is the author of such books as *Sasquatch: The Apes Among Us*.) A few years ago, I wrote an article for a magazine in which I casually mentioned that Bigfoot is, you know, fictional. A week after the story was published, I received a very angry letter from John Green, noted Sasquatologist, accusing me of having besmirched the good name of John Greens everywhere.

Fortunately, my reputation survived enough for you to want to write this book with me. So we wrote our first chapters with no idea of what the other person was writing and no idea whether the story would work. What were you thinking when I read my first chapter to you and you were introduced to Will and Tiny and Jane and the problem of picking one's friends and/or their noses?

DL: I don't want to sound easy, but you pretty much had me at the opening line. I mean, the minute you read it, I knew your chapter was going to start the book. And then when Tiny appeared . . . well, I certainly thought, "Oh, I can use this character." What I love is that it's a character everyone would have expected from me; but it's actually you who invented him, and in such an amazing way in relation to your Will. I was also surprised when Neutral Milk Hotel popped up. Because, you know, I'm supposed to be the music obsessive in this relationship. Had I known that I would suddenly be spending five or so years with "Holland, 1945" stuck in my head, I might have reacted differently. (Look, there it is again.)

Most of all, though, I was struck by how you and I had created two very different Wills but at the same time decided to grapple with some very similar ideas. (Note: I don't say "themes" here, because neither of us writes with "themes" in mind.) What was your reaction when you heard my first chapter?

JG: I loved it. I was shocked how immediately and completely I was inside your Will's head. Your half of the novel is very funny but also roaringly angry. One of the things I still love, even rereading your chapters for the millionth time, is how completely you're able to inhabit the mind of someone living with major depression. This is not a question; I just want you to say something about that.

DL: I wanted my will to be very much in the middle of things, because I don't feel there are enough books written about teens caught in the middle of things. I didn't want him to be full of self-loathing about being gay—he's fine with being gay but wants to keep it to himself, not out of fear, but out of a feeling that it's nobody else's business. He's lost a dad, and he's not completely over it; but he's not hung up on it either. And, most important, he lives with depression, but he's at the stage where he's living with it, not discovering it. So many novels—many of them excellent—are written about teens who first grapple with their depression and get help. There are very few about what happens next, when you have to live the rest of your life.

JG: I wonder if you can talk about the lower casedness of your will grayson.

DL: Oh, you noticed that, did you? The reason my will writes in lowercase is simple—that's how he sees himself. He is a lowercase person. He is used to communicating online, where people are encouraged to be lowercase people. His whole self-image is what he projects in that space, and his one comfortable form of communication is when he's anonymous and sending instant messages. It's not even something he thinks about. It's how his self-expression has formed. Is it stunted in some way? Absolutely. But at the same time, it's a true expression; and by the end of the book, I'd bet you don't even notice it. It's only jarring at first. But then you enter his world completely, get used to the rhythms of his life; and hopefully it makes sense.

I'm curious how Schrödinger's cat came into play in your chapters. If I remember correctly, it wasn't in the first draft. What sparked you to add it into the mix with Will and Jane?

JG: I think initially I was looking for another way to think about my Will's aversion to attachment; i.e., so long as you don't open the box, the cat is still alive. (Of course, the cat is also dead.) But I think a lot of the novel is about the weird relationship between identity and existence: In some ways, you are who you are because other people observe you; but in some ways, you are who you are in spite of other people's observations of you. One of the reasons nonphysicists have latched on to Schrödinger's thought experiment is because we all feel that tension between observed identity and interior identity.

DL: When we started talking about the book, neither of us had very many fans—my second book had just come out, and your first book was about to be published. Now we have more fans. And you have nerdfighters. What influence do you think that has on your work and your life?

JG: Well, my half of *Will Grayson, Will Grayson* is dedicated to a particular nerdfighter, but it could have been dedicated to all of nerdfighteria, because I am deeply inspired by their intellectual engagement and also their celebration of all things nerdy. (For those of you who don't know what a nerdfighter is, I make videos with my brother on YouTube; our fans are called nerdfighters because they fight for nerds and nerdiness.) I also learn a lot from them. It's really only because of nerdfighters that I am even aware that teenagers still like musicals.

DL: I couldn't have been more thrilled to marry into the nerdfighter family. Perhaps especially because so many of them like musicals. When you first wrote about Tiny and his musical, did you have any idea how much of it we would end up having in the book? And perhaps can you speak a little about the genesis of "The Nose Tackle (Likes Tight Ends)"?

JG: I had no idea we would ever see the musical in the book when the thought of it first occurred to me; but then as we moved forward, it seemed a good fit for the story we were telling. As to the genesis of "The Nose Tackle (Likes Tight Ends)," it's an old homophobic locker-room joke that I wanted to twist into a proud and celebratory observation. By the way, shouldn't there be an IRL musical?

DL: I'm working on it! Now, it may never, ever see the light of day. But slowly I've been putting on my enormously gay, gaily enormous thinking cap and have been composing some further show tunes. For example, the opening number. Now, I don't know if this will end up being it. But what I have right now is:

Act One, Scene One

It's a dark stage, and at first all you hear are murmurs, a heart-beat, and heavy breathing. Like, serious Lamaze. Then we see, in the middle of the stage, a large piece of paper showing two bare, spread legs, discreetly covered with a hospital sheet. The heartbeat gets louder. The breathing gets heavier. Lamaze on crack. And fi-nally, as it all crescendos, TINY COOPER enters the world, crash-ing through the piece of paper and entering spectacularly onto the stage.

We are not going for realism here. He should not be naked and covered with amniotic fluid. That's gross. He should not be wear-ing a diaper. He's not into that. Instead, the person who emerges should be the large, stylish Tiny Cooper who you will see for the rest of the musical. If you want to delineate him from Tiny at other ages, you can have him wearing a button that says AGE: 0.

Most babies come into the world crying or gasping or snotting.

Not Tiny Cooper.

He comes into the world singing.

Cue: Opening chords of "I WAS BORN THIS WAY." This is a big, lively, belty number—because, let's face it, if Elphaba got to sing "Defying Gravity" at the start of *Wicked*, she would have been much, much happier throughout the whole show. Tiny has just crashed into the world—some would say he was pushed—and al-ready he has a sense of who he is and what he's going to do. The music and the production value must reflect that. Sparkles, people. Think sparkles. Do not get stingy about the sparkles. The reason drag queens love them so much is that you can get them for cheap.

TINY (spoken):
Hello, my name is Tiny Cooper . . . what's yours? I've just been born; and, man, it feels good!

[Cue music.]

["I WAS BORN THIS WAY"]

TINY (singing):

    I was born this way
    Big-boned and happily gay
    I was born this way.
    Right here in the U.S. of A

    It's pointless to wonder why
    I ended up so G-A-Y
    From the very first day
    The rainbow's come my way

    I've got brown hair,
    big hips,
    blue blue eyes.
    And one day
    I'm gonna make out
    with guys,
    guys,
    guys!

    Why try to hide it?
    What good would that do?
    I was born this way
    And if you don't like it
    That says more about you

    If you find it odd
    Take it up with God
    Because who else do you think
    Could make me this way?

    All God's children wear traveling shoes whether you've got
    flat feet or twinkle toes. I'm going to dance right into this
    life And keep dancing as it goes

    I've got genes that fit me well
    And a spirit all my own

I was born this way
The rest is the great unknown

[really belting now]

I.
was.
born.
this.
way.

And I love.
the.
way.
I.
was.
born.

The rest
is the great unknown.
But I'm ready
Oh yes I'm ready
for it
to
begin!

DL: Now, I have to admit, this was written in August 2010. In September of this same year, at the MTV Video Music Awards, Lady Gaga (also enormously gay) announced that the title of her new album would be *Born This Way*. Coincidence? I think not. (Okay, I think so.) As of this writing, in November 2010, I have yet to hear her version. We'll see how it goes.

Turn the page to read an excerpt from
John Green's #1 *New York Times*
bestselling novel

THE FAULT IN OUR STARS

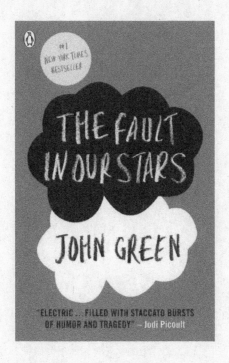

CHAPTER ONE

Late in the winter of my seventeenth year, my mother decided I was depressed, presumably because I rarely left the house, spent quite a lot of time in bed, read the same book over and over, ate infrequently, and devoted quite a bit of my abundant free time to thinking about death.

Whenever you read a cancer booklet or website or whatever, they always list depression among the side effects of cancer. But, in fact, depression is not a side effect of cancer. Depression is a side effect of dying. (Cancer is also a side effect of dying. Almost everything is, really.) But my mom believed I required treatment, so she took me to see my Regular Doctor Jim, who agreed that I was veritably swimming in a paralyzing and totally clinical depression, and that therefore my meds should be adjusted and also I should attend a weekly Support Group.

This Support Group featured a rotating cast of characters in various states of tumor-driven unwellness. Why did the cast rotate? A side effect of dying.

The Support Group, of course, was depressing as hell. It met every Wednesday in the basement of a stone-walled Episcopal church shaped like a cross. We all sat in a circle right in the middle of the cross, where the two boards would have met, where the heart of Jesus would have been.

I noticed this because Patrick, the Support Group Leader and only person over eighteen in the room, talked about the heart of Jesus every freaking meeting, all about how we, as young cancer survivors, were sitting right in Christ's very sacred heart and whatever.

So here's how it went in God's heart: The six or seven or ten of us walked/wheeled in, grazed at a decrepit selection of cookies and lemonade, sat down in the Circle of Trust, and listened to Patrick recount for the thousandth time his depressingly miserable life story—how he had cancer in his balls and they thought he was going to die but he didn't die and now here he is, a full-grown adult in a church basement in the 137th nicest city in America, divorced, addicted to video games, mostly friendless, eking out a meager living by exploiting his cancertastic past, slowly working his way toward a master's degree that will not improve his career prospects, waiting, as we all do, for the sword of Damocles to give him the relief that he escaped lo those many years ago when cancer took both of his nuts but spared what only the most generous soul would call his life.

AND YOU TOO MIGHT BE SO LUCKY!

Then we introduced ourselves: Name. Age. Diagnosis. And how we're doing today. I'm Hazel, I'd say when they'd get to me. Sixteen. Thyroid originally but with an impressive and long-settled satellite colony in my lungs. And I'm doing okay.

Once we got around the circle, Patrick always asked if anyone wanted to share. And then began the circle jerk of support: everyone talking about fighting and battling and winning and shrinking and scanning. To be fair to Patrick, he let us talk about dying, too. But most of them weren't dying. Most would live into adulthood, as Patrick had.

(Which meant there was quite a lot of competitiveness about it, with everybody wanting to beat not only cancer itself, but also the other people in the room. Like, I realize that this is irrational, but when they tell you that you have, say, a 20 percent chance of living five years, the math kicks in and you figure that's one in five . . . so you look around and think, as any healthy person would: I gotta outlast four of these bastards.)

The only redeeming facet of Support Group was this kid named Isaac, a long-faced, skinny guy with straight blond hair swept over one eye.

And his eyes were the problem. He had some fantastically improbable eye cancer. One eye had been cut out when he was a kid, and now he wore the kind of thick glasses that made his eyes (both the real one and the glass one) preternaturally huge, like his whole head was basically just this fake eye and this real eye staring at you. From what I could gather on the rare occasions when Isaac shared with the group, a recurrence had placed his remaining eye in mortal peril.

Isaac and I communicated almost exclusively through sighs. Each time someone discussed anticancer diets or snorting ground-up shark fin or whatever, he'd glance over at me and sigh ever so slightly. I'd shake my head microscopically and exhale in response.

So Support Group blew, and after a few weeks, I grew to be rather kicking-and-screaming about the whole affair. In fact, on the Wednesday I made the acquaintance of Augustus Waters, I tried my level best to get out of Support Group while sitting on the couch with my mom in the third leg of a twelve-hour marathon of the previous season's *America's Next Top Model*, which admittedly I had already seen, but still.

Me: "I refuse to attend Support Group."

Mom: "One of the symptoms of depression is disinterest in activities."

Me: "Please just let me watch *America's Next Top Model*. It's an activity."

Mom: "Television is a passivity."

Me: "Ugh, Mom, please."

Mom: "Hazel, you're a teenager. You're not a little kid anymore. You need to make friends, get out of the house, and live your life."

Me: "If you want me to be a teenager, don't send me to Support Group. Buy me a fake ID so I can go to clubs, drink vodka, and take pot."

Mom: "You don't *take* pot, for starters."

Me: "See, that's the kind of thing I'd know if you got me a fake ID."

Mom: "You're going to Support Group."

Me: "UGGGGGGGGGGGGGGG."

Mom: "Hazel, you deserve a life."

That shut me up, although I failed to see how attendance at Support Group met the definition of *life*. Still, I agreed to go—after negotiating the right to record the 1.5 episodes of *ANTM* I'd be missing.

I went to Support Group for the same reason that I'd once allowed nurses with a mere eighteen months of graduate education to poison me with exotically named chemicals: I wanted to make my parents happy. There is only one thing in this world shittier than biting it from cancer when you're sixteen, and that's having a kid who bites it from cancer.

Mom pulled into the circular driveway behind the church at 4:56. I pretended to fiddle with my oxygen tank for a second just to kill time.

"Do you want me to carry it in for you?"

"No, it's fine," I said. The cylindrical green tank only weighed a few pounds, and I had this little steel cart to wheel it around behind me. It delivered two liters of oxygen to me each minute through a cannula, a transparent tube that split just beneath my neck, wrapped behind my ears, and then reunited in my nostrils. The contraption was necessary because my lungs sucked at being lungs.

"I love you," she said as I got out.

"You too, Mom. See you at six."

"Make friends!" she said through the rolled-down window as I walked away.

I didn't want to take the elevator because taking the elevator is a Last Days kind of activity at Support Group, so I took the stairs. I grabbed a cookie and poured some lemonade into a Dixie cup and then turned around.

A boy was staring at me.

I was quite sure I'd never seen him before. Long and

leanly muscular, he dwarfed the molded plastic elementary school chair he was sitting in. Mahogany hair, straight and short. He looked my age, maybe a year older, and he sat with his tailbone against the edge of the chair, his posture aggressively poor, one hand half in a pocket of dark jeans.

I looked away, suddenly conscious of my myriad insufficiencies. I was wearing old jeans, which had once been tight but now sagged in weird places, and a yellow T-shirt advertising a band I didn't even like anymore. Also my hair: I had this pageboy haircut, and I hadn't even bothered to, like, brush it. Furthermore, I had ridiculously fat chipmunked cheeks, a side effect of treatment. I looked like a normally proportioned person with a balloon for a head. This was not even to mention the cankle situation. And yet—I cut a glance to him, and his eyes were still on me.

It occurred to me why they call it eye *contact*.

I walked into the circle and sat down next to Isaac, two seats away from the boy. I glanced again. He was still watching me.

Look, let me just say it: He was hot. A nonhot boy stares at you relentlessly and it is, at best, awkward and, at worst, a form of assault. But a hot boy . . . well.

I pulled out my phone and clicked it so it would display the time: 4:59. The circle filled in with the unlucky twelve-to-eighteens, and then Patrick started us out with the serenity prayer: *God, grant me the serenity to accept the things*

I cannot change, the courage to change the things I can, and the wisdom to know the difference. The guy was still staring at me. I felt rather blushy.

Finally, I decided that the proper strategy was to stare back. Boys do not have a monopoly on the Staring Business, after all. So I looked him over as Patrick acknowledged for the thousandth time his ball-lessness etc., and soon it was a staring contest. After a while the boy smiled, and then finally his blue eyes glanced away. When he looked back at me, I flicked my eyebrows up to say, *I win*.

He shrugged. Patrick continued and then finally it was time for the introductions. "Isaac, perhaps you'd like to go first today. I know you're facing a challenging time."

"Yeah," Isaac said. "I'm Isaac. I'm seventeen. And it's looking like I have to get surgery in a couple weeks, after which I'll be blind. Not to complain or anything because I know a lot of us have it worse, but yeah, I mean, being blind does sort of suck. My girlfriend helps, though. And friends like Augustus." He nodded toward the boy, who now had a name. "So, yeah," Isaac continued. He was looking at his hands, which he'd folded into each other like the top of a tepee. "There's nothing you can do about it."

"We're here for you, Isaac," Patrick said. "Let Isaac hear it, guys." And then we all, in a monotone, said, "We're here for you, Isaac."

Michael was next. He was twelve. He had leukemia.

He'd always had leukemia. He was okay. (Or so he said. He'd taken the elevator.)

Lida was sixteen, and pretty enough to be the object of the hot boy's eye. She was a regular—in a long remission from appendiceal cancer, which I had not previously known existed. She said—as she had every other time I'd attended Support Group—that she felt *strong*, which felt like bragging to me as the oxygen-drizzling nubs tickled my nostrils.

There were five others before they got to him. He smiled a little when his turn came. His voice was low, smoky, and dead sexy. "My name is Augustus Waters," he said. "I'm seventeen. I had a little touch of osteosarcoma a year and a half ago, but I'm just here today at Isaac's request."

"And how are you feeling?" asked Patrick.

"Oh, I'm grand." Augustus Waters smiled with a corner of his mouth. "I'm on a roller coaster that only goes up, my friend."

When it was my turn, I said, "My name is Hazel. I'm sixteen. Thyroid with mets in my lungs. I'm okay."

The hour proceeded apace: Fights were recounted, battles won amid wars sure to be lost; hope was clung to; families were both celebrated and denounced; it was agreed that friends just didn't get it; tears were shed; comfort proffered. Neither Augustus Waters nor I spoke again until Patrick said, "Augustus, perhaps you'd like to share your fears with the group."

"My fears?"

"Yes."

"I fear oblivion," he said without a moment's pause. "I fear it like the proverbial blind man who's afraid of the dark."

"Too soon," Isaac said, cracking a smile.

"Was that insensitive?" Augustus asked. "I can be pretty blind to other people's feelings."

Isaac was laughing, but Patrick raised a chastening finger and said, "Augustus, please. Let's return to *you* and *your* struggles. You said you fear oblivion?"

"I did," Augustus answered.

Patrick seemed lost. "Would, uh, would anyone like to speak to that?"

I hadn't been in proper school in three years. My parents were my two best friends. My third best friend was an author who did not know I existed. I was a fairly shy person—not the hand-raising type.

And yet, just this once, I decided to speak. I half raised my hand and Patrick, his delight evident, immediately said, "Hazel!" I was, I'm sure he assumed, opening up. Becoming Part Of The Group.

I looked over at Augustus Waters, who looked back at me. You could almost see through his eyes they were so blue. "There will come a time," I said, "when all of us are dead. All of us. There will come a time when there are no human beings remaining to remember that anyone ever existed or that our species ever did anything. There will be no one left to remember Aristotle or Cleopatra, let alone you. Everything that we did and built and wrote and thought and discovered will be forgotten and all of this"—I gestured encompassingly—"will have been for naught. Maybe that time is coming soon and maybe it is millions of years away, but even if we survive the collapse of our sun, we will not survive forever. There was time before organisms experienced consciousness, and there will be time after. And if the inevitability of human oblivion worries you, I encourage you to ignore it. God knows that's what everyone else does."

I'd learned this from my aforementioned third best friend, Peter Van Houten, the reclusive author of *An Imperial Affliction*, the book that was as close a thing as I had to a Bible. Peter Van Houten was the only person I'd ever come across who seemed to (a) understand what it's like to be dying, and (b) not have died.

After I finished, there was quite a long period of silence as I watched a smile spread all the way across Augustus's face—not the little crooked smile of the boy trying to be sexy while he stared at me, but his real smile, too big for his face. "Goddamn," Augustus said quietly. "Aren't you something else."

Neither of us said anything for the rest of Support

Group. At the end, we all had to hold hands, and Patrick led us in a prayer. "Lord Jesus Christ, we are gathered here in Your heart, *literally in Your heart*, as cancer survivors. You and You alone know us as we know ourselves. Guide us to life and the Light through our times of trial. We pray for Isaac's eyes, for Michael's and Jamie's blood, for Augustus's bones, for Hazel's lungs, for James's throat. We pray that You might heal us and that we might feel Your love, and Your peace, which passes all understanding. And we remember in our hearts those whom we knew and loved who have gone home to you: Maria and Kade and Joseph and Haley and Abigail and Angelina and Taylor and Gabriel and . . ."

It was a long list. The world contains a lot of dead people. And while Patrick droned on, reading the list from a sheet of paper because it was too long to memorize, I kept my eyes closed, trying to think prayerfully but mostly imagining the day when my name would find its way onto that list, all the way at the end when everyone had stopped listening.

When Patrick was finished, we said this stupid mantra together—LIVING OUR BEST LIFE TODAY—and it was over. Augustus Waters pushed himself out of his chair and walked over to me. His gait was crooked like his smile. He towered over me, but he kept his distance so I wouldn't have to crane my neck to look him in the eye. "What's your name?" he asked.

"Hazel."

"No, your full name."

"Um, Hazel Grace Lancaster." He was just about to say something else when Isaac walked up. "Hold on," Augustus said, raising a finger, and turned to Isaac. "That was actually worse than you made it out to be."

"I told you it was bleak."

"Why do you bother with it?"

"I don't know. It kind of helps?"

Augustus leaned in so he thought I couldn't hear. "She's a regular?" I couldn't hear Isaac's comment, but Augustus responded, "I'll say." He clasped Isaac by both shoulders and then took a half step away from him. "Tell Hazel about clinic."

Isaac leaned a hand against the snack table and focused his huge eye on me. "Okay, so I went into clinic this morning, and I was telling my surgeon that I'd rather be deaf than blind. And he said, 'It doesn't work that way,' and I was, like, 'Yeah, I realize it doesn't work that way; I'm just saying I'd rather be deaf than blind if I had the choice, which I realize I don't have,' and he said, 'Well, the good news is that you won't be deaf,' and I was like, 'Thank you for explaining that my eye cancer isn't going to make me deaf. I feel so fortunate that an intellectual giant like yourself would deign to operate on me.'"

"He sounds like a winner," I said. "I'm gonna try to get me some eye cancer just so I can make this guy's acquaintance."

"Good luck with that. All right, I should go. Monica's waiting for me. I gotta look at her a lot while I can."

"Counterinsurgence tomorrow?" Augustus asked.

"Definitely." Isaac turned and ran up the stairs, taking them two at a time.

Augustus Waters turned to me. "Literally," he said.

"Literally?" I asked.

"We are literally in the heart of Jesus," he said. "I thought we were in a church basement, but we are literally in the heart of Jesus."

"Someone should tell Jesus," I said. "I mean, it's gotta be dangerous, storing children with cancer in your heart."

"I would tell Him myself," Augustus said, "but unfortunately I am literally stuck inside of His heart, so He won't be able to hear me." I laughed. He shook his head, just looking at me.

"What?" I asked.

"Nothing," he said.

"Why are you looking at me like that?"

Augustus half smiled. "Because you're beautiful. I enjoy looking at beautiful people, and I decided a while ago not to deny myself the simpler pleasures of existence." A brief awkward silence ensued. Augustus plowed through: "I mean, particularly given that, as you so deliciously pointed out, all of this will end in oblivion and everything."

I kind of scoffed or sighed or exhaled in a way that was vaguely coughy and then said, "I'm not beau—"

"You're like a millennial Natalie Portman. Like *V for Vendetta* Natalie Portman."

"Never seen it," I said.

"Really?" he asked. "Pixie-haired gorgeous girl dislikes authority and can't help but fall for a boy she knows is trouble. It's your autobiography, so far as I can tell."

His every syllable flirted. Honestly, he kind of turned me on. I didn't even know that guys *could* turn me on—not, like, in real life.

A younger girl walked past us. "How's it going, Alisa?" he asked. She smiled and mumbled, "Hi, Augustus." "Memorial people," he explained. Memorial was the big research hospital. "Where do you go?"

"Children's," I said, my voice smaller than I expected it to be. He nodded. The conversation seemed over. "Well," I said, nodding vaguely toward the steps that led us out of the Literal Heart of Jesus. I tilted my cart onto its wheels and started walking. He limped beside me. "So, see you next time, maybe?" I asked.

"You should see it," he said. "*V for Vendetta*, I mean."

"Okay," I said. "I'll look it up."

"No. With me. At my house," he said. "Now."

I stopped walking. "I hardly know you, Augustus Waters. You could be an ax murderer."

He nodded. "True enough, Hazel Grace." He walked past me, his shoulders filling out his green knit polo shirt, his back straight, his steps lilting just slightly to the right as he walked steady and confident on what I had determined was a prosthetic leg. Osteosarcoma sometimes takes a limb to check you out. Then, if it likes you, it takes the rest.

I followed him upstairs, losing ground as I made my way up slowly, stairs not being a field of expertise for my lungs.

And then we were out of Jesus's heart and in the parking lot, the spring air just on the cold side of perfect, the late-afternoon light heavenly in its hurtfulness.

Mom wasn't there yet, which was unusual, because Mom was almost always waiting for me. I glanced around and saw that a tall, curvy brunette girl had Isaac pinned against the stone wall of the church, kissing him rather aggressively. They were close enough to me that I could hear the weird noises of their mouths together, and I could hear him saying, "Always," and her saying, "Always," in return.

Suddenly standing next to me, Augustus half whispered, "They're big believers in PDA."

"What's with the 'always'?" The slurping sounds intensified.

"Always is their thing. They'll *always* love each other and whatever. I would conservatively estimate they have texted each other the word *always* four million times in the last year."

A couple more cars drove up, taking Michael and Alisa away. It was just Augustus and me now, watching Isaac and Monica, who proceeded apace as if they were not leaning against a place of worship. His hand reached for her boob over her shirt and pawed at it, his palm still while his fingers moved around. I wondered if that felt good. Didn't seem like it would, but I decided to forgive Isaac on the grounds that he was going blind. The senses must feast while there is yet hunger and whatever.

"Imagine taking that last drive to the hospital," I said quietly. "The last time you'll ever drive a car."

Without looking over at me, Augustus said, "You're killing my vibe here, Hazel Grace. I'm trying to observe young love in its many-splendored awkwardness."

"I think he's hurting her boob," I said.

"Yes, it's difficult to ascertain whether he is trying to arouse her or perform a breast exam." Then Augustus Waters reached into a pocket and pulled out, of all things, a pack of cigarettes. He flipped it open and put a cigarette between his lips.

"Are you *serious*?" I asked. "You think that's cool? Oh, my God, you just ruined *the whole thing*."

"Which whole thing?" he asked, turning to me. The cigarette dangled unlit from the unsmiling corner of his mouth.

"The whole thing where a boy who is not unattractive or unintelligent or seemingly in any way unacceptable stares at me and points out incorrect uses of literality and compares me to actresses and asks me to watch a movie at his house. But of course there is always a *hamartia* and yours is that oh, my God, even though you HAD FREAKING CANCER you give money to a company in exchange for the chance to acquire YET MORE CANCER. Oh, my God. Let me just assure you that not being able to breathe? SUCKS. Totally disappointing. *Totally*."

"A *hamartia*?" he asked, the cigarette still in his mouth. It tightened his jaw. He had a hell of a jawline, unfortunately.

"A fatal flaw," I explained, turning away from him. I stepped toward the curb, leaving Augustus Waters behind me, and then I heard a car start down the street. It was Mom. She'd been waiting for me to, like, make friends or whatever.

I felt this weird mix of disappointment and anger welling up inside of me. I don't even know what the feeling was, really, just that there was a *lot* of it, and I wanted to smack Augustus Waters and also replace my lungs with lungs that didn't suck at being lungs. I was standing with my Chuck Taylors on the very edge of the curb, the oxygen tank ball-and-chaining in the cart by my side, and right as my mom pulled up, I felt a hand grab mine.

I yanked my hand free but turned back to him.

"They don't kill you unless you light them," he said as Mom arrived at the curb. "And I've never lit one. It's a metaphor, see: You put the killing thing right between your teeth, but you don't give it the power to do its killing."

"It's a metaphor," I said, dubious. Mom was just idling.

"It's a metaphor," he said.

"You choose your behaviors based on their metaphorical resonances . . ." I said.

"Oh, yes." He smiled. The big, goofy, real smile. "I'm a big believer in metaphor, Hazel Grace."

I turned to the car. Tapped the window. It rolled down. "I'm going to a movie with Augustus Waters," I said. "Please record the next several episodes of the *ANTM* marathon for me."

He just wanted a decent book to read ...

Not too much to ask, is it? It was in 1935 when Allen Lane, Managing Director of Bodley Head Publishers, stood on a platform at Exeter railway station looking for something good to read on his journey back to London. His choice was limited to popular magazines and poor-quality paperbacks – the same choice faced every day by the vast majority of readers, few of whom could afford hardbacks. Lane's disappointment and subsequent anger at the range of books generally available led him to found a company – and change the world.

'We believed in the existence in this country of a vast reading public for intelligent books at a low price, and staked everything on it'
Sir Allen Lane, 1902–1970, founder of Penguin Books

The quality paperback had arrived – and not just in bookshops. Lane was adamant that his Penguins should appear in chain stores and tobacconists, and should cost no more than a packet of cigarettes.

Reading habits (and cigarette prices) have changed since 1935, but Penguin still believes in publishing the best books for everybody to enjoy. We still believe that good design costs no more than bad design, and we still believe that quality books published passionately and responsibly make the world a better place.

So wherever you see the little bird – whether it's on a piece of prize-winning literary fiction or a celebrity autobiography, political tour de force or historical masterpiece, a serial-killer thriller, reference book, world classic or a piece of pure escapism – you can bet that it represents the very best that the genre has to offer.

Whatever you like to read – trust Penguin.